D0261868

GOLD, SILVER AND GREEN

GOLD, SILVER AND GREEN
The Irish Olympic Journey, 1896–1924

KEVIN McCARTHY

CORK UNIVERSITY PRESS

First published in 2010 by
Cork University Press
Youngline Industrial Estate
Pouladuff Road, Togher
Cork, Ireland

This publication has received support from the Heritage Council under the 2009 Publication Grant Scheme.

British Library Cataloguing in Publication Data
A CIP catalogue record for this book is available from the British Library.

ISBN 978-1-85918-458-5

Typesetting by Red Barn Publishing, Skeagh, Skibbereen, Co. Cork
Printed in Ireland by ColourBooks Ltd.

www.corkuniversitypress.com

CONTENTS

ACKNOWLEDGEMENTS

The many staff members of the National Library with whom I have had dealings over the past five years could not have been more helpful to me in my researches. The same is true of the various local libraries and of the staff members at the Colindale newspaper division of the British Library and at the New York Public Library.

The willingness with which the archives of the GAA, the British Olympic Association and the American Irish Historical Society were opened to me was as close to spontaneous as it could have been, with particular thanks owing to William Cobert of the American Irish Society, who had the grace to facilitate me while he was in the midst of organising a major fundraising banquet in late 2005. The Olympic Council of Ireland was essentially founded after the core period of my research and hence was unable to assist me with archival material, although I certainly thank the staff I spoke with there for their efforts in any respect. Professors Joe Lee and Marion Casey at NYU were also most supportive when called upon for assistance on the American front and secured me access to the NYU Irish archives.

The staff at the Olympic Studies Centre in Lausanne have always been much more than helpful. From the moment I made contact with Ruth Beck-Perrenaud and Patricia Ekert, no stone was left unturned to provide assistance to my work. In total, I believe I had dealings with at least twelve different staff members in Lausanne, often in my pidgin French but always with the most helpful of people. For anyone interested in researching the Olympics, or just in the Olympic Games themselves, the centre and museum, attached to the IOC headquarters on the shores of Lake Geneva, are a must.

On a more localised level, the assistance of Marie McMahon and Julia Walsh at the South Tipperary Museum in Clonmel, of Rosemary Ryan at the Treasures Museum in Waterford, and of Sophia McNicholas at the Bohola Cheshire Home must be recorded. Waterford County Library staff have also been very supportive, none more so than my local librarian, Mary Tobin. Countless people have assisted with anecdotes, snippets of information and just supportive words during this sporting odyssey. People like Peter O'Connor's grandson, Mark Quinn, Con Tarrant (Banteer), Tom Aherne, the Ahearne family and Tim

Quaid (Athea), Patsy McGrath and the society members in Kilfinnane, the Sheridan memorial group (Bohola), Michael McGrath and Mary Burke (Charleville), Sean O'Donnell (Clonmel), Michael Walker (Dublin), Michael O'Dwyer (Bansha), Edward Walsh (Carriganimmy), Colm Murphy (London) and official GAA historian Marcus de Búrca are very happily numbered among these 'consultants' and providers of material. My sincere apologies if I have left anyone out of the list.

A number of schools and history teachers whom I have worked with have been forthcoming with material on Olympic alumni, for which much gratitude is heartily offered. Ger O'Sullivan did great work in trying to track details of the plans (in 1900) for Olympic hurling with Cork County GAA Board. Those who deserve my thanks also include several of my colleagues at the Department of Education and Science, whom I have certainly bored silly with my obsession over the years.

At the UCC History Department, Professor Dermot Keogh and Dr Gabriel Doherty have given me tremendous advice and encouragement over the duration of my research and I am very fortunate indeed to have had not only two such fine historians but also sports fans into the bargain, to supervise my work. I am hugely indebted to Professor Keogh for his ongoing interest in my work, not least in the transforming of the original thesis into the work you now hold. I can only hope the book has done justice to his faith in me.

My heartfelt thanks must go to the members of the Hibernian Athletics Historical Association, the self-styled 'HAHAs'. Dr Cyril White, Larry Ryder and Ronnie Long have added so much to my enjoyment of this topic since I met them and have, in my opinion, enhanced its quality beyond recognition with their knowledge, insights, human-interest details and photographs. These men are amazing ambassadors for Irish athletics and athletic history. They have also acted as guides and proofreaders when required and I have no doubt that the service people like these have given to Irish sporting history is beyond the scope of my mere words to properly recognise. My thanks also to Tony O'Donoghue of RTÉ (and the HAHAs) for his background support and great work on Irish championship records.

My wife, Patricia, and my daughters Elaine and Carole have been great supports to me and tolerated years of disruption, boxes of documents and general disorder in the completion of this work, for which they have my undying love and gratitude. Such disruption has gone back much further than this project, in fact, involving textbooks and local history books, but it is now, hopefully, at an end. I must thank my sister Lily also, particularly for her intrepid adventures with her husband Michael in South Boston on the trail of James Brendan Connolly, and for overnight accommodation on visits to the National Library. Sincere thanks are also due to my sister-in-law Caroline Bosshard for her practical assistance with accommodation and travel arrangements in Switzerland.

Thanks to Dr Cyril White and Vincent Hoban (UCD Photographic Reproduction Department) for preparing the certificate awarded to John Pius Boland for his victory in the tennis competition, (see p. 3 of colour section).

The core research on this book has been carried on over a period of close on five years. In reality, it may well have commenced twenty-five years ago, on the evening that John Treacy, who went to secondary school just up the street from my house in Cappoquin, won a silver medal in the Los Angeles Olympic Marathon in 1984. As Treacy came into the finishing straight, commentator Jimmy Magee made one of his most famous summations, deciding on the spur of the moment to list off the twelve previous Irish medallists at the Olympics and announcing John Treacy from Villierstown in County Waterford as the thirteenth. At this point, my eighty-two-year-old father, who had been sitting watching Treacy's success with every bit as much delight as I had, declared, 'He forgot about Peter O'Connor and the others!' While Jimmy Magee might possibly have forgotten about O'Connor *et al.*, and that is *very* unlikely, I had never even heard of them, though I had been an Olympics 'buff' since the days of Bob Beamon and Dick Fosbury in Mexico 1968. My father duly enlightened me, he having been a personal acquaintance, through judging with them at local athletic meets, of both Peter O'Connor (1906 Olympic triple jump champion) and Pat O'Callaghan, twice hammer gold medallist in 1928 and 1932. For his inspiration in terms of the love of the Olympic Games, which I inherited, and for his stories about the likes of O'Connor and Kiely, I would like to dedicate this work to the memory of my late father, Jack McCarthy. He loved all sports but none more so than the Olympic Games, which he and Danny McGrath had attended in 1948. If there is an athletic heaven, I can just picture my father introducing his old friend, Pat O'Callaghan, to his personal hero from 1948 and 1952, Emil Zatopek, and the two of them impressing even the mighty Czech runner with tales of the great Irish athletes whose story this book seeks to do some justice to.

Finally, my heartfelt thanks to all who have worked on this project at, and for, Cork University Press for their painstaking professionalism, support and courtesy to me at all times.

THE OLYMPIC GAMES, 1896–1924

1896 Athens

1900 Paris

1904 St Louis

1906 Athens*

1908 London

1912 Stockholm

(Berlin 1916)**

1920 Antwerp

1924 Paris

*Intercalated Games, held on the tenth anniversary of the first Athens Games

**Berlin Games abandoned following the outbreak of the Great War in 1914

Note: the term 'Olympiad' is generally used for the period of four years following the inaugural Olympic Games in 1896, not specifically for the number of the Games themselves. Accordingly, while the Berlin Games were not held, the period from 1916 to 1920 is still known as the sixth Olympiad. To avoid confusion, the term 'Olympiad' has not been employed in this book, with the name of the specific Olympic Games held being the normal means of identification.

ABBREVIATIONS

AAA – Amateur Athletic Association of England
AAU – Amateur Athletic Union of the USA
AOH – Ancient Order of Hibernians
BOA – British Olympic Association
DMP – Dublin Metropolitan Police
FA – Football Association of England
GAA – Gaelic Athletic Association
GACU – Gaelic Athletes' and Cyclists' Union
GNYIAA – Greater New York Irish Athletic Association
IAAA – Irish Amateur Athletic Association
IAAC – Irish American Athletic Club, later name for the GNYIAA
IAAF – International Amateur Athletic Federation
IARU – Irish Amateur Rowing Union
IASA – Irish Amateur Swimming Association
ICA – Irish Cyclists Association
IOC – International Olympic Committee
IRB – Irish Republican Brotherhood
IRFU – Irish Rugby Football Union
MAPA – Munster Athletes' Protection Association
NACAI – National Athletic and Cycling Association of Ireland
NYAC – New York Athletic Club
OCI – Olympic Council of Ireland
OSC – Olympic Studies Centre, Lausanne
SAAA – Scottish Amateur Athletic Association
WAAA – Welsh Amateur Athletic Association

INTRODUCTION

This chapter will attempt to set the scene for the Irish Olympic journey prior to independence. In some respects, the word 'journey' is far too restrictive for the story we are about to embark upon. Perhaps 'odyssey' might do it more justice, were it not for the fact that even the original Odyssey appears almost a mere pleasure cruise by comparison with the sporting and political trials which those who sought Olympic success for Ireland undertook. For this is a story spanning three decades of political and sporting change, where what might appear on the surface to be a relatively straightforward matter of sporting representation became a complex set of obstacles, some self inflicted, to Irish involvement at the Olympic Games.

The Dawn of International Sport

The last quarter of the nineteenth century saw major strides in the development of organised international sport. From the 1870s, international competition in sports like rugby and association football commenced, particularly in the British Isles, while in some circumstances such contests even began to cross continental boundaries, including the commencement of the Ashes competition in cricket in 1877 between England and Australia. In many respects, it was inevitable that such developments in team sports between pairs of nations would in time evolve into multi-event and multi-national sports contests. Initial moves in this direction saw the very first international athletic contest take place between Ireland and England in 1876 and, just four years later, the formation of the Amateur Athletic Association (AAA) in England and the holding of its first championships, open to international entries.[1]

By the 1890s, a significant degree of international sporting competition developed, and already the linkage between national identity and international sport was well established. Then, in 1894 the first steps were taken towards the foundation of the greatest international sporting competition of them all, the modern Olympic Games.

The ancient Olympic Games have long been thought to epitomise peace and reconciliation, based on the notion that all rival Greek states ceased their warring tendencies for the great festival at Olympia once every four years. To what degree this cessation actually occurred remains open to dispute by historians the world over. It is, of course, true that the ancient Games contributed to inter-state rivalries, by the competitive nature of the sporting contests themselves. Victors were certainly lauded in their home states for their individual prowess but also for the fact that they had beaten the representatives of rival states into the bargain:

> The idea of winning was of far more significance in these Games than in the Olympic philosophy established by Pierre de Coubertin more than 2500 years later. In fact, victory was of paramount importance, with defeat bringing disgrace for the whole *polis* [city state].[2]

To some extent, the modern Olympic Games just 'appeared' on the international sporting horizon in the mid-1890s, the brainchild of one idealistic mind. The modern Olympics' founding father, Baron Pierre de Coubertin of France, was quite genuinely seeking to promote international rather than simply French physicality and sporting excellence in founding the Games at the Sorbonne University in Paris in 1894. De Coubertin had many sporting theories, some might say a full-blown philosophy of the importance of sport in the human condition. However, even for him, national issues in an era which saw the rise of nationalism globally were impossible to escape from. In many respects, it was France's defeat in the war with Prussia in 1870–1 that had spurred the young Coubertin to consider how he could contribute to the re-establishment of French grandeur and improve the physical conditioning of its men.[3] Likewise, it is most obvious that the organisers, participants and spectators at the first modern Games saw them as vehicles for national pride. The inaugural Athens Olympics were permeated by displays of national pride, from loudly chanting and flag-waving American enthusiasts to those who used the ceremonies to reinforce the prestige of royal rulers, such as the Greek royal family at the same Games, and so on:

> With origins that located sport so clearly in the midst of competition between nation states, with all the accompanying symbolism of anthems and flags, it is difficult to see how the Olympics could ever be free of nationalism.[4]

National pride came to the fore too in the notion that certain sports or sporting events were a sort of natural preserve of specific nations. It explains, for instance, the relative unconcern of the Greeks when their sportsmen at the Athens Games in 1896 failed against Americans, Germans and others, as long as redemption came in the end via the Greek shepherd Spiridon Louis winning the marathon race. As we examine the development of the Games after 1896 from an Irish perspective, it will remain a constant that many issues of nationality and nationalism permeated the modern Olympic movement. As historian Allen Guttmann puts it:

> Although the Olympic Charter proclaims that the games are contests between individuals, not between nations, the IOC [International Olympic Committee] created an institutional structure based on national representation . . . The danger of rabidly nationalistic partisanship was there from the start.[5]

The Irish Sporting Context

For the Irish who participated at the Olympic Games from 1896 onwards, it was perhaps inevitable that they would become caught up in symbolism and patriotic demonstration like many others. The Irish experience at the first modern Olympics between 1896 and 1920 had, in fact, several parallels with emerging nationalities such as the Finns, Hungarians, Bohemians and the Australians, and these will illuminate the Irish story in different ways during our study. In other respects, particularly given the massive Irish diasporal dimension in the United States of America, and to a lesser extent in Canada and South Africa, the impact of Irish identity on the early Olympics and vice versa was quite unique.

While we will see that the modern Olympic movement under Baron de Coubertin was itself riddled with confusion and complexities on the issue of national identity, Ireland's Olympic involvement was further complicated by the fact that we were under British rule. Wherever the arousal of national pride posed any sort of threat to ruling establishments, the conservative and aristocratic International Olympic Committee (IOC) and the leaders of what became the British Olympic Association (BOA) made concerted efforts to dampen such sentiments. What made the emerging national identity of Irish Olympians even more of a threat to the establishment was that the demand for separate recognition was coming from people who were generally drawn from the lower social orders. The IOC motives for upholding its amateur regulations should not be underestimated – they had at least as much to do with maintaining the control of the establishment over society generally as with preserving the supposed purity of the sporting contest:

> The concept of amateurism as it was then understood was an invention of the Victorian middle and upper classes. Its freely acknowledged purpose was to exclude the 'lower orders' from the play of the leisure class.[6]

Of the twenty-five Olympic titles won by Irish athletes between 1896 and 1920, only three were won by 'professional' people in the old sense of the word. Two titles were won by a final-year law student in 1896 (John Boland) and the third in 1906 by a law clerk at the time, Peter O'Connor. The Irish and particularly Irish-American track and field athletes, several of whom were de facto professional athletes, were a severe challenge to accepted IOC norms of aristocratic dominance, whatever about the nationalistic threats they may have posed otherwise.

The modern Olympic Games provided an opportunity for the emergent Irish identity to establish itself on a stage far larger than either internal native sport or relatively restricted international team sports had to offer. The English-language literary works of people like Yeats and Synge had a much greater impact in terms of portraying Irish identity internationally in this period than Irish-language works by writers like an Pádraig Pearse or Douglas Hyde. This was because the medium of the message was an international one, the English language. The Olympic

Games had a similar potential for Irish identity to reach a global sporting audience. It is this opportunity, and the degree to which it was seized upon, which is a central preoccupation of this book.

Sport and the Irish Diaspora

One important feature in the early Irish Olympic story is the fact that it relates to Ireland but also to the Irish post-Famine diaspora. By the 1890s, this diaspora was well established in a number of places around the globe, but particularly in North America. The other great centre of Irish global emigration, Australia, produced one famous female swimmer of an Irish-Australian background, Fanny Durack, but otherwise the sporting Irish in the southern continent gravitated towards sports like Australian Rules football and cricket, which did not have an Olympic dimension.

Irish-American sporting heroes were already well established in the USA, particularly in boxing, before the Olympic Games were mooted in the 1890s. However, individual achievements of the likes of John L. Sullivan, Jim Corbett and others lacked an international dimension in many instances. Their main opponents were often fellow Americans, meaning that the possibilities of using sport to arouse a sense of national fervour were not high, as a rule. The same was true of the Irish who starred in 'American' sports like baseball and American football – international competition was a non-entity in these sports. This all changed quite significantly through track and field athletics. By the later nineteenth century and beginning of the twentieth, through international athletic competitions such as the AAA and Olympic championships, America seized major opportunities to demonstrate that it had surpassed, in sporting terms, anything which the old world had to offer. To the fore of this American change in track and field athletics were the Irish-Americans. As will be seen, the success of Irish-American athletes in the Olympics gave a significant boost to various forms of Irish national identity within the USA itself and also to the American acceptance of Ireland as one of its 'melting pot' components.[7] This was achieved through sporting excellence, through very definite identification with the athletes' adopted country (without losing Irish identity either) and to occasionally fighting battles against the more negative elements of Irish identity, in order to challenge the bias of others in the USA towards Irish identity. For the Greater New York Irish Athletic Association (GNYIAA) in particular, later known as the Irish American Athletic Club, the welcoming of non-Irish athletes to the club, as well as the promotion of a positive image of Ireland, were important concerns. An interesting cameo of the latter concern can be seen when, in writing of an unsavoury match during the GNYIAA carnival at Celtic Park, which included the final of the Hurling Championship of New York, the *Gaelic American* newspaper warned:

> The Daly Hurling Club should not allow this man to play with their team again, as such a rowdy as he proved himself to be will do much to discredit and put a damper on Irish field sports, as well as give American athletes and patrons of field sports the idea that Irishmen cannot enter into competition in any manly pastime without finishing the game in a riot, and thereby giving the Jew newspaper proprietors and reporters a chance to ridicule and belittle Irishmen and Irish sports, as anyone may see by reading an account of the above-mentioned hurling match in the New York *World* of Monday, July 5.[8]

Clearly, this concern derived from more than a mere distaste for unsporting behaviour. In cities like New York, groups like the Jews were often rivals of the Irish in terms of seeking acceptability as new 'Americans'. For many Irish in the USA, America came very quickly to represent what they had never had in Ireland – wealth, prestige, influence, democracy – and they came to use this 'Americanism' very pointedly, particularly when Olympic competition against or in Britain was concerned.

The Irish Sporting Context
Before we delve any further into matters of politics or organisation in Irish sport prior to the modern Olympics, one point must be made very forcefully. By any yardstick one chooses – depth of sporting talent, records, consistency, prize winning, etc. – the standard of athletic sports in Ireland in the latter half of the nineteenth century was phenomenal, and athletics was to be the lifeblood of the modern Olympic Games. Considering that the nation was experiencing prolonged post-Famine decline, falling birth rates, massive emigration and rural depopulation, the number and quality of top-class athletes that Ireland produced was

Tom Davin (left) and Tom Kiely with some of the weights they threw as younger men around Deerpark in south Tipperary, the Davin family home.

startling. Perhaps even more remarkable is that a huge proportion of the great athletes who established Irish fame in this period came from a very small pocket of rich countryside, often known as the Golden Vale. North Cork, west Tipperary and much of County Limerick may well have produced more world records, more international and Olympic champions than any other rural area in modern times. This is particularly true of traditionally strong Celtic sports like weight throwing and jumping, and will be borne out as we read of the Leahys, Flanagans, Ahearnes and Davins, of Tom Kiely, Con Walsh, Paddy Ryan and so many more in the coming chapters.

The most significant work of recent years on the emergence of sport and national identity in Ireland from the 1890s has focused on the Gaelic Athletic Association (GAA) and association football. Its central definition of nationalism is of 'a multifaceted expression of identity which, while having some common constituents, functions as both a mobile and historically contested ideology'.[9] In the Irish and Irish-American Olympic experience, it will be seen that this definition is largely accurate, although the word 'mobile' must be interpreted quite literally, perhaps better as 'transferable' in the context of Irish and Irish-American national identity. This multifaceted nature also included many people who were just proud to be Irish, some who were quite narrow and certainly parochial about it, some whose 'nationalism' can be seen merely as patriotism or even anti-Englishness, some who sought to use sport as a weapon in the struggle for independence, and many who did not. There was also a lot of fluidity in people's opinions. Just because someone was a supporter of GAA games did not always mean that he or she was an opponent of non-GAA sports, whatever his or her political leanings otherwise. Many people, whether extreme nationalists, moderate nationalists or unionists, were comfortable in acknowledging Irish sporting success at the Olympics, regardless of the political persuasions of the contestants.

At this juncture, a second constant of the times deserves mention. Irish sportspeople of all political and perhaps even religious persuasions enjoyed beating their neighbours, none more so than the English. For those of more extreme national viewpoints, if an Irish team or athlete was not in a position to achieve such a victory, support transferred itself very often to whomever the opponents of England happened to be. This was, perhaps, something which was to be found in many nations with close neighbours or in nations under the rule of others, but it was strongly present in the Irish sporting consciousness from the very early stages of international competition.

A particularly clear example of how international sport was a vehicle for Irish national identity lay in the reaction in Ireland to the great contest of September 1895 between the New York Athletic Club (backboned by several athletes of Irish extraction) and a London Athletic Club selection.[10] The first issue of interest here arose in the make-up of the London team. *Sport* reported on the proposed London line-up, commenting:

> It will be seen that the list includes Horgan, Kiely, and Ryan; but ... it is hardly likely that they will go. Perhaps one might, but it is not a point about which there is likely to be any great enthusiasm in Irish athletic circles. Their presence would probably turn the tide in favour of London, and should the victory come off I wonder to whom the credit would be given.[11]

The palpable reluctance to see Irish athletes represent an English team hardly needs comment here. It was felt in extreme nationalist circles and among many of more moderate viewpoints. The same article continues:

> We in Ireland would have every confidence in the issue of the meeting as far as the Irish representatives are concerned, but it would be desirable that the occasion were a better one.

It was also clear that the Irishmen representing New York were in no way seen as competing for a foreign/alien body, in the way representing London was viewed. An additional reason for the reluctance to see Irishmen compete for London was offered:

> While again they would practically be opposing their own countrymen, for a very large percentage of the New York representatives will be Irishmen or the descendants of Irishmen.

The Irish reaction to the decisive victory which New York eventually scored over the London team (for which, as anticipated, none of the aforementioned Irish athletes turned out) was jubilant. *Sport* reported on a 'crushing defeat of Englishmen . . . who failed to score a single point,' while a sub-heading declared, in reference to the Irish-Americans on the New York squad, 'Irish well to the fore'.[12] The emergence of some patriotic fervour did not take long either:

> . . . we have very good reason to be proud of the part our countrymen took in the contest, and the very large share indeed which they had in the victory. For out of the eleven events of which the contest consisted no less than six fell to men born in Ireland or with a large amount of Irish blood in their veins.[13]

Irish Sporting Organisations and Tensions

'Sport has played a hugely important political role in Ireland since the late nineteenth century, it has had a central function in constructing different ideas of what it is to be Irish.'[14]

From the commencement of the AAA championships in England in 1880, Irish athletes began to travel and achieve notable international successes, particularly in the sports which had been popular activities in rural Ireland for many decades before the AAA was founded. In the 1881 championships, Pat Davin of Carrick-on-Suir won the AAA long jump and high jump titles, while his brother Maurice (one of the founders of the Gaelic Athletic Association in 1884) won the shot and hammer events.[15] Political divisions, differences of views on the appropriateness of holding competitions on Sundays, giving cash prizes and other factors soon caused a division in Irish athletics. The formation of the Gaelic Athletic Association in 1884, and of the Irish Amateur Athletic Association a few months later, gave renewed organisational impetus to Irish athletics. Although these associations had significantly different political and, often, social and demographic backgrounds, they helped to formalise Irish athletic sports and ensured that, by the 1890s, Irish athletics was at least on a par with the best on offer in any other nation capable of competing on the international stage.

The GAA began in the 1880s with the stated intention of promoting Irish athletic excellence but this very soon became a body which promoted local rivalries even more strongly. The national identity which evolved within the GAA had a limited international focus and, through its intermittent bans against other sports and organisations, was often reactive rather than proactive. The association's reluctance to commit to the Olympics in the 1890s stems not just from its narrow focus but also from other factors, such as financial constraints, the timing of competitions and the simple lack of appeal of the early Games. One modern Irish historian makes a very convincing argument that what 'Irish Irelanders' in the 1890s felt to be the threat of anglicisation was, in point of fact, really modernisation.[16] In ways, the same can be said of the GAA when its stance on athletics is examined. The world was changing, with the Olympics offering a whole new international vista in an age of greater ease of transport and communication. The GAA's efforts to revive athletic pastimes would see it shun the modernisation and international-isation of sporting competition in part because it did not distinguish such modernisation from anglicisation. Instead, the association chose the more readily Gaelic route of developing football and hurling and basically abandoned the national and international potential of athletics in the process.

In the 1880s and 1890s, Irish involvement in international sporting competition outside of occasional athletics contests with Scotland or individual participation in international championships was largely down to conservative-dominated bodies like the IAAA in athletics or the Irish Rugby Football Union (IRFU). Irish national teams competed regularly in anglo-sports like hockey and rugby and generally against the home countries. Frequently, too, the focus of such international sport was on beating 'brother Celts', not necessarily just Britain or England. One commentator on a rugby victory over the Scots explained:

> It is with feelings of great satisfaction and complacency that I at last find myself in the position of recording angel of a most decisive victory for the wearers of the green over their brother Celts . . .[17]

Yet the fact that such sporting organisations, including the IAAA, were dominated by people of less extreme political sentiment, hovering between moderate nationalist and staunch unionist, did not prevent them from wanting to establish an Irish identity through sport. As early as 1895–6, the evidence suggests that the identification of international sport as a national vehicle was, in fact, quite strong in all parts of Ireland.

Rivalry between the GAA and other bodies would be a constant feature of most of the years between 1896 and 1920 and was extremely damaging to Irish Olympic efforts. In some respects, Irish athletic activity at this time was hugely fraught with divisions in ways far outside of matters of identity and politics too – the threats of legal action between athletes over claims of use of inappropriate weight-throwing equipment, for instance, populate the pages of the main Irish sporting chronicle from the 1890s, *Sport*.[18] The historian of pre-1884 Irish athletics has even gone as far as to suggest that there is something almost intrinsically self-destructive in Irish athletic circles:

> Ireland is a land of contradictions. There is the propensity for greatness as there is for self destruction. It was Brendan Behan who, at a meeting to establish a society, made the first proposal that the 'official' split [of the society] should now be made and got over with immediately. Although for Behan this was a jest there is an element of truth behind the tale. Irish athletics suffered tremendously because of the splits and dissensions – official and otherwise. Whatever benefit the administrators drew from their command of various associations, it was the athlete inevitably and the sport generally that suffered.[19]

While the above statement referred to the 1870s in the main, it was just as correct of the period from 1884 to 1896, and the frightening thing is that the statement remained quite true of all Irish athletic organisations for the duration of the period under study here. The GAA promoted nationalism, sometimes extremism, Sunday sports meetings, acceptance of payments to certain athletes and a largely rural support base. By contrast, the politics of the IAAA and Irish Cyclists Association (ICA) were more conservative. They tended to be more unionist than separatist, against Sunday competitions or any form of professionalism. The support base of these organisations was also more urban than the GAA's. These are broad generalisations, no more. However, the extent to which there was, in fact, a sort of begrudging co-operation too between the rival athletic bodies in Ireland before the Olympics has often been underestimated. Certainly, the GAA had been and would be again at loggerheads with both of the moderate 'unionist' bodies, the IAAA and its sister body, the ICA. I am using the term 'unionist' very warily here, and will do so throughout this work. In many respects, the word 'unionist' was used by more extreme nationalists to describe nationalists who were willing to accept less than full independence and hence might otherwise be described as 'conservative'. As such, while a body like the IAAA was often termed as 'unionist' in the 1890s and later, most of its members were firm Home Rule supporters and some were to make more potent nationalist demonstrations at the Olympic festivals than extreme nationalists were able to do.

In any event, by the mid-1890s, the GAA's bans of 1885 and 1887 against co-operation with the other bodies had both been lifted and it would be 1905–6 before the association moved again in the direction of banning co-operation with organisations like the IAAA or ICA.[20] The plethora of athletic meetings held in August 1895, for example, showed at least a willingness to co-operate on rules and regulations. The sports meetings held at Castlerea, Castlebar and Portadown were under joint IAAA and ICA rules, which was not terribly surprising politically, perhaps. On the other hand, the Durrow sports were held under GAA and ICA rules.[21] In the same edition of *Sport,* GAA stalwarts like Kiely, Horgan and Ryan, who would later reject the idea of competing for London, were reported to be competing on an Irish team, alongside 'unionist' athletes from Dublin and Ulster, against a Scottish selection at Parkhead in Glasgow. The newspaper merely described Kiely and others as 'the Southern members of the Irish team' and noted that the team overall were 'a fairly representative lot'.[22] There is, perhaps, a further point of interest about the Parkhead venue itself, home of Glasgow Celtic FC. Michael Davitt, one of the original patrons of the GAA, also became a patron of Celtic in 1892 – evidence again of the fluidity of Irish sporting identities, whatever bans were to be in place from time to time.

The issues of national identity, in terms of what the Olympic movement itself fostered and what British Olympic officials were willing to tolerate, will be shown to be central matters in the forthcoming chapters. So, too, will the complexities which beset the Irish viewpoints of national identity, mingled with the political wranglings within Irish athletic circles, and including the Irish-American identities and nationalism. Irish and Irish-American sportsmen achieved magnificent heights at the Olympic Games between 1896 and 1920, in sporting terms and also in terms of establishing an Irish identity often in the face of either apathy or vehement opposition in official circles, including those in Britain particularly. This is the story of an often-forgotten but certainly glorious chapter in Irish sporting history, and of the political division and confusion which ultimately helped ensure that the great achievements of Irish competitors at the early Olympics were never to be repeated after independence.

CHAPTER ONE

THE ATHENS OLYMPICS OF 1896

The inaugural modern Olympic Games of 1896 in Athens had limited impact on Ireland. A central reason for this was simply the newness and smallness of the fledgling Olympics. They lasted just ten days, had representatives of barely fifteen countries and a total of just 245 competitors, all of them men. Several national teams at the Beijing Olympics had more competitors than all of the participants at the 1896 Games put together.[1] The remoteness of Athens, the lack of available media coverage of the Games, except for bland Reuters and International Press Association reports, and the lack of an identifiable 'Irish' team were further contributing factors in the general ignorance of these Games in Ireland before, during and after them.

Although there was basically only one Irish-born competitor in Athens, and a couple of Irish-Americans representing the USA, there is still a lot to learn from these first Olympics, including insights into the nature of Irish sport, the degree of division which existed in Irish athletics and the Games' links to national identity on both sides of the Atlantic. The first Olympics also contributed to a form of national awakening, though embryonic, and this should not be dismissed lightly, even though nationalist politics was in a particularly disjointed state in 1895–6. One noted historian has described nationalist parliamentary politics of 1895 as:

> Parnellism without the overwhelming personality of Parnell, without the favourable political position of 1885, without the

support of a united and enthusiastic country, without the inspiration and imagination which had lifted the earlier movement from obscure beginnings to be the embodiment of the national cause.[2]

Matters of Invitation

One Irish Olympic historian has suggested that both the GAA and IAAA received invitations to get involved in the inaugural Olympic Congress, at the Sorbonne University in Paris during 1894. The text of the letter from Baron de Coubertin to the IAAA honorary secretary, Edward J. (Ned) Walsh, survives. Walsh, from County Offaly, was a founding member of the IAAA and a one-time national 120 yards hurdles and high jump champion, as well as winner of the Canadian championships in these events in the same year, 1885. He also won seven caps in rugby union for Ireland between 1897 and 1893. As IAAA secretary in 1894, Walsh was told by the baron:

> The Congress has been called by the Union of French Sports Clubs for the purpose of studying the question of Amateurism and of making a first effort towards the unification of sports regulations. Thus preparation will be made for the restoration at an early date of the Olympic Games, on bases and in conditions suited to the needs of modern life.[3]

Walsh's reply, dated 28 May 1894, referred to having received de Coubertin's letter on 12 May, and informed the baron of his committee's decision:

Baron Pierre de Coubertin, founder of the modern Olympic Games, pictured in 1900. Courtesy of the IOC Research and Reference Service at the Olympic Studies Centre, Lausanne.

This photograph of the Lansdowne Rugby Club team which won the Leinster Senior Cup in 1891 shows Edward J. Walsh, the man who received the IAAA's invitation to the 1896 Olympics, standing third from the left at the back. Seated at the left of the middle row is Michael Bulger, who later became the IAAA's representative on the Council of the British Olympic Association. Courtesy of Dr Cyril M. White.

> They will accept your invitation to send delegates with pleasure and will be represented by D.D. Bulger, Vice President or J.T. Magee of the Race Committee or perhaps both.[4]

A copy of the letter to the GAA, if it existed, has not been located during the research on this book. However, de Coubertin's only confirmed visit to Ireland was during the 1880s, when both the GAA and IAAA had been founded. Thus it is very likely that he knew of the existence of both organisations.[5]

In the end, there were two representatives of the IAAA – Dan Bulger and Jim Magee – and none from the GAA present at the inaugural meeting of the Olympic movement at the Sorbonne in Paris.[6] In attending, they at least made the new International Olympic Committee aware of the existence of the IAAA and of Irish athletics. We may even speculate that the Irish pair must have been more central to proceedings than that, as Bulger at least, like E.J. Walsh, was a past student of the French College, now Blackrock College, and would have been more than comfortable in his francophone surroundings at the Sorbonne. The serious sporting pedigree of the two IAAA representatives also showed that the association was very interested in Irish involvement on this international stage. Bulger was the winner of five AAA championships in long jump and hurdles, as well as twenty-five Irish titles, and once held the world record in the 120 yards hurdles. Magee, furthermore, won two rugby caps for Ireland within a year of attending the Sorbonne congress.[7] Whatever the Irish involvement, however, these men were also to be the last Irish representatives to attend as delegates at an IOC forum for over a quarter of a century, although Bulger's brother Michael in particular would play a central part in quite a deal of Olympic history subsequently, as will be seen in later chapters.

The outcome of the Sorbonne gathering of seventy-eight representatives of nearly forty national sporting bodies was to be, basically, the setting up of the Olympic movement (the International Olympic Committee, henceforth IOC) and the decision to hold the first modern Olympic Games in Athens during 1896. In the end, neither the IAAA nor the GAA would be represented there.

Co-operation?

As seen in the previous chapter, there was some evidence of improving relations between the GAA and IAAA on the eve of the first modern Olympics. In July 1895, a three-man delegation from the GAA was authorised to meet with their IAAA counterparts. Why this meeting did not occur until December remains a mystery. However, when it did occur:

> . . . after only some hours' discussion, agreement was reached on a joint GAA–IAAA records committee. The GAA central council at once ratified this and appointed the three GAA delegates as its members on the joint committee.[8]

These were essentially practical, administrative matters. Where there remained a potentially unbridgeable gap, of course, was in the political differences between the GAA and an organisation like the IAAA. A letter from the Dublin GAA board to its flagging members in the metropolis stated:

> To every Irishman worthy of the name, and believing in an individual national existence for his country, our appeal for support to the GAA should carry increased force, because the athletic pastimes which we seek to revive, have, from earliest ages, been a main characteristic of our native land, and the means by which the muscular superiority and fame of her people were established.[9]

Co-operation on record-keeping, rules or even on sending teams to defeat the Scots reflected a limited degree of co-ordination between the GAA and other sporting bodies, though a far cry from total co-operation across the political chasm. However, the issue of entering an Irish team at the 1896 Olympics was unlikely to be blocked by political differences alone. In fact, relations between the GAA and the IAAA and ICA were a lot better in the mid-1890s than they had been in the 1880s or would be when bans were subsequently introduced in the early twentieth century. It has also been argued that far from everyone in the GAA during the pre-revolutionary period was an extremist in nationalist terms:

> In the early years of its existence the GAA was a solid supporter of Parnell's vision of a constitutionally achieved home rule. In 1900, with the rise of John Redmond, and the electoral process whereby the Irish were left holding the balance of power, the GAA was again highly supportive (officially at least) of the constitutional route.[10]

The GAA certainly developed a more radical, anti-conciliatory strain of leadership in the initial years of the twentieth century, something which impacted negatively on its attitude to Olympic participation. However, the notion of the GAA as some form of homogeneous and narrowly nationalistic entity in the 1890s is simply wrong. In fact, there can have been few periods in the organisation's history when its sense of political direction was more confused than it was in 1895–6. One commentator has pointed out that the GAA was in 'a sharp, if temporary decline in the early and mid-1890s as a result of both the confusion within parliamentary politics and of divisions within the militant Irish Republican Brotherhood'.[11] Therefore, to simply ascribe some form of narrow nationalism as the sole reason for the GAA's Olympic abstension is also unreliable. The organisation, and indeed the IAAA, had much more practical concerns, not least of them being money.

No Olympic Entry
The original invitations to the 1896 Olympic Games went out from the IOC to various athletic bodies which might have been interested, and in a position to organise teams for Athens. This was the case, for instance, with the USA, where the invite appears to have been taken on board specifically by the Boston Athletic Association.[12]

While IOC records and the official report of the 1896 Games carry definitive lists of the nations who competed at Athens, no extant records have been unearthed to show those who were actually invited. In the Irish context, it is certain that the IAAA did receive an invitation to compete, no doubt due to its representatives having been at the Sorbonne congress in 1894. The IAAA secretary, E.J. Walsh, submitted what was described as 'a circular from the executive of the Olympian Games' at a general committee meeting of 10 October 1895. The communication, in French, issued the core invitation:

> . . . the Grecian committee, established at Athens . . . have the honour to invite you to take part in the Olympic Games of 1896. The invite was signed by Timoleon T Philemon, Secretary General of the Grecian Olympic Games Committee.[13]

It is unclear whether such an invite ever issued directly to the more nationalist GAA, not to mention who exactly Mr Philemon meant by 'you' in the invitation. Even though no definitive evidence has been found at IOC level, it is highly likely that the GAA received no Olympic invite. Certainly, de Coubertin had visited Ireland during the 1880s and must have known of the GAA's existence. Nor should we forget that the quality of any Olympic athletic competition would be adversely affected by Irish absences, as in 1896 no fewer than twenty world 'records' were held by Irish athletes.[14] However, it is a matter of fact rather than speculation that, in matters relating to British sporting associations, de Coubertin deferred from the start almost entirely to the then AAA secretary, Charles Herbert. This was a man whom de Coubertin once described, along with

William Sloane of the USA and the baron himself, as one of 'an immovable trinity' who founded the Olympic movement. It is hard to imagine that Herbert recommended invitation of any other Irish organisation except the one he had regular contacts with, not to mention an acceptable political viewpoint: the IAAA. It was difficult enough to create enthusiasm within British sporting circles for the untested Olympic ideal, making it less than likely that Herbert would have sought the involvement of an organisation perceived to be more separatist than the IAAA. *The Guardian* newspaper bemoaned the lack of real British enthusiasm for the Athens contests. However, the tone adopted by the Manchester newspaper shows how far from allowing the Olympic Games to become vehicles for any sort of anti-British organisation or sentiment the British establishment was in 1896:

> With our usual slowness to seize an opportunity and our usual indifference to the rest of the world, England and in particular the older universities, are but poorly represented at Athens, but still it is from England that the impulse to these things in modern Europe has come . . . The Olympic Games may yet do for Europe what cricket does for the sea-divided Anglo Saxon race.[15]

The IAAA committee's reaction to the Olympic invitation was cautious, citing the expense of the venture as being a major concern. The committee on the night decided that 'the opinion of the leading supporters of athletics throughout the country should be invited through the Press before any definite action be taken in the matter'. The final paragraph of this aforementioned *Sport* account of the meeting mentioned plans to rearrange a meeting which had previously fallen through with the GAA. Yet it would be overly speculative to assume that the Olympic invite had necessarily prompted this effort to rearrange the meeting now. No outstanding GAA Central Council minutes contain a reference to this invitation. Certainly as far as the Irish press records:

> It was apparently the IAAA which first mentioned the possibility of an Irish team participating in the first revived Olympic Games fixed for March 1896. This idea was discussed by the [GAA] central council – although not recorded in the

minutes – and a decision taken to canvass clubs on the chances of forming a team; but by December the project had been abandoned.[16]

It has elsewhere been suggested that the GAA was uninterested in the 1896 Olympics because the holding of the Games, in the month of April, meant that GAA athletes would not be sufficiently fit/prepared to do themselves or the organisation justice.[17] *Sport* recorded the GAA's eventual decision to reject participation as having been taken at the very meeting which approved the joint GAA–IAAA committee on record-keeping:

> The Council had under discussion the proposed scheme of sending out a team of athletes to compete in the Olympian Games at Athens. The programme of the games was submitted to the meeting, but the Council decided to take no further steps in the matter as there were only two events in the programme, namely the putting the shot and the high jump, which Irishmen would be likely to win, the meeting then adjourned.[18]

Although not stated in the press, it is important to consider the relatively tight financial constraints the GAA operated under in 1895. The annual convention at Thurles in April that year was informed that during the previous year the receipts of the association amounted to £284. 8s. 2d., and the expenditure to £299. 19s. 10d.[19] Although some extenuating circumstances were identified, it is highly probable that the GAA did not have the money to spend on an Athenian adventure in 1896, any more than the IAAA did. This is not otherwise documented in GAA archival material but must be taken into account, especially with the psychological and financial legacy of the disastrous 'American invasion' of the late 1880s. This 'invasion' involved sending a large group of GAA athletes to compete in American venues. It had been anticipated as a money spinner for the association but, in fact, had all but bankrupted the GAA, leaving it incapable of even funding All-Ireland championships for a year. It is not unreasonable to suggest that the untried and untested Olympic Games of 1896 seemed to both athletic bodies to be an unwise investment of scarce resources.

Missed Opportunities

The timing of the Athens Games was cited as a factor in the GAA's lack of interest in forming a team, due to the lack of training that its top athletes would have done by that early stage of the year. However, serious doubt is cast on this notion by GAA-inspired events elsewhere in April 1896, just a week before the Athens Olympics. The *Irish Independent* carried lengthy accounts of what it termed 'the Invasion of London'.[20] This was a GAA-organised festival of Irish sport at Stamford Bridge. The national triumphalism of the accounts was very palpable, but so too is the evidence that GAA athletes, even in April, were world class and would have been well capable of holding their own in Athens. The *Independent* tells us:

> If the Gaelic Tournament were memorable for nothing else, it will long be referred to in world-wide sporting circles with keen interest, for J. Flanagan of Kilmallock beat his own [hammer] world record by more than eight feet.

Later in the same article it was reported that 'This event was followed by the throwing from the nine foot circle and again a world's record was broken – that of T.F. Kiely – the length of the throw being 147 ft. It was won by Flanagan.'[21] Admittedly, there was no hammer event on the schedule at the Athens Games the following week, but the prowess of Flanagan and others surely casts doubt on the idea that Athens was too early in the season for GAA athletes, particularly as the dates of the Olympic events had been notified in 1895, giving ample preparation time if needed. As an aside, the Stamford Bridge event was of interest in that both John Flanagan and Tom Kiely, who would become Olympic champions in time, played in the Munster hurling team against Leinster there, with Munster winning in the end by 5–7 to 2–8. Although Flanagan's two world records overshadowed Kiely in the athletic events, it is worth noting that Kiely also won the long jump at Stamford Bridge.[22]

Further evidence of the significant opportunity which was missed by neither the IAAA nor the GAA sending athletes to the Athens Olympics comes when we compare the winning times and distances at Athens with those achieved in Irish championship events later in 1896. It is not possible to compare all events, given that the rules varied quite a lot in many weight-throwing and jumping contests. Also, Irish distances tended to rely on imperial measurements whereas Olympic competitions were always in metric distances. Yet some events bear reasonable comparison.[23] In the 100 metres at Athens, Harvard's Irish-American student Thomas Burke took twelve seconds to get to the finish. Irish 100-yard titles were won in the same year in 10.2 seconds (IAAA) and in 10.6 seconds (GAA). With a difference in the respective distances of just over seven metres, the Irish times would have won at Athens, with some comfort. Similarly, 400 metres is just over two metres shorter than 440 yards. The Athens winning time for the 400 metres, 54.2 seconds, would have been no match for the 51 seconds flat achieved by James Meredith in the IAAA 440 yards championships. Meredith recorded the same time in the annual match against Scotland in the same year. Thomas Burke of Boston University was not a specialist 100-metre runner, although he and his coach were credited with the 'invention' of the modern sprint start position. Thus, it could be reasonable to suggest that the Irish 100-metre times were not exceptional by world standards. Burke, however, was also to become the Olympic winner in the 400 metres and had been considered the top American 400-metre runner of the day, making the achievements of Meredith, in an event for which Ireland was not particularly noted, all the greater. It also bears consideration that the Athens track was a then-modern cinders one, while Irish championships tended to be run on grass, a significantly slower surface.[24]

The same pattern emerged in the jumping and throwing events which could be compared directly, having identical rules. The Olympic high jump was won at 5 feet 11.5 inches. While the IAAA championships were particularly low in standard in 1896, with a winning jump of 5 feet 6 inches, the GAA title was won by Murty O'Brien at 6 feet and half an inch, even though the weather was showery, while James M. Ryan cleared 6 feet 2 inches when winning the Ireland v. Scotland match in July. In the long jump, the Olympic title was won in 20 feet 10 inches. The GAA championship of 1896 was won in 21 feet 6.5 inches, the IAAA mark was half an inch further, while 22 feet exactly was reached by Walter Newborn in the Ireland v. Scotland match. Finally, in the shot put, the Olympic record of 36 feet 9.75 inches would not have kept pace with the achievements of Denis Horgan in 1896. In the IAAA championship, the man from Lyre, near Banteer in north Cork, threw 44 feet 7 inches, in the

GAA championship he recorded 44 feet 11 inches and in the Ireland v. Scotland match he marked 44 feet 7 inches again. If anyone was to merit the title of greatest Irish athlete never to win an Olympic title, it would be Horgan. Yet, as we will see when we get to the one Olympic Games he did compete in, those at London in 1908, he was to be attacked in some quarters for doing so as part of a British and Irish team.

These five events were the only ones which could be compared directly with Olympic athletic events in 1896. The comparison suggests one important message: whatever the standards of many of the original Olympic champion athletes, in every single case the marks achieved in the same year by Irish athletes were far ahead of those achieved in Athens. The opportunity to establish Irish identity in an indelible way, through multiple victories at the first Olympic Games, by the GAA, the IAAA or both, was certainly lost.

If the GAA particularly missed a national opportunity at Athens, the organisation was not oblivious to the nationalistic, indeed revolutionary impact which sport could have. After the London tournament, Mr Arthur Lynch, on behalf of the London Gaelic clubs, said:

> Wellington had truly said that the battles of England were won by the muscular training which obtained on the playing fields of England. They should all hope that some national results would accrue from the physical training on the athletic fields of Ireland, which were superior to those of England. The bone and muscle of the Irish race was superior to that of any other nation and he hoped it would always be diverted into national channels.[25]

Another edition of the *Irish Independent* criticised the decision to separate Irish and British lawn tennis bodies, the writer being moved to point out:

> As one of the great national games of this age, lawn tennis has been accorded a place in the New Olympian contests . . . Had not Dr. Pim, obedient to the higher claims of the Aesculapaen art, abandoned all intention of further tournaments, Ireland undoubtedly would have had the honour of presenting the first Olympic lawn tennis champion to the world.[26]

This writer was most certainly conservative in political sentiment, yet expressing quite clear views on the desirability of Irish representation in Athens. More ironically, Ireland was, in fact, about to present the first Olympic lawn tennis champion (twice) to the world.

John Boland and Irish Representation at Athens

In 1896, the difference between constitutional nationalism and unionism, particularly for someone from a well-to-do Catholic background, was nothing like as clearly defined as it later became. John Pius Boland was to become Ireland's first Olympic champion in 1896 and came from a conservative, moderately nationalist background. His daughter, Bridget, undoubtedly recounting what her father had told her of his early years, tells us that our first Olympic champion had a particularly strong link to the Catholic Church, not least because of being orphaned young:

John Pius Boland in more formal attire than he wore in competition at Athens From Bridget Boland, *At My Mother's Knee.*

> Their parents both dying when their seven children were very young, the family were brought up by their guardian, uncle on their mother's side, who was assistant Bishop of Dublin, making a strange household for a Catholic prelate. Even their family jokes had an ecclesiastical flavour, a particularly good one, my father told me, being awarded a 'pontifical high laugh' of three times three, from the fact that a High Mass in the presence of a bishop has three priests at the altar.[27]

Patrick Maume has identified a strong tendency for sections of the higher clergy in middle-class Dublin, whose schools produced servants of the state, to defer to the social hierarchy surmounted by the crown. 'The capture of the St. Stephen's Green constituency by a Catholic unionist MP in 1892 and 1895, for example, reflected a local middle class Catholic vote.'[28] In the aftermath of Parnell and, from 1895, of Gladstone, it was even reasonable for nationally minded Catholics to seek as much solace in embracing unionist allies as in persevering with a seemingly hopeless Home Rule cause. Redmond and Tim Healy epitomised this sense too by supporting the work of the Recess Committee set up by Horace Plunkett, a liberal unionist, to promote nationalist and unionist co-operation in economic development.[29]

Ireland's first Olympic champion was born at 135 Capel Street in the heart of Dublin, the original address of the family business, Boland's Bakery.[30] The story of Boland's invitation to Athens by a Greek friend and fellow archaeology enthusiast, Konstantinos Manos, has been widely accepted as his *raison d'être* at the Games.[31] Boland's daughter has also suggested, though in occasionally inaccurate memoirs, that her father's trip to Athens was inspired by a need to recuperate from a six-week cramming session, assisted by the Jersey air and a private tutor, before scraping through his final law examinations at Oxford.[32] Good tennis player as he undoubtedly was, Boland actually appears to have preferred the shot put. He made no effort to enter the latter event, however, even though it took place just before the tennis and he was surely in Athens on the day.[33]

A further irony about the involvement of John Boland in the first Olympic tennis tournament was that Ireland was, at the time, quite well supplied with top-quality tennis players. Dr Joshua Pim (mentioned earlier) won Wimbledon twice, while Willoughby Hamilton (1890) and Harold Mahony won a Wimbledon title apiece, Mahony from Kenmare actually winning the 1896 All-England Championship just months after the Athens Games.[34] Whatever Boland's reasons for being in Athens, his entry into the tennis tournament was, according to himself, quite unplanned and chaotic and he was not even close to being Ireland's best tennis player. In his own unpublished diary, Boland recounted:

> On Monday evening an English speaking Greek called Lagli who was sitting opposite me at dinner asked if I thought of going in for the tennis as the contestants were very few in number. I said I should be delighted to go in as his partner in the Doubles and in the Singles . . . owing to his being a Greek he was paired off with another Greek and I was paired off with a German called Traun . . . I was totally unprepared for tennis and spent until 12 in hunting up the various requisites . . . An Australian gentleman named Broughton, who happened to be in one of the shops came

to my assistance and brought me to an Austrian tailor, where I secured a pair of ready made slacks . . .'[35]

Some modern research has suggested that Boland was really quite an accomplished tennis player and that some of those he beat were also very well-respected players.[36] However, everything about the tennis event, its chaotic organisation and small scale in particular, suggests that it would be unwise to give the competition too high a quality rating. Relatively unprepared or not, after four days of haphazard competiton, Boland certainly won the tennis singles title on 11 April. Olympic records show that the singles final ended in a win for Boland over the Egypt-based Greek, Kasdaglis. This same Kasdaglis was in fact the man whom Boland had met with the nickname 'Lagli' at dinner a few evenings before. For some reason, the official Olympic Games report suggests that the tennis was played inside a shed of some sort, erected for the occasion. Curiously, however, Boland never mentions playing indoors and the only extant pictures of tennis at Athens are definitely outdoors, so the nature of this 'shed' remains a mystery, beyond the possibility that it was a temporary tent-like structure designed to keep the sun's heat at bay.[37]

The casual nature of the tennis competition is shown in the fact that the only reliable record of the final score comes from Boland's own diary, giving the Irishman victory by 6–2, 6–2. The official report merely records that in tennis, 'Single Game I.P. Boland, England. Double Game I.P. Boland, England and F. Thraun [sic] Germany.'[38] The standard of the singles tennis cannot have been very high. Not one of the recognised top players in international tennis was competing, and some of the competitors were specialists in other events entirely, including Edwin Flack, the Australian athlete, while Boland's doubles partner Friedrich Traun was also an athlete first and foremost.[39]

Boland's doubles partnership with the German Traun typified the fluid nature of national representation in Athens tennis particularly. This was due to the small entry list forcing the cobbling together of pairings simply to make the competition happen. While there were thirteen entries in singles, there were only five pairings in all contesting the doubles.[40] Thus, it would be unfair to suggest that the tennis competition saw some sort of effort to de-nationalise the Games – such national boundaries were

A scene from the 1896 tennis championships, purported to depict Boland in action (© IOC Lausanne).

crossed in no other sports in 1896, although they would be again in other Games, largely for the sake of making up adequate numbers, up to and including 1908. In any event, Boland and Traun won through to the doubles final which was played immediately before the singles. Remarkably, Boland recorded that the doubles final at the Athens velodrome started at just before five in the evening, following the cycling events, with Boland and Traun winning by 5–7, 6–3, 6–3, before Boland and Kasdaglis played each other in the singles and the whole thing was apparently finished by 6.30! Boland's diary displays a few confusions, not least in getting the name of one of his doubles opponents wrong, but it also seems to have erred somewhat in the suggestion that the singles and doubles finals (five sets in all) were both run off in the space of one and a half hours. Boland's confusion in his diary could well have come not only from the numerous and lengthy Greek names but from the possibility that his diary entries were not necessarily written on the actual day in question but some time later. This could also account for the error, if there is one, in suggesting that the two finals were run off in just ninety minutes. Dr Cyril White, authenticator of Boland's diary, has pointed out that the Dubliner was a notoriously poor timekeeper, which would offer the simplest explanation of all for the apparently frenetic speed of play in the finals.[41] Boland has given us a remarkable description of the victory ceremony, in a near-full stadium on marathon day:

> Each winner received a huge diploma in a large circular cardboard case, a medal in a case and a branch of olive a couple of feet long. These latter I believe had been brought specially from Olympia itself. Lawn Tennis was the last on the list, but as the Singles were read out first, it remained for Traun to be the last man to go up for his reward. On mounting the platform, the King shook me by the hand and said, in English, 'I congratulate

One of Boland's medals, back and front, showing the Greek deities Zeus and Nike on one side and the Acropolis on the other.

you' + then handed me the two diplomas, two medals + two olive wreaths. So full were my hands that I forgot, as indeed did the majority, to descend the steps backward, but I made up for the omission by bowing when I got to the bottom.[42]

Boland's Identity Crisis

Boland's initial intentions of competing at Athens were not in any way nationalistic, yet the official reaction to his victories at the Games created in him something of an Irish identity crisis. Bridget Boland mistakenly thought her father's doubles partner to have been Austrian – Traun came, in fact, from Hamburg – but her account is otherwise worthy of note on the issue of national identity:

Officials ran up the Austrian flag and the Union Jack. My father objected: the Irish flag, he explained, bore a gold harp on a green ground. They apologised profusely and said that they would have one ready in future; whereat he went on to beat his doubles partner in the finals of the singles [it is debatable which final came first – Mallon lists both for 11 April but with no time given]. 'Never mind,' said my father to the distressed officials, 'the Union Jack will do to be going on with; but maybe you'd better just have a flag ready with "J.P. Boland" on it, it'll be easier to make . . .'[43]

Taking Bridget Boland's account here as based on stories recounted to her later by her father, the polite sense of injured Irish identity it portrays does not really tally with Boland's own diary and scrapbook entries for 1896. There is little doubt that some degree of urban legend has built up around the Irish participation at the Olympics and Boland's case is worth a closer look in this regard.

While in Athens, Boland at no stage recorded his Irishness in his diary, beyond a reference to an Irish companion, Miss Hayden, persuading him to purchase a green sash on 11 April, which he is not thought to have worn subsequently, although the wearing of such a sash would not have been uncommon at the time.[44] In fact, given that he had travelled with several companions from Oxford, we find the Dubliner on a number of occasions call himself 'English'. For example, 'Meanwhile Flack and Robertson were beaten in the Doubles and they were also out of the singles. I was accordingly the only Englishman left in.'[45] Later, we see him mention that at a royal luncheon for the athletes, 'led by Mr Boucher we English gave the King a rousing hip, hip, horrah.'[46] Two days later, regarding attendance at a ball at the Schliemann home, 'A good many of the Germans and all the Americans were there, but of the English only Robertson, Flack and myself, the others having left Athens.'[47]

These examples suggest considerable comfort in Boland's mind with being considered part of an English grouping. They also hint at something more fundamental about the confusions within Irish nationalism at the time. The mid-1890s in particular were years of inherent paradox in the Irish political psyche. The moves towards unionism in some nationalist quarters have already been noted. Home Rule was also undoubtedly the main political vehicle in the country and was an umbrella movement for many different strands of national sentiment and expression. As a rule, the movement (and Boland) was comfortable in accepting membership of the British Empire hand in hand with promoting Irish nationality.[48] Boland at Athens felt both sentiments, though not quite simultaneously.

It is too simplistic to infer that such declarations of Englishness implied that Boland considered himself 'English'. For example, Boland knew well that Edwin Flack was not English, telling us: 'Flack, an Australian, won one of the heats of the 800 metres . . .'.[49] Yet he sometimes included the self same Flack with himself in the 'English' contingent, as can be seen from the diary entries quoted in the previous paragraph. In large part, Boland was simply identifying himself, and Flack, as part of the English contingent, not of the English nation per se. Similarly, Boland knew well that his fellow Oxford student G.S. Robertson was a Scot, though part of the 'English' group in Athens. It was when he was 'accused' subsequently of actually being 'English' that Boland's identity crisis struck home.

Boland's victories were never likely to be seized upon at the time by the Irish press as some sort of triumph for an Irish identity. The *Irish Independent* happily printed a Reuters report on 9 April listing 'Boland (England)' among the tennis entrants. Yet even as Boland's Irish identity became known, Irish papers contented themselves with merely printing Reuters reports of the victories, occasionally inserting sub-headings like 'Victory of a Dublin Man' but making no other editorial comment.[50] The notion of these being 'Dublin victories' is an interesting and possibly accidental foretaste of things to come, in the sense that early Irish Olympic victories were often seen first and foremost as victories for home towns or counties, and only secondly, even incidentally, as victories for an Irish 'nation'.[51] In the overall context, Boland's wins being in a minority sport like tennis, and one in which no major international tennis stars had competed, contributed greatly to the lack of impact in Ireland of his successes. To most Irish observers who even knew that these Olympic Games were going on, this was little more than a distant sporting contest which bore no connection to Ireland or its sporting traditions.

It would be unjust to accuse those contemporaries who hailed Boland's victory at Athens as a British one of some form of anti-Irish campaign. It was probably a genuine mistake – Boland had been unheard of and everything identifiable about him – his language, sport, university – was British. *The Guardian,* for instance, listed 'Boland (England)' when it first reported his tennis exploits but within days had at least acknowledged that he was from Dublin.[52]

Technically, of course, Boland was British, as was any other Irish person in 1896. On the other hand, a poor British showing at Athens was made to look better in some quarters by claiming Boland as British. The same happened with the previously mentioned first Australian Olympian, Edwin Flack, who won both the 800 metres and 1,500 metres in Athens:

> He was not selected by a colonial sporting association nor was he funded by a colonial government. Flack was able to attend the Games because he was working in an accountancy firm in London and was nominated by the London Athletic Club. Flack had made his own way to Athens. After his success, although Boland recollects it differently, the Union Jack was raised and some British newspapers believed that he was an Englishman who had helped to thwart the American dominance of track and field. This error was perpetuated until 1936.[53]

Whatever the John Boland of his later Irish Party days might have claimed, the Boland of 1896 was no flag-waving nationalist. His initial lack of interest in declaring his Irish identity appears to have changed mainly because of a subsequent dispute which arose with some of his Oxford contemporaries after the Games. In response to an article criticising the lack of publicity of the Athens Games and the lack of an invitation to England's top athletes, Boland was moved to write:

> England, the leading sporting nation of the world, held aloof because she was not entreated to go and make the Games a success, and because Greece did not forego her dignity and play the part of beggar for England's favour . . . Surely the role of spoilt child does not become an athletic nation![54]

More notable is the comment Boland made in response to previous claims in the *Oxford Magazine* that England had scored successes at Athens: 'The winner of the 1500 and 800 metres is an Australian who has been in England little over a year, and the "stray lawn-tennis player" [as Boland had been called in the initial magazine article] is proud of his Irish birth.'[55] Now the battle for national identity was well and truly joined, with the 'stray tennis player' engaging in a witty yet, occasionally, pointed exchange of views in subsequent editions of the magazine. Boland's interlocutor, signing himself 'The Writer of the Article' but in fact his fellow Athens competitor, G.S. Robertson of New College, and Scotland, responded the following week:

> I refuse to reckon Mr. Flack as anything but an Englishman. The Union Jack was hoisted for his victory, and he is an English subject. What more can one want? Did my critic desire to see an Australian flag (which I am told consists of a kangaroo passant regardant, gules, an emu's egg dormant on a hatchment, argent, and a boomerang hurlant, au naturel) sent afloat to celebrate his victory? Why did not my critic himself take a green flag with him in his pocket, in case the committee should forget (as indeed they did) to provide themselves with something distinctive of his Hibernian origin? If pure Celtic origin debars a man from being reckoned an Englishman, several of us are no more English than he is; but we are only too proud to bear the name.[56]

The tone of Robertson's article was an obvious mix of fun-poking and patriotism. He had certainly aroused a sleeping Hibernian tiger in Boland. The latter firstly defended his Australian colleague, Flack, claiming rightly or wrongly that an Australian flag had been raised in his honour at Athens. Flack's identity is not much clarified either by the fact that when he attempted (unsuccessfully) to complete the marathon course on the last day of competition, he was accompanied on a bicycle by the same Mr Broughton who had helped find a tennis outfit for Boland. Broughton was certainly an Australian but one who worked as an assistant to the British ambassador in Athens.[57] Then, however, Boland addressed the more pertinent issue of Irish identity in sport:

> ... in matters of sport, as for instance on the football field, Irish and Scotch are not regarded as English, and I claim that the

John Boland later in life, in his barrister's attire and wig. Courtesy of Dr Cyril White.

distinction still holds good in such meetings as those at Athens. Australia is in these matters even more distinct from England than Hungary is from Austria . . . When England's honour is on defence, I am as proud of bearing the name of Englishman as your correspondent, but I refuse to forswear my 'Hibernian origin' and the green flag in the field of sport; and, as the pure Colonial [Flack] is not beholden to England for his athletic prowess, he occupies a precisely similar position.[58]

Robertson ended the argument eventually, declaring: 'Must one employ the smile or the shillelagh to answer him? Perhaps the safest course is to get out of his way as rapidly as Celtic dignity permits.' The *Magazine* editor also put an end to the correspondence, having apparently arranged for a personal meeting between the two, expecting 'lawn tennis bats and boomerangs at ten paces'.[59] Robertson would cross the paths of Irish Olympians again and again, as we will see in later chapters.

These exchanges show the emergence of a form of injured Irish pride in Boland, an Irish patriotism which had no link with separatism or nationalism in a political sense – he has been seen to be more or less conservative (of the Catholic variety) in his 1896 sentiments, whatever about his subsequent engagement with Home Rule, the Irish language and the Irish universities. Boland's change here was essentially a reactive one – his Irishness emerged from the shadows only when it was accused of being 'Englishness', in effect. This concept of Irish sporting identity as anti- or at least non-Englishness is a significant one. When taking the well-trodden path of linking the GAA, for example, with more extreme Irish nationalism – a linkage which does not always hold up to scrutiny – it would be completely wrong to assume that people of non-extreme viewpoints were in some way unpatriotic. One historian has argued quite strongly that the GAA in its pre-1914 incarnation was substantially a solid supporter of Parnell's vision of a constitutionally achieved Home Rule, a philosophy which continued well into John Redmond's tenure as well.[60] People like Boland felt, perhaps, a more submerged and moderate national identity, but one which, through their greater participation in international competition than their GAA equivalents, actually emerged abroad more clearly and forcefully than did the GAA's brand of nationalism. Time and again, the sporting successes of people from a particular country/nation or locality, and well beyond Ireland or the Olympic model too, produced an almost automatic rise in nationalism or what we will call 'localism'. Boland was nonchalant about whether his tennis victories were 'Irish' or 'English' wins. It was only when an English label was imposed on him that his national identity was aroused. In subsequent Olympics, when Irish representatives in sports with much greater popular appeal suffered the same fates, the result was similar.

Even more strikingly, the *Irish Independent* carried an illustrated article on the 1896 Games at the time of the Intercalated Games (1906), written by none other than John P. Boland MP. In it, Boland declared:

I was privileged to take part and, in the absence of representative players, to secure for Ireland the singles in lawn tennis. The doubles were a joint victory for Ireland and Germany.

Boland went on, ten years later, to list the victories of each nation, allocating 'Ireland' two (his own) and 'England' just one. Boland's brush with G.S. Robertson in the *Oxford Magazine* had clearly started him on the road of national identification. By 1906, as an MP in an Ireland much more aware of the import of the Olympics and perhaps much more aware too of its own identity, Boland was happily applying some retrospective greenery to his exploits. Boland had, by 1906, embraced both the Irish language and the cause of Irish third-level educational independence, so it was unsurprising that he closed with an almost Byronic assertion of what the Olympics had done for Greek national identity:

> . . . though entertaining guests of all nations, Greece rightly asserted her own nationality throughout . . . Greece was, and is, a nation.[61]

Irish-America in Athens

John Boland was one of at least three competitors at the Athens Games with Irish links. American athletes James Brendan Connolly and Thomas Burke, as their names tend to suggest, had Irish roots. Connolly's parents came from Inis Mór in the Aran Islands while both of Burke's parents were Irish too, living then in South Boston, as were Connolly's.[62] Connolly had the distinction of winning the very first title in Athens, in the hop, step and jump (as well as a third place in the long jump), while Burke was a double champion, winning the 100 metres and 400 metres. The fact that the rules allowed Connolly to take two hops and a jump is an interesting reminder of how loose the regulation of sport still was in 1896. Tom Burke was, in fact, the only reigning American AAU champion to compete in the first Olympics, again showing the lack of import which was attributed to the early Games by serious athletes. Some information on his later career in law and journalism has been found but nothing on his family or Irish background. Burke was a student at Boston University and their records show him to have later practised law in Massachusetts for six years and to have worked as a sportswriter for the *Boston Journal* and *Boston*

Post. He also enlisted in the US army during the Great War, at the age of forty-three.[63]

One might have expected the feats of Connolly and Burke to arouse some sense of pride in Ireland but this was not to be borne out in the national press. The *Irish Independent,* for example, merely listed the Reuters-sourced results which included the mention of 'Burke (America)' with no additional comment.[64] Connolly's treatment was identical, with even the Galway-based newspapers ignoring his triumph and links with the county completely.

There are a number of reasons for this ignoring of Burke's and Connolly's Irish connections, apart from the obvious lack of general interest in and awareness of the Olympic Games to begin with. The men were essentially students, little known in Ireland, as indeed was Boland. Furthermore, as in Boland's case, the national press relied exclusively on internationally sourced news of the Olympics and sub-editors rarely, if ever, tinkered with a Reuters text. As seen earlier, Tom Burke's Irishness had been celebrated in 1895 when he participated in what was perceived as a crushing victory over the 'English' (London) selection – competing and winning against international or non-British opponents at the Olympic Games clearly did not merit the same claim to be an Irish success story. This idea that Irish sporting identity was, to an extent, about anti-Britishness rather than necessarily promoting 'Irishness' is one which will recur more forcefully in the early twentieth-century Games.

If the Irish press took little or no note of the Irishness of some of the American champions, what of the Irish-Americans themselves? Irish-American newspapers like the Boston *Pilot* were very 'Irish' – full of tales inspired by Irish legends, news from Ireland (county by county), and so on. Furthermore, there was a very strong Irish nationalistic thread running through the American-Irish press. The *Pilot* in 1896 carried articles on the progress of the memorial to Fenian John Boyle O'Reilly, on the heroes and battlefields of 1798 and on how Boston was helping Irish political prisoners.[65] The strong Catholicism which blended with this Irish nationalism was well demonstrated in comments like: 'It is the honourable privilege of the Irish blood to be, beyond any other, in America, at least, identified with the True Religion.'[66] Here we can detect the presence of what was essentially Irish prejudice, rather than merely nationalism, as occasionally seen in the press in Ireland. Finally, and most crucially in Irish-America, the *Pilot's* pages displayed a vehement anti-Britishness, positively delighting in the American opposition to Britain's encroachment upon the Boers, for instance.[67]

The emergence of the Olympic Games as a vehicle for American anti-British sentiment was, in 1896, still over a decade away in real terms. The British involvement in Athens was neither sufficiently noteworthy nor nationally representative for it to arouse rivalry or antipathy. A more genuine surprise, from the perspective of Irish-American press coverage, was the lack of association between the likes of Burke and Connolly and their Irish origins. Although the celebrations on their return were dominated by the presence of Irish-American dignitaries like Alderman Barry and included such as an ode called 'To our laurelled sons' by Henry O'Meara, the 'nationalism' which exuded in Irish-America was 'American' and fundamentally parochial. From the outset, the *Pilot* bore the heading: 'Boston Athletes to Contest in Olympian Games at Athens,' followed by the affirmation that 'Boston is sending six young men to represent her'.[68] After the Olympic Games, the governor of Massachusetts announced at the celebratory function for Burke and his colleagues:

> . . . we recognize that these men carried to Athens the will and indomitable pluck which belongs to America, Massachusetts and Boston . . . we of Boston and Massachusetts share in their glory.[69]

While efforts to establish significant detail on Burke's Irish roots or connections have not been very successful, it was notable that he too saw himself as representing his university first, over and above his country. In taking his six weeks leave of absence from Boston University School of Law, Burke wrote to the dean and promised: 'I shall wear the colors of B.U. in these games and hope to uphold the reputation of the university.'[70]

Connolly's Legacy

When he returned to Boston in May of 1896, James Brendan Connolly (who came back later than the other Olympians) found himself being lauded as a hero of the neighbourhood, certainly not of the 'old country'. Presented with a gold watch, at an official banquet given by the City of

James Brendan Connolly pictured beside the American flag during the 1896 Games (© IOC Lausanne).

Boston in Faneuil Hall, the first modern Olympic victor was most noticeably touched by the citizens of South Boston who staged a parade on his behalf. Connolly remembered:

> . . . many carriages and a double line of policemen from curb to curb, to clear the way . . . with red and blue and green lights and sky rockets flaring up from in front of drug stores, clothing stores, private homes and barrooms and the band all the while playing 'See the Conquering Hero Comes!' . . .[71]

Much has been written of Irish-American assimilation. To a large extent, the drive in Irish-America to have the immigrant population accept America and be accepted by it was led by middle-class representatives. Kevin Kenny has pointed out that:

> Most of the Catholic organisations were led by the Irish urban middle class . . . emphasising hard work, self-discipline, thrift and sobriety. They therefore acted as a vehicle for Irish-American assimilation, defined in a specific, middle class, respectable manner.[72]

However, the example of Connolly was an important exception. He certainly did not fit the mould of middle-class Irish-America and yet his assimilation could hardly have been more complete. Other Irish-American Olympians from non-middle-class echelons would follow – Sheridan, Flanagan et al. – and will be dealt with in later chapters. Connolly's experience perhaps shows that assimilation was very much a local concern in the first place. Connolly won for Boston first and only secondly for America. Ten years later, Irish-Americans were winning medals for New York and America in more equal measure, partly through greater assimilation of the Irish into American life but also because the Olympics of 1906 and particularly of 1908 would simultaneously arouse American patriotism and anglophobia.

In Athens itself, Connolly, according to *Boston Herald* reporter Beverley Cronin, had 'yelled in a burst of emotion, "Here's for the honour of County Galway", and then jumped the 44 feet 11¾ inches that won him the title as the first modern Olympic victor'.[73] Interestingly enough, Ellery Clarke Jnr recounted a quite different story of Connolly's winning jump, as told to him by Ellery Clarke Snr, who had also competed in Athens:

> Just before Connolly's second jump in the Olympic hop, step and jump, in his own words, 'Before I started down the path I breathed on my hands and looked down at the jumping pit. I recall a rush of energy that came over me like a warm wave going through my blood. I gripped my fists tight and took off. The next day the Greek papers joked about the incident. When they saw me breathe on my hands they reported: "No wonder Connolly won. He was praying just before he jumped." '[74]

A huge difference between Connolly and most of the other Boston Olympians, Burke apart, was that his origins, as one of a family of twelve children, were very much rooted in working-class Irish South Boston. Connolly in Athens had remained the sole representative of the Suffolk AC of South Boston. He later explained:

> I had been elected to membership in one of the powerful athletic clubs of the country [the Manhattan AC of New York] without my knowing anything about it before I went south, but I had never competed for them. I never was strong for those big clubs who were always taking promising athletes away from poor clubs, and keeping them like stables of horses, paying their way and giving them a good time so long as they brought prestige to the big club. I chose to compete for the little Suffolk Athletic Club of my own home town of South Boston, and I was paying my own expenses.[75]

In several sources, Connolly is referred to repeatedly by his last name while other team members are addressed by title, first and last name, perhaps reflecting a difference in perceived social status. Nor was this merely Boston snobbery. Even the *New York Times* reflected the class distinction between the athlete from working-class Irish stock and the old Bostonians. While it mistook Connolly for a member of the Boston Athletic Club (BAA), the paper consistently referred to 'Connolly', neither using his initials nor his Christian name, whereas all Princeton athletes were given more formal titles and 'Captain Robert Garrett' even had a pen picture about his family pedigree inserted at the end of the article.[76] The *Boston Post* showed its local knowledge and pride on the same date with the heading 'Boston Boys Victors' and noted more accurately that Connolly hailed from the Suffolk Athletic Club, not the BAA.[77]

A rare photograph of the 1896 American Olympic track and field team, found in the James Brendan Connolly Papers, shows Connolly seated on his own to one side of the team. With one athlete, Garrett, paying the passage of his Princeton teammates, and the Boston Athletic Association providing for its members, Connolly was left to pay his own way in the amount of $700. Connolly had worked and saved to earn his place in Harvard, so spending such money on getting to Athens was a major decision, certainly no mere whim. In going, he was perhaps unintentionally setting a precedent for increased representation by Irish-American athletes of the lower socio-economic strata in future Olympic Games.[78] Connolly was also considerably older than his compatriots, having worked in a number of jobs (including as a prize-fight promoter) prior to enrolling at Harvard, where he paid his own fees until he dropped out at the time of the Athens Games, never to return as a student. While Connolly always claimed he spent his own savings on getting to Athens, it is also highly likely that some of the funding he required came from the local (and Irish) Catholic parish, which was the main sponsor of the Suffolk Athletic Club.[79] Connolly, furthermore, laid much of the credit for his athletic prowess on his Irish heritage:

> In the . . . district of the city where I was born and brought up most of all the men were interested in an athletic sport of some kind. Most of the older people of the district were of high blood still keen for the field sports of the old country. You could find the old men unable to read or write [but] could argue keenly, intelligently on any out door sport whatsoever. And among those old men were many who had been themselves athletes of fame; hurlers, bowlers, wrestlers . . .[80]

Connolly's strong identity and affinity with his Irish heritage were also seen in his later life. He observed the War of Independence in Ireland first hand. For his services as commissioner, in Ireland, for the American Committee for Relief in Ireland, in which capacity he regularly associated with members of the IRA, Connolly was awarded the Medal of Honor by the American Irish Historical Society, and received the annual medal of the Ireland Society of Boston. Part of the surprisingly strongly worded citation which was read at Harvard upon the university's conferral of an honorary degree on one of its most celebrated 'drop-outs' read:

> At the darkest hour of the mother country's last uprising against the oppressor, with the nation in an agony of violence and its leaders in hiding or dead, he proclaimed in Dublin the failure of the invader and the coming independence of Ireland . . . Mindful of the trust reposed in them by the Commonwealth of Massachusetts, the President and the Trustees of the University confer on James Brendan Connolly the degree Doctor of Letters.[81]

As an American, Connolly fought with the 9th Massachusetts Infantry at San Juan Hill during the Spanish–American War (the Irish Fighting 9th of Civil War fame), was granted a private audience with Pope Pius X in Rome in 1911, and ran for the US Congress on the Progressive Party ticket in 1912 and again in 1914. It is worth noting Connolly's close affinity with Theodore Roosevelt, one-time US president and founder of the short-lived Progressive Party. Roosevelt was also one of the founding members of the American Irish Historical Society and had strong Irish ancestral roots.

All this said, it is another step entirely, in the context of the time, to suggest that Connolly's Olympic success acted as some sort of springboard for his later fame in a meaningful way. This sort of political involvement may have had no more connection with Connolly's Olympic achievements than Boland's subsequent membership of parliament had with his tennis wins. In Connolly's case, his political and revolutionary work was merely an extension of his incredible energy and zest for living. He continued to travel the world, wrote over two dozen seafaring novels, worked on trawlers and even managed to get back to win another Olympic placing four years after Athens.

Connolly showed that the bond with Ireland was very strong among working-class Irish-Americans. In him a vehement anti-Britishness, based in no small part on its sporting snobbery, was also evident. Irish-

Americans embraced sport as a passion but also as a financial enterprise, wholly anathema to British (and indeed Olympic) ideals of amateurism. This 'gentlemen and players' friction would emerge again when Irish-American Olympians encountered British administrators in 1904–8. Connolly's denunciation of the British was both scathing and unceasing. Written in the wake of the controversial London Olympic Games of 1908, Connolly took direct aim at Anglo-Saxon control over sport, as well as their very national character. Providing 'tongue in cheek' descriptions of global intrusions into the Englishman's aristocratic traditions of rowing, tennis, yachting, track and field, and even boxing, Connolly went on to systematically criticise the willingness of other nations to tolerate the 'sharp practice', decadence, hypocrisy and excuses of the English sporting establishment. Connolly concluded that in England:

> If your father wasn't a curate, or a barrister, or if he wasn't a brewer, or a wholesale dealer in jams, or in some way making his living off the Government, or if he did work with his hands for a living . . . be sure your entry won't be accepted.[82]

The localisation of the Olympian victories didn't occur in Ireland with Boland, largely because he was not a widely known local athlete to begin with, nor was his sport a widely popular one.[83] However, the localisation as opposed to the 'nationalisation' of Olympic pride would become very obvious indeed in Ireland too once some 'people's champions' achieved glory, as in 1904 and 1906. Connolly's story was also evidence of how the Irish in America transferred their national allegiance very comfortably to their new homes – the longing and love for the motherland was all very well but America had given them everything which Ireland had not – wealth, status, university education – and America very easily became 'home'. Connolly himself was to sum up this easy transferal of loyalty for Irish-Americans:

> It matters not what country a man chooses to call his own, he must, if he would wish that country well, hold in reverence her institutions. Patriotism will preserve a nation when nothing else survives . . . And it is such a tremendous country, this of ours, a country into which new millions are ceaselessly pouring; and

while these new millions which to them, as yet, mean nothing, but which to us of older citizenship, when we do not forget, mean so much. It is for us to give the lesson . . .[84]

The Irish-American identification with the USA as a surrogate motherland would be seen in vivid relief by the time the 1908 Games were held in London. John Boland's victories were never likely to be seized upon by the national press as some sort of triumph for an Irish identity. The fact that his victories had been in non-national, non-popular sport and on a distant plane which was not in direct confrontation with Britain were contributory factors. On the other hand, the 'nationalism' which exuded in Irish-America was 'American' and, in 1896, fundamentally localised and Bostonian. Yet the case of James Brendan Connolly had introduced a theme which would become much more significant later, especially in the huge controversies of 1908 – working-class Irish-America's anti-Britishness and its abhorrence of what it considered British sporting snobbery.

CHAPTER TWO

THE PARIS GAMES, 1900

T he second modern Olympic Games were awarded to Paris, despite Greek demands that Athens be their permanent home. There were nearly twice as many countries represented at Paris by comparison with Athens, while the total number of competitors was well over five times the Athens figure, including twenty-two women.[1] For all this, the Paris Olympic Games of 1900 were the most disorganised and diluted Games ever held, lost in the mists of a five-and-a-half-month world exposition. Partly due to this, the Games also had a very low level of Irish involvement, little better than in Athens before that. In this chapter, we will explore that involvement and its impact on Irish identity. We will also look at how 1900 itself marked a sort of watershed in Irish Olympics-related sports, involving recognition of a need for international competition that pre-supposed Irish athletics dominance was under serious threat from America, including Irish-America. In some respects, it was such developments and the disappointing nature of the 1900 Olympics too, which galvanised at least some of the remaining Irish athletics greats to attend future Olympic Games when they came around.

An Invitation Accepted
Although evidence of a national engagement with the Olympic movement during or immediately after the 1896 Games is scarce, the prospect of another opportunity for Ireland to display its athletic prowess in Paris was a welcome one in some quarters. The geographical closeness of Paris, the

fact that the Games would not be held as early in the year as the Athens ones had been, and the realisation that the Olympics were an established entity now, not a once-off novelty, all played a part in awakening Irish interest. One historian reported: 'The British, Irish, and Scottish amateur athletic associations were the first to enter, followed by several American universities and clubs.'[2] Searches at the Olympic Studies Centre at Lausanne have failed to confirm this entry through documentation. There are many individual invitations, to Olympic dinners and balls for instance, but no list of invited countries or organisations appears to be extant. Although the *Cork Examiner* was a little 'previous' with its report, this Irish decision to send a team was confirmed by the paper on 16 July 1900, citing that:

> Fourteen nations have sent their chosen representatives. America sending 48 . . . England and Hungary 7 . . . Ireland, Norway and Greece 2 . . . England is represented by Bennett, Rimmer, Robinson, Tysoe, Lee and Eliott; and Ireland by Leahy and O'Connor . . .[3]

The Irish Amateur Athletic Association, as we saw in the last chapter, received an invitation to attend the inaugural Games in 1896 and there is no doubt that the same happened in 1900, despite the lack of official invitation lists. A letter from Charles Herbert of the AAA, unfortunately not dated, showed him listing likely officials who might participate in an upcoming congress.[4] Among ten names, nine from the south of England – including W.H. Grenfell, the future Lord Desborough – Herbert listed E.J. Walsh of Rhodaville, Churchtown, Dublin. Walsh, as we saw previously, was the secretary of the IAAA. This letter was undated but contained Herbert's suggestion that holding the international championships in Paris on Sunday 8 July would not be a good day because it was the day after the AAA championships.[5] The only year between 1896 and 1906 when 8 July fell on a Sunday was 1900, not to mention the fact that the Paris athletics contests were eventually held on the following Sunday, 15 July, in the main.

Other national and local papers likewise backed up the notion that the Paris Games were the first for which an actual Irish team was to be entered.[6] The most authoritative Olympic records extant cite the representation of Ireland in athletics, polo and tennis, though enshrined in the caveat that 'Two other "nations" could be considered to have been represented in 1900. Algeria and Ireland had athletes competing, but neither country in 1900 was an independent nation.'[7] In the end, whatever the original invitation or intention, Irish representation in Paris was to be so small that it was subsumed into the British representation in the minds of all those involved – all the contemporary documentation in the Paris 1900 files at the Olympic Studies Centre in Lausanne listed the Irish competitors as 'Grande Bretagne', although Australian medallists were recognised as Australian (in contrast to what happened with Edwin Flack in 1896), as were Norwegians, even though Norway did not gain independence from Sweden until 1905 and the Swedish aristocrat Victor Balck was a very powerful IOC member.[8] As the British Olympic Council was not in existence in 1900, the considerable influence of English AAA officials on the Olympic movement generally and on de Coubertin specifically appears to have come about informally and through personal contacts. De Coubertin had great admiration for many things English, while he and Herbert had mutual fears of growing professionalism and anti-imperialism (which posed a potential threat to both Britain and France, of course). The largely Tory-led AAA would certainly have felt a little uneasy in 1900 due to moves to reunite the Irish Parliamentary Party, adding another potential reason why a separate Irish team would not be welcomed in official circles. Herbert and de Coubertin would eventually share antipathy towards American, often Irish-American, attitudes to Olympism for very similar reasons. It is unsurprising that the baron did not seek to push for a separate Irish representation at Paris, which he was mainly absent from in any event and where just one Irish-based athlete ultimately competed.

Growing International Viewpoints in Irish Athletics
The press talk of an Irish Olympic entry is some evidence that a separate Irish identity had continued to emerge in international athletics after 1896. The idea that an Irish team of athletes could represent Ireland in international competition was certainly still current – the official competition against Scotland was now in its sixth year and the AAA championship by 1900 had become a sort of Ireland v. England challenge, in the same way as the Cheltenham festival is viewed today in horse-racing

circles. Following one local victory, the *Waterford News* purred with pride in announcing that: 'P. O'Connor [Peter O'Connor, the long-jumper] of Waterford has received the hearty congratulations not only of his many friends but of hundreds who watch the athletic achievement of Irishmen.'[9] The following week, the same newspaper informed readers that:

> This dashing athlete [O'Connor] will compete in the English Championships on the 25th, and with P. Harding, Carrick-on-Suir, and T.F. Kiely, Ballyneale, will do battle for the Shamrock in the international contest against Scotland at Belfast on the 29th inst.[10]

The significance of having locally known athletes to support, which did not happen in an Irish context in the Olympics of 1896, has already been noted. The likes of Boland, through his anonymity and the minority nature of his sport, and Connolly and Burke through their youthful American-ness, could not arouse the interest of the average Irishman in the same way as men who represented the pride of the district did in rural Ireland. O'Connor, Harding and Kiely actually lived less than twenty miles away from each other, one in Waterford city and the other two in County Tipperary along the County Waterford border. Yet the importance of having local heroes to cheer on was not the only factor which aroused interest in Ireland. Sometimes, the holding of international competition locally had a similar effect. When the international match was held in Belfast in 1900, even the ultra-unionist *Belfast Newsletter* was replete with coverage of the Irish struggle with Scotland. The paper was comfortable in acknowledging both Ulster athletes and the likes of Kiely and O'Connor as being Ireland's representatives:

> As this was the first contest of its kind ever held in Belfast, the greatest interest was evinced in the meeting, and while it was hoped that we would be able to retrieve our defeat of last year, it was generally felt that the contest would be a close one . . . both countries were represented by the best men and it was evident that on the part of the home contingent no effort would be spared to decisively wipe last year's defeat by one point from the slate.[11]

This form of 'patriotic' sentiment was certainly evidence of the sort of pride in Ireland that was also found in rugby contests from the same period. The Belfast contest was, of course, IAAA-organised, and one which that association felt every right to feel proud of:

> After the event – Mr E.T. Walsh, in returning thanks, said that these trials of strength with Scotland had been the best meetings the country had engaged in for years, and if the IAAA had made many mistakes in its time, certainly one of its proudest triumphs was the promotion of these international contests.[12]

A considerably more nationalistic tone was also found in some of the southern coverage of Irish athletics in 1900, particularly in the *United Irishman*. In June 1900, for instance, the paper reported:

> The members of the Major McBride National Athletic Club held its inaugural ceremony at their new rooms, 75 Aungier Street, on last Friday night. There was a large attendance of members. The President, Mr G. Ryan, occupied the chair. The chairman, on rising, said it gave him great pleasure to propose the toast of the evening, which was dear to every true Irishman's heart: 'Ireland a nation.' The toast was drunk amidst the greatest enthusiasm.[13]

Later in the article, reference was made to the singing of 'God Save Ireland' and some Boer songs, again showing that, for more extreme nationalists, the desire for a formal Irish identity, i.e. an independent nation, was inseparable from anti-Britishness and support for whomever Britain's enemies happened to be at any given time.

Another feature of the Irish identity which was clearly in existence in 1900 was the inherent pride felt in our athletic tradition, a tradition which was, as yet, largely untested against the might of the new world, whatever about those who took on Irish athletes at competitions like the AAA championships. The tribute paid on the death of J.M. Ryan, a famous athlete, in the *United Irishman* typified this sentiment:

> He sprang from a race of genial Gaels, whose physical abilities astound the world and wins it homage, and though meteoric performers may compass greater feats under extraordinary

favourable conditions, Ryan's fame as a jumper will be a standard of merit for all time, as he himself will be a type of all the nobility of the Gael – *sans peur et sans reproche.*[14]

Ryan also merited a brief obituary in the Boston *Pilot.*[15] This was significant in that it was the only comment made in the *Pilot* on either Irish or Irish-American athletics at the time of the Paris Olympics. While the novelty of the first Games had worn off, the lack of Boston interest in 1900 was obviously due in part to the fact that the same local connections could not be made as had been in 1896 (even with Connolly, an independent traveller, winning a second place in the Paris hop, step and jump). The great enthusiasm of the Bostonians in 1896, in welcoming home their victorious athletes from Athens, including Burke and

This picture of prominent athletes competing at a Castlebar sports must date from around 1900. The two athletes on the right are wearing the traditional three-sprig shamrock work by IAAA athletes in internationals. The man at the back right is Con Leahy while his brother Pat is in plain clothes in the front centre. Apologies for not managing to identify the others as yet, or to identify whether the shamrock-wearing athlete on the front left is sporting a GAA vest, though that is what it appears to be. Courtesy of Larry Ryder.

Connolly, had dissipated in 1900, assisted by the fact that the *Pilot* had become even more focused on narrow Catholic issues by then.

This decline in American interest was effectively the reverse of what had been seen in the Irish context regarding Kiely, O'Connor and Harding, and reinforced the importance of local issues in the emergence of national pride via the Olympics and international sport in general. Sometimes, even when the opportunity for the exploitation of local interest presented itself, the bias and interests of local papers did not always mean that the local or topical athletic achievements were covered. Pat Leahy, for example, would become the only Irish athlete of note to compete in Paris. Yet, although Leahy came from just inside the County Limerick border with Cork, the *Limerick Leader* completely ignored him and the *Limerick Chronicle* never once mentioned his achievements at either the AAA championships of 1900 or the Paris Games, contenting itself with occasional articles on rowing and just one set of results from an athletics meeting in June 1900.[16]

Pat Leahy's brother Con was to win even greater Olympic fame later, as we will see, but their story bears consideration here from the political perspective. The Leahy brothers were mainly able to compete at the Olympic Games because of their affiliation with the IAAA. Yet, theirs was a strongly nationalist tradition. Local historians in Charleville can also point to the fact that the Leahy home lay on the Limerick road out of Charleville, and that the younger members of the family were often accompanied for the initial part of the journey home from school at Charleville CBS by the young Éamon de Valera. Who is to say but that the youthful de Valera may well have witnessed one of the legendary feats of the Leahys, the day that Con Leahy (five years de Valera's senior) high-jumped over the Mannix family gate, standing on the outskirts of Charleville and still measuring well over six feet at its highest point? All history is local, lest we ever forget that.[17]

Paris – an Organisational Disaster

Despite the inconsistency of press interest, the evidence thus far suggests that the Irish 'nation' was much more ready to embrace the Olympic Games of 1900 than it had been in 1896. One very important obstacle to this demonstration of Irish athletic prowess presented itself, an obstacle which had nothing to do with Irish nationalism, professionalism or anything else. Quite simply, the Paris Games were an organisational disaster, a situation which was to impact hugely on Irish ambitions. The athletics contests were poorly organised, the events were held in dismal facilities, and there was mass confusion among the athletes because of the plethora of events conducted. An Australian competitor, Stanley Rowley, summed up the feelings of many for his country's national press:

> . . . to treat these events as world's championships would really be an insult to the important events they are supposed to be. They are treated by most of the competitors as – A HUGE JOKE – and when it comes to it that one has come all this way from Australia to compete in them, it really seems ridiculous.[18]

In advance of the Games, a new organising committee was appointed to rescue them, but with little effect:

> They also proposed an entirely new list of events and new places to hold them . . . Organisations all over the world had made plans in accordance with the original program announced by Coubertin and most of them refused to have anything to do with the new committee.[19]

Baron de Coubertin himself toured many European capitals in advance of the Games, trying to ensure participation by the leading nations in a Paris event which was already destined to become horribly diluted by its association with the great world fair in the city. De Coubertin did not make his way to Ireland at this time, nor did the message that the original schedule of events in which the Irish had hopes of excelling was hugely altered. The letter from Charles Herbert to de Coubertin, already referred to, had suggested that 7 July was the original date intended for the athletics events but that it clashed with the AAA events.[20] Whether this communication had caused the organisers to propose moving the Games from July all the way to September is impossible to ascertain. However, that is how it was perceived in Ireland, so the news that they were being brought forward from September to mid-July again reached Irish athletes at a very late stage. The shocking blow to Irish hopes of Olympic glory was announced by one commentator on 14 July:

I cannot account for the misconception over the Olympic Games at Paris today. Everyone thought, because it was advertised, that September 2nd was the date, and I hold letters to that effect. However, one new disappointment more or less won't make much difference to me, and it is pleasing to know that Pat Leahy, Pat [sic] O'Connor, J.C. Meredith and Horgan have gone . . .[21]

It has not been possible to identify the degree to which work commitments could have tied Irish athletes down in 1900. Going to Paris immediately after the AAAs, without prior warning, would have been a challenge to farmers like Kiely and Horgan, or to O'Connor, working in a busy legal office, but there may have been at least one other factor in the decision not to attend the Games, as we will now see.

Developing the American Connection

It has already been noted that Ireland tended to ignore the Irishness of American athletes in Athens, and that likewise the Irish-Americans were very happy to see themselves as American, not Irish. This changed somewhat after 1896, though not dramatically. Some of the Irish press carried general celebrations of Irish-Americanism. For instance, a *Limerick Leader* article, entitled 'the Irish American Boys', lauded the bravery and chivalry of Irish-American soldiers from Chicago who went to fight on behalf of the Boers.[22]

In purely sporting terms, an interesting development had occurred in that the Irish-Americans had gone from having their Irishness ignored in the Irish press to being portrayed as the main threats to Irish dominance in the forthcoming Olympics. John Flanagan, who had been breaking world records as an 'Irishman' at the GAA's 'Invasion of London' prior to the 1896 Olympics, was given honourable mention in the *Cork Examiner* under the heading: 'World Record by the American Flanagan.'[23] Although this story was based on a special telegram from the AAA championships at Stamford Bridge, the headline writer was almost certainly a Corkman in this instance. Flanagan was actually competing on the newly arrived American athletics team, hence his being described as 'American'. Yet the absence of any form of claim to his Irishness was interesting. The *Waterford News* repeated the Americanisation of the Limerick man,

A picture of some great American and Irish athletes. At the back, from left are Dennis Carey, Irving Baxter (USA) and T. Mullaney, a DMP sports official. Front, from left are Pat Leahy, Alvin Kraenzlein (USA) and Peter O'Connor. The picture appears to be from a year or two after 1900, as neither Baxter nor Kraenzlein wore moustaches in Penn State pictures of its athletes at the Paris Games. Courtesy Larry Ryder.

merely listing Flanagan as part of the American team for the forthcoming USA v. England match.[24]

The main Irish Olympic hopefuls went to London for the AAA contests in early July 1900, still thinking that the Olympics were due in September. The likes of Peter O'Connor and Tom Kiely went to London fully hopeful of victories over whatever England or America had to offer. Irish press reports suggested that the stories which had reached Ireland about the feats of American athletes at home had been taken with a large grain of salt. At the AAAs, the Irish were in for a rude awakening as the Americans, spearheaded by Flanagan and a cohort of athletes from the University of

Pennsylvania, won almost everything, with the great Irish champions reduced to minor placings. Ironically, the coach to many of the US athletes was the legendary Irish-American, Mike Murphy. The reaction of the *Kerry Sentinel* to this humiliation was interesting, in that the Irishness of the Irish-Americans was now seized upon to a degree not seen before:

> America got all the credit but as far as I can make out there was never an American in America as they are sold now. Flanagan hails from Kilmallock, Duffy is not of Parisian origin and Sheldon's people will be found in Trim.[25]

At last, albeit coming as a straw-clutching exercise on a dark day for Irish athletics, here was an acknowledgement in Ireland of the Irishness of these American athletes. The success of the Americans, including the Irish-Americans, at Stamford Bridge before the Olympics brought satisfaction to the more extreme nationalists, again because much of the success had been achieved against British athletes or against Irish athletes who, simply by virtue of their competing at the AAA championships, were deemed 'West British'. The *United Irishman* reported that:

> A very lively sense of satisfaction seemed to pervade Irish Gaelic circles at the brilliant victories of the American athletes in the English Championships. This, of course, was largely due to a feeling of kinship to that body amongst whom so many of our exiled Gaels found a hospitable home and fitting opportunity to demonstrate their innate prowess. Not a little of it, however, had its origin in the fact that one eternally hears doubts and sneers cast upon American performances and American sportsman-ship by the 'unco guid' English amateur and his repulsive West British imitator.[26]

The similarity between these views and those of James B. Connolly earlier was striking. The allusion to the 'West British imitator' added another dimension to the anti-British dimension of Irish identity, as felt by people who agreed with the *United Irishman*. The fact that the Irish athletes such as O'Connor and Kiely, for instance, had competed as IAAA representatives in London made them effectively considered to be less acceptable Irishmen than the Americans were: 'That some Irish-born performers, sailing under the IAAA colours, got beaten with as little ceremony as the veriest Saxon aborigine in the island, takes not a whit off our enjoyment.'[27] Although most of the American team had no Irish connections, the more extreme nationalist was happy enough to gloss over this and claim what he could as Irish, while also decrying (neither for the first nor last time) the English opposition to America and its 'professionalism':

> We can see many typical Irish names amongst the winners, but make no apology for singling out Flanagan (late of Kilmallock) for special congratulations . . . We would just, however, warn our readers to be on the look out for a cry of 'professionalism' against some of the Americans. It is sure to come in its due season, and will appear in good time in the Irish sporting press.[28]

Flanagan's case in particular demonstrated one final twist in the Irish national identity crisis in sport. Previously, the Irish abhorrence of the possibility of Tom Kiely and others competing for an English representative team against Irish-Americans in New York in 1895 was noted. If the AAA championships of 1900 did nothing else, they showed the Irish champions that their true opponents in international competition were not English or Scottish, but American representatives like Alvin Kraenzlein (still the only man to win four individual athletics gold medals in one Olympic Games) and Flanagan.[29] There was also intense anticipation of a rematch between Kiely and Flanagan after the AAAs:

> A well-informed friend of mine has assured me that Kiely and Flanagan are certain to meet in the hammer throw at the Paris Exhibition meeting, adding: 'When they do meet, Flanagan will win and don't you forget it, for there is not the slightest difference between the present American hammer and the Irish one . . .' I reserve my own opinion on this matter as I have reason to believe that this American hammer does afford a greater handle leverage . . .[30]

Whether Kiely would ever have gained revenge on Flanagan in Paris is immaterial, as the great Ballyneale athlete never made it to the French capital. What is significant, however, in the above extract was that Irish sporting nationalism had essentially grown up. No longer was it just

Peter O'Connor taking off in 1901, during one of his world-record-breaking jumps at this time. Courtesy of Larry Ryder.

looking at a narrow desire to beat the 'ould enemy' or even brother Celts. The Americans had set new heights and if Ireland was to regain its much-prized reputation for athletic excellence then this new challenge had to be met. Nor could it be argued that this was still just a sort of parochial rivalry – with the exception of the Kiely–Flanagan duel, most of the Americans in 1900 had no Irish connections at all – Kraenzlein, who beat O'Connor and Leahy comfortably at Stamford Bridge in the long jump, was born in Germany. This was not the end of narrow sporting nationalism, where beating neighbouring rivals was paramount, because that was and still is essentially a worldwide phenomenon. It was, however, some evidence of the beginning of a more global view in Irish athletics.

To Go or Not To Go . . .

The success of the Americans over all-comers at Stamford Bridge had an impact not just on Irish national pride but on athletics training methods here too. First of all came a sort of national debate centred on the lack of proper preparation of Irish athletes vis-à-vis the Americans: 'The Americans have been two years training for this visit, and have their special men to look after them – doctors, cooks, etc., etc.'[31] A feeling began to emerge that the Irish needed to specialise more, that the top athletes tended to try to compete in everything, to win everything and that, at the highest level, this was causing them to fall between several stools:

> A correspondent writes – Take for instance Keily [sic], who has won the All-Round Championship of Ireland for several years. Were he to give over hurdle racing, jumping and throwing heavy weights, and confine himself exclusively to throwing the hammer, I venture to assert that he would vanquish his countryman, Flanagan, and create a new world's record. Again, Leahy and O'Connor, two brilliant performers on the long and high jump, go in for all round athletics, particularly O'Connor. If Leahy would confine himself exclusively to the high jump and O'Connor to the long jump, I again assert that they would, with proper training create world's records in these events.[32]

A lengthy letter in the pages of *Sport* espoused similar sentiments. The ultimate ironies in all this, of course, were that Kiely was to persist with his all-round athletics and become the Olympic champion at St Louis four years later, while O'Connor did indeed specialise more in the long jump (subsequently holding the world record for nearly two decades and the Irish record for three-quarters of a century), but was to win his only Olympic title in the hop, step and jump in 1906.[33]

The AAA championship failures of the Irish, when allied to the mistake over the starting dates of the Olympic athletics programme at Paris, cast some additional light on the non-appearance of most of the top Irish athletes at the Paris Games. The athletics columnist in *Sport*, who had certainly backed an Olympic entry, admitted:

> It is a pity that Kiely, Horgan, O'Connor etc. did not go to Paris as intended; but perhaps they got enough of the opposition at Stamford Bridge and in any case they are satisfied that they are 'not in it' with the Americans as far as training goes.[34]

Thus, rather than some sort of grand imperialist conspiracy, 'Ireland' was poorly represented at Paris because of confused organisation and perhaps because the Irish faced up to realities. Another clue that this was the case came in a subsequent issue of *Sport*, when an account of the RIC sports at Belvedere College told of Peter O'Connor winning the long jump with an effort 'just one inch worse than Newburn's accepted record, and I am certain that if O'Connor was only half in proper condition that he would have jumped a foot further'.[35] Perhaps the GAA's belief back in 1896 that its athletes were not in good condition early in the year is partially borne out by this statement. To add further grist to this particular mill, O'Connor later in the summer set the first of four consecutive world records.[36] It is absolutely no exaggeration to see Peter O'Connor as the Jesse Owens or Carl Lewis of his generation in long jump terms. O'Connor's performance at Belvedere was in an RIC sports meeting, again showing that athletics was transcending the narrower boundaries set out by the GAA. This would happen again and again up to 1908, though much to the annoyance of the more narrowly nationalistic advocates.

The best-organised sports in the country were often the RIC or DMP (Dublin Metropolitan Police) sports, leaving athletes with the choice of sticking to particular political ideals or not getting sufficient high-level competition. It should also be remembered that the DMP and RIC were essentially two different police bodies, and the acceptance of one by largely rural athletes did not necessarily imply support, or dissent, towards the other body. There was, after all, just one police body in whatever area you lived, and the members of that body were as Irish as anyone else. One leading police officer and athlete of the day was Dennis Carey, a cousin of John Flanagan's and a native of Kilfinnane where Flanagan hailed from, who later went on to compete in the Stockholm Olympics of 1912 and also to train Irish athletes for the Paris Olympic Games post-independence.[37]

Irishmen in Paris

The only top Irish amateur athlete who eventually competed in Paris was Pat Leahy, who participated as part of a British team.[38] This seems to be at odds with the idea that a separate invitation was sent to an Irish team by the IOC and certainly suggests that such an invitation had anticipated all along that Irish entrants would be accredited as British AAA representatives anyway. It has also been suggested that O'Connor may have missed Paris because he was not happy about competing on a British team.[39] This seems unlikely given what has already been discussed in this chapter. Considering the level of the competition he was up against, Leahy did superbly well. He placed second in the high jump and third in the long jump, the events held in the grounds of the Racing Club de France in the Bois de Boulogne, near where Longchamps racecourse is located. Pat Leahy had generally played second fiddle to O'Connor in Irish competitions, and to win two Olympic placings in such chaotic circumstances was some achievement. In some respects, Leahy's second place in the high jump behind the American, Baxter, was a disappointment, one biographer describing it as the only break in a glorious record of success for him in that event, contributed to by his arriving in Paris at 2 a.m. that morning. [40] The same source suggests that Leahy had to battle through a competition of fifty-six competitors, jumping many times to reach the last few. This is not substantiated in more official records, with the general belief being that there were eight entrants in the high jump, coming from seven different countries.[41] Leahy had been AAA high jump champion in both 1898 and 1899, although Baxter had defeated him at the 1900 AAA championships referred to earlier in this chapter.

While the AAA had a well-established policy of awarding medals to those who finished in the top three placings in events, the Paris Olympic Games were much less uniform. John Boland and James Brendan Connolly had received silver medallions, not gold, for winning Olympic titles in 1896 (second place in 1896 garnered a bronze medal, incidentally). In 1900, the first three placed in the high jump, and in all other athletics events, received objects of art of unspecified value. It has not been possible to identify what Pat Leahy received exactly, but it was certainly not a medal.[42] The other item of interest was that the prizes in Paris were awarded for a 'World Championship' (Championnât du Monde) rather than using the term 'Olympic', even though few have actually questioned the right of the Paris Games to be considered Olympic, and even those who have questioned elements of the Games have accepted that any events which had international competitors, as all of Leahy's did, should be accepted as 'Olympic' in history.

When Pat Leahy finished third in the long jump he was among twelve entrants from six different countries, and his fourth in the hop, step and jump was in a field of thirteen from six countries. This latter event had not been on the original programme, and some sources do not list Leahy as participating at all, but most recognise him as finishing fourth, after arriving late for the competition.[43] In detailing Leahy's successes, *Sport* commented:

> Then we have Paris World's Championships in which only one Irishman competed, viz. Pat Leahy of Charleville, and he won two prizes against the multitudinous opposition of all comers . . . after a sick passage, he only arrived in Paris on Friday night, and had to compete at 9 o'clock on Saturday morning.[44]

Before leaving Pat Leahy, there is a lovely cameo of his role in Peter O'Connor's world-record-breaking performance in May 1901. O'Connor was disappointed that the Irish record holder of the time, Arthur Newburn, had failed to turn up to the IAAA championships in Ballsbridge that year. Pat Leahy, who had not intended to take part in the long jump, did so in order to provide competition for O'Connor. Throughout the competition, although he knew he had little chance himself, Leahy apparently encouraged O'Connor, helped him cope with erratic judging and generally provided huge support as the Waterford-based athlete eventually soared to a world record on his fifth jump, 24 feet 9 inches.[45]

Turning to Irish-America, we get another insight into how small the Irish athletics world was in reality. Given that James Brendan Connolly, the 1896 Athens champion, finished second in the hop, step and jump, with Pat Leahy fourth, the two undoubtedly met. Similarly, with Leahy's events taking place on 14–16 July and the hammer being on the 16th, there is every likelihood that Pat Leahy and his near neighbour John Flanagan met each other and reminisced about sporting days in south Limerick while in Paris.

John Flanagan would go on to become one of the most successful single-event Olympians of all time, winning three hammer titles in all. In Paris, he won his first Olympic hammer title, with his best throw of 167 feet 4.5 inches being over fifteen feet further than the runner-up. Legend has it that one of Flanagan's efforts ended up in a tree. Flanagan would eventually hold not only three Olympic titles but also seven American hammer championships and six American titles for throwing the 56-pound weight.[46] Flanagan's success in Paris some weeks after the AAAs awoke the people of his home town too. 'Flanagan is coming home on a visit to Kilmallock next week and really, although time is short, we ought to give him a welcome of some sort.'[47] This occasion represented the first official function in Ireland honouring the achievements of an Olympic victor. Here was a victor who just weeks previously was considered 'American' by some Irish press commentators and not mentioned at all in the *Limerick Leader* before, during or even after the Olympics at Paris. *Sport* acknowledged Flanagan under the heading of 'Gaelic Pastimes':

> At a meeting of the Kilmallock Sports Committee . . . the chairman said they may rest assured that Mr. Flanagan would be well received by his fellow townsmen. It was due to him at their hands to receive him in a suitable manner, as his prowess had reflected credit on Kilmallock and on Ireland.[48]

Flanagan has sometimes also been hailed as a Kilfinnane native. In point of fact, his homestead still stands in the Kilbreedy/Martinstown area of County Limerick, between Kilmallock and Kilfinnane, where a magnificent statue of him in full flight was unveiled some years back.[49] Flanagan was a very accomplished hurler as well, winning a Limerick County Senior medal in 1893 with Bruree. Who is to say that the then eleven-year-old Éamon de Valera, himself then living in Bruree, was not in the crowd that day?

There were almost certainly several others on the American athletics team in Paris who were of Irish extraction. The Edmund Minihan who finished fourth in the 60 metres was only seventeen years old in 1900, one of the youngest American track and field athletes ever. He later played major league baseball for a brief spell with the Cincinnati Reds.[50] It has not been possible to trace his Irish links but the phone directory for west Cork could well be a place to start. Similarly, an athlete named Frederick Moloney finished third in the 110 metres high hurdles and with a name like that he must have had Irish ancestry. Neither of these men can be recorded as yet as being 'Irish' because their origins have not been identified, but it is as certain as it can be that Ireland can make some sort of claim to both based on their surnames alone.

The only clue unearthed thus far to the fact that Richard Sheldon of the US team had Irish ancestry comes from a previously quoted *Kerry Sentinel* reference to his people being from Trim. Assuming this to mean that he was second-generation Irish-American, the same Sheldon proved

Three great athletes of the 1900 Games: John Flanagan seated on left, Pat Leahy standing and on the right is a great friend of Irish-America, Ralph Rose. Courtesy of Larry Ryder and Dr Cyril White.

himself a fine performer in Paris. He won the shot put very easily on 15 July, aided by the fact that his nearest rivals in the qualifying round refused to compete on the 15th as it was a Sunday.[51] This suggests that Sheldon was probably of Catholic stock, although sufficiently well established to have been able to send the young Sheldon to Yale. The fact that his closest rival in the shot, Josiah McCracken of the USA, had a very Irish-sounding name and may well have been of Ulster non-Conformist stock, would explain McCracken's abstention from competing on a Sunday. Apologies if this reasoning seems over-speculative, not least because no details of McCracken's origins have been identified by this author's researches. Sheldon also won a third placing in the discus event on the same day, incidentally, an event in which some sources, but not all, list John Flanagan as competing and finishing seventh.[52]

Another Irishman, Mike Sweeney of Kerry but domiciled in New York, actually won two first places in Paris, but in the 'professional' high jump and long jump events. These were never recognised as Olympic events and received no comment in the Irish press. Ironically, Sweeney had lost his amateur status for taking a coaching job with a New York school prior to the Games.[53] Yet, typically of the Olympic movement's own anomalous position on professionalism at the time, James Brendan Connolly, who had taken on an identical role with a Boston school since 1896, was allowed to compete again in the 'amateur' hop, step and jump and won second place this time. As a footnote, even though he lost his amateur status, the high jump record set by Sweeney in 1896 lasted until 1908. His professional mark in Paris, 1.80 metres, would have been good enough to pip Pat Leahy for second place in the high jump but would still have been ten centimetres behind Baxter.[54] Sweeney's two victories in Paris won him money prizes, although the amount of the purse has not been verified, and his titles were called 'Championnât du monde professionel'.[55]

Irish reaction to Irish successes in minority sports was on similar lines to the reaction to Boland's tennis successes in 1896 – essentially non-existent. The only reference to Irish tennis victories found in the national press was a transcript of a Reuters report in the *Cork Examiner*.[56] The paper did not even seem to notice that one of those listed, Harold Mahony, was from Ireland, although he won a second place in the men's singles, second in the mixed doubles in partnership with Hélène Prévost of France and a joint third place in the doubles when partnering Arthur Norris from Britain. Unlike John Boland from four years previously, Harold Mahony was an international tennis player of some renown, having won the Wimbledon singles title in 1896 and the European Championship just the year before the Paris Olympics.[57] The tennis entries were small, as in Athens, but the overall quality of the competitions was certain to have been far higher also than had been the case in Athens – the top British players, Reggie and Hugh Doherty, won all before them in Paris, as they did at Wimbledon and elsewhere in the 1900s. Even the *Kerry Sentinel,* so ready to comment at length on Irish athletes going to Paris or not going, completely ignored the success of Mahony from Kenmare, County Kerry. There is no reason to assume that this had anything to do with him being from a landed gentry family – Boland's Catholic and relatively nationalist background four years earlier had won him no more attention in Ireland than Mahony got. The main problem was that tennis was just not a sport of the masses and the Paris competitions did little to capture Irish imaginations. If the 'Britishness' of the sport was the issue, then how could we explain the coverage given in Irish papers to rugby, fox-hunting and so on? Nor was there any evidence of unionist press acknowledgement of the Kerryman when the nationalist press had ignored him. The *Belfast Newsletter* carried no coverage of the Olympics at all, while *The Irish Times* merely listed the results, with no comment on Mahony's Irishness, or even his being 'British'.[58] Efforts to gather more information on Harold Mahony locally in Kenmare came to nothing, largely due to the fact that much of the records held at the family home had been destroyed in a fire in recent times. He did, however, die tragically due to a fall from a bicycle in later years.[59] Like Leahy, Mahony's prizes were objects of art, otherwise unspecified, although the term 'World Championship' was not used, the prizes being simply presented for the 'Championnât'.[60]

If the tennis achievements of Mahony went unnoticed in Ireland, it is even less surprising that the presence of two Irish gentry on the winning polo team at Paris were ignored. Both Dennis St George Daly and John George Beresford represented the Foxhunters Hurlingham Polo Club, together with two Americans and a Briton. Although the polo competition at Paris has always been accorded official Olympic status, only one of the four participating teams here was comprised of players of a single nationality.[61] It is also a matter of some dispute as to whether the aforementioned polo tournament merits the title 'Olympic' and it seems to depend entirely on which set of criteria one adheres to.[62] There is no evidence to date to suggest that the 'Georges A. Dillon-Cavanagh' who finished sixth or seventh in a fencing event was anything other than a Frenchman, though descended from a wild goose or two, perhaps.[63] Dillon-Cavanagh was one of a total of fifty-four competitors in the foil competition, held nearly two months before the athletics events in La Grande Salle des Fêtes de l'Exposition. He was awarded an art object as a seventh prize, even though for some strange reason the prizes in other fencing competitions varied between art objects and medals of different hues.[64]

Taking Stock

Before leaving the results at Paris, a brief look at the performances in comparable athletics events at the Olympics, the AAA championships and the Irish championships may shed some light on the fact that Irish athletics would have to raise the bar, metaphorically and in some cases literally, if it was to compete on the world stage. An insight into the already declined interest in athletics within GAA circles comes from the fact that there were no GAA championships held in 1900, beyond four individual events which were 'farmed out' to different meetings around the country. The illness of just one very prominent administrator, Frank Dineen, was seen as a major factor in this non-holding of the championships and showed how tenuous the GAA's commitment to athletics really was at this time.[65] It may also be significant that Dineen was then the owner of the main athletics venue used by the GAA, at Jones's Road, Dublin, latterly Croke Park, although this was certainly not the sole venue used for GAA athletics championships at that time.[66]

The running events at Paris were in metric distances and, as we saw previously, were somewhat difficult to compare with the standards achieved in the other national championships of 1900, those of the IAAA. However, taking normal adjustment methods into account, no victor at the IAAA championships, and no Irish competitor in the Ireland v. Scotland match of the same year would have finished in the top three of any Olympic running event in Paris.[67] The IAAA 220 yards champion ran 23.8 seconds, while the almost identical 200-metre distance in Paris was won in 22.2 seconds. There was a difference of exactly four seconds between the Olympic 800-metre winning time and the IAAA 880-yards winning time, although the actual difference in distance is less than five yards, while the 400 metres–440 yards comparison saw a gap of three seconds between the respective winners.

Field events compare considerably more favourably (here using imperial equivalents for the Olympic measurements). Pat Leahy's second place in the Paris high jump was at the same height as won the IAAA championships, at 5 feet 10 inches. Peter O'Connor's winning long jump at the IAAA championships would have tied with Alvin Kraenzlein's leap at Paris while Denis Horgan would have finished a close second at Paris if his IAAA mark of 45 feet 9 inches had been replicated there. Tom Kiely's IAAA hammer mark of 141 feet 6 inches would not have come close to Flanagan's winning effort in Paris but this does not take into account the variations in regulations and hammer types which obtained at the different events.[68]

Olympic Hurling

Given the 'exhibition' nature of much of what happened at Paris in 1900, it is not surprising that the Games were used to showpiece some 'ethnic' competitions. Pelota Basque was played between Spanish and French Basque teams and has been accepted as an official Olympic competition to this day.[69] There is no suggestion that the game was considered inappropriate by the French organisers, though it may well have provided a sort of fillip to Basque identity or nationalism. What is hugely interesting from an Irish perspective, however, is that an invitation was issued to Ireland to send some hurlers to Paris for an exhibition. The *Kerry Sentinel* reported:

> The exiled Gaels of London are sending teams to the Paris exhibition, Cork being unable to accept the invitation to do so. It will be a novel experience for most *Boulevardiers* to witness the games that were played in Ireland when its soil belonged to a free race, the games that are played today by those who live on memories – and hope. There, in the intellectual capital of the world, the brilliant home of wit and gaiety . . . will be heard the crash of the camán, and I hope the music of the Gaelic tongue on the lips of excited hurlers.[70]

The inability of the Cork GAA board to send a team may well have reflected financial difficulties. This assumes that the responsibility for such a team rested with the county board, simply in that it is hard to see what other sporting body might have taken responsibility for entering a Cork hurling team in Paris. In commenting at length on the Olympic hurling plans for Paris, the *United Irishman* was hugely optimistic about the possibilities for even Irish independence which this proposed match offered:

> We understand that arrangements are to be made to have a hurling match played in Paris this season between the Chicago and the London Gaels, although the original idea was that the Cork and the Chicago men should play. There ought to be no difficulty in arranging for two teams to play on the friendly soil of France. It goes without saying that the Gaels would get a hearty reception in the French capital. In bygone days, Ireland's prowess was exhibited, though perhaps in a different way on France's plains, and may be again. An exhibition of the national pastime of Ireland would, no doubt, be appreciated. The London men would be glad to meet their brothers from 'Greater Ireland' at this famous trysting place, and the meeting would have its advantages too, and, perhaps, help the men 'from one bright island flown' to realise the ties which bind them together, their duty to their motherland, and the necessity for unity and strength in striking a blow in her name and for her freedom.[71]

Nothing has been unearthed in either Olympic records or contemporary accounts to suggest that these 'exiled Gaels' ultimately made the trip and entertained the *Boulevardiers* at Paris. However, the above excerpt is so laden with nationalist passion – the sense of loss and exile, love of the mother tongue, the longing for freedom – that it deserves serious attention in its own right. It may well be that the GAA had missed another opportunity to establish an Irish identity on a world stage, as it did in rejecting the invitation to send a team to Athens four years earlier.[72]

A number of Irish press articles from this period echo the desire for renewed French aid for Irish freedom. Fanciful as it may have appeared, it is important to bear in mind that the Paris Games came just two years after the Fashoda Incident, which had almost brought France and Britain to war in Africa. Adding further to the Irish hopes was the fact that an Irish delegation on a form of state visit to the French capital coincided with the Games:

> The Irish delegates to France have been publicly received by the Municipal Council of Paris. Such an incident has never previously taken place in connection with Ireland, and taken along with several other unmistakable tokens of French interest in Ireland as evidenced by the enthusiastic reception of our fellow-countrymen is an augury of the greatest hope for the future.[73]

Whatever else, this statement linking sport with national identity and an appeal for independence remains the most potent expression of Irish sporting nationalism which we have yet seen regarding the Olympic Games.

Political Olympians

The year 1900 was not just the year of the Paris Olympics but also one which saw the reunification of the Irish Parliamentary Party. Links between party members and the Irish Olympic movement would indeed emerge, although the most prominent supporters of Irish Olympism, certainly as a separate entity, came invariably from the ranks of non-parliamentary, though not physical force, nationalists. The reunification of the Irish Party was, in some respects, an artificial one, given the number of factions, and even greater prevalence of differing opinions in relation to national identity and preferred tactics to bring about whatever form of national identity individual members sought. The story of the Irish Parliamentary Party is one of an evolving and disparate group, bound together philosophically at times as loosely after 1900 as they had been in the days of Isaac Butt. The same degree of variance is evident when it comes to the views of people with political interests in relation to the Olympic Games and Ireland's involvement in them. Around 1900, two initial links between the Olympic movement and the Irish Parliamentary Party were forged, though in very different manners and neither of which linked the Irish Party generally to the Games.

John Pius Boland, as we saw, was the Olympic tennis champion of 1896. There is no known record to suggest that he ever played a serious tennis match after 1896. In 1900, he commenced a lengthy and distinguished career in politics, representing South Kerry at Westminster continuously up to 1918. The local press coverage of the selection of Boland as MP for South Kerry in 1900 sheds light again on the lack of nationalistic significance ascribed to his Olympic successes in a minority sport. Evidence from newspapers of the time suggests that a high degree of nationalism prevailed in Kerry sporting circles, particularly within the GAA. On one occasion, the *Kerry Sentinel* lauded the fundraising done within the county for the planned Wolfe Tone memorial, declaring:

> We in Kerry have taken the initiative in this matter . . . why should not the other County Boards also identify themselves with the project . . . the Kerry Gaels . . . have subordinated sport to patriotism, and in doing so have set a high example to the Gaels of every other county to follow.[74]

Against this background, one might have been forgiven for anticipating that a double Olympic champion, known by now to have objected to being treated as 'British' in Athens, might at least have aroused the curiosity of sporting Kerry folk. Not so. When he was proposed for the nationalist seat in South Kerry, Boland was effectively an unknown. The *Sentinel* politely accepted him because 'Mr. Boland, though not so well known in the constituency, is possessed of scholarly attainments, and it is claimed for him that his political views are attuned to the National ideal.'[75] This was hardly a rousing endorsement from the local newspaper. Furthermore, the paper's report of the South Kerry selection convention gives the clear impression that it was the support of the local Catholic clergy which won the unopposed nomination for Boland:

> The Convention Chairman, Monsignor O'Sullivan, was hardly impartial in declaring: 'Mr. John Boland . . . was a thorough gentleman, a sound scholar of Oxford, a sincere Catholic, a Barrister by profession and a sterling Nationalist' (cheers).[76]

Not one reference has been found linking Boland at this time to the Olympic victories of 1896. This is confirmation of the small impact the Games, and tennis within them, had on the national consciousness in these early years.

A second Irish political figure with Olympic links also emerged as an MP around this time. The highly colourful Alfred Arthur Lynch won a seat for Galway City in the parliament of 1900.[77] Unfortunately for him, his prior involvement in, among other activities, leading the 2nd Irish Brigade against British forces in the Boer War meant that he was arrested, charged with treason and sentenced to death upon his arrival in London to take up his seat. The sentence was afterwards commuted to a short term of imprisonment, leaving Lynch to pursue a highly chequered career as a politician, journalist, doctor and even critic of Einstein's theories before his death.

The connection of Lynch to the Olympic movement is a philosophical one rather than one of direct sporting involvement. Recent research has uncovered much to suggest that Lynch, writing in the period 1894–5, was the originator of the concept of 'religio athletiae', the notion linking sporting involvement with spiritualism which was so fundamental to Baron de Coubertin's Olympic ideals. Although de Coubertin never acknowledged the influence of Lynch on his original Olympic philosophy, much circumstantial evidence has been unearthed to suggest that this most unusual sometime member of the Irish Parliamentary Party was, in point of fact, a huge influence on the Olympic movement without, perhaps, ever intending to be so.[78] As a microcosm of the disparity of viewpoints which characterised much of the Irish Party, one could hardly have found two MPs with Olympic connections but with such widely differing viewpoints. Boland was and remained a staunch Redmond loyalist throughout his parliamentary career, with him later recalling 'my great leader, John Redmond'.[79] Lynch, by contrast, even in the midst of a mini posthumous revival of Redmondism, was still happy to declare of Redmond that 'He was the worst leader Ireland ever had.'[80] Even when Irishmen with Olympic connections went outside of the sporting arena, it seems that divergence of viewpoints was to be the norm there as it was in matters sporting.

In Conclusion

Even without a significant popular impact as yet, the developments of 1900 show that there had already been significant shifts vis-à-vis the emergence of Irish identity around the Olympics. Firstly, an embracing of Olympism is evident in the apparent acceptance of the invitation to compete, an invitation which had been rejected by unionist and nationalist sporting bodies in 1896. Secondly, this Olympic entry coincided with a growing commitment to international competition, certainly in athletics events, as evidenced by the continued involvement in such as the annual Scottish match and the AAAs, and by the growth in local press coverage of the feats of O'Connor, Kiely et al. The Irish involvement at Paris, and the medal haul, would undoubtedly have been greater had it not been for the organisational muddle about timing of events and, perhaps, the Irish realisation at the same time that they were just not as well prepared as they needed to be.

This last point brings us, of course, to the Americans. It was in 1900, more so than in 1896, that the Irish press significantly embraced Irish-Americans as brother Irishmen, though partly in an effort to ease the pangs of defeat in the AAAs. Yet 1900 also saw the emergence of America as a rival of the Irish, challenging Ireland's preconceptions about its athletic prowess but simultaneously making the point that international sport was now seen among the Irish to be about more than just beating the English or 'brother Celts' in Scotland. Indeed, the evidence suggests that Irish abstension from Paris arose in part from a realisation of American might and a sense that the Olympics, even in 1900, were actually about winning, not just taking part.

Of the Irish who did compete in Paris, competitors in minority sports or from ascendancy backgrounds had no impact on the Irish consciousness. Yet, the coverage in nationalist circles of the plans to stage hurling in Paris certainly showed that the potential of the Olympics as a national or patriotic vehicle had been realised, albeit in a rather idealistic manner. The seeds had, at least, been sown in Paris for the development of this idea over the next eight years, when Ireland's top champions did eventually make it to the Olympics and Irish-America got its chance to express itself most forcefully through the Games.

CHAPTER THREE

IRISH-AMERICA AND THE 1904 OLYMPICS

While the Paris Olympics of 1900 had major problems, at least they were held where they had been scheduled for. The next Olympics were due to be held in Chicago, USA, in 1904 but for a number of reasons, some of which we will touch on here, they were changed to St Louis. St Louis had not even been one of the four US candidate cities to begin with. Again, the Games were linked to a world fair, with roughly one sporting event held each day, causing them to be dragged out from 1 July to 23 November. Only twelve countries were represented here, including 'Ireland', and just 630 athletes.[1] The disastrous mess that the Games of 1904 became could have destroyed the Olympic movement for good. However, for a number of reasons, the St Louis Games marked major advancements for the Irish and Irish-Americans, as we will see in this chapter and the next.

The years prior to the St Louis Olympics of 1904 were quite traumatic ones for the International Olympic Committee (IOC), not least because of great tensions between the IOC and the head of the Amateur Athletic Union (AAU), James E. Sullivan, the son of an Irish labourer from County Kerry. Sullivan was a fiery character who seemed to delight in antagonising de Coubertin and challenging some of the IOC's principles of amateurism and decorum. An early example of the tensions was seen in an open letter from de Coubertin, attacking James E. Sullivan for apparently wanting to set up an independent athletics body in opposition to the IOC, for criticising the 1900 Paris Games and de Coubertin's relative absence from them, and for suggesting that Athens was better organised in 1896 than Paris was in 1900.[2]

Hostility to Sullivan was equally strong among the British members of the IOC, including the Reverend Robert de Courcy Laffan. Ironically, de Courcy Laffan's father was Irish, just as Sullivan's was, but the two men were worlds apart in every other respect. There was still no British Olympic Association in existence but a very strong and aristocratic British presence on the IOC nevertheless. It bears explanation at this stage that the term 'member' has very specific connotations within the IOC. Members of the IOC came from different countries but not as representatives of those countries, strictly speaking. Instead, the IOC invited people like de Courcy Laffan to become 'members' (often with a capital 'M' in IOC documentation) of the IOC and then appointed them essentially as IOC ambassadors to the countries they came from. It was a clever way, devised by de Coubertin, of seeking to ensure that IOC members owed their first loyalty to the IOC, not necessarily to their country of origin. A nice cameo of the socio-political sentiments of de Courcy Laffan, a most influential and long-serving British IOC member, was found in his note to de Coubertin regarding plans for London's hosting of an IOC meeting in June 1904:

> Could you give your luncheon on Friday 24th instead of Wednesday 22nd? Friday is the King's birthday, and if we lunched with you on that day we could drink the King's health and send him a telegram of congratulations; which would be a pretty compliment from the International Committee. Try to arrange this ...[3]

The American sporting philosophy, embracing as it did professionalism, nationalism, anti-aristocratic sentiment and often bluntness, was anathema to people like de Coubertin and de Courcy Laffan. After the mess of the Games at Paris and their dilution by the world exposition, it was a worrying development for the Olympic establishment when news reached them that the selected host city for 1904, Chicago, had given way to a largely Sullivan-inspired plan to switch the 1904 Olympics to St Louis, coinciding with the world fair there. De Courcy Laffan complained to de Coubertin:

> This decision seems to me even more regrettable . . . Today the impression the Chicago committee has given – I don't mean among our colleagues but among public opinion generally – will be of trying to extricate itself from a disagreeable task . . . the joining of the Olympic Games with the Universal Exposition is not made to enhance the dignity of them. The Olympic celebration should, in my opinion, be independent of all other meetings.[4]

Although no direct comments from the IOC members have been found in printed archives for 1903–4, the news that Sullivan himself was to be the de facto head of the Olympics at St Louis must have been a serious blow. Despite his long and powerful association with American athletics, Sullivan was most certainly not considered IOC member material in the eyes of the committee's leaders. The background chaos and the presence of Sullivan at the helm did little to encourage Britain to send an Olympic team. These Games marked the start of a quite serious rift between the Americans and the British, a rift in which Irish-Americans played a major part by 1908. In the end, neither Britain nor France competed as nations at St Louis, a fact the Americans were to accept with some detachment:

> Neither France nor England were missed from the games of 1904, however, and it is doubtful, indeed, if a single Frenchman could have finished even fourth in any of the events. In fact, only one Englishman would have stood a chance of winning any event whatever, and that man was Shrubb, who holds several world's records in the distance events.[5]

The St Louis Games afforded Irish-America an opportunity to express itself, both in its Irishness and in simultaneously establishing its 'American-ness'. Even before St Louis was selected instead of Chicago, for instance, it was fully intended to hold Gaelic sports at the 1904 Games. The *Chicago Tribune* reported as far back as 1901:

> It is proposed that the games shall cover a period of two weeks and shall consist of contests in baseball, cricket, basket-ball, track athletics, feats of strength, cycling, turning, bowling, polo, tennis, wrestling and the peculiarly national games of different

countries. Both Gaelic and American football is to be played. Exhibitions of lacrosse will be given by Americans, Canadians and Indians . . .'[6]

In this list, the plan to include the German tradition of 'turning', a form of group gymnastics, in the Olympic programme is also notable, no doubt influenced by a desire to appeal to the substantial Germanic immigrant population of the mid-west.

The Chicagoans, in making their preliminary preparations, made contact with sporting bodies in Montreal, seeking assistance and advice. This may well have influenced the decision to place lacrosse on the Olympic programme, and the huge Irish involvement in Canadian lacrosse should not be forgotten. Records show that hurling was played in Newfoundland in the eighteenth century and it is a very real hypothesis that the Irish took to the native American game as a sort of trans-Atlantic hurling substitute. A glance at the top scorers in the Canadian lacrosse league at this time shows a clear predominance of Irish surnames. The Montreal Shamrocks were the team of the year in Canada, backboned almost entirely by Irish immigrants. Ironically, when the Canadian team eventually took the field and won the title in the St Louis Games, it was drawn from members of the Winnipeg Shamrocks but had only a few members with possibly Irish surnames.[7]

Whatever about the unfulfilled plans for hurling in the Bois de Boulogne in 1900, the move of the Olympics from Chicago to St Louis was not going to deflect the organisers from including Gaelic games in the programme. In New York, a year before the Games, 'Great Plans for Olympian Games' were reported, citing that association football, Gaelic football and hurling had been given two days each in the programme.[8] In St Louis that same summer, it was announced that Irish sports, including hurling and Gaelic football, would take place between 20 and 28 July in 1904. Interestingly, there were no other nation-specific sports listed in this official programme of events.[9]

It was important, at the risk of overstating the Irish influence on the St Louis programme, that the Irish sports were specially designated and were not to form part of any so-called 'anthropological days' planned for St Louis, events involving tribal participants from Africa, Asia and

North and South America. The plans for German turning events did not survive the shift away from Germanic Chicago. While James E. Sullivan's influence was undoubtedly significant in the retention of Irish sports on the Olympic programme, demographics must also have been considered. Chicago had, for instance, 70,028 inhabitants of Irish birth in 1890, almost as many as Boston. The city's Irish population, not taking second-generation Irish into account, was actually the fastest-growing Irish group in any American city – the Irish population there had been little over half this number in 1870. St Louis, too, was a major Irish centre, holding the seventh-largest Irish population of all US cities in 1890.[10] President Theodore Roosevelt was a founding member of the American-Irish Historical Society, and had maternal roots in Ireland. His acceptance of the honorary presidency of the Games may also have been influenced by the heavy Irish-American dimension to the St Louis events. He had, after all, finished third in the 1886 New York mayoral election behind not one but two Irish candidates.[11] If he had one eye to the Irish-American electorate in 1904 – he also sent his daughter to present the medals at St Louis – it would not be the last time, as will be seen in 1908.

There was another reason why Irish sports were assigned such pride of place on the St Louis programme. In turn-of-the-century urban America, the Irish were the leading proponents and exponents of athletic sport. While the *Irish American* newspaper may be considered a biased source in this regard, the advert for the James E. Sullivan-organised 'Irish Games at the Garden' in February 1903 at least showed that Irish athletics was a mecca for many non-Irish athletes as well. It referred to: 'James S. Mitchell, world record holder in throwing 56lb weight for height, and John Flanagan. Mitchell is a man of the NYAC but these games are being organized by the GNYIAA.' The GNYIAA referred to here was the Greater New York Irish Athletic Association, already becoming a central plank in Irish-American identity. The advertisement also promised that college races were to be very much to the fore, involving the cream of the Ivy League – Yale, Cornell, University of Pennsylvania, Columbia and others. A separate article, again perhaps biased in its commentary though not inaccurate in its facts, reported on plans to enlarge facilities at Celtic Park, New York, home of the GNYIAA:

Nearly all of the important athletic fixtures this year will be held at Celtic Park. The Greater New York Irish Athletic Association will hold three sets of games, the all-round carnival on Decoration Day, the all-round championship of the Amateur Athletic Union of the United States on July 4, and the usual sports on Labor Day.[12]

Another World Fair but with an Irish Twist
The 1904 Olympic Games were staged during the St Louis World Fair. This created the same sort of confusion as had occurred in Paris, with Olympic historians and statisticians arguing to this day about the 'Olympic' nature of many of the St Louis events. In terms of the sports events, athletics became additionally disparate because of the holding of several college, high-school and other sports at St Louis in the summer of 1904. On the other hand, the schedule for events as announced in mid-1903 remained very tight. The Irish sports, for instance, predicted for the week between 20 and 28 July were eventually held on 20 July.

The main Irish-American newspaper to cover the events at St Louis was the *Gaelic American*. This began publication in New York in September 1903, under the editorship of John Devoy, driving force behind the republican organisation, Clan na Gael. The paper's voice was most definitely a loud and nationalistic one, with the publication quickly becoming the largest-selling Irish newspaper in the USA. Devoy soon engaged Tom Clarke, later to become one of the 1916 Proclamation signatories, as manager and assistant editor of the paper. Clarke also became John Devoy's secretary at the Clan na Gael headquarters and correspondence secretary of the United Irish-American Societies, until he returned to Ireland in December 1907.[13]

Three giants of Irish-American athletics. This picture may have been taken at St Louis or at one of the subsequent championships or picnics in the USA. From the left are John Flanagan and Martin Sheridan, sporting the winged fist of the Irish-American club, with James Mitchell on the right in the New York Athletic Club vest. Courtesy of Colm Murphy, who used it on the cover of his lovely book, *The Irish Whale.*

Devoy used the events in St Louis, both sporting and those linked to the world fair, to considerable effect in 1904. While the fair itself was not directly relevant to an Olympic focus, it afforded many opportunities to portray Irish industry and culture. The 'Irish village' was to become the central meeting point for the Irish-Americans around the St Louis Olympics, including the members of Irish national organisations and the athletes themselves. It contained reconstructions of the Irish house of parliament, Blarney Castle (complete with kissable stone) and Cormac's Chapel. It housed a restaurant and, most importantly, a theatre where traditional Irish music, dance and drama were to be performed. This theatre was, in fact, the venue for a very controversial variety show about Ireland, one upon which the *Gaelic American* reported with considerable vehemence because of the portrayal of what it considered 'stage Irishmen' and a generally very negative image of the country. The controversy is mentioned here simply in that it resonated with a previous one in which Irish-American athletes had become embroiled and had shed light on the strong Irish identity which the athletes about to win glory for the USA in St Louis had still retained. In 1903, the *Irish American* newspaper had reported:

> The movement to clean the vile and vulgar caricatures of the Irish off the stage took recent and drastic forms in this city [New York] and in Philadelphia. On the evening of March 20th, the low travesty called *McFadden's Row of Flats* which was put on at the New Star Theatre received the first attention from an organized effort carefully planned by members of the Clan na Gael and the Ancient Order of Hibernians, reinforced by members of the Greater New York Irish Athletic Association. The actors were driven off the stage by bad eggs and decayed vegetables. A boycott on all such theatres and players as offend in this manner will have a healthy and quick effect in putting a stop to the evil.[14]

When turning to the activities and considerable achievements of members of the Greater New York Irish Athletic Association, at St Louis and beyond, clearly this was an organisation dedicated to athletic excellence but also to the promotion of Irish identity and prestige within the USA itself. In fact, the twin aims were often inseparable.

Irish-American Athletes and the Olympic Games

By 1904, Irish-America had begun to win respectability, to different degrees, in a number of urban environments. In Philadelphia, for example, the social problems that had plagued the post-Famine Irish had moderated considerably. The Irish had begun to dominate the construction industry, much of city politics and, of course, the Catholic Church. The Irish influence on the Church was very important, especially because Catholicism eventually attracted and held masses of other immigrants through its schools and influence.[15] This acceptance was, by the start of the twentieth century, also quite evident in Boston, where the traditional anglophobia of native Bostonians found a resonance among the Irish. However, the largest concentration of Irish in the USA lay in the great melting pot of New York and it was here that the greatest battle for

John Flanagan on his way to his second Olympic title in the hammer, at the St Louis Olympics (© IOC Lausanne).

acceptance was fought, with sport and Olympic success playing a vital role in the first decade of the twentieth century.

The difficulties for the Irish in gaining acceptance among the elite of such as the New York Athletic Club had led the immigrants to effectively set up their own club, the Greater New York Irish Athletic Association, which received its charter in 1897. The club subsequently purchased and developed what became known as Celtic Park, spiritual home of Irish-American sport for the next three decades.

By the early twentieth century, a lot of circumstantial evidence suggests that the GAA back in Ireland had begun to lose interest in the promotion of athletics. Among Irish-Americans, however, the contrast was quite significant. Where hurling and football matches had basically taken centre stage at GAA events in Ireland, they remained very much late-evening, almost novelty events with groups like the GNYIAA. Athletics remained the principal attraction of Gaelic sporting events in Boston, New York and other Irish centres. This helps to explain the success of Irish-American athletes in the first five or six incarnations of the Olympic Games in the twentieth century. It also helps to explain the massive crowds which flocked to Irish athletic meetings in New York and along the east coast.

It would be pointless to try to identify all of the competitors at St Louis who came from Irish backgrounds. Relying on Irish surnames alone and thereby discounting those who had Irish maternal backgrounds only, a glance down the list of competitors shows that there were dozens of Irish-Americans. The St Louis AAA lacrosse team which finished runners-up to the Winnipeg Shamrocks was peopled by men called Grogan, Dowling, Murphy and Sullivan.[16] The association football tournament was won by Canada but both the second- and third-placed teams represented the USA and were drawn from Christian Brothers College (St Louis) and the St Rose parish, also of St Louis. It is certain that Joseph Lydon, born in County Mayo, was a member of the Christian Brothers team which won second place, while St Rose in particular looked to be a very Irish outfit, including a Brady, an O'Connell and a Cosgrove in their ranks. Interestingly, Lydon also went on to win a bronze medal in welterweight boxing at St Louis. It has been suggested that Lydon, later a successful oil dealer, may well be the only Olympian to have won medals in both association football and boxing, certainly at the same Games.[17]

The real impact of Irish-born American sportsmen at St Louis, of course, was on the athletics field. This was not necessarily a numerical issue, however. A number of Irish-born athletes achieved places in athletics events, including the giant James Sarsfield Mitchell of Emly, County Tipperary, and the New York Athletic Club, third in the 56-pound weight throw. Mitchell also had a fifth place in the hammer and a sixth in the discus, no mean feat for a man already forty years old. Otherwise, the Irish-American victors, outside of any who had come over to represent Ireland itself, were actually confined to just two. John Flanagan, formerly of County Limerick, won first place in the hammer – following on from his win in Paris four years before – and also won second place in the 56-pound weight-throwing event. Flanagan's hammer-throwing technique used two turns only within a seven-foot circle, unlike the three-turn technique perfected a quarter of a century later by another Irishman, Pat O'Callaghan of Banteer. The third-placed athlete in the hammer, Ralph Rose of the USA, actually only took one turn and was anything but a specialist hammer thrower. In the 56-pound event, Flanagan had broken the world record in July 1904 with an incredible 40 feet 2 inches. In St Louis, however, his best of 33 feet 4 inches was a foot behind the winner, Desmarteau of Canada. Flanagan's failure to win a second Olympic title in this event is partly explained by the event being confined to the same seven-foot circle, whereas Flanagan had broken the world mark with an unlimited run-up. In addition, having won the hammer on 29 August, by the time the 56-pound event was held on 1 September, Flanagan had contracted a bout of flu.[18]

St Louis also saw the first Olympic triumph of the greatest Irish athletic export of all, Martin Sheridan from Bohola, County Mayo. Sheridan won the first of what would eventually be nine Olympic placings in St Louis, triumphing in the discus over Ralph Rose after the only throw-off in Olympic discus history. John Flanagan, whose bulk made for a slower discus technique, finished fourth in the event. The Mayo man had already made a dramatic entrance to American athletics on 4 June 1904 when he won both the shot and the discus titles at the AAU meet. In doing so, he spearheaded the victory of the GNYIAA in the team championship for the very first time. The club defeated their arch rivals of the NYAC by a substantial margin of sixty-one points to forty-five.[19] Sheridan had

Martin Sheridan, again wearing the winged fist crest of the GNYIAA, contesting and winning the first Olympic title of an eventual total of five, the freestyle discus at St Louis (© IOC Lausanne).

emigrated to the USA in 1899 and spent a few years working as a sports instructor at the Pelham Bay Park Athletic Club before becoming a New York policeman in 1906. He was only twenty-two when he won the Olympic discus title, all the more remarkable when one considers that he apparently took up the event by accident:

> Shortly after he arrived in America, he went with his brother Richard and John Flanagan to the grounds of the Pastimes Athletic Club, New York . . . Martin's interest was keenly aroused and when the other two retired to the dressing rooms, Martin tried his hand at the discus. To his amazement, his throw beat the others' best by 5ft. He kept his own counsel, entered for the next athletics meeting, and beat his nearest rival by 9ft . . . from

that time until his retirement from athletics he was never beaten in his favourite event, the throwing of the discus.[20]

Sheridan came to be known as one of the greatest discus throwers of all time but it is significant that, in common with many great Irish athletes of the day, he was an all-rounder of great ability. He finished fourth in the St Louis shot put event too. Although he did not compete in the all-round championship at St Louis, he was to go on to win three Amateur Athletic Union (AAU) all-round titles, in 1905, 1907 and 1909.[21] A pole used by Sheridan in a pole vault competition when visiting home again in 1908 still hangs on the wall of Micksie Clarke's former public house, a stone's throw from the giant memorial to Martin Sheridan which graces Bohola today.

These St Louis athletics victories did much to gain sporting prominence for Irish-America. For American Olympic enthusiasts of the early twentieth century, athletics was the lifeblood of the Games. That both Flanagan and Sheridan were natural leaders who helped bring the Irish to the fore in US athletics was equally undeniable. Heretofore, the typical Irish-American sporting great had been much better known as a prizefighter representing himself for money than an athlete representing his adopted country for little more than the honour of doing so.[22]

The 'Irish sports' which took place as part of the St Louis athletic programme had been planned at least three years in advance of 1904. These sports were intended as a homage to Celtic athleticism and had nothing of the racism which surrounded the 'anthropological days' also held in St Louis, which saw African pygmies and other tribes brought half way around the world for little more than fairground sideshow entertainment. Yet, strangely, when they did occur, there was an element of anti-climax about the Irish sports, certainly from the nationalistic perspective. One obvious reason was that it was intended to involve Irish athletes, or athletes with Irish connections, competing against each other. One of the constants in Irish and Irish-American Olympism during this period was that the level of nationalistic engagement in competitions increased almost proportionately according to the level of British involvement. Similarly, Irish-Americans were more attracted by the possibility of scoring triumphs over Ivy League athletes than over each other. With none of the 'old enemy' or 'new enemy' to compete against and defeat, the profile of the Irish sports at St Louis was lessened anyway in Irish and Irish-American eyes.

The organisers sensed that the Irish sports were not going to be a major draw for the top athletics clubs, deciding in advance that no banners were to be awarded for the athletics contests.[23] That they were held on 20 July did nothing to help either, as the great Irish-American athletes were not due in St Louis for their main events until late August. As a result, the standards reached at the Irish sports were relatively poor by comparison with Olympic levels. In fact, two Tipperarymen whom we will read more on shortly, Tom Kiely and John Holloway, relying entirely on their previous training for the all-round championship of 4 July, amassed more points under the then-scoring system than all other competitors combined.

Ultimately the Irish sports did not draw sufficient numbers of Irish-American competitors and a number of entries were accepted from athletes with non-Irish backgrounds. This was the logical explanation for the lack of distinctly Irish names among the participants, at a time when most Irish immigrants were still marrying other Irish immigrants. Of the nineteen athletes named among the laurels, only seven had distinctly Irish names or were definitely Irish. Several of the athletes who competed in the Irish sports were also involved in the Western AAU handicap (29 July) and 'Special Athletic Events' (2 July), suggesting that they were simply in or around St Louis and entered the Irish sports as just another opportunity for competitive action. Similarly, of eleven different clubs represented at the Irish sports, only the Chicago Fenian AC (one athlete) and the GNYIAA (represented this time by Kiely and Holloway) were specifically Irish clubs. One other athlete named Barrett is listed as a GNYIAA representative in one event, unattached in another and as a member of St Leo's Gymnasium, Baltimore, in a third.[24]

The first and still only Gaelic football and hurling matches played as part of an Olympic programme were also held on 20 July. The Chicago Fenians beat the St Louis Innisfalls by a total of ten points to nil in football, while in hurling the Innisfalls of St Louis won. It is not known who their hurling opponents were – neither the *Spalding Review* of 1905 nor the researches of Bill Mallon has identified a runner-up, suggesting that the match itself may have been a walkover of some sort.[25] While James E.

Sullivan was happy to record in the *Spalding Review* that banners were awarded to the winning teams in these championships, the Gaelic team events inspired even less enthusiasm from likely competitors than the athletics contests did.[26] The cost of transporting an entire team to St Louis, as opposed to individual athletes, militated against entries from outside the mid-west. The relative peripherality of football and hurling in comparison to athletics among the Irish-Americans, as previously mentioned, was another likely factor.

Irish Revolutionaries and the St Louis Champions

If the Irish sports themselves did not succeed well as events, they did have a very important impact on Irish-American nationalism. Because the 20 July date had remained fixed for some considerable time, it gave the Ancient Order of Hibernians (AOH) an ideal opportunity to organise their national convention and participate in a day of celebration of Ireland, both at the world fair and at the Irish sports events:

> The delegates and visitors went in a body to the World's Fair in streetcars to participate in the Irish Day celebration. At 2 o'clock the Hibernians assembled in the Stadium to witness the Irish games and athletic contests. Later in the afternoon, a trip to the Pike was made, ending at the Irish industrial exhibition, where a special performance was given. In the evening, a splendid banquet was tendered the delegates in the Irish Pavilion by the local members of the Hibernians, at which State President John J. O'Connor, of St Louis, State President of Missouri, presided . . .[27]

This same John J. O'Connor was president of the Amateur Athletic Union of America Western Division and a central figure in the organising committee of the 1904 Olympics. The AOH delegates were inspired by the day, the sports, the show and the Irish village itself to enhance their nationalistic instincts:

> The resolutions adopted were even more strongly national than those passed by the Denver convention, but left every individual Hibernian free to exercise his judgment in regard to Irish

movements . . . The convention adjourned sine die with the singing of 'God Save Ireland' . . .[28]

This Games-linked AOH convention at St Louis was huge. Six hundred delegates, a quarter of them women, attended, some coming from Australia, New Zealand and other places. Two thousand people attended the banquet on the evening of the Irish sports:

> The keynote of the banquet and the convention was the independence of Ireland. No matter how many favors England may grant Ireland, still her people will be satisfied with nothing less than complete independence. The convention represented 250,000 members of the AOH and was a grand success.[29]

In terms of Irish-American athletic sports themselves, there had long been a linkage with nationalist movements. Even before the successes of Sheridan and Flanagan, in July 1904 the *Gaelic American* was able to report that 'fully fifteen thousand persons' were in attendance at the Brooklyn Clan na Gael athletics meeting and picnic at Ridgewood Park, Long Island.[30] As further evidence of the Irish-American commitment to professionalism in sport too, it was reported that 25,000 attended a Philadelphia Clan na Gael picnic and professional sports contests on 4 July the same year.[31]

Both of these events were Clan na Gael fundraisers. Perhaps it suited the John Devoy-edited *Gaelic American* to exaggerate attendances somewhat, but this is really quite unlikely. Devoy, Clan na Gael's driving force along with Justice Daniel Cohalan and others, was meticulously accurate when it came to fundraising and fund management and fought numerous battles over the need for scrupulous accounting within Clan na Gael over fifty years. He had a major argument with the so-called 'Triangle' leaders over their financial irregularities.[32] Devoy kept a clear eye on money being transferred from the USA to Ireland.[33] He later, most famously, took de Valera to task, partly over his alleged financial extravagances while in the USA.[34] De Valera, in turn, suggested that Devoy was interested in having personal control over the funds raised and the ends to which they were to be put. One way or another, in 1904 and afterwards, it would have made things very difficult for someone like

Devoy were he to claim that a crowd of a certain amount attended a fundraiser and subsequently the financial returns were not to bear this out. It is much more logical to accept the figures given by his newspaper as relatively accurate reflections of attendances.

In 1904, the interest among Irish-Americans in athletics contests was undeniable. Another such picnic advertisement, for the Irish Volunteers of Yonkers, told that the admission charge was 25 cents.[35] Taking this as a standard admission charge – even if the purported attendance figures were halved, and likely additional revenue from food and beverage sales at the picnics were not included – each one of these social and sporting events generated thousands of dollars for staunchly nationalist organisations. The role played by Irish-American and Irish athletes in headlining the entertainment at these picnics, given the prominence they achieved in the summer of 1904, was a central factor in drawing such large attendances. The *Gaelic American* itself, to a considerable extent, was reaching out to quarters of middle-class Irish-America in terms of circulation. The newspaper, on one occasion, sought potential advertisers by announcing that the paper circulated to 'the homes of people who needed servants'. This offered all the more reason for Devoy and Clan na Gael to use the athletics picnics to reach the masses.[36]

The financial element of these athletics festivals-cum-picnics needs to be more broadly contextualised. Between 1905 and 1916, the Clan largely financed the supreme council of the Irish Republican Brotherhood in Ireland, giving an annual subsidy of around £350.[37] The exchange rate between the dollar and pound at this time was approximately five to one, so this translated into around $1,750. That, in turn, related at the most conservative of estimates to the proceeds of just one substantial 'picnic' on the eastern seaboard of the USA. Devoy later estimated that a total of $100,000 was sent to Ireland in preparation for the 1916 Rising, including $25,000 immediately before Easter week.[38] Roger Casement signed a financial statement in Berlin, on 24 September 1915, acknowledging receipt of a total of $7,740 from Devoy in 1914–15. It is no exaggeration to suggest that the events which the likes of Flanagan and Sheridan headlined at in the first decade of the twentieth century went a long way towards raising the kind of money known to have been sent to Ireland by Clan na Gael before 1916.

More importantly, these picnics involved huge numbers of Irish-Americans in supporting 'the cause' in a way which a more dispersed, though larger, organisation like the AOH could never match. The figure quoted above for Philadelphia's picnic represented approximately one in five of the entire Irish-American population of that city.[39] If thousands of Irish-Americans were to be drawn back to foment rebellion in Ireland, mass gatherings like the athletics picnics were ideal vehicles for imparting the doctrines of the Clan, the IRB and republicanism generally. The nationalistic tone of such athletics meetings-cum-picnics inevitably reached a more extreme note than the AOH did. The speech by Major John McBride at the Boston Clan na Gael field day is just a sample of what was involved: 'We have been told recently to bury the hatchet and come to terms with our enemies. Yes, let us bury the hatchet, but let it be in the skulls of the enemies of our country . . .'[40] The impetus given by Irish-American (and indeed Irish) involvement in the June AAU championships at St Louis was substantial. *The Gaelic American* reported:

> The festival and games of the Irish Revolutionary Brotherhood Veterans to commemorate the 141st anniversary of the birth of Theobald Wolfe Tone attracted a goodly crowd to Celtic Park on Sunday last. John Flanagan was a 'head liner' in the athletic events and his exhibition throw of the fifty six pound weight and the sixteen pound hammer showed the champion to be in great form . . .[41]

Once Flanagan and Sheridan won their titles at the St Louis Olympics, they naturally became even bigger fundraising draws than before for nationalist organisations. The *Gaelic American* carried not just an article but also an advert for the Irish Volunteers of Yonkers military and athletic tournament at the Empire City race track, specifying: 'John Flanagan, Champion Weight and Hammer thrower of the World, and Martin Sheridan, Champion Discus Thrower of the World, will compete in the Weight-Putting Contest.'[42] While Sheridan went on record many times, especially in 1908, regarding his support for Irish nationalism, the old adages that all history is local and, indeed, that Ireland is a very small place come to mind in relation to Flanagan. The Martinstown man was, by all accounts, quietly spoken and uninterested in matters political. However, it has been confirmed that members of Flanagan's maternal family, the Kincaids, were close allies of John Devoy, ensuring his presence at nationalist fundraising events for personal if not necessarily political reasons.[43] Equally remarkable is the fact that Martin Sheridan's brother Joseph, three years older than Martin and supposedly an even better athlete, had by this stage married a Cork-born school teacher in Bohola. She was Kitty Collins, sister of Michael Collins, who went on to win fame as a Sinn Féin and IRA leader.[44] The only time after 1904 that Martin Sheridan visited Bohola again was in 1908 and it remains unverified that he ever met his brother-in-law from Clonakilty. These are two remarkable connections between Irish athletes and Irish nationalists, nevertheless.

Reviving the Tailteann Games

Irish newspapers of the late nineteenth and early twentieth centuries carried occasional references to the great Celtic festival at which the Tailteann Games were held in pre-Christian Ireland. However, the first modern attempt to revive the Tailteann Games, inspired by the news of the Olympics coming to the USA, was by the Irish-Americans of New York. In a speech by Thomas Lonergan, the connection between the Olympics and Tailteann Games was established, with the very clear suggestion that it was the Irish, not the Greeks, who had invented international athletics contests:

> We know that the Olympic Games were first held at Olympia, in Greece, 1,200 years before Christ. So you see Ireland, not Greece, was the birthplace of athletic sports, and has been the home of famous athletes for well-nigh forty centuries . . .
>
> Those to whom I have referred this evening are all amateur athletes and world record holders, but I desire to say that the professional athletes of Irish birth and extraction more than hold their own wherever athletic games are held or championships are to be won.[45]

Nor was Lonergan speaking in some sort of personal vacuum. The Greater New York Irish Athletic Association, in fact, staged a revival of the Tailteann Games in 1903, attempting to establish continuity with their Celtic past and, logically, to raise funds for their activities:

GREAT TAILTIN GAMES AT CELTIC PARK.

In Spite of Heavy Rain and Muddy Tracks an Immense Crowd Witnesses the Performances of the Irish-American Club's Fine Corps of Athletes—Weight Throwing, Running, Wrestling and Gaelic Dancing—Monaghan and Eccentric Firemen's Games.

This is the headline from the *Gaelic American* of 9 September 1905, referring to what was by then the third holding of the Tailteann Games by the Irish-American club (i.e. GNYIAA).

> On Labor Day, September 5 [1904], at Celtic Park, the Greater New York Irish Athletic Association will hold its annual renewal of the Tailtin [*sic*] games, Ireland's ancient athletic festival. This will be the 2951st celebration of these games, the 2950th having been held by the Association last Labor Day. As the event last year was a decided success, and proved very interesting, the officials of the Irish organization have decided to make it an annual fixture . . .[46]

Such was the enthusiasm in Irish-American athletics circles for this effort to revive the Tailteann Games, thus linking up with the old country and even with mythological supremacy theories, that some of the top athletes had to return from the St Louis Games by train and make a dash that very afternoon to Celtic Park for the 1904 Tailteann festival. Ten thousand spectators saw the athletics events that day.[47] Again, as with the controversy over the Irish village programme and the commitment to Clan na Gael fundraisers, a real impetus in terms of reviving Irish nationalism as a reincarnation of a Celtic past was coming from within Irish-America. When John Devoy in 1924 made his first trip back to Ireland in over half a century, it was no accident that it coincided with the Free State government's inaugural effort to revive the Tailteann Games in Ireland.[48] This was an interesting reminder of the import both the Olympics and the Tailteann Games had for Irish-America in 1904, and of the use Devoy and Clan na Gael made of both to stir up Irish nationalism and quite a few funds for republican action as well.

The success of the GNYIAA in winning the club's first AAU title in 1904, along with the exploits of Irish-Americans in American vests at St Louis, were major steps on the road to integration in the USA. It mattered little whether these were second-generation athletes, like James Connolly in 1896 had been, or newer arrivals like John Flanagan or Martin Sheridan. It would not be until 1908 that the fullest incarnation of Irish-American transferal in tandem with Irish anti-Britishness would surface, in the London Olympics, dubbed by many in America as the 'Battle of Shepherd's Bush'.

Linking with the Old Sod

Another great Irish athlete won an athletics title in St Louis. However, he essentially did so for 'Ireland' and was not a representative of the USA at all. We will examine the story of Tom Kiely in the next chapter in much greater detail. For now, retaining a focus on the Irish-American dimension alone, it is useful to look at how Irish-America took to Kiely, dubbed 'Erin's Champion' while he was in the USA, and how he too was brought into the nationalistic impetus from the St Louis Games.

Following the arrival of world-renowned Kiely to compete in the St Louis all-round championship on 4 July, Irish-Americans were quick to see the possibilities of using the Tipperaryman, whether Kiely agreed or not. The *New York Sun* reported on an IRB veterans' meeting in late June:

> For the past week or so, the management of the games spread the news around that Kiely and Flanagan would meet and their names adorned the programme to substantiate the report. Kiely did not appear, however, and when asked last night by a reporter of the *Sun,* said he never promised to meet Flanagan and the use of his name on the programme was absolutely unauthorised.

By the time this article appeared, Kiely's name had done its work as a promotional ploy in any event. When Irish-American athletes like John Flanagan and Martin Sheridan returned triumphant from the AAU championships at St Louis, their fame was again employed to raise funds for national causes. The *Gaelic American* advertised a meeting to raise funds for the Irish Christian Brothers training college at Marino, Dublin, declaring:

This advert from the *Gaelic American* of 11 June 1904 highlighted the forthcoming contest between Tom Kiely and John Flanagan, with all profits going to the IRB memorial fund.

Among the famous athletes who will take part are: Thos. F. Kiely, the all-round world champion, who has postponed his departure for Ireland until after the event; John Flanagan, M.J. Sheridan, John J. Joyce, Richard Cotter, Meyer Prinstein, and John J. Holloway.

The paper explained that this was 'truly national work' because:

> The Irish Christian Brothers have a stronger claim on the support of Irish Nationalists than any other body, political or religious, in Ireland, which seeks aid in the United States. The teaching in their schools is of the very best, and it is calculated to make good Irishmen of the pupils. They are taught the history and language of Ireland and their pride of race is cultivated.[49]

Another article on 30 July again stated that Kiely would attend. In the end, Kiely again did not compete but the day attracted 7,000 spectators who saw Flanagan break the world hammer record.

It will be noted that the purported list of athletes due at the Christian Brothers event included Irish-Americans and Irish. It also included a great athlete who had no Irish connections at all, Meyer Prinstein. He was, however, a member of the GNYIAA. Tom Kiely's absence from these and other nationalistic sports in the USA should not be read as some sort of stance against them, although the extreme nationalism of Irish-America may well have been anathema to him. Serial competitor as Kiely was, his non-attendance could well have been on purely athletic grounds. He had peaked specifically for the all-round championship on 4 July, whereas the likes of Flanagan, Sheridan, Daly and others were then readying themselves for late August's main athletics events in St Louis and needed the competition. Kiely elsewhere admitted that he had put on a stone in weight in the weeks after 4 July.[50] Although he later changed his mind, Kiely had always intended in 1904 that the all-round championships would actually be his last major competition, at nearly thirty-five years of age.

Whatever about reconstructions of the Rock of Cashel, flawed re-enactments of Irish history and legend or revivals of the Tailteann Games, Irish-American athletics saw in Tom Kiely, all-round champion at St Louis, the personification of their national consciousness:

> Tom was brought up on the farm under the influence of the factionless home life characteristic of the Irish . . . if you have any doubts as to his being Irish all that you have to do to be convinced of his native country is to hear him talk. Then your

doubts pass into oblivion and you realize with a vengeance that he is truly a son of Erin . . .[51]

The fact that Kiely was, quite genuinely, a sportsman only endeared him further to his American hosts. They readily forgave his absence from the aforementioned fundraisers for nationalist causes. Even John Devoy forgave his apparent non-appearance at a June IRB fundraiser, announcing:

> The news that Thomas F. Kiely, the champion all-round athlete of Ireland, had won the all-round AAU championship of the world at the Stadium, St Louis, on July 4th, was received with the greatest of enthusiasm in Irish and Irish American sporting circles throughout the country . . . His individuality, and his prestige, has done more to uplift athletic Ireland than any man, excepting Maurice Davin of Carrick-on-Suir. Kiely's wealth of laurels has been no detriment to the sacrifices he has made in the interest of one of the heritages of his race – the instinct of sport . . .[52]

Following his victory at St Louis, Kiely travelled first to Buffalo, where the reaction to him was to typify Irish-American sentiments across the eastern seaboard too:

> President Walsh of the Gaelic Athletic Association, and Adam Gunn, Buffalo's representative all-round athlete, met Messrs Kiely and Fleming [a member of Kickham's Football Club of New York who travelled to and from St Louis with Kiely] at the station and the quartet were driven to the Iroquois [presumably a hotel] . . . Several members of the Irish Nationalists Association and AOH men called during the evening and paid their respects to the noted Irish athlete. . . . Mr Kiely has been the guest of the Nationalists in all of the American cities he has visited, and that organization has been planning for his coming for some time . . .[53]

Kiely was basically 'adopted' by the GAA in America. This was unsurprising, given his links with the organisation in Ireland and the close links between athletics and GAA games in the USA. The flocking of

Reception and Presentation of a

Loving Cup

....TO....

THOMAS F. KIELEY

....Champion Athlete of the World....

ON THE EVE OF HIS DEPARTURE FOR HOME

At Sulzer's Harlem River Casino

127TH STREET AND 2D AVENUE

Saturday Evening, September 24th, 1904

MUSIC BY BAYNE'S 69th REGT. BAND

Irish and American Dancing Will Commence at 8 O'clock Sharp

Annual Field Day and Games

OF THE

First Regiment, Irish Volunteers

UNDER THE AUSPICES OF

Company O, of Yonkers, N. Y.

TO BE HELD AT

EMPIRE CITY RACE TRACK,

Sunday, September 25th, 1904

John Flanagan, Champion Weight and Hammer Thrower of the World, and Martin Sheridan, Champion Discus Thrower of the World, will compete in the Weight-Putting Contest.

MUSIC AND DANCING

M. DROHAN Captain.   **Tickets. - - - 25 Cents**

This 24 September pair of adverts from the *Gaelic American* detail both the ceremony presenting a loving cup to Tom Kieley [*sic*] as he left for Ireland and below it an Irish Volunteers fundraiser using the match-up between John Flanagan and Martin Sheridan as the headline event.

Telephone: 128 Bay Ridge

Athletic Games,

REVIEW AND DRESS PARADE

OF THE

First Regiment Irish Volunteers

Major Charles J. Crowley, Commanding,

AT CELTIC PARK,

Laurel Hill, L. I.

ON SUNDAY, AUGUST 20, 1905.

Music by Somerset's I. V. Band.

Dress Parade and Review at 6 P. M.   **Games at 2 P. M.**

Dancing.   **Prize Bowling.**

The following Events are Open to all Registered Athletes, A. A. Rules to Govern:

100 Yards Run, Handicap.   880 Yards Run, Handicap.   One Mile Run, Handicap.
Prizes—Solid Gold Die Medal to First in Each Event. Solid Silver Die Medal to Second in Each Event. Bronze Die Medal to Third in Each Event.

Entry Fee, 50 Cents for Each Event.

Events Closed to Members of the Irish Volunteers.

Medal of Honor Race.   Sack Race.   Shoe Race.   Obstacle Race. ¼-Mile Scratch.
Prizes—Gold and Silver Medals for First and Second in Each Event.

Entries close on **Monday, August 14, 1905,** with JOHN J. McHUGH, 412 East 50th Street, and DIEGES & CLUST, 23 John Street. Closed Events with Capt. EUGENE J. FLOOD, 682 Sixth Avenue, New York City.

Gaelic Football Championship.

ADMISSION - - - - 25 CENTS.

This advert from the *Gaelic American* of 12 August 1905 shows how varied the activities on offer during some of the Irish picnics were, though with the Gaelic football match well down the order of priority.

'respectable' middle-class Irish-Americans from such as the AOH to greet Kiely is also noteworthy. When combined with the previously mentioned adoption of him by Clan na Gael, albeit as an overt fundraising ambassador, Tom Kiely became a rallying point for all Irish nationalists in America. He was a representative of Ireland who, quite unintentionally, helped to reinforce the exiles' sense of racial distinction and superiority. He was, for them, a sort of living embodiment of what Irish-America had always dreamed the Irish race to be. Before Kiely's departure for Ireland, Irish-America paid its last homage to him at a grand occasion in New York. At a special 'Summer Night's Festival' in his honour, Erin's Champion was feted and presented with a special 'loving cup', which cost $1,000. By 1904 standards, this was an incredible sum of money and certainly testified to the impact Kiely had had in reinforcing Irish-American pride. One dignitary, Police Commissioner McAdoo, summed this impact up when he said:

> Kiely had shown himself to be the greatest athlete in the world. Kiely typified many of the best qualities of the Irish people; he was the representative of the race. Not only did he possess skill and physique, but moral and staying qualities. It was the courage, skill, with moral courage added, that had made the race invincible. The civic records of the United States bore out that although in many cases handicapped by poverty, the Irish race had acquitted itself with the utmost credit in the performance of public duties and second to none in the performance of domestic duties.[54]

There is no known record of the subscribers to the American fund for Kiely's presentation but it is conceivable that the list went even beyond the Irish-American forum itself. In many ways, Kiely summed up the American dream, the notion of the hero emerging from humble origins to achieve remarkable success. He was, of course, also one who had shown great loyalty to his own nation's identity. The *New York Daily News*, a paper with an appeal far beyond Irish-American readership, captured this in a cameo, recording the Irishman's moment of departure for home:

> Of two men who walked up the gang-plank of the *Celtic*, which cast off her lines at 9 o'clock this morning, there was one who

possessed what the almost unlimited wealth of the other could not buy. He who was accompanied to the dock by scores of friends, and was given a parting ovation seldom recalled, was Thomas F. Kiely, world's champion athlete, who returns to his native land, the Emerald Isle. The other was William Waldorf Astor, former citizen of the United States, but a subject now of his majesty King Edward, who boasts of wealth beyond computation . . .[55]

In conclusion, the St Louis Olympics were almost as disorganised and drawn out as the Paris Games had been. Yet, they had a huge impact on Irish nationalism in America. The Games, and even their linkage with the world fair, provided a sort of rallying point for the activities of Irish-American organisations during much of 1904. In the athletics contests, St Louis provided an uninhibited opportunity to stage Irish sports for the first, and only, time in the modern Olympics, albeit with limited promotional success. The successes of Irish-American athletes did much to cement the growing status of the Irish in American sporting society, at least as much as any political, commercial or administrative roles they played. These athletes also served as important, indeed hugely important, promotional elements in nationalist fundraising efforts in the USA, and in attempts to revive a sense of Celtic tradition. That Tom Kiely came to St Louis and beat America's best was, for Irish-America, merely a reinforcement that their own place in American society and Ireland's right to nationhood were deserved.

CHAPTER FOUR

ST LOUIS – IRELAND'S OLYMPIC AWAKENING

I n the previous chapter, the extent to which Irish-America utilised the St Louis Olympic Games, and events around them, to promote a very powerful sense of its own identity was clear. Naturally, this was aided by the fact that the Games were hosted by America and that more traditionalist Olympic powers, chiefly the French and British, had abstained from having anything to do with St Louis. We now turn to look at the impact of St Louis on the Irish back in Ireland and particularly on Irish national identity. These were definitely the first Olympic Games to impact with significance on the national consciousness, despite their chaotic nature. More remarkable still is the fact that the bulk of this impact came through the success of one individual, a quiet and unassuming champion from south Tipperary.

The absence of British officials and of de Coubertin from St Louis definitely left a gate open for independent Irish representation, regardless of how loosely that particular gate might have been shut previously. Whatever qualms some Irish athletes had prior to this about having to compete under a British flag, there could be none if Britain's flag was not there to begin with. Furthermore, we have seen in the last chapter the degree to which there was Irish influence permeating the St Louis Games. For certain, America was ready to give recognition to Ireland's athletes as representatives of Ireland itself.

Still No Irish Team
On an administrative level, Irish sporting bodies once again failed to see

the Olympic Games as an opportunity to send a team and establish an Irish identity, separatist or not. There is little doubt that part of this was down to the limited impact of Olympism generally in Ireland thus far and in the Irish press, and must have been influenced by cost considerations too. The GAA Central Council's minutes for the years prior to July 1904 contained no references to the Olympic Games or any plans to send athletes to St Louis. Press coverage of GAA meetings and Central Council minutes both showed that the organisation was focusing increasingly on the promotion of hurling and football and less on athletics. What athletics issues arose at Central Council level tended to centre around disputes over handicapping, keeping a watching brief on the IAAA and ICA and, occasionally, dealing with the disciplining of individual transgressions, as in a celebrated 'encounter' between John James Daly and an athlete named Hynam at the 1904 cross country championships, which will be referred to later. In effect, the GAA's attitude to athletics was now reactive, not proactive.

The GAA's reversion to a ban on 'foreign sports' in the early years of the twentieth century was detrimental to any chance of entering an Olympic team in co-operation with the different Irish athletic bodies. The venom with which the renewed 'ban' was to be enforced was evident throughout nationalist press articles, for example in this response to a plea for sporting flexibility:

> I have no intention nor would it serve any useful purpose to enter into a controversy with 'Sean Ghail' [anti-ban journalist] . . . I resented, and still resent his wanton and unwarranted sneer at those who have endeavoured and succeeded in stamping out seoinín games – native or foreign – and will be content to take my place with those Gaels in the field, not in the library, who think hurling and Gaelic football good enough for any Irish youth with physical vigour and national spirit . . . If 'Sean Ghail' can start a hockey club, I wish him success, but it would never satisfy a Gael. It is, I repeat, an emasculated form of hurling fitted for the weaklings who play it, and incapable of standing the healthy air of a Gaelic arena. It and such exotics befit the atmosphere they have developed in; any other would kill them.[1]

GAA Central Council minutes showed that in 1904 Ireland's foremost sporting body again viewed athletics as something that had to be administered rather than promoted, as a weapon with which to fight the conservative Irish athletic bodies rather than promote Irish national identity on an international stage.[2] One GAA columnist wrote of non-GAA sports as being the cause of the destruction of athletics by the emphasis placed on glittering prizes, destroying the chances of parish sports being attractive alternatives:

> To see a prominent athlete leave his native hillside the day preceding the local meeting, and travel half Ireland to compete at a much-advertised sports is provocative of uncharitable thoughts regarding the purity of our 'amateur' athletics.[3]

The writer's warning that the GAA itself needed to get its act together in athletics was, however, to be a prophecy few were prepared to listen to. Regarding non-GAA sporting events, he said:

> They are, admittedly, a public attraction, but as we do not desire that, when their time is over, we should have to hawk around their relics of portraits and exhibit them as the last of the jumpers and weight throwers, we must encourage a new growth of champions, for the material is plentiful if only we provide encouragement and facilities for its development . . .

The early years of the twentieth century saw the GAA grow significantly in popularity around the country. There were many factors involved here but the organisation's increasing focus on developing inter-club and inter-county competition and rivalry, particularly in Gaelic football, has been seen as a vital force in this growth.[4] Whether intentionally or not, the GAA made the call: survival and development depended on growth within Ireland and through the promotion of team games, not outside of Ireland in international competition. The importance of this GAA position cannot be overstated. All of Ireland's world-class athletes in the era of the first five Olympic celebrations, with the exception of Peter O'Connor, were most closely linked to the GAA in their initial years of competition. Despite the efforts of some GAA leaders like Frank Dineen to keep athletics going, the organisation's apathy towards the Olympics was a major reason for the complete failure of some Irish athletes to ever attend the Games or only do so when in the twilight of their careers.

Restored Athletic Pride

Despite obviously declined GAA interest in athletics, Irish athletes had done much to regain their international standing in the aftermath of the Stamford Bridge disaster against the Americans prior to the 1900 Olympics. This was particularly true of the successes of Peter O'Connor and Tom Kiely at the AAA championships at Huddersfield in 1901. It bears reiterating that, at least until 1908, the AAA championships were more highly regarded and had a higher standard in athletics than the Olympics. The pique in Irish athletics circles when the English press claimed Irish wins as English successes was self-evident. The Home Rule-oriented *Waterford News,* edited by C.P. Redmond, echoed the sentiments of even moderate nationalists:

> The English papers are loud in their praise of the great English success . . . but surely it is a stretch of the imagination to describe O'Connor as a common or garden Saxon. A truer, a better or a prouder man because of being an Irishman, is not alive today. Kiely's great victory in the hammer throwing is also put down as a success. How our friends on the other side clasp us to their bosoms when they pretend to claim 'Kudos' because of our efforts. Kiely, like O'Connor, is an Irishman who loves the dear old country, and who fought at Huddersfield not for England but for the land he loves so well.[5]

Not for the first, or indeed last, time did an anomalous national perspective arise here. The most extreme nationalist sporting body in Ireland, the GAA, because of its introverted ethos, financial difficulties, etc. continued to play no direct part in furthering a national identity abroad through sport. On the other hand, the more conservative IAAA had some form of international vision and actively promoted an Irish identity through the annual match against Scotland and through fostering Irish participation annually at the AAAs, even when some of its athletes had been much more strongly identified with the GAA, as the likes of Kiely and Denis Horgan were.

While the IAAA continued to promote its own brand of international competition through the now annual match with Scotland, this suffered some severe blows by 1904, including a major row which erupted between the association and world long jump champion, Peter O'Connor. The origin of this related in part to a dispute in 1902 around the paying of American athletes to attend a Dublin Metropolitan Police (DMP) meeting while the likes of O'Connor apparently had to make do with a prize of a second-hand clock.[6] Further fuel was added to the row subsequently when O'Connor, who missed the IAAA national championships due to a funeral, was passed over for selection on the IAAA team for the annual match against Scotland, prompting him to write:

> Owing to the scandalous way I have been treated by the IAAA, without any cause, I have ignored their championship sports ever since and instead have gone to the English Championships, which are open to the world, where, I must admit, I have received respect, fair play and sportsmanlike treatment.[7]

While the annual match with Scotland continued without O'Connor, there is little doubt that the event was in decline after a zenith around 1901–2. Regardless of the likely lack of political will in the IAAA to enter a separate Irish team at St Louis in possible opposition to a British one, the organisation was, if anything, in an even less likely position to provide an Olympic team than it had been when invited to Athens eight years before. Nor could the Irish Cyclists Association (ICA) fill any such role. It had been engaged in a protracted dispute with the English and Scottish cycling bodies and this dispute dominated its affairs from 1901 to the middle of 1904, when a sort of truce was declared.[8] The upshot of all the above was that, while few Olympic hosts could have been more welcoming of an Irish team than the Americans, no Irish athletic body was in a position, either separately or in co-operative manner, to enter a team for the Games. In the end, the three athletes who competed for 'Ireland' at St Louis were more closely associated with the GAA than the IAAA but in fact were entered by neither association.

Individual Entries

Given that there was to be no Irish team entry at St Louis, despite the positivity towards it in the USA, the way was still open for individual entries by Irish athletes. In the midst of detailing the prospects of Irish-American athletes at St Louis, the *Gaelic American* even in late August 1904 expected participation by major Irish athletes in the St Louis events:

> Peter O'Connor, of Waterford, who holds the record in the broad jump, will cross the Atlantic and try for a new mark. Denis Hogan, the shot putter, and the two Leary [*sic*] brothers, the famous high and broad jumpers, are also expected to be at St Louis.[9]

Not one of the Irish athletes mentioned above made it to St Louis. A major difficulty around this was probably one of cost, but this should not be exaggerated. For one thing, the cost of travelling to St Louis was kept down considerably, presumably because of the sheer volume of people willing to travel from Europe for the world fair. In July 1904, for instance, Thomas Healy, The Mall, Tralee, was offering tickets via Cunard, White Star, etc. to the St Louis exposition at £13 single for first saloon accommodation and starting from £8 for second cabin.[10] The value of even one first prize at some of the larger sports meetings in Ireland (though not of O'Connor's second-hand clock) would regularly have exceeded at least the second-class fare, suggesting that transport costs were not insurmountable. The Aberdeen Cup at the RIC sports carried a value of £25 even in 1901. Peter O'Connor won a seven-guinea gold medal for himself, in addition to the perpetual trophy, for the 1905 AAA long jump title.[11]

These calculations do not take account of the prospect of having local supporters organise testimonials for potential St Louis participants. The GAA's near demise because of the financial disaster that the American invasion of 1888 turned out to be was unlikely to be repeated should a team of perhaps eight or ten top athletes be sent to one venue for a defined period. There was also the possibility of American athletic clubs sponsoring Irish athletes, though such athletes would be expected to compete as representatives of those clubs, not of Ireland per se. For the athletics championships held in conjunction with the previous world fair at Chicago, it was known that representatives of top American clubs had come to Britain and Ireland seeking talented athletes who could bolster their clubs' chances of success.[12] Peter O'Connor had spent some months on the athletics circuit in the USA in 1901, with his expenses, both for travel and accommodation, being covered by the Greater New York Irish Athletic Association.[13] If an athlete from Ireland did not receive or want support from an athletic club in the USA, there were always county associations, friends and relatives who could offer support. Even in relation to loss of income, it should be pointed out that the majority of Ireland's top athletes in 1904 came from farming stock – Kiely, Horgan, the Leahys – so loss of regular weekly wages or of pensionable employment might not have been as much of an issue either.

Of the top Irish athletes in 1904, Peter O'Connor was not really in a position to go to St Louis. Despite rumours that he would go and try to break the magical 25-foot barrier in the long jump, O'Connor was very much preoccupied with planning and effecting, in relative secrecy, his marriage on 28 September 1904.[14] The case of Denis Horgan is a little more peculiar. For one thing, the great shot putter from Lyre had been practically unbeatable, winning seven AAA titles prior to 1904 – he would win another six between 1904 and 1912. Horgan had also been to the USA before, winning the shot title at the AAU championships of 1900. What is particularly odd about Horgan's non-participation at St Louis is that a testimonial was, in fact, set up by the people of Navan – nearly 200 miles from Lyre – to facilitate his participation. *The Irish Times* in advance of the Games carried a short article headed: 'Proposed testimonial to Denis Horgan, World's Champion 16lbs shot putter':

> On last evening a meeting was held in Central Hotel, Navan, Mr W. Curry, Co. C. in the chair for the purpose of inaugurating a testimonial to Denis Horgan, of Banteer, on his departure for the United States, where he competes in the Olympic Games. A committee having been duly appointed, it was arranged that subscriptions for the district would be received by the Hibernian Bank, Navan. Other meetings will follow.[15]

There were no further reports on this testimonial in subsequent editions of *The Irish Times*. One possible explanation for the plan, and for it originating in County Meath, was that Horgan had by then competed a number of times against the 1900 Paris Olympic shot champion, Richard Sheldon of the USA. We saw two chapters back that Sheldon's people came from Trim in County Meath and it may simply have been that Meath people wanted to see the Irish champion compete against their man in the USA. That Horgan did not go to St Louis had almost certainly nothing to do with injury – he won his eighth AAA shot put title that same month, with a distance against inferior opposition which would have earned him an Olympic medal at St Louis. The only Olympics that the Lyre man would attend were to be the 1908 London Games, where he finished second at thirty-seven years of age. Two latter-day Olympic historians have been moved to comment that: 'Horgan could possibly have won the shot put gold medal in the Olympics of 1900, 1904 and 1906 if he had competed at those Olympics.'[16]

As both O'Connor and Horgan attended and won titles at the AAA championships in England during the summer of 1904, it must be argued that the less arduous journey, the high profile of the AAAs and the prospect of being able to take on Britain's best – who were not, after all, at St Louis – were factors which contributed to the non-attendance of some great Irish athletes at the 1904 Games. However, the core point remains: 1904 was a golden opportunity for Irish representation on the Olympic stage, one which was to be seized upon with zeal by one man in particular, Tom Kiely.

Erin's Champion

There is no evidence that Tom Kiely decided to go to St Louis on some sort of national crusade, to establish Ireland's identity in the great pantheon of Olympism. That this is very close to what happened as a result of his participation should not deflect from this initial truth. With deference to O'Connor, Kiely was the closest Ireland had to an individual sporting hero in 1904. Indeed, given the state of flux and torpor that Irish politics found itself in during these last years of Tory rule, it is not unrealistic to argue that he was a national hero in ways beyond the sporting fields too.

There are several reasons why Ireland's greatest all-round athlete made it to his one and only Olympics in 1904. His age meant that this would be his last chance to take part in the Games. With an eventual tally of some thirty-six Irish athletics titles in GAA championships alone and twenty-eight world record marks, Kiely had not taken part in an Olympics as yet and, perhaps just as importantly, he had not taken on the Americans in

Tom Kiely in a famous athletic pose, practising with a timber-shafted hammer. Courtesy of South Tipperary County Museum.

their own back yard either. Memories of the defeats at Stamford Bridge in 1900 stuck deep in the Irish athletic psyche – painful memories which Peter O'Connor's trip to the USA in 1901 had not entirely eased either.

Kiely might have been heading for the St Louis Olympics, and his gold medal clearly states that his event was part of the 'Olympic Games', but he also knew that he was competing in the 'all-round championship of the world'. While this might seem to dilute the notion of his 'Olympic' participation, we need to bear in mind that 'Olympic' was more an adjective than a recognisable brand name at this time, and that in the Paris Games of 1900 the phrase 'world championship' had also been used interchangeably with 'Olympic' for many of the events. Essentially, the Olympics were the world championships and vice versa and the fact that Kiely's event was more often called a 'world championship' did not mean it was different from an 'Olympic' event.

It was one of the tragedies of Irish involvement in the early Olympics that so many of the nation's greatest performers were at the ends of their careers when they got to participate. Peter O'Connor would be thirty-four in 1906 and Denis Horgan thirty-seven in 1908. At close to thirty-five years old, Tom Kiely saw St Louis as his last chance to win the equivalent of a world title. He apparently funded his participation by selling some of the 3,000 prizes he had won during his career.[17] From his arrival in the USA in May up to his departure in October, Kiely had little difficulty in finding people to stay with, most notably the former secretary of the GAA, William Prendergast, who had been a close friend back in south Tipperary. Prendergast was a very wealthy property investor by now, as well as being a member of the New York police force, and had made a fortune in real estate to the extent that he was the main financial backer for the GNYIAA's acquisition of Celtic Park.[18]

Whatever about the ambiguities of Boland's participation in 1896 or Leahy's in 1900, there is one certainty about 1904. Tom Kiely went to St Louis to represent himself, his county and, when nationality came into it, Ireland and no other country. The *Cork Examiner* explained:

> He challenged as a representative of Ireland. He refused to be identified with any American-Irish or Irish Clubs in America. He was pressed by various clubs to compete under their auspices but he absolutely refused, and declared that he went to America as an Irish athlete and as such he would compete. In that, he acted very differently from many Irish athletes who went before

him. He preferred that the old country should have the honour, whatever it might be, of the great contest.[19]

This idea is supported by quite a deal of evidence. Kiely's near-legendary declaration to the St Louis officials that he was representing 'Tipperary and Ireland' is reported in so many different sources from the time that it must be taken as fact.

Kiely was certainly a GAA man but one of the moderate Maurice Davin persuasion.[20] He had been elected a vice-president of the GAA in 1896 but he was no extremist. He actually opposed the organisation's links with 1798 centenary commemorations and left his vice-presidency in 1898 as the GAA once again lurched in a more extreme direction. Kiely's participation in a famous Sunday athletics contest in Belfast had much more to do with a desire to set sport free from extremism of any persuasion than it had with a political statement:

> The tournament organised by the Red Branch Hurling club on the Celtic Football Club Ground at Belfast on Sunday last was a signal success. Everything possible to crush the initial effort of the club was done by the Irish Football Association, the Orangemen, and the Sabbatarians without number. Efforts were made to have the sports proclaimed by the Lord Mayor of Belfast. Even the Lord Lieutenant was invoked to come to the rescue. Notwithstanding all this, no less than seven thousand persons assembled and cheered to the echo the splendid performances of Kiely and Leahy.[21]

William Prendergast, Kiely's mentor and supporter for most of his American sojourn, was also a moderate nationalist. When Maurice Davin, Kiely's relative, family friend and mentor, was elected president of the GAA in 1888, Prendergast (although only twenty-three) had been elected secretary. 'Their election was perceived as a victory for the moderate nationalists over the IRB element in the association.'[22] Prendergast spent a time in the USA following the Gaelic invasion fiasco before returning and being elected to Clonmel Corporation as an anti-Parnellite member from 1890 to 1892, after which he returned to America for good. As with Davin, as with everything seen about Kiely himself thus far, the athlete's close association with Prendergast probably marks him down again as a moderate rather than an extreme nationalist. Never should we forget either that the two men from south Tipperary may just have been good friends and that politics was not a major issue between them at all!

Kiely was also an athlete who had represented the IAAA in numerous international matches against Scotland and took part in many AAA championships. One account of an Ireland–Scotland match from 1895 gives an interesting insight into the parochialism of Irish sporting patriotism:

> Points were equal on both sides and one event, the long jump, remained for decision. Ireland relied on a Limerick man to save the day, he was beaten and the Scots were jubilant. Tom Kiely was an onlooker; so far he had taken no part in the contest. But with the Shamrock trampled upon, his Tipperary heart throbbed, the blood quickened in his veins and he felt it his duty to throw off his coat . . . the Scot was defeated and away to the listening hills went an Irish cheer for the standard bearer of Knocknagow.[23]

Kiely's representation of Ireland at St Louis was not to be the representation of one political philosophy or another, it was simply a representation of Ireland. He duly won the all-round athletic title at St Louis. The conditions were atrocious on 4 July for the competition, and Kiely managed first place in four of the ten events to take the title. The competition that day (all ten events took place in one day) was mainly from the three American champions, Adam Gunn, Truxton Hare and Ellery Clarke, although Clarke was to pull out through illness part of the way through. Kiely was only lying in fifth place after the first four events but came to the fore in the second half of the competition when the heavyweight throwing events took place. Overall, Kiely scored first places in the 880-yard walk, the 120-yard hurdles, the hammer and the 56-pound weight throw. He had a second place in the long jump and third placings in the shot and pole vault. The times and distances achieved are of no great relevance, given that ten events took place consecutively and conditions were horrendously muddy all day. Clarke and Gunn had each won two

AAU all-round championships prior to 1904, so there is no doubting that Kiely's victory was against top-notch opposition.[24]

Kiely had a fellow Tipperaryman in the field, John Holloway. Holloway was several times an Irish pole vault champion but in Olympic records, he is usually listed as from the United States. He had, indeed, emigrated from Bansha to the USA some years previously, his last Irish title having been won in 1898. However, there is no doubt that he represented Ireland alongside Kiely in the all-round event. One photograph of Kiely in the high jump event shows him wearing what appears to be a GNYIAA vest, despite not affiliating with the club.[25] However, another photograph of the two Tipperarymen on the field at St Louis shows Kiely's jersey partially obscured but with what *may* be a shamrock moniker on the chest. Much more clearly visible on Holloway's striped jersey is a large Irish shamrock, the first time that an Irish emblem was photographed in Olympian competition.[26] Holloway finished fourth overall. Vest changes may well have been due to the muddy conditions during the day anyway.

Controversy has remained since 1904 as to whether Kiely had, in fact, won an 'Olympic' title in St Louis. It basically seems to depend on which source you read. There was no 'official report' as at other Olympic Games. There were, in fact, two unofficial reports. One, by a man named Lucas, does not refer to Kiely or his event at all. The other, the *Spalding's Official Athletic Almanac, Olympic Special*, was published by James Sullivan and gives the clear message that all the events in St Louis, from the interscholastic meet held on 14 May onwards, were considered by the chief organiser to be Olympic contests. The all-round championship is included in a list of events with the opening description: 'The entry that was received for the Olympic games shows conclusively what interest was taken in the different athletic fixtures . . .'[27]

Perhaps most importantly of all, the medal which Tom Kiely won in St Louis still survives, having pride of place at the South Tipperary Museum in Clonmel. On its face are five words: 'St Louis Exposition: Olympic Games.' The fact that the later, main athletics championships held in August did not have within them a separate all-round championship must also be taken into account, and it seems appropriate that most Olympic record books today accept that Kiely's victory was in the equivalent to the modern Olympic decathlon.

John J. Daly

John J. Daly from Corofin, County Galway, competed later that summer, becoming the third competitor representing Ireland at St Louis. While not in the same league as Kiely in terms of national popularity, he was a very well-known and be-medalled athlete, and even more closely associated with GAA athletics than Kiely was. The predictions of Daly's success prior to St Louis suggested a certain degree of arrogance about his chances in the Irish sports media:

> J.J. Daly has arrived at New York and has joined the Greater New York Irish Athletic Association. He leaves New York today for St Louis, where he will compete in the two miles Steeplechase of the world on Monday next. Daly should win, for it was only by a mere accident that he was beaten in the English championship in this event . . .[28]

Following Daly's achievement of second place in the St Louis steeplechase, the same paper was able to offer both a form of excuse and, significantly, some measure of compensation in recognising the triumph of an Irish-American athlete:

> J.J. Daly (Galway) did very well on Monday at the Olympic games at St Louis. He only arrived there on Sunday, and succeeded in getting second in the 1,000 metres [*sic*] steeplechase . . . In the same meeting John Flanagan threw the hammer 168 feet, 1 inch . . .[29]

Daly's steeplechase was, in fact, a 2,590-metre race which included a mighty 14-foot water jump on every lap. Had it been as the newspaper thought above, he would probably have won, as he is reported to have led by forty yards after two laps. Even with one lap remaining, Daly's lead over the American James Lightbody was reported as being at least fifteen yards but he was caught and lost by one second, roughly ten yards, in the end.[30] While Daly had joined the GNYIAA, unlike Kiely, he most certainly represented Ireland at St Louis. The only photograph extant of him crossing the line in the steeplechase has him in a white vest with no emblem. This contradicts a notion voiced elsewhere that Daly wore a

This picture of participants in an Irish Canadian Athletic Club event in 1910 includes, second from the left at the back, Adam Gunn, Tom Kiely's rival in St Louis, with the tall John Daly of Ireland to our right of him. Seated at the left is Tom Longboat, native Canadian distance runner, with John Flanagan beside him and, two to the right, also with arms folded, is Pat Flanagan, John's brother. Courtesy of the Flanagan Memorial Committee.

green vest in St Louis.[31] This is not very significant – in many respects, the national emblems of Kiely and certainly of Holloway were unusual, not Daly's lack of one, for 1904. Ironically, his participation may be said to have been thanks to the GAA back in Ireland. Daly was known for his aggressive running and could have had some difficulty competing at St Louis had the GAA authorities decided to suspend him for rough tactics at the national cross country championships earlier in 1904:

> The report of Mr Dineen in reference to the running of J.J. Daly and M Hynam in the Cross Country championships held at Finglas was next considered. Letters were read from each enclosing doctors' certificates certifying that Hynam was under medical treatment at the time. Also a certificate from J.J. Daly showing that his ankle was severely sprained in the race. Both athletes' explanations were considered satisfactory . . .[32]

At St Louis, Daly proved no shrinking violet either. His second place in the official Olympic event was one thing. He competed in and won a subsequent non-Olympic one-mile handicap a few days later, with the *St Louis Star* reporting:

The One-mile Handicap brought out a new star – John J. Daly of Ireland. Daly was beaten on Monday by Lightbody in the Mile-and-a-Half Steeplechase. On the flat he is a wonder . . . John J. Purcell, the erstwhile famed English distance champion, made his appearance in this race, but after one lap of chasing the Irishman he had enough and chucked it up. After the race Purcell remarked: 'The English never liked to defeat the Irish anyway.' This race was characterised by rough work by both Daly and Munson. These two indulged in a bumpy match at every opportunity. The Irishman proved that he also knew this game . . . [33]

After St Louis, Daly rushed back to New York with his new clubmates in the GNYIAA and took part in several meetings under their banner. The significance of his participation should not be underestimated, as it forged yet another link between Irish-American athletics and Ireland itself. Furthermore, Daly achieved considerable success in a string of meets and helped the GNYIAA to win its first AAU national club title. The import of this achievement in earning respect for the GNYIAA among the more established atheltic clubs and universities in the USA has already been alluded to. Daly also continued to endear himself to his audiences by his ability to scrap things out in a close race – yet again. While competing at the final GNYIAA meeting of the season, against another athlete of Irish background named Joyce, we find that, after the race:

> Joyce entered a protest with the referee. President P.J. Conway of the Greater New Yorks, who refused to uphold the protest on the grounds that both men had done some elbowing from the back stretch up to where Joyce fell, and as the latter was at Daly's shoulder when the accident happened he could not see that he had suffered by the crowding.[34]

Conway had been involved in officiating at St Louis and, as GNYIAA leader, was almost certainly involved in getting Daly to sign up with the club in the first place. He would also play a significant role in fuelling Anglo-American discord after the 1908 Games in London, which we will see later.

Localised Reaction in Ireland

The success of John James Daly, unlike the performances of Boland in 1896 or Pat Leahy or John Flanagan in 1900, did at last arouse interest in his native county. With an interesting but not unexpected jibe at the Americans whom Daly had beaten, it was reported in a national daily that:

> A committee has been formed under the presidency of the Rev. Mark Eagleton, PP, in Corofin, Daly's native parish, for the purpose of presenting him with a suitable address on his arrival. The Galway City Harriers, his old club, also intend to have a presentation. But Daly deserves it all. He is an athlete of great courage and one who can be always relied on to run his races. He has done much in America to keep Irish Athletes to the front, and his visit to the States, when taken in connection with T.F. Kiely's victory, must have made the Yankees think that, after all, the US is not the whole world, and that their best men can be whipped by mere Irish boys.[35]

A curiosity around the local reaction to Daly's successes in the USA is that we find absolutely no reference to either the Olympics or to Mayo/Galway victors in the *Connaught Telegraph*. This partly reflects the low degree of impact which the Olympics had had on sports enthusiasts in Ireland and far beyond it. Neither the 'American' Mayo man, Sheridan, nor the 'Irish' Galway native, Daly, merited a word of recognition, not to mention congratulations, in the region's main paper. Such an omission could also relate to a possible anti-nationalist bias in a paper, as in the case of the *Clonmel Chronicle* and Tom Kiely. That paper had no reference to Kiely's success whatsoever in any of its editions after 4 July, even though it carried articles on such events as a Limerick tennis tournament and a cricket match between two army teams.[36] There was more cricket on 20 July, numerous articles in later editions on the meetings of huntsmen and even one in the week prior to the remaining Olympic athletics contests on a prize fight between Munroe and Jeffries in the USA.[37] In Daly's case, however, it is not realistic to suggest that the *Connaught Telegraph* had an anti-nationalist bias. The truth may be simpler. Given that Daly did not return to his native land for several months after the Olympics, and adding in the still-fledgling nature of the Games, the paper simply seems to have 'missed' the local story.

If the nationalist press in west Connacht missed Daly, and the non-nationalist press in south Tipperary ignored Kiely, the nationalist press in south Tipperary certainly did not when it came to its local champion. When news of Kiely's triumph in the all-round championship reached home, the local and appropriately named newspaper was immediately ecstatic. Under a heading of 'Bravo Kiely', the Clonmel *Nationalist* reported:

> Thomas F. Kiely, of Carrick-on-Suir, Ireland, has won the All-Round Championship of the World at the World's Fair, St Louis, under the auspices of the American Athletic Union, scoring four firsts in nine [*sic*] events. This is the crowning glory in Kiely's wonderful career as an athlete, and we join with his many friends in congratulating him on the honour won by his mighty prowess.[38]

The news was the signal for the unleashing of a host of different strands of national pride, not unexpectedly in Tipperary itself. It was not long before a proposal was made, through the *Nationalist* newspaper, to raise a testimonial fund to present to Kiely whenever he returned home. The newspaper's support was clear:

> *The Nationalist* will subscribe, and help in every way, for it is only right that the Premier County should suitably honour this splendid Tipperaryman, born and reared 'neath the shadow of Slievenamon, and who, by his prowess, has added luster to our county, and to Irish manhood, by winning the proudest title in the highest athletic arena of the world.[39]

While the paper did add some lines on Kiely's success, typifying the view 'that the world's best men come from the simple, godly homes of the Irish Catholic peasantry', there was no way that Ireland was going to be accorded the glory that was primarily Tipperary's. Among Tipperarymen abroad too, the surge of local pride was both evident in and fuelled by the local newspaper. It reported a speech given by Thomas F. Lonergan in the USA that, in the main, celebrated the local aspect of the achievement, while merely giving polite acknowledgement to national pride:

> It seems that the premier county of Ireland, during the past fifty years, has produced as many famous athletes as all the other counties combined. Now, I do not refer to this in any spirit of county pride, because I do not believe in local or geographical distinctions. Every county, yes every foot of Irish ground, is equally dear to me.[40]

According as the weeks passed after the news of Tom Kiely's gold medal, the sense of local pride was to focus even further in the pages of the *Nationalist*. As the subscriptions to the testimonial fund flowed in, the paper carried many letters from readers. One Tom O'Grady from Littleton stirred the local pot a bit more, in urging further donations:

> Sir – Bravo Tom! Knocknagow is not gone yet. It surprises me why the boys are not coming in. Is it in the want of courage to subscribe their names to the modest sum of 5s?[41]

Later in August, with the triumphant Kiely still on a sort of US grand tour on the eastern seaboard, exiled Tipperary again expressed its pride and its purported superiority over the rest of Ireland too:

> Tipperary may well boast that she is the Premier County of Ireland. 'Well done gallant Tipperary!' is the cry of thousands of Irish dwellers in the Eastern States, at the performances of Tom Kiely. Away, far away today from dear old Slievenamon this great achievement of Tom Kiely's will gladden the hearts of many an exile from the Valley of the Suir.[42]

The outpouring of local pride as part of, or separate from, national pride has been seen before. Something similar happened when the Bostonian athletes, including James Connolly, returned to Massachusetts after the 1896 Games. That it had not happened in Ireland prior to 1904 is due to a combination of the anonymity of Irish competitors, the minority status of their sports and the lack of Olympic impact, as in Boland's case, or to the neglect of local press, as with Leahy in 1900. Kiely, as already stated, was in a league of his own, both in terms of athletic prowess and popularity. His was a success which seemed to prove Ireland's (and Tipperary's) right to status, acceptance, even superiority. Consistently in Tipperary, given the relative lack of impact of Olympism thus far on the Irish sporting psyche, Kiely was celebrated much more as the 'world's champion', or as 'Erin's champion' than as the 'Olympic champion'. Perhaps the most intriguing example of 'Tipperaryism' after Kiely's victory in St Louis came in an article by J.M. Wall, originally published in the *New York Daily News* and reprinted, naturally, in the *Nationalist:*

> Kiely comes from Carrick-on-Suir, that fiery centre in fiery Tipperary. Thurles, in that county, exactly midway between Dublin and Cork, is not inaptly known as 'the pulse of Ireland'. Tipperary is a great place and the kind of Irishmen found there are fine fellows. It was at the Battle of Chillianwalla, I think, during the mutiny that the English commander, seeing a regiment composed mainly of these powerful fellows storm the enemy lines, roared out in unrestrained emotion, 'Magnificent Tipperary!' And it was Thomas Davis who wrote:
>
> > Tall is his form – his heart is warm;
> > His spirit light as any fairy.
> > His wrath is fearful as the storm
> > That sweeps the hills of Tipperary![43]

In many respects, this article summed up much about national identity and the Olympics to date. National pride was very evident, particularly when it had a national hero to worship, but it was not restricted to a particular political persuasion. In this instance, Mr Wall had no difficulty in quoting Thomas Davis, Young Irelander and a British commander during the Indian mutiny, as supporting evidence of the might of Tipperarymen. The fact that one source was an ardent nationalist and the other an epitomy of imperialism seemed to matter not a jot.

Although Tom Kiely himself was certainly not a militant nationalist, it was natural that militant nationalism also sought to seize on his success as a vehicle to promote the separatist, revolutionary agenda. As we saw in the previous chapter, the Irish-Americans attempted, with limited success, to do just that by using Kiely as a promotional advertisement for Clan na Gael and other fundraising events. In Ireland, and coincidentally from another Tipperaryman, the separatist drum was beaten loudly and echoed back to Brian Boru.

Tom Kiely struck on the right lines . . . this time he has unfurled the old banner at the masthead in the world's exhibition to flutter above the National colours of the earth. There it was again, the flag of Brian, before which the Danes fell back at Clontarf, etc. . . . . The *English Globe,* which heretofore would scarcely admit that the green flag was the emblem of a nation, now admits that as a nation and as a race, the Irish are first in the world in physique – a strange admission from the *Globe.* But the green flag flying proudly above the banners of the world at St Louis, forced England and the world to believe that behind the grass-green banner there is still a nation. Since 1890 no athletic gathering in the south or east of Ireland was considered complete without Tom Kiely. 'And Tom Kiely is coming' was the boast of every sports committee, for his presence brought crowds, and increased gate receipts . . . But now Tom Kiely is coming – coming home to Ireland and Tipperary – the champion of the world, and that honoured green banner which, to the envy of the nations, fluttered proudly over the broad waters of the Mississippi, he is bringing with him to hand over to his country.[44]

Some Anomalies in the National Perspective

The Tipperary reaction to Kiely contained some cameos of national politics too. For one thing, the role of the clergy, or rather lack of it in post-Croke and McHale times, as a vehicle of national expression was called into question. The archbishop of Cashel at this time, Dr Fennelly, was one of a very small group within the hierarchy who had given active support to the GAA around the turn of the century. Despite a prolonged clerical boycott of the GAA nationally, 'because of the involvement in the GAA of Archbishops Croke and Fennelly, priests in Tipperary fully participated in GAA activities'.[45] This being so, it was perceived in Kiely's case that the clergy were not supportive enough of the testimonial. On this point, some women of Tipperary were most vocal, both in their praising of Kiely as the fruit of a Tipperary woman's womb but also in the attacks on the reluctant clergy. Although it was a member of the Tipperary Catholic clergy, C.F. Ryan, CC of Drangan, who first proposed and contributed to the Kiely testimonial in the *Nationalist*, Fr Ryan's confrères were seen as a little slow to use their resources in assisting the testimonial:

> We continue to receive encouraging letters regarding the Kiely testimonial. One, signed 'A Clanwilliam Girl,' states that the girls will find the bits of silver to subscribe if the boys will only go manfully about the collection. She hopes to see more of the priests helping in the movement, and winds up with the capital suggestion, that the presentation should be made by that patriotic prelate, Most Rev. Dr. Fennelly, Patron of the GAA and of Irish Ireland.[46]

Another woman's letter in the same edition of the *Nationalist* was more directly critical of the lack of Church support for the cause:

> A 'Tipperary mother' writes – 'With reference to Mr. Kiely's presentation, your correspondent of last issue depended much on the boys and girls, but he forgot the Tipperary matrons, who are each and every one of them, as far as I know, proud of that Tipperary mother who reared the champion of the world. We are there, and we will be there, if the young men of the country only form parrish [*sic*] committees and collect. It would be well if more of our good *soggarths,* and particularly those under the jurisdiction of the great patron of athletics in Ireland, would throw themselves into the project. We know that every *soggarth* is proud of Tom's mother, and we have confidence in movements in which the *soggarths* lead.'[47]

By the time of Kiely's arrival back in Ireland, the number of subscribers to the *Nationalist* testimonial ran to over a hundred but only Fr C.F. Ryan, the Drangan curate, and Archbishop Fennelly of Cashel (who gave the largest individual contribution of £3) were among the clerics on the list of subscribers.[48]

Kiely's testimonial casts significant doubt on the notion that the clergy were universally respected for their championing of national causes. The Tipperary reaction to Kiely's success threw up an even more important question, namely to what extent was Kiely seen as a victor for a nationalist/separatist Ireland, rather than a moderate or conservative one?

In the unionist press at national level alone, a fairly limited view emerged. The *Cork Constitution* had no coverage at all of Kiely's win. *The Irish Times* simply stated:

> Thomas F. Kiely of Carrick on Suir has won the All-Round championship of the world at the World's Fair, under the auspices of the American Athletic Union, scoring four firsts in nine events.[49]

The poor coverage of Kiely's triumph in the conservative press was otherwise surprising. He had many supporters in unionist and Home Rule circles. He was largely apolitical and was as happy competing at RIC sports as at GAA ones, or for Ireland's IAAA against the Scots as much as in the GAA championships. More localised moderate nationalists responded with ardour to Kiely's success. Lifelong athletics supporter and Home Ruler C.P. Redmond of Waterford wrote:

> We are proud indeed to be able to announce the receipt of a cable from St Louis to the effect that Mr T.F. Kiely of Ballyneale has won, on Monday, the all-round championship of the world . . . Wherever throughout the wide world an Irish athlete has found a home, or where there exist admirers of magnificent athleticism, the name of Thomas F. Kiely is familiar and esteemed. There will be none, we fancy, ready to gainsay that in the person of the subject of our sketch, the premier county has given to the world one of the finest all-round athletes of recent times, in addition to a characteristic specimen of an Irishman of the best type – upright and amiable, generous and trustworthy and a sportsman from sole to crown.[50]

In making a contribution to the testimonial fund for Kiely, Redmond added a few weeks later:

> He has been appropriately described as the 'hero of athletics who has so well upheld the traditions of the old country' . . . I think that if ever an Irishman deserved popular recognition it is the same good old Tom . . .[51]

A few weeks later again, the *Nationalist* printed a letter from M. Baldwin, donating ten shillings to the Kiely testimonial fund. Significant here was the fact that the same Mr Baldwin was the Home Rule chairman of Carrick-on-Suir Urban Council. Reaction in Carrick-on-Suir – geographically, a little closer to Kiely's home than Clonmel – was summed up when:

> At the last meeting of the Carrick Urban Council, Mr M. Baldwin (chairman) presiding, Mr. O'Brien said – I have been asked what steps the urban council are going to take with regard to the home coming of Mr. Thomas F. Kiely, the champion of the world. We are all aware that he has reflected some glory on Carrick-on-Suir, because he always appeared as T.F. Kiely, of Carrick-on-Suir . . . Last night the Young Ireland Society decided to present him with an address, and it would be a very nice thing to meet this young gentleman on his return from America and present him with an address from our Urban Council (hear, hear) . . . Mr. Grubb seconded the proposition, which was cordially adopted, and it was decided to hold a special meeting of the council in connection with the matter.[52]

This account highlighted the degree of comfort felt by local moderate nationalist politicians in following the lead of the more extreme Young Ireland Society in honouring Kiely. Local legend had it that Kiely, in fact, was quite overcome by the welcome organised in Carrick on his eventual return and slipped quietly homewards soon after alighting from his train. The Mr Grubb mentioned as cordially seconding the proposition to honour Kiely was a member of a most staunchly unionist family in south Tipperary. He was also a leading member of the Quaker community, shedding further light on Kiely's cross-cultural popularity. For Ireland's new Olympic and 'world' champion stood for nothing that was a threat to any political or social grouping. Clonmel at the time had two rowing clubs, the Clonmel Rowing Club and the Workmen's Club. There was a considerable social divide between these clubs, with Clonmel Rowing Club being particularly middle and upper class in its make-up. Yet, ironically, it was the Clonmel club and not the Workmen's which subscribed to the Kiely testimonial. The fund received a letter as follows:

> Dear Sir – Will you please take charge of the enclosed cheque, value two guineas, from the Clonmel Rowing Club towards the Kiely presentation. In voting this sum, the committee wish to mark in a small way their appreciation of a Tipperary man who has beaten the world in open competition. T. Foley, J. Peacocke (Hon Secs)[53]

The local situation which gave rise to such support was an interesting one. Throughout the 1890s, the Clonmel Rowing Club regatta at the Island featured athletic sports as well. Maurice Davin and Tom Kiely had been regular participants and supporters. It was not unknown for GAA national championships to be incorporated into these sports, placing, in a way, the GAA under the temporary and local auspices of possibly south Tipperary's most anglicised sporting body.[54] From as far back as 1893, Kiely's own scrapbook held a cutting which recalled his links with the rowing club and its central place in Clonmel life, regardless of politics:

> As already announced, the annual Clonmel Sports and Regatta will take place on the Island on next Monday, August 7th . . . Mr Kiely, the all-round champion of Ireland, will also attend, and compete in several of the events. The energetic hon. secretaries – Messers T. Foley and T. Power – are leaving nothing undone to make the meeting a success. The splendid band of the 10th Hussars will attend, and a display of fireworks will be given at the Gashouse Bridge in the evening by Mr. Hodsman, of Dublin . . . The day will be observed as a general holiday in Clonmel . . .[55]

A later cutting refers again to the Clonmel meeting and to the fact that Murty O'Brien of Buttevant won the GAA championship in the high jump at these Island sports.[56]

Even a cursory glance at the subscribers on the final *Nationalist* list verifies the cross-political response to Kiely's success. The likes of James and John Britton and Maurice Wolfe were prominent Gaelic Leaguers in Clonmel; Jeremiah Condon and John Dalton were known Fenians. On the other hand, James Reidy was very anti-republican, famously slamming the door on Archbishop Mannix as he was about to be given the freedom of

Clonmel, while the local Irish Party MP, J.J. O'Shee, and over a dozen county council members of moderate nationalist persuasion also contributed.[57]

In a nutshell, the reaction across south Tipperary to Tom Kiely's Olympic triumph reinforced the point that 'localism' rather than necessarily nationalism was a powerful force in Irish life. This local pride, when it emerged, transcended social and political barriers to a huge degree, focusing individuals firstly on the victory of the local man and only secondarily on the victory of the Irishman. To an extent, this greater emphasis on the local origins of the victor rather than the nationality he represented was the unifying factor, allowing nationalists of the extreme variety to unite in celebration with moderate nationalists and indeed unionists. However, it was also true that the response to Kiely particularly shows that, where genuine sporting and personal popularity were involved, political beliefs were quite readily swept aside. The more profound polarisation of Irish political persuasions which affected the country after 1916 could never have tolerated such a *mélange*.

GAA Reaction Further Afield

Before leaving the 1904 Games, the reaction of the GAA in general to the first Olympic victory of one of its athletes merits consideration. At local level, it was unsurprising that GAA members joined in the adulation of Kiely. A local report shows that the Carrick-on-Suir Gaelic Football Club was a major subscriber to the testimonial:

> At a meeting of the committee of the above club, held at the town hall on Wednesday, 10th inst., it was unanimously resolved, on the motion of Mr. William Galvan – 'That we subscribe £5 to the T.F. Kiely Testimonial, as a token of our esteem for his having so nobly represented our town and country at the far-famed St Louis Exhibition.[58]

Slightly further from Carrick, there was considerable support for the testimonial from GAA people in Waterford, among them Dan Fraher, a Central Council member and ardent nationalist.[59] Yet this too was essentially localism, in that Kiely's home was within sight of County Waterford and there had been many contacts between him and Dan

MO'D

comairle co. portláirge
(County Council of Waterford),

seosaṁ 5. ua ouṅlaıṅs,
Rúnaí

J. G. DOWLING, A.S.A.A.,
County Secretary.

Oıṗıs Rúnaıṫe an Conntae,
(County Secretary's Office).

ı nouṅ 5aṅbáın,
(Dungarvan),

5uṫáṅ : ʋıṁ, a 12.

Telephone No. 12.

Please quote the following Reference

Co. Poṛtláıṅse.
(Co. Waterford).

No. ....

13th November, 1951.

Mrs. Kiely,
Shawfield,
Ballyneale,
CARRICK-ON-SUIR.

Dear Mrs. Kiely,

I am directed by the Waterford County Council to convey to you, and to your family, the following copy of a Resolution passed at yesterday's meeting of the County Council of Waterford:-

"Proposed by: Denis Heskin
Seconded by: Michael Harty

AND RESOLVED:-

That this Council express to the relatives of the late Mr. Thomas Kiely, their deepest sympathy on his recent death, and that we place on record our appreciation of the fame which he brought to this County, by his outstanding achievements in the athletic field, and that this Meeting do now stand adjourned until 12 o'clock Noon as a mark of our respect".

The County Manager, on his own behalf and on behalf of the staffs of the Council, associated himself with the Resolution, which was passed in silence.

As a mark of their respect, the Council adjourned their meeting until noon.

I am, dear Mrs. Kiely,

Very sincerely yours,

Runai.

This letter of condolence to Tom Kiely's family, upon his death nearly half a century after St Louis, shows the degree to which the athlete won respect outside his native Tipperary also. It is worth noting that County Waterford thanked the family of Tom Kiely for the fame the Tipperaryman had brought to Waterford. An interesting transfer of local pride, perhaps. Courtesy of South Tipperary County Museum, Clonmel.

Fraher over the years, not least because Fraher was the owner of one of the most popular sporting venues of the early twentieth century, the Fraher Field in Dungarvan. Elsewhere:

... at a meeting of the Tipperary County Board on the motion of M. Brennan, seconded by M. Landers, a vote of congratulations to Mr. T.F. Kiely, his father, and Maurice Davin, upon his recent success at the St Louis Exhibition in winning the world's championships was unanimously passed, and promising the hearty support of all Tipperary Gaels in any project to honour one of Tipperary's worthy sons.[60]

The GAA Munster Council meeting on 10 July decided:

On the motion of Mr Hayes, seconded by Mr O'Reilly, Mr TF Kiely was awarded a special vote of thanks for his brilliant performance in America. It was also decided that a delegation from the council would meet Mr. K on his arrival at Queenstown.[61]

It is tempting to be a little cynical about such GAA effusiveness, given the organisation's contribution to Irish athletic decline during Kiely's career. In fairness, this was less true of the Tipperary and Munster boards than it was at national level, where there was little positive interest in athletics or Olympics by 1904. Yet, a 'special meeting' of Central Council was held on 17 July:

It was decided that an address be presented to Mr TF Kiely on his landing at Queenstown. The President trustees and Sec to attend as a deputation to present the address. Messrs Dinneen [*sic*] and O'Toole were appointed to draft the address for next meeting of council to be held in Dublin on July 30.[62]

The illustrated address which the GAA presented to Tom Kiely at Queenstown is now on display at the South Tipperary County Museum in Clonmel. It told much about the organisation's commitment or otherwise to athletics, at times unintentionally. The address is illustrated, for one thing, with symbols of both Irish-American accord – the bald eagle and Stars and Stripes rest at its head – and of nationalist tradition – wolfhound, harp, a female figure and a sunburst flag generally associated with extreme nationalism. A four-provinces crest lies at the base. Local pride was given a look-in too via a miniature of the Rock of Cashel.[63] All this symbolism was considerably at odds with the persona of Kiely himself, who shunned so much of the trappings of adulation, had not participated in many of the more nationalistic functions while in the USA and had, on the St Louis park, associated himself with the traditional Irish emblem of the shamrock, an emblem with no political/militant connotations at the time.

The text of the GAA's welcome address contained more nationalistic words, referring to Kiely's 'mission', telling him 'you had the earnest wishes of every Gael, for the honour of the old land was in your keeping . . .' Kiely was informed that he had 'shed honour on your country and race' and was 'the living embodiment of our Gaelic manhood . . . upholding our pretensions before the world, and against all comers . . .' Given the GAA's own reluctance to promote athletics, or Ireland's image abroad through athletic contest, there is an irony in the address announcing that 'the athletic chronicles of the world contain in your performances an epitome of the ability of the Gael in all branches of athletics'.

It might be suggested that the triumph of Kiely marked some form of awakening for the GAA, where the organisation finally realised that athletics was a vital part of its own mission and could be a significant force for national identity. The events of 1906 and afterwards proved the reality to be somewhat different.

CHAPTER FIVE

THE 1906 INTERCALATED GAMES

lthough the Olympic Games of ancient times and in their modern reincarnation were held at four-year intervals, the International Olympic Committee agreed to hold what became known as the 'Intercalated Games' on the tenth anniversary (i.e. 1906) of the inaugural Athens Games, once again in the Greek capital. This was in part intended to ease Athenian disappointment that the Games had not been granted a permanent home in the Greek capital. In the broader context of the modern Olympic movement, following on two sets of Games which had been linked to world fairs (Paris and St Louis), these 1906 Athens Games went a long way towards rescuing the Olympic movement from becoming a form of side show, with sporting and particularly athletic contests given centre stage with no distractions. Huge crowds attended the 1906 Games, over a compact eleven-day period and with many of the world's top athletes gracing the ancient Panathenaen stadium. While the IOC has never felt fully comfortable in acknowledging these Games as official Olympics, there is no doubting their importance. Many modern Olympic historians have continued to challenge the IOC on its subsequent denial of 1906 as a full Olympic Games, arguing that the IOC had in fact approved these Games as far back as 1901 and that the Games themselves were much more 'Olympic' in sporting terms that either Paris or St Louis had ever been.[1] These 1906 Games had a huge importance in the Irish context also, particularly in the role played at Athens by world long jump record holder Peter O'Connor and his supporting cast.

The notion of GAA representation on the international stage had been established by Tom Kiely and his compatriots in 1904, however unintentionally at the time. Yet, the seeds of the continuing failure of Irish athletics to see the struggling Olympics as a vehicle for national identity were sown even before Kiely went to St Louis. In early 1903, after years of relative calm between Irish athletic bodies, the feud re-ignited with the founding of the Gaelic Cycling Association under the umbrella of the GAA. The intention was to challenge moderate nationalist/unionist influence in the ICA. One GAA supporter wrote:

> The Irish Cycling Association, a West-British body, had hitherto had sole control of cycle-racing in Ireland, but it will have that sole control no longer . . . The cycling element in Ireland can be of enormous service in promoting the national revival.[2]

This move was closely linked to the resurgence of the GAA ban on 'foreign sports' from 1901 to 1905, setting out in very clear terms that anyone participating at non-GAA athletic and cycling meetings, or playing association football, rugby or cricket, would be barred from any participation in the GAA:

> Let no Gael forget that the truce with the neutral and the supporter of alien games ceased on the 31st ult. Henceforward it is 'with us or against us'. The sport of hunting with the hounds and running with the hare must cease, native or alien; that is the alternative. Every man of worth will make his choice; dissemblers, tricksters and knaves will plead, argue, shiver and succumb.[3]

The article also decried the playing of these alien sports in some middle-class Catholic boarding schools. A fine, though admittedly hindsight-based, irony in this respect was that Éamon de Valera was lining out for Rockwell College within a year of this, on the rugby pitch, as a teacher-member of the school team. This move by the GAA came in no small measure from a desire to reinvigorate the association, which had been struggling in quite a few rural areas in the early twentieth century. Given that this reinvigoration focused substantially on developing parochial rivalries through hurling and football in the main, it was again of no assistance to athletics or, by implication, involvement in international or Olympic athletic competition.

By 1906, the situation had deteriorated, with both the GAA and IAAA/ICA at loggerheads. The president of the IAAA Northern Branch, Mr W.W. Campbell, told its monthly meeting:

> The IAAA had an agreement with the ICA and also with the GAA, but as the latter had gone outside that agreement the IAAA had decided to stand by the ICA and in the event of matters being pushed to a finish he [Campbell] wished merely to mention that there would be a battle between the ICA and IAAA, as against the GAA . . .[4]

Shortly afterwards, the IAAA basically placed a reciprocal ban on its athletes competing at GAA meetings. Any sort of united Irish effort for the next Olympics was now impossible to envisage. C.P. Redmond of the *Waterford News* summed up the feelings of nationally minded lovers of athletics on the matter of the GAA ban, expressing the hope that officialdom might relent:

> Probably the men in question will ultimately be brought to their senses by their own followers – for those Gaels who feel that in some branch of athletics they are equal to the task of competing with the world, as most of them are – will get sick of performing in their own back yard, and in all likelihood they will kick out the men who have made a parochial organization of an association that ought to be world famous, and who have made it impossible for the Gaelic Association to be recognised by the other governing bodies of athletics in the world.[5]

Ironically, in one way the GAA–IAAA/ICA split actually gave a boost to Irish Olympism, specifically in the case of world long jump record holder Peter O'Connor:

> At the beginning of 1906, there were further fresh grounds for [O'Connor] calling it a day when the IAAA and the GAA fell out and dissolved the working arrangement they had maintained since 1888. If he was to continue competing,

O'Connor would have to align himself with one of the two associations. So close to the end of his career, the world champion was loathe to become a political pawn in a game of intrigue played out between the IAAA and the GAA.[6]

Having missed two previous opportunities to compete at the Olympics, Peter O'Connor determined that the Intercalated Games of 1906 in Athens would be his last hurrah in athletics, a hurrah which would be independent of the wranglings within Irish athletics but more profoundly declare an Irish identity at the Olympics than even Tom Kiely had done.

The GAA and the Athens Games

It has been suggested that the GAA persuaded John J. Daly to represent it at Athens. Certainly, the GAA set up a distinct Athletic Council in 1905, with the intention of promoting athletics. There is, however, no mention of either Daly or the Athens Games in any minutes of the Central Council or Athletic Council. It has been speculated that the Athletic Council was instrumental in getting O'Connor, at last, to go to the Olympic Games. This is very hard to accept. O'Connor and Con Leahy would have been completely at odds with the GAA ban on participation in IAAA meetings, and all of the circumstantial evidence from O'Connor suggests that these

Contestants on the 'Great Britain' team in Athens, with John Daly clearly wearing a single white shamrock, probably derived from the GAA logo, on his vest three from the right in the back row. From Theodore A. Cook, *The Cruise of the Branwen*.

two, if not Daly, had patchy connections with the GAA in 1906.[7] The only known suggestion that the GAA sponsored Daly at all came from the pen of Peter O'Connor thirty-five years after the event, when he wrote to a GAA historian that the association had 'influenced him [i.e. Daly] to represent them'.[8]

It is unclear whether Daly wore GAA-specific athletic clothing or badges in Athens, although circumstantial evidence which we will address later suggests that he may have had a shamrock on his vest in the marathon race. Regardless, this man was quite an individual, well capable of going to Athens with or without GAA sponsorship. He had, after all, paid his own way to St Louis just two years before. In addition, he had been known to fall foul of the GAA authorities previously because of his somewhat robust style of competing. Like many top athletes prior to the GAA ban, Daly competed in IAAA events too, including international competitions against other nations of the United Kingdom, as in Wales in March 1906:

> The Irish International team will take some beating on Saturday next at Newport. The list is headed with J.J. Daly, the famous Galway man, who says 'form was never better' and signifies his intention of taking part in the Olympian games.[9]

An account of the Irish Senior Championship, held at Elm Park by the Irish Cross Country Association barely a month before the Athens Games, tells of John J. Daly winning the event as an individual entry.[10] This was clearly a non-GAA and very much an IAAA athletics event. It occurred after the GAA 'ban' had been imposed. Yet Daly took part and then went to Athens just four weeks later as the apparent representative of the GAA at the Olympic Games. Even if it was possible that Daly was the first pre-selected GAA athlete ever to represent Ireland at the Olympics, it would have been another leap altogether to see this as the association finally pre-engaging with Olympism.

Another factor in the GAA context was that the association's stance on refusing to allow its athletes to compete in non-GAA competitions automatically called into question the appropriateness of a GAA entry at Athens. Its athletes would have had to compete against not only non-GAA athletes but also British ones, under the auspices of an association in which members of the British gentry were influential, and under rules which differed from the GAA's own rules. This was pointed out prior to Athens by the president of the Irish Cyclists Association:

> The original object for which the GAA was established was the fostering of games and athletic contests which are traditionally Irish, and in the furtherance of this programme no one could have for them anything but praise . . . But it might be expected that in the working of these rules the GAA would at least be consistent and deal out equal justice to the men who stay at home in the country and never roam, and yet allow their champions to compete in America, England, Scotland, and even in Ireland without questioning who they compete against or who organises the sports, let him be a policeman, Russian, Turk or Jew. If some of our Gaelic champions are selected to go to Athens this year, will the GAA dare to select who their opponents should be? I think not.[11]

An Unusual Sponsor for Irish Olympians

While Daly's status remained somewhat unclear in 1906, the IAAA would use the Athens Games of that year to promulgate Irish identity. Both Peter O'Connor and Con Leahy were sponsored by the IAAA, even being kitted out in very distinctive green blazers, as O'Connor later recalled:

> Con and I were supplied with blazers with gold braid around the sides, cuffs, collar and lapel, with a gold shamrock on the left breast and green caps to match and shamrock on the front.[12]

The IAAA's choice of the *Erin Go Brágh* logo deserves some consideration here. This was the maxim which had been adopted by the Home Rule movement since the demise of Parnell. It also had direct links to the Fenians and particularly to the 1798 rebellion and the United Irishmen.[13] It was reinvigorated by the centenary events of 1898, the same events which Tom Kiely had opposed GAA participation in, as we saw in the last chapter. It was, by 1906, the slogan of the majority nationalist opinion in Ireland, though not specifically of extreme nationalists. Both the harp and shamrock were, essentially, the emblems then in vogue as representative of Ireland. The shamrock was used on the ceremonial keys used for the visit of Edward VII to Dublin in 1906, on Munster Fusiliers' cap badges in the Great War, on the crest of the Irish rugby team and in St Louis by John Holloway and probably Tom Kiely. The harp was, in fact, much more of an emblem associated with Irish militancy in the early twentieth century than the shamrock was. The harp was particularly prominent in much of the regalia emanating from Irish-America in and after 1898.[14] Its placing with both the shamrock and *Erin Go Brágh* on the regalia of the IAAA athletes was quite a telling reflection of the lack of clear divisions in most Irish people's minds at the time between extreme and less extreme nationalist sentiment.

The issue of the cash-strapped IAAA funding the sending of O'Connor and Leahy to Athens could have been an insurmountable obstacle in 1906. The resolution to this came from an unusual source, spearheaded by the Irish-American politician 'Boss' Croker. Croker achieved near-legendary status in New York's Tammany Hall, mostly for uncomplimentary reasons, but by 1906 was in semi-retirement in Ireland. Some accounts described his sense of hurt at being excluded from the horse-racing circles of the English gentry as being a motivating factor in his involvement in backing an Irish athletics entry at Athens. This was not improbable, particularly as the same personnel were very much to the fore in the British Olympic Association, founded in 1905. Some were even taking part at Athens:

> The Olympian games which will take place at Athens in April are attracting the attention of all classes of society, and Lord Howard de Walden (the owner of Zinfandel) and Lord Desborough have announced their intention to take part in the fencing competitions.[15]

In the case of Croker, Peter O'Connor's biographer summed up his interest:

> Not only was he well connected to the affluent Irish racing fraternity, but the notion of a renegade team of Irish crack athletes travelling to Athens, independent of the English AAA, no doubt appealed to him after the cold reception he had received in England.[16]

Croker was said to have instigated the idea of a national subscription for the Irish athletes when approached on the matter of making a donation at a race meeting. For those who seek interesting connections, it was apparently one of the Coll family from Bruree who first approached Croker at a race meeting.[17] The Colls were, of course, the maternal family of Éamon de Valera, and one of the family, Robert 'Bob' Coll, was a most accomplished athlete in pre-1884 days.[18]

Organising a subscription to fund a sporting event, or an individual athlete's participation in a sporting event, was quite common in Victorian and Edwardian society, although this was the first directly and successfully linked to an Irish Olympic entry. Croker's move also helped to explain why the newspaper campaign he began the following week was through the *Irish Field* and not a more mainstream or nationalistic publication. *Irish Field* readers would not generally have supported GAA athletes competing in Athens but the likes of O'Connor and Leahy were at least as much associated with the IAAA as with any other body. Croker cared little about the political niceties within Irish athletics and more for the demonstration of Irish athletic prowess at the Olympics, which he knew had done so much for Irish-America already. Croker's Irish-American background enabled him to promote Olympic involvement without having to be seen on one side of the athletics divide or the other. He donated £10 to the Athens fund and proposed that top athletes, including Kiely and Horgan, should be sent 'to uphold the prowess of Irish athletes at Athens.'[19] His suggestion of these two was significant in that they were chiefly seen as GAA athletes and, as such, showed the apolitical nature (or lack of sport/political understanding) of Croker's intentions. They also showed the lack of insight he really had into Irish athletic activity, as Kiely was now thirty-six and in semi-retirement. His particular sights in 1906 were probably already set on America and another tilt at the All-Round Championship of the AAU (which he was to be successful in), while Horgan may then have been in New York, where in late 1907 he would receive a severe head injury in a brawl with an Italian shopkeeper, possibly while the Irishman was doing police duty.

In looking at the people who responded to Croker's plea to support an Irish team, it was striking how different the make-up of the list was in comparison to the many who supported the testimonial for Tom Kiely a year and a half before. Among the subscribers of a total of £43 were the cream of the Irish horse-racing establishment and industrialists. These could not have been men inspired by a separatist desire to see the country represented at Athens. Delving a little deeper into the coverage of Croker's campaign by the *Irish Field* may give the answer. The editor wrote of Croker's initial contribution of £10:

> He has forwarded us a cheque for £10, and, as it will only cost £25 a man for the trip, it should not be hard to obtain the wherewithal to send three, or at least, a couple of our best athletes . . . We notice that Mr. S. R. Guggenheim, Mr J. Pierpont Morgan, and Mr August Belmont are amongst those interesting themselves in the getting together of the American team.[20]

The following week, a further snippet under 'Items of Interest' recounted that:

> The committee who are organising the American team for the Olympian Games require £5,000 for expenses. They obtained £1,000 of this amount in one visit to Wall Street.[21]

Croker's appeal met with success partly because it was seen as a means of displaying a sort of philanthropic spirit, though perhaps not quite in the same league as the Guggenheims and Pierpont Morgans. In fact, no other donor gave more than £1 to the fund. If this was the motive for donations, rather than a nationalistic instinct of any significance, it also explained why the *Irish Field* neither covered the Olympic contests themselves nor any of the national identity issues that emerged. The newspaper's generally conservative leaning explained why the two athletes it promoted most as the Irish entrants to be sent were O'Connor and Con Leahy. One writer to the paper took this selection to task:

> Will you kindly allow me to suggest that a selection committee be appointed, say by you, and that they meet early next week, as the entries close on March 23. The committee should include representatives of the IAAA and GAA. Both these bodies would, no doubt, contribute to the fund. Personally, I don't agree with the selection I have seen. A representative committee, however,

would undoubtedly select the best men in the country at their respective events. Yours truly, Athlete (Dublin).[22]

By the time the subscription fund closed, readers of the newspaper had sponsored O'Connor and Leahy to the tune of £55.10s., certainly sufficient to send the two athletes to Athens.

Irish or British Representatives?

Sending Irish athletes to Athens was one thing; having their entries accepted as Irish, not British, would be quite another. As English AAA champions in the long jump and high jump respectively, O'Connor and Leahy were almost certainly invited to be part of the British team for Athens. This had occurred the last time a British team went to an Olympic celebration in 1900. What form their refusal of this invitation took is unclear. On the one hand, there is no evidence of the Irishmen applying for assistance from the grant of £208 that the Greek government had given to the English AAA to fund the British team.[23] However, they still took passage on the same train and boat journeys to the Games, even posing for group photographs with the British competitors. One photograph, taken of the contingent heading for Athens, also shows John Daly wearing a dark (presumably green) vest with a light-coloured shamrock on it. Neither O'Connor nor Leahy is in the photograph. The photograph in question, headed 'The English competitors at Athens', also shows other athletes wearing localised vests – some with St George's cross, some with the Union Jack, one wearing an unidentified emblem and one with what looks like a red ensign or flag of Australia.[24] The *Waterford News,* for instance, a Redmondite newspaper in its editorship and ownership, saw no contradiction at all:

> Con Leahy of Charleville and Peter O'Connor of Waterford, the Irish and English high and long jump champions respectively, will represent the Emerald Isle ... The English, Irish and Scotch athletes will travel in a party together.[25]

A week later, the paper again comfortably accepted the Irishness of O'Connor's entry:

> I am sure that every reader will join with me in wishing Peter O'Connor bon voyage, and the fullest measure of success in the

classic city whither he is going to uphold the name and prestige of the Emerald Isle.[26]

The approaching Olympics again gave rise to outbreaks of Irish patriotic fervour, both in terms of what O'Connor, Leahy and Daly might achieve and also latching on to the Irishness of several of the American competitors. An Irish sports commentator noted: 'Ireland claims more than outside rank. For the backbone of the American team is of Irish build, many of its members taking their descent from Irish parentage.'[27] In terms of the actual participation of O'Connor, Leahy and Daly at the Athens Games, none of the Irish newspapers made a distinction between the 'Ireland' being represented by either IAAA or GAA men. The *Waterford Chronicle,* naturally enough, focused more on O'Connor because of his local connection:

> Peter O'Connor, the World's Champion long jumper, left on Thursday night for the Olympic Games at Athens, where the pick of athletes of all nations will be found competing in this great carnival of sport. O'Connor is confident of winning his favourite event and has been training quietly for some time past.[28]

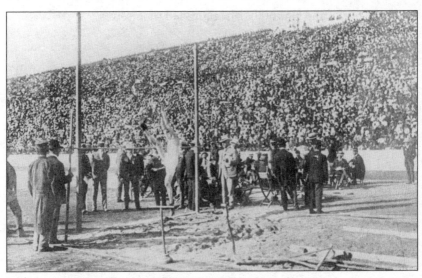

Con Leahy winning the high jump at Athens in 1906 (© IOC Lausanne).

It is slightly more surprising that the main newspaper in O'Connor's home county – although born in Millom, England, he had been reared in Wicklow – did not claim him at all. It merely reported the concern that other papers reported about an injury scare in advance of the long jump: 'It will be regretted by many to learn that Mr. P O'Connor sprained his foot in practice . . .' There was also a complete lack of commentary by this or other Irish papers on the fact that several non-independent nations were being represented at Athens. The *Wicklow People* continued: 'Hungary has sent 43 champions, Denmark 87, Sweden and Norway 140, Bohemia 20 and Austria 42.'[29] While Hungary had a form of home rule in place at this time, Bohemia certainly did not. Yet no newspaper noted any relation between this and Ireland's situation.

The *Irish Independent* was the national newspaper most interested in the 1906 Athens Olympics.[30] It relied substantially on international press reports but tailored many of them to the Irish circumstance. In anticipating Irish successes, the paper commented:

> So far the Irishmen, who are represented by three formidable champions, have not competed. It will be remembered in the games of 1896 we were only represented by one champion, Mr John P. Boland, the present MP for Kerry, who won the lawn tennis singles. At that time, several Irish Americans, including Burke and Connolly, distinguished themselves.[31]

Note the change which had occurred in ten years. In 1896, even Boland himself was quite uninterested in declaring his Irishness, while newspapers like the *Irish Independent* had more or less ignored his nationality or indeed the Irish-American connection.

International Barriers

Behind the scenes of all this Irish preparation for Athens, two crucial events took place which brought the Irish athletes into direct confrontation with the Olympic movement and into prominence as representatives of Irish nationality. The first was the foundation and early development of the British Olympic Association (BOA) in 1905–6. From the outset, its administrators saw the association as a promoter of conservative values, including the unity of the United Kingdom. It intended to support no division within United Kingdom athletics, as the letter written by its first secretary, the Reverend Robert de Courcy Laffan, to Baron de Coubertin, demonstrates:

> I send a line to say that after a great deal of preliminary work we have got our Council of the British Olympic Association fairly constituted and are actively at work promoting the attendance of British athletes at Athens . . . Now I want you to send me an official statement that you regard this Association as the representative in Great Britain of the International Olympic Committee, and as the medium of communication between the IOC and all British Associations, whether athletic, sporting or educational.[32]

Having failed completely to attend at St Louis, the British Olympic enthusiasts were determined to be represented by a strong team at Athens. Furthermore, de Courcy Laffan was leaving no doubt that the new BOA regarded itself as the sole representative of sporting associations in these islands vis-à-vis the Olympics. Whatever about the opportunities not taken in the first three celebrations of the Olympics, it would no longer be easy for Irish athletes to be recognised independently of the BOA. The list of those invited to form the inaugural council of the British Olympic Association also left no doubt that this was to be a sporting organisation very much dominated by establishment figures, most unlikely to be supportive of any effort to establish a separate Irish identity at the Olympics.[33] On a list of nineteen invitees to the inaugural meeting, all male, there were four Tory MPs, three army officers, two lords and a clergyman. Of the others, those whose backgrounds could be identified, such as Theodore Cook and Charles Herbert, showed themselves also to be very clearly establishment figures. Not one invitee came from part of the United Kingdom outside of England, and the sports represented were establishment-dominated, with the exception of association football.

A further but equally important matter came into the equation at this point – Baron de Coubertin himself. He was very close to British IOC members like Desborough and de Courcy Laffan. Their copious correspondence held numerous reflections of close personal friendships, extending to spouses and other family members. The baron was also a conservative and known admirer of the English. He was unlikely to be tolerant of any Irish attempts to establish a separate team or identity, at Athens or anywhere else. De Coubertin's adherence to the idea of nations having to be independent to be represented at the Games was otherwise a very arbitrary one. The baron, for instance, tolerated and absolutely defended the right of Bohemia to enter its own team in 1906, even though Bohemia was entirely within the Habsberg Empire and had no more right to independent representation than Ireland had. De Coubertin defended the Bohemians against Austrian protests after 1906 by stating to the protesting official:

> . . . if there was in your country another such 'province' which trained such number of gymnasts, we would love to have its representatives among us. We have to take into account the athletic autonomy of a country . . . we did not consider it a state but a centre of sports.[34]

De Coubertin reiterated this argument some years later, again in relation to supporting Bohemian sporting independence, by declaring:

> The fundamental rule of the modern Olympiads is summarised in these terms: 'All games, all nations.' It is not even within the power of the International Olympic Committee, the highest authority in this matter, to change this. I must add that a nation is not necessarily an independent State. There is an athletic geography that may differ at times from political geography.[35]

Here was an insight into the vital but arbitrary attitude of de Coubertin and the IOC to non-independent nations. The identity of Bohemia was recognised in 1906, not least because Austria-Hungary was neither a political friend of France and Britain nor did it have an IOC representative. Finland too, although under Russian rule even more directly than Ireland was under British, managed to sneak separate representation for its four athletes at the 1906 Games. Several Greek city states which were actually within the Ottoman Empire in 1906 were given recognition, both as Greek and individual cities, at the Athens Games.[36] Ireland, however, was a different scenario. Its athletes were not going to get the support of the British Olympic Association, nor in all likelihood of de Coubertin, if they were to seek independent recognition. It was one thing to risk offending the Austrians, Russians or Turks, it was quite another for either de Coubertin or the IOC to upset the British Olympic representatives by allowing the Games to become a vehicle for furthering a separate Irish 'athletic geography.'

In Ireland, Arthur Griffith pointed out that the GAA had 'missed one of its finest opportunities by not sending its representatives to compete in the name of Ireland at the Olympian games'.[37] This comment from Griffith also adds credence to the notion that John Daly was not seen as representing the GAA, as previously suggested. Griffith was, however, taking little account of the difficulty which now faced any possible Irish entry following the foundation of the British Olympic Association, although it was a valid criticism of GAA athletic apathy. Griffith's grasp of the broader international situation saw him contrast the Bohemian position with the Irish one very perceptively:

> As a result, Ireland was almost the only country in Europe whose flag was not accorded official honours in Athens last week by the Government of Greece . . . Bohemia, a country in circumstances of similarity to our own, declined to permit its representatives to appear under the flag of Austria, and the Bohemians, carrying their national banner, were saluted by Greece as a distinctive nation. Ireland, with a better opportunity than Bohemia, was smothered in the Union Jack, and the men who were supposed to represent Ireland were, therefore, officially catalogued as 'English.'

Battling for Irish Recognition

It appears that the three Irishmen, O'Connor, Daly and Leahy, only discovered that they had been entered as British competitors when they arrived in Athens.[38] They had heard nothing of the new regulations about affiliations of Olympic committees and were genuinely shocked. It is unclear whether their entry as 'British' competitors was down to the AAA, which had after all invited at least two of them to represent it at Athens already, or to the Greek hosts. The Greeks might well have pleaded ignorance of the political squabbles within the United Kingdom. The close relationship between the Greek and British royal families made ignorance unlikely, just as it made Greece wanting to avoid any embarrassment for the British royals, including Edward VII, attending the Games all the more likely. No direct evidence of IOC involvement in this decision has been unearthed, although its official policy on national identities was now in existence. De Coubertin didn't even attend the Athens Games in 1906. When it came to the opening ceremony of the Games, the three Irishmen walked to the rear of the British delegation, O'Connor and Leahy wearing the special green blazers that had been presented to them.[39] Some nationalistic reports suggest that the Irishmen effected almost a separate parade during this opening ceremony, waving green flags around the stadium.[40] Nothing found thus far in contemporary newspaper reports, official documentation or photographs has borne this out, although such insubordination would have been unlikely to make it to the official records of the IOC or Greek organisers.

O'Connor drafted an appeal to the International Jury for the Irishmen to be designated as representing Ireland but this appeal was turned down. So too was a direct appeal he made to Prince George of Greece. The prince reportedly replied: 'When Ireland has a parliament of its own, you can hoist the flag but not before. Perhaps there will be an Irish parliament by the time the next Games come around.'[41] As with de Coubertin, Prince George's position here was an ambivalent one. On the one hand, he was a friend of Britain, a relative of its royal family and an upholder of Olympic rule. Yet, on the other hand, he was well aware of the independent representation being afforded to several Greek city states which at the time were firmly under Ottoman rule.

The failure of the Irish to gain entry as a separate team caused some degree of confusion in the media at home. If Daly was a GAA athlete and the other two were IAAA-affiliated, no commentary on this being at odds with the bans on co-operation then in force in both organisations has been located. More curious still was the fact that O'Connor's long-time ally, the *Waterford News*, found the non-acceptance of an Irish entry quite tolerable in the circumstances, merely commenting:

> A rather unusual excitement was created by our townsman, Peter O'Connor, and some more of the Irish representatives, who

tried to insist that the wins registered by Ireland should be marked by the raising of the green flag as against the Union Jack. However this may be in sentiment, the protest could by no means hold good, as O'Connor and his confreres were part and parcel of the English team.[42]

The same editorial contented itself with rejoicing in the fact that many Irish were among the laurels for other countries, including the British team. He was, however, taken to task the following week by a letter writer:

> Dear sir – I don't think it is quite correct to say that messers. O'Connor, Leahy and Daly went to the Olympic Games as 'part and parcel of the English team.' These three Irishmen had their expenses paid out of a fund specially raised in Ireland for that purpose, and O'Connor's spirited protest against being classed as a Briton, shows that the competitors themselves considered they were representing Ireland and Ireland alone. It is a pity this country could not have sent a team of Irish-speaking athletes, as in that case it would have been much easier to convince the Athenian officials of their distinctive nationality. TFH Jacob, 20 Newtown Hill [Waterford] 7th May 1906.[43]

In New York, the *Gaelic American* was in no doubt as to what had happened in the denial of Irish representation and put a far more extreme perspective on things than any Irish newspaper. Noting (incorrectly in the first two cases at least) that the 'Greco-Danish Prince' had also ruled that the athletes of Australia, Canada and Scotland would be classed as 'English', the paper commented:

> The royal coterie which promulgated this ruling was composed of the reigning families of Greece and England. The King and Queen of England were present, and no doubt the ruling of Prince George voiced the wishes of the rulers of England . . . Ireland is an unwilling partner in the blood-stained Empire, the nations are aware of her sorrows and of her many struggles for freedom, and the struggle will continue until Ireland takes her place among the nations.[44]

It was rare enough for the other great organ of Irish-America, the *Irish World,* to be in agreement with John Devoy. While Devoy's newspaper was clearly separatist in its philosophy, the *Irish World* remained much more a Home Rule supporter, harking back to its halcyon days of backing Parnell when he went to the USA in the early 1880s. However, on this occasion the *World* too sought to highlight the non-Britishness of Ireland's competitors, under a sub-heading 'They Won't be English': 'They are paying their own expenses and proclaim on all occasions that they are in no way identified with English athletes.'[45]

British Victories?

Between them, the three Irish athletes made the 1906 Games the most successful yet for the 'old distressed country', regardless of the entity they ended up representing. Leahy won the high jump and was second in the hop, step and jump on the same day. It remains open to contradiction, but Con Leahy's success appears to make the Leahys the first brothers in Olympic history to achieve top three placings in athletics (Pat was placed in two events in Paris 1900). Leahy's high jump win came at the end of a very long contest, dragged out over two days. This happened because the bar started at just 1 metre 37.5 centimetres, well under five feet, and was only raised by a centimetre at a time throughout most of the first day. Nor were contestants allowed to pass at any height. The result was that darkness fell on day one when most competitors were still in the field. By agreement, the bar was raised in 2.5-centimetre intervals after that, eliminating a couple of contestants before dark and some more the following morning. Eventually, only Con Leahy and Lajos Gönczy of Hungary were left at 1 metre 77.5 centimetres. Leahy went clear and Gönczy failed in three attempts. In joint third place was the American AAU champion, Herbert Kerrigan, who had suffered an injury when on board ship to Athens, and whose name suggests Irish origins but these have not been confirmed.[46]

Peter O'Connor was second in the long jump and won the hop, step and jump. In the latter event, he had actually trailed Con Leahy all the way through with Leahy having four efforts which were better than anyone else's over the first five rounds. In the very last round O'Connor became the only one to clear fourteen metres and beat Leahy by nearly ten centimetres.[47] Contrary to popular belief, neither O'Connor nor Leahy received gold medals for these Olympic victories. In 1906, the winners' medals were made of silver.

The defeat of O'Connor in his favourite long jump event was to cause major controversy and, from the perspective of this study, provide some interesting insights into the issue of national identity and allegiance at Athens. The merits of O'Connor's claim that he was effectively cheated out of the long jump title are not for investigation here. However, there were, at the very least, serious irregularities which had a significant impact on Irish perceptions of both American and British Olympism.

For the long jump, a British judge was scheduled to officiate, along with an American. In fact, the British judge, Perry, disappeared from the pit side and the main part of the event was officiated at by only one recognised judge. Perry has been accused of leaving deliberately to thwart O'Connor's chances but it is much more likely that his expertise as a starter was the reason for his being called away at that particular time.[48] Of greater significance than the absence of the judge, however, was the reason given by O'Connor for the absence. The Irishman chased down the missing judge during the event in another part of the stadium, being told that the judge was refusing to officiate at the long jump because of O'Connor's attempt to represent Ireland and not Britain.[49]

The subsequent difficulty for O'Connor was that the sole judge of the long jump was an American, Matthew Halpin. The ironies abounded here from a national perspective. Halpin was an Irish-American, and a cousin of James Sullivan, the US team leader. According to O'Connor and several independent accounts, Halpin adjudicated in a fashion which helped to ensure that the Irish athlete did not stand an even chance of winning.[50] A second irony was that the Irishman who had tried in vain to represent Ireland was actually defeated by an American, Meyer Prinstein, who represented the Greater New York Irish Athletic Association (by now the Irish American Athletic Club). A third point was that the person who alerted O'Connor initially to the dubiousness of having Halpin alone officiate at the long jump was not only an American, but the famous Irish-American, James B. Connolly, attending the second Athens Games as a journalist. It is worth pointing out that Connolly had a long and vitriolic relationship with many of the prominent Irish-Americans in the AAU, not least James E. Sullivan and Halpin (who both sued Connolly for libel in 1910). Connolly was one of the first and most vocal critics of Sullivan's use of athletics to promote the use and advertising of Spalding sporting goods (see Connolly's article, 'The Capitalisation of Amateur Athletics', published in the *San Diego Sun* newspaper, 1910). However, most of the evidence for Connolly's dislike of Halpin relates to events in 1908 and therefore cannot be used to suggest a particular bias on Connolly's part in 1906. O'Connor's 1956 interview quotes Connolly telling him that, with Halpin as judge, he stood no chance of beating Prinstein.[51]

The outcome saw British judges deserting an overtly (if unwilling) British competitor and an American journalist attacking the partiality of an American judge. The incident led O'Connor to appeal directly to Prince George of Greece, even while the long jump was in progress, but with no success:

> When O'Connor informed Prince George of his complaint, most judges present were probably already involved in officiating other events. As such, he was probably reluctant to interfere with a competition already underway. In addition, the removal of Halpin, apart from creating logistical problems, could be perceived as an admission that certain improprieties may have taken place. Such decisive action would not necessarily bring the matter to a close, since the American delegation would be sure to protest the removal of Halpin without strong evidence of malpractice.[52]

Prince George also had to consider the importance of maintaining friendship with the American officials, who were among the most vocal supporters of having the Olympic Games based permanently in Greece. Refusing the appeals certainly helped the Prince to maintain his friendship with Britain and America, a dual aim which was very difficult to achieve otherwise in Olympic circles in the early years of the twentieth century.

Arthur Griffith's previous warning that Irish successes would be claimed as English ultimately came true as well, adding fuel to the flames. *The Times* of London may be regarded as the newspaper of record for the British establishment of the day. It did note that J.J. Daly was 'the Irish champion' but carried news of the long jump with 'P. O'Connor (England) being second' and, most glaringly, a few days later recounted that: 'The hop, skip and jump resulted in a triple English success. O'Connor won, with 14.75 metres, while Leahy was second with 13.98 metres and Cronan third with 13.7 metres.'[53]

Ceremony and Symbolism

More striking than the long jump affair itself was the protest which O'Connor, abetted by Leahy, initiated at the victory ceremony. Given that the two athletes still had events to compete in, thus risking the wrath of officialdom yet again, it was a quite remarkable expression of national identity. O'Connor described what happened:

> When I climbed the pole about 20 feet in height and remained aloft for some time, waving my large flag and Con waving his from the ground underneath the pole, it caused a great sensation. It occurred just as the official hoisted on the Olympic masts the three flags indicating the nationality of the first, second and third

Peter O'Connor junior and younger family members hold the flag that Peter senior brought to Athens in 1906. Courtesy of Larry Ryder.

winners of the long jump, the British Union Jack being flown for my being second. It was only the section of the spectators in the seats near where the jump came off that fully appreciated our demonstration as Irishmen as objecting to the Union Jack being hoisted claiming my being second in the long jump as a win and a point gained for the British team. I had a very excitable temper and was simply furious over the English judges' [note the plural, *sic*] refusing to officiate as judges because of my letter to the Olympic committee, over the sarcastic remarks of Prince George and over the way I was robbed of victory. I was an accomplished gymnast in my youth and my active climbing of the post excited the spectators who had observed my violent protest to Halpin being sole judge and declaring my best jumps foul.[54]

Yet again, the Irish media remained silent on this very dramatic gesture, identified by O'Connor's biographer as the first overtly political act to take place at an Olympic Games.[55] Irish newspapers certainly highlighted the fact that the marathon winner at Athens had Irish ancestry. One commented that Billy Sherring was an Irishman:

> He is 28 years old and a member of the St. Patrick's club, Ontario. His mother is a county Roscommon woman. During the race Sherring wore a white jersey with a white [means green] shamrock embroidered on it, and while he was approaching the winning post his identity was mistaken by many of the assembled thousands, who shouted Daly! Daly! However, the latter, who was Ireland's hope in the race, had dropped out a long time previously.[56]

The Times (3 May) managed to point out, incidentally, that Sherring's father had been a Londoner. The Irish press collectively wrung their hands at the fact that so many Olympic champions had come from Ireland but represented other lands. (They did, however, collectively miss the fact that John McGough, second placed in the 1,500 metres for Britain, had been born in Monaghan before his family emigrated to Scotland.) However, the notion of publicising the actions of athletes who had sought to do something practical to address this issue seems to have eluded Irish newspapers, particularly those with an otherwise nationalist tendency.

Even *Sinn Féin* contented itself with using the flag protest as a means of reminding the GAA of its failure to enter a team in Athens and so strike a blow for Irish identity:

> The sequel to the victories of the Irish athletes at the Olympic Games enhances our regret that the Gaelic Athletic Association did not officially participate in those games. The three Irishmen objected to being classed as British, and asserted their distinctive nationality by waving green flags for their victories, although the official recognition was the hoisting of the Union Jack. If the Irishmen had been sent officially from Ireland their distinctive nationality would have been recognised by Greece, as it recognised the distinctiveness of Bohemia and, apart from the athletic kudos accruing to Ireland, she would have gained a political advantage by impressing her distinctiveness on what has now come to be an assemblage of Europe in Athens . . .[57]

The somewhat simplistic viewpoint of Griffith on the matter of how easy it would be for Ireland to have competed as a nation at Athens has already been referred to. Yet, in terms of media coverage, his was ultimately the only Irish newspaper to carry at least some detail on the affair. Griffith was vehemently opposed to the IAAA as a promoter of 'garrison sports and Britishness' and, perhaps consequently, neglected the fact that what had been achieved at Athens in terms of establishing Irish identity had, in fact, been achieved by the IAAA's representatives:

> Then, on Friday week, when Mr. O'Connor obtained second place in the broad jump, a Union Jack was waved to indicate his nationality to the spectators. Mr. O'Connor at once protested against this, and . . . waved a green flag of his own. It is to be noted that there were several English amongst the officials, and one can be certain that a word from any of them would at once have put the matter right. The English competitors, of whom there are over twenty, have made a very poor figure in the contests all round . . . But they made up a little of their leeway by claiming the achievements of the Irishmen as their own. Of the supineness [i.e. GAA non-involvement] which permitted

this to take place there should be no trace left when the Olympic Games again come round.[58]

The silence, both of local and mainstream national papers, was so remarkable that one might be forgiven for thinking that the whole 'flag incident' was little more than an urban legend, not least because O'Connor himself remained publicly silent on the matter until his interview with the *Limerick Leader* nearly half a century later. The official Olympic Report for 1906 carried no mention of the incident, unsurprisingly. In fact, in seeking contemporary verification of the incident, it was once again the *Gaelic American* in New York which provided it. In attacking the anti-Irish bias of the English news agencies' coverage of the Athens Games, Devoy's paper quoted what it termed 'the Devil's News Bureau' as saying: 'There was some amusement after the long jump because of the protest made by O'Connor that the British flag should be run up to show that he was second in the event.' The *Gaelic American* commented:

> It is evident that this *amusement* aroused the ire of the news bureau. Although O'Connor's protest was not allowed by the Greeks, whose sovereign is a protégé of England's King, the protest has had the desired effect. O'Connor waved Ireland's flag with his own right hand, not alone when he was *second* but also when he was *first* in another event. The thousands of spectators from all parts of the world know now, if they didn't know it before, that Britain's blood-stained banner is not respected nor recognised by the Irish people.[59]

The *New York Sun* also bore testimony to the fact that there were actually two occasions when O'Connor displayed his Irish flag, climbing the flagpole after the long jump and then, following his hop, step and jump win: 'O'Connor, although the British flag was hoisted when he won, walked about the stadium waving his Irish flag to show the assemblage where he hailed from.'[60] The *Irish World* was a little more general but made essentially the same point about Irish flag-waving:

> The authorities in charge of the games have classed the Irishmen as members of the English team. This the Irishmen resent. They refuse to be included under the Union Jack and when the

Greeks, in announcing an Irish victory, wave the British flag the Irishmen immediately wave the green and gold of their native country.[61]

An area of national symbol deployment which has received no documentary coverage to date relates to the clothing worn by the Irish athletes in competition at Athens. Apart from the IAAA blazers already referred to, and Daly's shamrock-decked vest in the photograph on page 143, pictorial evidence shows that O'Connor wore what was, for the time, an unusually dark singlet over his white shorts during competition but it is impossible to detect whether this was a green one symbolising Ireland or not. More certain was the picture of Con Leahy going over the high jump bar, dressed in the more traditional white athletic outfit but with the triple shamrock logo of the IAAA clearly visible on the top left corner of his singlet.[62] Searches at the IOC archives in Lausanne have failed to find an image of John Daly in competition, although he must also have worn a shamrock-emblazoned singlet, given that the Greek crowd along the marathon route began to shout 'Daly, Daly' when they saw the shamrock-wearing Sherring of Canada approaching.

Billy Sherring of Canada running in the final straight in the 1906 marathon, with Prince George of Greece jogging alongside (© IOC Lausanne).

How Ireland Reported the Games

O'Connor's brush with officialdom was reported in some peremptory comments in the Irish press. That said, the reliance on Reuters reports in the main meant that most papers missed anything controversial. At local level, the *Waterford Chronicle* lamented the news that O'Connor had sprained his foot prior to competition but completely ignored his achievements or national demonstrations afterwards.[63] The *Waterford News* merely reported: 'We learn with pleasure from Athens that our popular townsman Mr. O'Connor has won the hop, step and jump, and that the running high jump was carried off by Mr. Leahy of Charleville.'[64] The *Wicklow People* was even more matter-of-fact: 'In the long jump many good jumps were registered. At first it seemed as if O'Connor (Ireland) would win, but eventually Prinstein (America) jumped 7.20 metres, and this proved too much for O'Connor . . .'[65]

Nationally, little differed. The *Cork Examiner* relied entirely on Press Association and Reuters articles on the Athens Games, only inserting the headings 'Remarkable Irish Successes – Southern men placed first and second' over the generic Press Association account of the triple jump and 'Another Irish Triumph – Con Leahy wins the High Jump' over the high jump results.[66] The *Cork Constitution*, meanwhile, was a significantly more unionist newspaper. It carried an article on the arrival of the king and queen of England in Athens prior to the Games but no more than one incomplete account of some athletics events, with absolutely no reference to Irish participants.[67] The *Freeman's Journal* had also noted O'Connor's sprained foot in advance of competition but missed everything subsequently, even including the Irish trio in its preamble on 'The British athletes who are to compete in the Olympic Games'.[68] Even *Sinn Féin* missed any of the controversy over judging, contenting itself with lamenting that, as predicted, the second place of O'Connor was attributed in the British media to 'England', not Ireland:

> It is thus Irish fatuity helps England in her policy of keeping Ireland concealed out of sight and memory of Europe, and permitted us to read in the London papers of Saturday how second place in a jumping competition was achieved by 'O'Connor (England)' . . . An Irishman instantly becomes British

when he performs any creditable action . . . Were Ireland only able to live her own life as Greece now lives it, she would, beyond all question, have had a contingent of athletes at these games who might not fear to meet against the picked competitors of the world and bear off many a prize.[69]

The most vociferous response to the Athens events found in the Irish press comes in the form of a letter to the editor of the *Waterford News,* from T.A. Rockett. Even his agenda was somewhat narrower than a mere nationalist one, seeing the achievements of O'Connor and the others as proof of the folly of the GAA's ban, though linked with broader political and historical issues:

This attempt to set class against class must fail if common sense has at least an innings. Divide and conquer has ever been the motto of our enemies, and the lessons of the fatal split in Irish politics have sunk too deeply in the hearts of Irishmen to be eradicated in a day. We want to live in peace with all men and, as sportsmen, to enter into rivalry with all nations.

It is not recognised by any athletic or cycling association in existence. Had O'Connor, Leahy or Daly subscribed to the new order of things in the GAA, they could not have so gallantly upheld the athletic prestige of Ireland at the Olympian games. No cyclist who competes now under GAA laws can enter the lists under the rules of any other association. This is the result of the crude and selfish legislation introduced, as I am aware, for handicappers' purposes at the recent Gaelic convention . . .[70]

Irish-America
The Athens Olympics of 1906 saw the beginning of Anglo-American rivalry which would erupt in London two years later. We have already seen that the Americans savoured victories over the representatives of Britain, even if they were Irishmen, in Athens. Even setting aside the Halpin–O'Connor controversy in the long jump, the head of the US team, James Sullivan, highlighted this American triumphalism in a telegram to President Roosevelt, dated 1 May 1906:

Americans won hurdles, half-mile and standing jump today. Final score stadium events: America eleven firsts, six seconds, six thirds; total 75 points; Great Britain and all her possessions four firsts, six seconds, three thirds; total 39 points; Greece and Sweden tied for third place. Great athletic victory for America.[71]

In looking at the reaction of Irish-America to the Athens Games, apart from its profiling of the O'Connor demonstration, there was a continued emphasis on the achievements of Irish-American athletes at the Games and the subsequent use of Martin Sheridan and others to promote fundraising activities of Irish nationalist organisations. There was no doubt whatsoever that the star of Irish-American sport by 1906 was Martin Sheridan, fresh from his second set of Olympic triumphs. At Athens, the Mayoman had won a total of five Olympic placings, two firsts and three seconds. Again, because the Olympics were still two years away from the idea of gold medals for the winners of events, these translated into two silver winners' medals and three bronze ones for the second places. Sheridan's wins were in his favourite freestyle discus event and in the shot. He was widely recognised as the world record holder in the discus at this stage, despite the lack of IAAF records until a few years later, and is credited with holding between seven and sixteen discus world records in all during his career. The shot victory was less impressive, with Sheridan not really being known as a shot putter at all and victory coming over a weak field missing the world's top putters, Ralph Rose of the USA and Denis Horgan of Ireland.[72] Sheridan's versatility as an athlete, which eventually won him three American AAU All-Round titles, was shown by the second places he won in the stone throw, the standing high jump and the standing long jump. Sheridan had not intended to compete in the 14-pound stone throw at all but filled in for the Irish-American specialist, James Mitchell from Emly, County Tipperary, who dislocated his shoulder when the ship lurched violently en route to Athens. The event was held at no other Olympics. Sheridan's standing high jump second place was won while he was competing at the same time in a 'Greek-style' discus event, in which no one seemed to understand the rules and where Sheridan finished fourth in the end.[73]

A particular cause of satisfaction to Irish-America was the fact that a traditional team points score allocated to Sheridan alone would have seen him single-handedly surpass the total points score achieved in athletics by competitors from England and Scotland combined.[74] He was eulogised in poems and articles, especially in the *Gaelic American*. The noses of the Greeks were well and truly rubbed in the dust of the Athenian discus circle:

> Soldiers of Salamis, heroes of Marathon, helmeted, sworded,
> Seeing the muscle-free grace of the Gael, and the mould of his
> torso,
> Look from the clouds in a shadowy phalanx, asking each other:
> 'Comes back to earth our Androsthenes, greatest at hurling the
> discus?'[75]

Patrick Ford's *Irish World* eulogised Sheridan in particular and used the opportunity to remind readers of the significance of Irish involvement in US history generally:

> The American team has acquitted itself so as to gain the applause of the world and Martin J. Sheridan has won honor not merely for himself and America, but for his Celtic race and fatherland, and shed further lustre on an Irish name already bright in the pages of American history.[76]

It was useful from the Irish-American perspective that the Games were over and done with by early May, allowing for the attendance of these athletes at nationalist picnic after picnic during the summer months on the eastern seaboard of the USA. Cross-national bodies like the Ancient Order of Hibernians (AOH) and Irish Volunteers, and localised ones like the Claremen's and Tipperarymen's associations, all used athletic contests to attract the masses of urban Irish-America to their celebrations. Given that most Irish immigrants came from disparate rural backgrounds where membership of any organisation, certainly of a political variety, was not common, the importance of these bodies in first shaping an Irish identity in the USA, giving the immigrants moral and social support, should not be underestimated. One historian has extended the argument on this issue further, in that:

most immigrant groups have not only discovered their 'ethnicity' in America, but that the development of some form of ethnic identity has been an integral part of the process through which immigrants have normally become American.[77]

The participation of the Olympic champions was headlined in the advertisements for such picnics. For instance, both the two-day athletic carnival of the AOH (25–6 August) and the eleventh annual sports and picnic of the curiously named Eccentric Association of Firemen (2 September) advertised their Celtic Park proceedings with the headings: 'World Champions To Compete' and 'World Champions Will Compete' respectively. These two advertisements, plus another for the First Regiment Irish Volunteers carnival to be held on 19 August, took up two-thirds of page 8 in this particular edition of the *Gaelic American*. The largest advertising space afforded to any single event or product in the newspaper was allocated to such events.[78] The *Gaelic American* ensured the high profile of events by writing lengthy previews and subsequent reviews of such picnics, again relying very heavily on highlighting the attendance and achievements of such as Sheridan and other Olympians.[79]

Naturally, Clan na Gael too held more 'athletic picnics' (if that is not a contradiction in terms) throughout the summer of 1906. New York Clan na Gael, with Sheridan, John Flanagan (who had not gone to Athens) and the visiting, semi-retired Tom Kiely headlining, reported that its annual picnic had the biggest crowd ever assembled at Celtic Park, with the largest gate receipts ever taken there, although no figures were specified on this occasion.[80] That this event had been 'revived after many years of an intermission' also points to the boost given to Clan activities in the metropolis by the Irish-American athletes' successes in the 1906 Olympics. Crowds of 10,000, according to the *Gaelic American*, attended the Long Island and Philadelphia picnics, both held on 4 July, a day when the Boston Clan's equivalent was partially washed out by rain. The 4 July date for the main Clan picnics has some significance. Being a date when all of the USA took a holiday anyway, it was a natural opportunity for the Clan both to attract large crowds and also demonstrate its love of America. The *Gaelic American* summed this up:

ANNUAL PICNIC AND ATHLETIC GAMES

OF THE

CLAN-NA-GAEL
Of New York
AT CELTIC PARK,
LONG ISLAND CITY,

ON SUNDAY, JULY 1st, 1906,
COMMENCING AT 2 P. M.

EVENTS.

THE FOLLOWING EVENTS ARE OPEN TO ALL REGISTERED ATHLETES.
A. A. U. RULES TO GOVERN:

100 YARDS RUN, Handicap.
300 YARDS RUN, Handicap.
600 YARDS RUN, Novice.
1,000 YARDS RUN, Handicap.

ONE MILE RUN, Handicap.
RUNNING HOP, STEP AND JUMP, Handicap.
THROWING THE DISCUS, Handicap.
THROWING 16-LB. HAMMER, Handicap.

THREE-MILE RUN, SCRATCH—INVITATION.

PRIZES.

SOLID GOLD WATCH FOB to First in each Event. SOLID SILVER DIE MEDAL to Second in Each Event. BRONZE DIE MEDAL to Third in each Event.

ENTRY FEE, FIFTY CENTS, WHICH MUST ACCOMPANY ENTRY.

Entries close on Wednesday, June 27, with John J. McHugh, 412 East 50th Street, and Dieges & Clust, 23 John Street, New York City.

HURLING AND FOOTBALL CHAMPIONSHIPS

Dancing Afternoon and Evening.

TICKETS   25 CENTS EACH.

A Clan na Gael picnic advert from the *Gaelic American*, 16 June 1906.

It was entirely appropriate that the Clan-na-Gael of Long Island should hold their annual picnic on the Fourth day of July, a day dedicated to freedom. The glorious fourth was an inspiration to the downtrodden the world over, for it commemorated the triumph of freedom over tyranny. In the celebration of this day, the Irish element in the population of this country take a just pride, for it was largely by Irish brawn and bravery that the fight for independence was fought and won.[81]

An element which entered the equation at the Long Island meeting on this occasion was the presence of an Indian delegation, of both Hindus and Muslims, 'to mark the drawing together of the Indian and Irish peoples to work against the common foe, England'. The financial significance of these picnics, and the import for future Clan hopes of getting mass Irish-American support for Irish revolution, have already been alluded to. The importance of numbers, in terms of people and not just dollars, to Clan na Gael's plans is worth restating. It was around this time that Devoy's newspaper began a series of 'special offers': 'For thirty annual subscriptions ($60 in cash prepaid) the Gaelic American will give a brand new Mauser rifle or for twenty subscriptions ($40 in cash prepaid) a second-hand Mauser rifle.' This appeared below a feature about teaching the young how to shoot with urgings that 'every Nationalist should have a rifle of his own – good shooting is one of the essentials in war – that was the secret of the Boer successes'. Below the advert, among other points, appeared: 'In Ireland the people can't practice rifle shooting. In America, every man can have a rifle and learn how to use it. The riflemen that will free Ireland must be trained here.'[82]

What the gatherings of 4 July, and other contemporary Clan activities did not show yet was a high degree of assimilation of Irish-Americans as 'Americans'. This was happening to an extent but it would be 1908 before the Olympics played a major role in such assimilation. The failure of organs like the *Gaelic American* to embrace and promote assimilation has long been identified. 'Instead of trying to turn the Irish into better Americans, the paper existed to propagate the gospel according to Clan na Gael.'[83] The period around the 1906 Olympics reinforced this view. When, for example, the San Francisco earthquake struck at the same time as the Athens Games, Clan na Gael gave $1,000, but specified it be used for the relief of Irish-Americans in the stricken area. The *Gaelic American* headlined Martin Sheridan's Athens triumphs on the top left of its front page, with the right-

A line-up of great Irish champions. From left: Pat Davin (one-time world record holder in high and long jump), Peter O'Connor, Tom Kiely, Con Power (a member of the GAA invasion of America in 1888) and Percy Kirwan, multiple AAA champion. Courtesy of Larry Ryder.

hand side announcing its disaster appeal with 'Our Own in San Francisco Need Relief'. To be fair, this 'looking after our own' mentality was not unique to the Clan or *Gaelic American*. Douglas Hyde, for example, was in the USA at the same time on a Gaelic League fundraising tour. He raised $5,000 from the Irish societies and businesses of San Francisco and, following the earthquake, made the significant gesture of returning that amount to the Irish societies of the city for disaster relief.[84] Even when a celebration of the victories of 'the American and Irish American athletes' in Athens was organised by the Irish American Athletic Club, it became an Irish affair, not an American one, to the point of the hymn 'America' being sung at the conclusion, but to a new air, replacing the old one which used the tune of 'God Save the King', so anathema to Irish nationalists.[85]

In conclusion, the 1906 Olympics saw the first organised and significant effort by Britain to stifle Irish Olympic identity. Those who sought or might have sought separate Irish identity at Games prior to this had, in truth, few barriers placed in front of them, beyond their own lack of resources, cohesion or vision. The 1906 Intercalated Games, however, brought about a significant change in this, not least because the British Olympic Association was by then in existence and its Council was highly influential within the Olympic confraternity. The aftermath of the Athens events again reinforced the role played by Irish-American athletes as fundraising vehicles for nationalist movements in the USA, particularly Clan na Gael.

CHAPTER SIX

LONDON 1908 FROM AN IRISH PERSPECTIVE

The months after the Athens Games in 1906 saw significant activity at the British Olympic Association, including discussion of Irish representation at, and involvement in, future Olympic celebrations. In late 1906, following the disastrous earthquakes in Italy, it was established that London, not Rome as originally planned, would host the 1908 Games.[1] Although evidence from both 1896 and 1900 showed that British officials, particularly within the Amateur Athletic Association, were happy to recommend the involvement of Irish organisations or athletes in the Olympic Games, the initial plans for 1908 suggested that the focus of organisational attention was going to be on English-based associations. The BOA's honorary secretary wrote to de Coubertin, declaring his joy at the news that the AAA was giving its full backing to the London Olympic project, anticipating that 'we shall carry the English associations as a whole' and listing nine sporting bodies, all English, which had been approached for support.[2]

The IAAA was not slow in seeking a role for itself at London. Initially this came in the form of a request to have an IAAA representative on the organising committee for the 1908 Games. At the final BOA meeting of 1906, the secretary, de Courcy Laffan, reported:

> That he had received letters from the Hon. Secs. of the AAA and the ARA [Amateur Rowing Association] of Ireland, expressing willingness to co-operate in the Olympiad of London. The Hon.

Sec. of the IAAA wrote – 'My committee respectfully suggest that a member of this Association might be given a place on your Committee.' It was directed that the consideration of this request should stand over pending the revision of the Rules.[3]

Neither the IAAA nor the Irish Amateur Rowing Union (IARU) were to be feared as vehicles of extreme nationalism. They were, however, independent-minded bodies. The IARA had a most intriguing blend of classes and political persuasions within it, although being very definitely conservative in the broad sense of the term.[4] They were also bodies which desired some form of Irish identity in the London Games, as the IAAA had done in Athens in 1906. That such a step would be anathema to the BOA was already obvious. It was further emphasised by the cameo detail that the very meeting which received the IAAA and IARA request also appointed, among others, G.S. Robertson to the council, the same G.S. Robertson who had exchanged pleasant hostilities with Boland after the first Athens Games and who had been an erstwhile official at the second Athens Games on the day of O'Connor's long jump controversy.[5] A similar (unminuted) request for representation on the organising committee came in around the same time from the Scottish Amateur Athletic Association (SAAA). Both the IAAA and SAAA had been engaged in international matches of their own for over a decade, so their requests for representation were not surprising. The official historian of the AAA actually credits Ireland with holding the first-ever international athletics match in 1876, when it hosted a visiting England team and competed in a return fixture in London the following year.[6] The BOA council's response was predictable. Its own rules were immediately redrafted and, on the recommendation of the Rules Committee, it was resolved at the very next meeting:

> To inform the Irish AAA and Scottish AAA that the Council regrets that it is unable, owing to the necessity of limiting its numbers, to ask them to appoint representatives, but that it will be happy to consult their wishes in every way.[7]

The Rules Committee had five members, including Robertson, de Courcy Laffan and Desborough, each of these at least having distinguished himself through correspondence or action on the issue of non-tolerance of separate Irish representation at the Olympic Games. The Rules Committee, and BOA as a whole, rejected Irish and Scottish representation in order to discourage separate identity demands. Evidence has been found to suggest that the BOA had begun to send invitations of interest to Olympic officials and bodies outside Britain as early as January 1907. No record of such a letter being sent to non-English bodies within the British Isles has been found.[8] The BOA also rejected representation from the British Gymnastic Teachers Institute but set up a sub-committee to draw up a gymnastics programme for the London Games. It actively sought out Major Egerton Green, manager of the Hurlingham Club, who was co-opted to the Council as a representative of polo.[9] Neither of these could lay claim to the sporting import or membership of either the Irish or Scottish athletic bodies. The difference, of course, was that gymnastics was never going to be a nationalistic threat of any sort while polo would, if anything, have helped in reinforcing the status of the Empire in sporting terms at the London Games.

The Scots were even more angry about the refusal than the IAAA appeared to be, with the BOA secretary fielding relatively annoyed responses from both the Scottish AAA and Scottish Amateur Swimming Association, while there was no evidence of an Irish response beyond a courteous one from the IARU, 'promising to do all in their power to co-operate with the council'.[10] In an effort to head off requests for separate Olympic representation, at the same meeting the BOA considered the idea of United Kingdom representation at London, with the proposal that:

> The British Isles would count as one country, and as the entries were presumably to be limited, the Associations representing the different portions of the Kingdom would be requested to arrange with each other the athletes who should be selected to represent the country in each branch of sport.

Decision in this matter was deferred but later it was decided:

> That the Council of the BOA is extremely desirous to meet the wishes of the various swimming associations of the British Isles, and hopes that they will favourably consider a system of

proportionate representation in the various individual events, and that they will meet with the ASA [Amateur Swimming Association] of England in conference to discuss the matter and settle teams for International Team Races and International Water Polo. This means that each Association shall nominate their own men for the individual events.[11]

This step was a sort of half-way house for those seeking national representation. On the one hand, it denied the admission of separate Scottish or Irish 'teams' for London. Yet, this quota system guaranteed these nations representation in different events but only under the United Kingdom flag. Further Scottish representations for the payment of expenses to athletes were rejected. This offered Irish and Scots at least a vehicle for acceptance into the British Olympic fold. The IAAA now took up the case for representation on the BOA, with the backing of the Welsh AAA as well, until:

... the resolution was adopted that the Council was willing to give representation to bodies governing sports in Scotland, Ireland and Wales which were recognised by the corresponding governing bodies in England.[12]

The decision here was a simply founded one. Only unionist or moderately nationalist bodies could have had previous recognition from or involvement with 'corresponding governing bodies in England'. There was no question, for example, of Irish GAA participation under this stipulation, whether the GAA applied or not. By early May, the BOA had opened its doors to acceptable Irish and Scottish representation on the Council, though not on the track. 'The Hon. Sec. reported the appointment of Mr. D. Scott-Duncan as representative of the SAAA and of Dr. M.J. Bulger as representative of the IAAA.'[13] Dr Michael Bulger, former athletics champion, rugby international and one of the founders of London Irish Rugby Club, was the brother of the man who had represented the IAAA at the inaugural Olympic Congress at the Sorbonne in 1894. This BOA policy of only dealing with sporting bodies that had links with English governing bodies affected more than Irish entries for London. For instance, we find the application of the Hungarian rowers to have the closing date for their entry extended, as had been done for the crews from Belgium, Canada and Germany, being rejected. The honorary secretary was directed to tell the Hungarians that the extension of time for entries was allowed only in the case of governing bodies of rowing having treaties with the Amateur Rowing Association, and therefore the council regretted they were unable to ask the Amateur Rowing Association to alter their rule.[14]

The Hague Conference of the IOC in May 1907 was an important one for the organisers of the London Games. Its regulation defining a 'country' was central:

> A 'country' is any territory having separate representation on the International committee, or where no such representation exists, 'any territory under one and the same sovereign jurisdiction'.[15]

This definition was to become an important defence mechanism in preventing the Olympics from becoming a vehicle for nationalism among non-independent nations. As Ireland did not have separate representation on the IOC and was certainly in 1908 under the same sovereign jurisdiction as the rest of the United Kingdom, this resolution effectively also shut the door on aspirations of bodies like the IAAA for separate representation. We will see in time, particularly between 1908 and 1912, that the British Olympic Association actively embraced the idea of gaining separate IOC representation for a number of dominions, particularly where it was able to ensure that the appointed representatives were the right sort of people from the BOA's perspective.

Perusing the BOA's own documentation of 1907–8, it becomes very clear that the definition of a 'country' was to be applied quite subjectively, as was previously seen to be the case with the IOC. The representation on the IOC of both South Africa and Canada was actively pursued by Britain. Moreover, the 'selected' representative of Canada in particular was to be a BOA choice:

> On the motion of the British members it was unanimously resolved that the British colonies in South Africa should be entitled to representation . . . The Chairman stated that Colonel

Hanbury-Williams, CMG, CVO, was organising the Canadian Olympic Committee, of which the Rt. Hon. Lord Grey, GCMG, Governor-General of Canada, has kindly consented to act as President.[16]

Grey was one of the original invitees to the inaugural meeting of the BOA. Hanbury-Williams was essentially imposed on the Canadians by the BOA and was certainly one who would support rather than challenge its principles and those of the IOC.

Hanbury-Williams . . . perfectly fit the de Coubertin model for IOC membership. He was urbane, of high social and professional rank, educated, well connected, and had seen enough of the world and its contemporary affairs to lend sage and experienced voice to IOC affairs.[17]

The BOA continued its efforts to develop a dominion lobby of its choosing within the IOC after 1908. For the moment, however, the examples above highlighted one important issue. Where the aims of the IOC and BOA were convenienced by bending the rules of Olympism, those rules were certainly bent. Ironically, this worked to the occasional advantage of Irish representation during 1908, but only where it also suited the needs of the Olympic organisers and never in mainstream athletics. This was because, in order to have meaningful competitions in some sports, the British Olympic organisers were again happy to waive the definitions of countries and sovereign states. In polo, Major Egerton Green was given the all-clear to invite some teams from the Native States of India, not even representatives of India as a 'country', as early as March 1907.[18] Where commitments to staging sports dear to BOA or imperial hearts, such as hockey, polo or, curiously enough, bicycle polo, had been given for the London Games, the acceptance of Irish teams was not to be a problem either.

Irish Anticipation of the Games
The 1908 Olympic Games were held on the site of the huge Franco-British Exhibition at Shepherd's Bush in west London. The exhibition, like St Louis, contained a replica Irish village and this provoked an isolated note of

discord among Irish nationalists. Pictures of 'Ballymaclinton' show it to be very typical of the sort of scenes being depicted in early twentieth-century Ireland by people like Father Browne or found in the Lawrence Collection.[19] Yet one anonymous 'Disgusted Irishman' took the village to task for its portrayal of apparently backward rural lifestyles and conditions. His attacks were answered most vociferously by one of the Irish people employed in the village, a blacksmith named Edward Keegan.[20] This incident apart, it is fair to say that Irish interest in the 1908 Olympics was focused on the sporting contests themselves in very large measure.

In Ireland, as the 1908 Olympic Games approached, the participation of Irish athletes as part of the team representing 'Great Britain and Ireland' was eagerly anticipated and, in the national press at least, not found to cause nationalistic odium to any significant degree. The *Irish Independent,* for example, reported that:

> At a conference between the representatives of the English Amateur Athletic Association, Scottish Amateur Athletic Association and Irish Amateur Athletic Association, held yesterday at the Albion Hotel Manchester . . . teams were selected to represent Great Britain and Ireland in the Olympic Games.[21]

In its lists of those selected, the paper made no effort to identify which were Irish, Scottish or English. A separate article on the cycling events commented that 'Ireland will be represented' by a number of named athletes. Perhaps this degree of acceptance of Ireland's representation under the banner of the United Kingdom, not as a separate entity, is indicative of the *Irish Independent*'s political viewpoint, but that could be exaggerated. The *Independent* had, since 1900, been under the ownership of William Martin Murphy and his political viewpoints generally reflected a Healyite acceptance of the union within its sometime-nationalist ethos. However, we have already seen that the *Independent* was the national daily which gave most coverage to Peter O'Connor's demonstration of his Irishness in 1906, so it may be best to accept that Murphy did not impose his political viewpoint on all aspects of the paper's commentary.[22] The paper did, for instance, identify the specifically Irish competitors when the Games drew nearer, on 13 July, while the supposedly more nationalist

Freeman's Journal only referred to Irish athletes as part of the Great Britain and Ireland team once, on 14 July, while merely listing them twice as British on 21 and 22 July.[23]

The *Cork Examiner* chose a quasi-local angle for much of its anticipatory coverage of the London Games. The famed Canadian distance runner, Tom Longboat, made his final preparations for London at the home of his Irish-American manager, Tom Flanagan. Longboat and Flanagan based themselves at Flanagan's home in County Limerick. Tom Flanagan was the brother of hammer-throwing great John Flanagan, and also trained the first black American world heavyweight boxing champion, Jack Johnson, and John Hayes, whom we will meet as the 1908 marathon victor in the next chapter.[24] It was this local link, rather than the fact that Longboat had been a member of the Irish Canadian Athletic Club since winning the Boston Marathon in 1907, that excited the newspaper's interest.[25] Longboat became a local celebrity, racing against horses and taking part in a lot of high-publicity runs while in Ireland before the Games. His preparations for London received coverage, and lengthy coverage, in the widest-circulating nationalist paper in Munster in seven articles in all between 3 and 21 July, while the matter of Irish representation or the lack of it at the same Games was a non-issue for the newspaper.

The lack of a cohesive Irish viewpoint on the London Games and Irish representation was symptomatic of the confusion and lack of clear viewpoint within Irish constitutional nationalism itself. Particular factionalism was seen within the Irish Party in 1908. It was a time of uncertainty about the prospects for greater national identity under the Liberals, or indeed of the merits of alignment with conservative interests in areas like land reform and the Universities Bill. The state of more extreme nationalism made it just as unlikely that any form of clear message about Irish sovereignty or independence, in sport or otherwise, would formulate in the Irish psyche in 1908. Sinn Féin, for example, was enjoying what one commentator has termed 'some sluggish growth' in 1908, with the caveat that even as late as August 1909 the total strength of that organisation came to 581 paid-up members, 211 of these based in Dublin.[26]

At one point, it seemed that a dramatic blow for Irish identity had been struck at the London Olympics. The *Irish Independent* reported as the Games began:

> The Council of the Olympic Games has at the last moment been
> compelled to extend to Ireland some share of national
> recognition in connection with the athletes from Ireland who are
> taking part in the Olympic Sports. It will be observed that the
> geographical description of 'Great Britain and Ireland' has been
> adopted, instead of 'United Kingdom' which had been decided
> upon to designate the territorial origin of British athletes.[27]

The paper congratulated itself on its role in this apparent breakthrough,
citing an interview which it had conducted with the Irish-Americans
James E. Sullivan and Martin Sheridan as being the catalyst for this change,
and concluding:

> . . . the Council felt that there was some substance in the
> rumours that the Irishmen would refuse to put in an appearance
> if Ireland did not receive the recognition due to her, and that the
> British combination would therefore lose one of its most
> important auxiliaries.

The *Independent* here was congratulating itself merely on getting the term
'Ireland' included in the nomenclature of the United Kingdom team. This
was certainly not strident nationalism. Of course, with Sullivan and
Sheridan leading the US charge for victory over the British in 1908, it
would have suited the Americans perfectly if the Irish contribution to the
British effort could have been hived off for scoring purposes, regardless
of nationalist aims. Nor did this recognise the efforts of the IAAA and
other moderate sporting bodies behind the scenes. The breakthrough of
getting IAAA representation on the BOA council was followed by the
admission of Dr Bulger in May 1907. That, in turn, was followed by the
appointment of E.J. O'Reilly of the Irish Cyclists Association to the
Council and of W.J. Leighton, vice-president of the Irish Amateur
Swimming Association, to the Programme Committee.[28] The
Independent's claim did not take account of the fact that the IAAA had
pressed for a separate Irish team at London. However, two days after the
Independent's claim that it was its publication of Irish-American disquiet
that had achieved the reference to Ireland at all, it was forced to climb
down:

> A propos the status of Ireland in the competitions, Mr H.M.
> Finlay, Hon. Sec. of the Irish Amateur Athletic Association
> reminds us that at a conference held in Manchester on the 7th
> February . . . it had been decided that all entries to the Olympic
> Games should be made in the name of Great Britain and Ireland.
> This disposes of the suggestion that the change was decided on
> after an interview with Mr J.E. Sullivan . . .[29]

Irish competitors on this Great Britain and Ireland team were also free to wear the emblem of their country, the shamrock. Photographs of London competitions showed that, while other nations, such as the USA and Canada, had adopted national athletic crests by 1908, Britain had not, allowing for another form of national demonstration by Irish athletes without any great fuss being required. Pictures of Athea's Tim Ahearne soaring to victory in the hop, step and jump clearly show him wearing the entwined shamrocks of the IAAA on his vest. From the BOA's perspective, there is no doubt that the acknowledgement of Ireland in name and through toleration of national crests was as far as it would go. The London Games generally saw a tightening up on what was acceptable as a 'nation'. Partly because of the new-found friendship between Britain and Russia since 1907 (the Triple Entente and an Anglo-Russian trade agreement), the sort of independent representation which Finland had achieved for itself in 1906 was denied it at London, forcing the Finns, who had been given independent recognition at previous Games, to parade around the stadium with no flag in the end, because they refused to parade behind the Russian one. Much more than the Irish, the Finns had long seen the Olympic Games as an opportunity to draw attention to Finnish nationalism.[30] Yet, again, the BOA (like the IOC) took a more relaxed view of national identity when the 'nation' involved was a friend. Bohemia, for instance, was still accepted as a separate participant, partly because it still had its own IOC representative but also, undoubtedly, because Austria-Hungary was not seen as a likely British friend of any meaningful description and had an alliance with Germany dating back to the late nineteenth century. The BOA showed its imperial side even more strongly in its efforts to facilitate the participation of the Natal and Transvaal lacrosse team in the 'Winter Games' section of the London competitions, although the logistics proved unmanageable in this instance.[31]

The London Olympics occurred at a time when the GAA had all but abandoned athletics, despite its formation of a separate Athletic Council in 1905 under Frank Dineen and subsequently J.J. Keane.[32] This was even more evident in the coverage of GAA activities by the radical press than in national or local media. The *Peasant,* for example, preferred to focus on the sort of witch-hunting of regulation breakers, which was seen in Central Council minutes previously, than on promoting athletics.[33] Arthur Griffith's *Sinn Féin* was much more forthright in its attack on the GAA for the association's failure to promote athletics:

> The Gaelic Athletic Association has allowed its athletics proper to become a secondary consideration . . . But the machinations of its enemies, the indifference of its members, and the absolute treachery of a few, handed over the athletic representation of Ireland to the pitiful coterie whose aping the GAA was founded to abolish . . .[34]

Griffith, as in 1906, attacked the IAAA for apparently usurping the GAA's earlier work in athletics, declaring:

> The Athletic Association in Scotland is (like the IAAA here) purely a sectional body, representing only the universities and urban athletes. It is composed of 'gentlemen amateurs' . . . When it pleased the IAAA to inaugurate an 'International' ('Exhibition style') contest, with these 'representatives' of Alba, the Gaels were utilised to win. So in the English Championships Gaelic-trained athletes were transported to wrest laurels for the IAAA, and the GAA neither protested against the deception, penalised the perfidy of the individuals, nor undertook (what was clearly its duty) the despatch of a team of athletes to win honours in England, America or elsewhere . . . the GAA is bereft of a 'real' athletic organisation, and its cardinal ideal is a dead letter.

Sinn Féin was somewhat unbalanced in that not one of the Irish athletes who had, at IAAA instigation, attended the Olympic Games up to and including 1908 was a university graduate or from the ranks of 'urban athletes', if we take Peter O'Connor's rural Wicklow background into account and discount John Boland, who had no connections with either the IAAA or GAA in 1896. To accuse athletes of 'perfidy' for not committing themselves solely to a body which had little commitment to their sport anyway would only add to athletic polarisation. Not all GAA supporters shared the GAA's policy of ignoring both the IAAA and athletics generally. W.G. Fallon wrote an open letter to GAA leader and proponent of athletics Frank Dineen (president of the GAA Athletic Council, 1905–9) in 1907:

> But for you, Irish agility and muscle would be little more than a tradition. This is the reason why you stand so high in the estimation of many Irishmen. With regret then I note that you have not considered it advisable to bring about a cessation of hostilities between the different Irish Athletic Associations . . . Surely our interests are wider and more patriotic than that we should imitate the IAAA. The latter body has never evinced the slightest interest in the welfare of purely native talent. It has ever concerned itself with a class only. We – instead of narrowing – should extend our scope, to enlist the sympathy of every Irish athlete. Our sphere of operations should be restricted only by the four seas of Ireland.[35]

More intriguing still was the viewpoint of Sir Roger Casement. In mid-1907, Casement wrote to Bulmer Hobson on the athletic prowess of the Irish:

> The Irishman has ever been an athlete and the greatest detractors of our people have not been able to deny us the possession of swift limbs and supple bodies . . .[36]

Casement specifically made the call for an Irish entry to the London Olympics, in the process betraying a lack of understanding of the internecine rivalries of Irish sport. He saw a pivotal role for dignitaries which GAA members would certainly have seen as unionist, like Horace Plunkett, or members of the affluent middle class like Richard Croker:

> Surely some of our kindly and leisured fellow countrymen will take the matter up. There are a host of Irish gentlemen, with a

traditional love of playing the game, who could ensure a great national representation of our country if they would only try. Sir Horace Plunkett would be an ideal President, to my mind, of such a gathering as this. Dr Douglas Hyde, Mr Talbot Crosbie of Ardfert, Colonel Moore – a host of names suggest themselves. And why not Mr Richard Croker? Surely an Irish youth is a nobler animal than an Irish horse. With a tithe of her thought, energy and training, and a hundredth part of the money, Ireland might send to the great Olympiad of 1908 a team of Irish youth and manhood as perfect in form and training as ever contended of old . . . for the priceless crown of wild olive.

Following more Griffith-backed castigation of the GAA for not going to London, the secretary of the Dublin County Board, M.F. Crowe, wrote to *Sinn Féin:*

> Permit me to say that the Athletic Council of the GAA wrote to the Olympic Association with the view to entering a team representing the Irish Nation, and was informed that 'for the purpose of these games, the United Kingdom of Great Britain and Ireland is reckoned as a Single Country.' Needless to say, the members of the GAA were not disposed to allow Ireland to be treated as an English shire in the athletic interests of England, and decided to take no part in the games. I may add that it was also decided to suspend such spiritless Irishmen as may be mean enough to abjure their nationality by competing under the conditions mentioned above.[37]

While there is certainly no reference in the minutes of the BOA to any correspondence from the GAA, this does not mean that Crowe was in error here. The views of the BOA in regard to national representation, even in its dealing with moderate groups like the IAAA, could well have meant that the secretary took it upon himself to reply without feeling it necessary to refer the GAA's request to the committee at all. Had he referred it, the BOA response to the GAA would have undoubtedly been the same. One isolated American source suggested that the GAA issued a decree to athletes urging them not to compete in London:

> The Gaelic Athletic Association of Ireland has very properly entered a strong protest against the arrangements [i.e. Irish athletes classed as British] and has backed it up with an order forbidding Irish athletes to take part in the international games unless as representatives of Ireland ... The English have never manifested a disposition to admit the Irish to any share of the glory or of the profit they have reaped from their own endeavours. A becoming sense of national pride should make the Irish practice a similar exclusiveness.[38]

Of the four athletes named by the paper as being urged to boycott the Olympics, Peter O'Connor had already retired while the other three competed anyway, perhaps showing the extent to which the GAA's role in Irish athletics had become diminished by this stage. It is impossible to ascertain any further the extent of the backing for this protest within the GAA. There was no reference to it in Central Council minutes of the time, or in any of the local or national press that has been examined from 1908. It remains possible that the *Irish World* may have been relying on hearsay on this occasion, given the lack of supporting evidence that such a significant decree was issued. It was certainly mistaken in thinking that athletes like Peter O'Connor or Con Leahy, two of those named, were single-mindedly GAA athletes, and indeed the newspaper also mistakenly referred to the GAA as the 'Irish Athletic Association' elsewhere in the article. However, the appearance on the British and Irish team of several Irish athletes was eventually to contribute to considerable worsening of relations in Irish athletics and, particularly, in Irish-America.

At the Games
Irish-based athletes performed outstandingly well in London, and in greater numbers than ever before due to the relative proximity of the venue, not to mention the strong tradition of Irish involvement in the AAA championships on English soil heretofore. The London Games were also the first in which the awarding of gold, silver and bronze medals for the first three places became standard, the gold medals being solid gold, a practice which lasted for just two Olympic Games before a more low-cost gold-plated medal was introduced, which is still used today. Among

those competing under the Great Britain and Ireland banner, Joseph Deakin, one time of Clonliffe Harriers, had emigrated to England for work in 1903 and was a member of the victorious British team in the 3-mile team race. In fact, he finished the team race in first place, some 30 yards ahead of the next competitor, Archie Robertson, also of the British and Irish team.[39] Nicknamed 'The Priest' by his Clonliffe clubmates in earlier times, he also lined up the same afternoon for the heats of the 5-mile race but failed to finish, perhaps due to the effects of the champagne victory lunch after the 3-mile team success.[40]

Tim Ahearne of Athea in west Limerick won the hop, step and jump, becoming the third athlete with an Irish background (following Connolly and O'Connor) to win the event. In second place was a Canadian jumper, T. Garfield McDonald, who may well have been of Irish or Scottish extraction given that he hailed from Nova Scotia. The jump pit where Ahearne trained is still identifiable at St Michael's College in Listowel, his alma mater. In winning at London, Ahearne broke the Olympic record with a leap of 48 feet 11.25 inches, six inches better than McDonald, who had led until the final round. In setting this Olympic record at the age of twenty-two, Ahearne became the youngest athlete to break an Olympic record. For his feat, he received not only the Olympic gold medal and olive wreath, but also two diplomas of merit and a royal sprig of oak from Windsor Forest. The latter was presented to Ahearne by the king himself, Edward VII.[41] Tim Ahearne was also eighth in the long jump at London, while there is no predicting what might have been achieved by Athea men had Tim's brother Dan not recently emigrated to the USA. Dan Ahearn (spelt without the final 'e' even before he left Ireland) held the world 'triple jump' record for years after this, and won seven AAU titles in America, where his brother Tim finished second to him on four occasions.[42]

Denis Horgan of Lyre, near Banteer, at last made it to an Olympic championship and won silver in the shot put. As with Kiely and O'Connor before him, the pity was that he competed in his only Games when in the twilight of his career. In 1908, Horgan was thirty-seven years of age and past his best, not to mention that he had had a silver plate inserted in his skull as a result of a brawl he tried to break up while working as a policeman in New York in 1907.[43] In London, Horgan lost to American giant Ralph Rose, on the only known occasion when the two competed

against each other. Con Leahy, despite his part in O'Connor's protest in 1906, was accepted back to the 1908 British and Irish team and won silver in the high jump. When added to his two medals in 1906, this silver medal made Leahy the first Irish-domiciled field athlete to place in three Olympic events, a distinction which no one has equalled to this day. With Leahy now thirty-two, it was again underlined that the greatest of the Irish

Two remarkable shots of Tim Ahearne, on the opposite page and above, in action during the London Games, with the entwined shamrocks of the IAAA clearly visible on his vest. Over the Irish logo is pinned a circular badge, depicting the emblems of England, Ireland (a harp), Scotland and Wales, with the text merely stating 'Olympic Games 1908'. That the British and Irish logo included a harp rather than a shamrock suggests that the team was meant to be representative of the United Kingdom rather than of constituent athletic bodies within the British Olympic Association, such as the IAAA. Courtesy of Tim Quaid.

champions at this stage were in the twilights of their careers. Of the seven first or second places won by Irish-domiciled athletes in the Olympic Games between 1904 and 1908, Ahearne's was the only one won by an athlete under thirty. The accusation that the GAA–IAAA dispute had contributed to standards falling so low that it would take over twenty years to regain Ireland's reputation in international athletics contests was not wide of the mark when one considered the age profiles of Ireland's best performers at the Olympics of these years.[44]

We will look at Irish-American involvement in London in the forthcoming chapter. Here, a mention deserves to be made of Robert (Bobby) Kerr, who won a gold medal at London in the 200 metres and a bronze in the 100 metres for his adopted Canada. Kerr was born in Enniskillen and his family emigrated to Canada when he was seven. A public park in Hamilton, Ontario, still bears his name today. From the Irish perspective, Kerr retained a strong sense of pride in the country of his birth. Indeed, he was believed to have embarrassed the IAAA organisers of the subsequent Dublin celebration of the Irish and Irish-

Bobby Kerr being chaired from the field after victory in the 200 metres for Canada in 1908 (© IOC Lausanne).

American Olympic triumphs by declaring there that he regretted not being able to represent the country of his birth. One way or another, Kerr did return to Ireland the following year and won two events for the Irish team in the match against Scotland.[45]

The involvement of specifically Irish teams in elements of the London Games aroused remarkably little interest in the Irish media, even in those papers with a conservative inclination. Irish teams participated in both competitive and exhibition sports, essentially in sports where it would have been difficult to find sufficient international competitors to make for meaningful Olympic competition. Ireland finished second to England in field hockey and joint second in polo. Some blows for Irish identity were struck within these sports too, regardless of their largely unionist tendencies. The English Hockey Association had initially proposed that a combined team from England, Ireland, Scotland and Wales should represent Great Britain at the Games. The Irish rejected the proposal at an emergency committee meeting on 21 November 1907, and after Scotland and Wales followed the Irish line, four separate teams from the British Isles took part.[46] All but three of the Irish team which won silver

Kerr in post-Olympic pose, representing his native Ireland and with the IAAA entwined shamrock logo clearly visible on his chest. Unidentified source.

were Dublin-based. In rugby union, where Irish international representation dated back to the 1870s, Ireland, Scotland and Wales were sent invitations to compete as separate entities at the London Games but seem to have completely ignored these invites. This is a surprise, which research to date cannot explain, given that Dr Michael Bulger of the IAAA and BOA had strong rugby affiliations himself. In the end, the rugby competition saw a largely Cornish team representing Great Britain being well beaten by an Australian touring team which included many descendants of Irish immigrants, if names like Russell, Carroll, Hickey, McCabe, Griffin and Patrick McCue are anything to go by.[47]

The Irish Cyclists Association both organised and won an exhibition bicycle polo event against Germany. In fact, the Irish cyclist Ralph McCready has been credited with the invention of bicycle polo. He definitely took part in the 1912 Stockholm Olympic road race but I have been unable to track down the names of the Irish team members in the 1908 bicycle polo, despite there being photographic records of the team in action.[48] While the bicycle polo did receive a mention from the *Freeman's Journal* of 14 July, no coverage or commentary on the other team events was found in the national media. That these events took place outside of the July weeks of heightened activity at Shepherd's Bush was an undoubted factor in this omission, as certainly was the fact that the sports were non-popular. The achievements of the evident unionist Joshua (Jerry) Milner, 61-year-old member of the Irish Ulster Rifle Association, in winning the free rifle gold medal were more or less ignored. Milner had actually represented an Irish shooting team in the USA as far back as 1874, and professionally was the last commanding officer of the Carlow Militia, disbanded in 1908.[49] Nor was much made of the success of James Parke, Dublin University, in winning a silver medal in the tennis (men's doubles) competition. Milner and Parke were ignored by all but the *Irish Independent*, in which there was a single reference to Parke's 'stubborn and plucky game' in being knocked out of the Olympic singles tournament.[50] Beatrice Hill-Lowe, definitely Irish but from a location I have not been able to identify, became the first Irish woman to compete at any Olympic Games and won third place in the double national round of the women's archery competition in London.[51] To suggest that the political/social background of these competitors was the reason for national media not celebrating their Olympic successes would be excessive. Their sports were not popular ones, certainly, and the competitors were not nationalists. However, as with tennis in 1900, difficulties here were sometimes linked to the rather hit-and-miss approach of the Irish media to sports coverage. This was especially when relying on international press reports. This is borne out also by the fact that the Irish national press missed the achievement of Edward Barrett, a Kerryman, who had the distinction of becoming the first, and still only, All-Ireland-winning hurler to also collect an Olympic gold medal. Barrett won the hurling medal for London against Cork in 1901 and was a member of the City of London Police team which won the gold medal in the tug of war against the Liverpool Police. Barrett also won a bronze medal in the heavyweight freestyle wrestling and even managed a fifth place in the shot put event, but was well down the field in the javelin and discus.[52]

The reliance of many Irish-based newspapers on Reuters or Press Association reports being acknowledged, it remains remarkable that a de facto protest by Irish athletes at the opening ceremony was picked up by no Irish newspaper, with the only evidence of it happening at all coming from part of the text of a political cartoon in one American publication, which noted that 'Denny Horgan and the other Irish athletes didn't parade' with the British team.[53] Overall, the quite detached sense of national identity in many Irish newspapers was striking. Even when a newspaper like the *Cork Examiner* used its own correspondent, there was limited national drum-beating in the media. Tim Ahearne's victory was celebrated in matter-of-fact tones, with added details about his 'pretty style' and of him being 'the wearer of the Triple Shamrocks'.[54] The most vocal publication when it came to Irish identity within the Great Britain and Ireland team was the *Cork Sportsman*. Its columnist 'Jayeff' indulged in the sort of hand wringing previously seen elsewhere in provincial papers as news of Irish victories on behalf of Great Britain filtered through:

> We have learned – with mingled feelings of pleasure tempered with regret – of the success of Irishmen at the Olympic Games; pleasure because our countrymen have demonstrated once again that Irish stamina and Celtic vigour are as much in evidence as in days gone by; regret because the laurels of triumph which should rightly encircle mother Erin's brow are given to other lands which, however great and prosperous, are not and cannot be as dear to us as our own Green Isle.[55]

The writer continued to berate Irish athletic officialdom for its failure to promote Irish teams in international competition and pleaded: 'How long, then, is Ireland to be exploited for the athletic advancement of other nations?' Before seeing this as an anti-British protest, we note that the same author then proceeded to list off the great Irish athletes who had had to represent other nations – all were on the US team! A week later, 'Jayeff' elaborated:

> It is sad perhaps to contemplate that Hayes [the marathon
> winner] ran for the Stars and Stripes, Hefferon [marathon
> runner-up] for South Africa, and Lynch for Australia . . . The
> exiled children of the Gael build up the greatness and prosperity
> of other nations.[56]

It was the impact of emigration rather than the imposition of British
identity on the Irish athletes which was being confronted here. Indeed, in
no newspaper, either national or local, was attack by an Irish-domiciled
journalist on the 'Great Britain and Ireland' umbrella of Irish-domiciled
athletes found. Such attacks would come from the other side of the
Atlantic. The *Cork Sportsman* carried several commentaries after the
Games, with its writer 'Carbery' calling on the ruling powers to 'allow a
team of athletes to go forth to defend Ireland's athletic honour, and
Ireland's only.' 'Jayeff' felt the matter rested more firmly in Irish hands: 'If
we now endeavour to secure recognition, I am confident that on the next
occasion Irishmen will go forth to do battle for unconquered and
unconquerable Inisfail.'[57] Important here was the lack of interest in
whether such an Irish team would be representative of the IAAA, GAA
or both, and the lack of understanding that the international situation had
changed considerably in terms of Irish entry prospects, particularly since
the foundation of the BOA. Only *Sinn Féin* of the Irish-based newspapers
attacked the involvement of Irish athletes on the Great Britain and Ireland
team:

> The Olympic Games of 1908 are over. England has won the ping
> pong and other garden party tournaments. America has won
> the Olympic Games . . . The officials who were guilty of breaches
> of duty in helping the Italian home in the Marathon race,
> because an Irish American was following close behind instead
> of a British favourite, admit they did wrong . . . England has
> learned one lesson from the Olympic games, if she has not
> learned any other. That is, that America is not, as was popularly
> supposed by England, the second great English people, but the
> second great English menace. Mr P. O'Connor of Waterford did
> not compete. It is to be hoped he refrained from doing so
> because of Ireland. It is understood some of the others from

Ireland who competed are now sorry for what they have done. It is the sorrow of the man who locks the stable door when the steed is stolen.[58]

As before, the half-accurate nature of the *Sinn Féin* commentary was striking. O'Connor, at thirty-six years of age, had never intended to compete in London; he had retired in 1906.[59] It is difficult also to reconcile the idea that British officials (including Dr Bulger of Dublin) tried to prevent the Irish-American from defeating Pietri, yet did not discover until two days later that Hayes had been 'born in Ireland'. Hayes was actually born in New York.

The GAA did participate in an international athletics competition shortly after the Olympic Games of 1908. It co-operated with the CYMS in sending a team of athletes to compete in the papal jubilee sports in Rome. One newspaper was at last able to declare: 'Ireland as an athletic country is now officially recognised and this important consideration will spur our boys to glorious effort.' However, the same writer anticipated the Leahy brothers being picked to compete, despite then-current GAA bans and the animosity of commentators like *Sinn Féin* to those who had competed under the Great Britain and Ireland banner in London.[60]

Bonding with Irish-America

We will look more directly at the huge Irish-American success in and reaction to the London Olympics in the next chapter. In terms of how Ireland itself saw Irish-America in London, little attention was paid in the Irish media to Irish-American victors, just as with Irish-domiciled ones. Negative commentary on the perceived poor sportsmanship of American officialdom (largely Irish-Americans) was never linked with Irish-American influence, although it was a feature of a number of articles in Irish papers. The *Freeman's Journal*, for example, despite its poor coverage of the Games in general and lack of interest in Irish or Irish-American performances, covered both the tug of war and 400 metres controversies between the USA and Britain, tending to side with the righteousness of the UK side much more often than not.[61] On the other hand, positive acknowledgement of Irish-American athletic prowess was rampant in all Irish newspapers which covered the athletic events:

> It was Ireland's day really at the Olympic games yesterday, when John Flanagan, the Kilmallock man, created an Olympic record by throwing the hammer 170 ft 4½ in. It must be admitted that big John is now a naturalized American, yet it cannot be gainsaid that he is a born Irishman.[62]

Flanagan himself later recalled his triumph:

> When it all came down to my last throw I knew I had to put everything into it and as it turned out I did. If I have any regret at all now, it is that I was not competing for Ireland on that day.[63]

Even here the hit-and-miss tendency in the Irish press continued. Flanagan, Matt McGrath and Con Walsh, for example, took the first three places in the hammer event. All were of Irish birth, although representing the USA or, in Walsh's case, Canada. They also garnered the distinction of winning the first official athletics gold, silver and bronze Olympic medals, all previous medals awarded being presented by the local organisers but not necessarily as part of official IOC practice or, as previously seen, not always in gold-silver-bronze denominations.[64] Yet this remarkable treble for Irish emigrants was missed completely beyond the insertion of headings like 'Flanagan's Record Throw – Walsh Third' over international press results listings, although Flanagan's Kilmallock background got a separate twelve-line reference.[65] On a human-interest level, Matt McGrath from near Nenagh had become hooked on hammer throwing while a boy, after walking to see John Flanagan throw at a sports meeting ten miles away and then trying his hand at the event when he had walked all the way back as well. He would go on to succeed his hero as Olympic champion four years later.[66] Con Walsh from Carriganimmy, County Cork, was not only a future world record holder in the hammer but also won the national championship for the longest kick of a Gaelic football in his time. He represented Canada, although he had emigrated to Seattle where he joined the police force and lived the rest of his days.[67]

Occasional interest was shown in the Irish press too in Irish-American administrators, with James Sullivan being frequently referred to and a lengthy interview with P.J. Conway, president of the Irish American

Athletic Club (the GNYIAA of old) being published by the *Cork Sportsman* on 29 August. In many respects, the Irish-American victory which had most impact in Ireland was by an athlete who, unlike Flanagan or Sheridan, was born in the USA of Irish parents, John Hayes. Hayes won the marathon race in spectacular style, after the sensational disqualification of Italy's Dorando Pietri. Pietri had crossed the line ahead of a fast-closing Hayes but only with considerable assistance from officials, who helped him on more than one occasion to regain his feet after he collapsed on the way to the line. It is worth recording that one of the officials who gave most assistance to the stricken Italian was Dr Bulger of the IAAA, who was the chief medical officer for the marathon at the London Games and who felt he had a duty to assist stricken athletes, especially amid fears that more than one marathon contestant had taken dangerous substances that day to help them to the finish.[68] While the little Italian won sympathy from all quarters, Irish newspapers immediately latched on to Hayes's Irish roots being in Nenagh, County Tipperary. Hayes was the subject of in-depth discussion and interview in Irish papers and the athlete himself was not slow to stress his Irish roots. In an interview with the *Evening Telegraph*, Hayes joked that he was 'a German from Nenagh', while a long article on him published in the *Cork Sportsman* reiterated the kind of local pride that was seen in several cases of Irish Olympic victory before this:

> Our hearts go forth to Charles Kickham's county; to Mat [*sic*] the Thrasher, Knocknagow, and all the others, and it is with love and pride that we think of Hayes. His glorious victory completely negatives the statement that the Celt lacked staying power . . .[69]

Nenagh too was quick both to acclaim Hayes and see his marketing potential:

> Our Nenagh correspondent writes: 'The winner is grandson of Mr. John Hayes of Silver Street, in this town, and the latter has been the recipient of the congratulations of the athletes and others of the town. It is expected that Hayes will be present with McGrath, Flanagan, and Sheridan, other noted American

athletes, and give exhibitions at the North Tipperary Hurling Championship matches next month.'[70]

The newspaper was, on this occasion, guilty of exaggerated anticipation, perhaps with its local correspondent even seeking to use Hayes to drum up support for hurling in north Tipperary. However, when Hayes did visit Nenagh, the reception was quite incredible, with thousands thronging the railway station to greet him:

> In fact, he was regularly mobbed, and it was with the greatest difficulty that Father Gunning prevailed on the people to allow him to enter a carriage awaiting. Immediately he entered the carriage the horses were taken from it, and it was pulled through the streets in a triumphal procession to the residence of his grandfather, Mr John Hayes, Silver Street, where the hero of the hour was presented to the members of the Urban Council and other public men, who congratulated him on his success as a Nenagh man.[71]

The native-born Nenagh man, Matt McGrath, had won silver in the hammer throw for the USA in London, and then broke the world record at Nenagh sports just a few days after Hayes's visit in 1908. That he was not afforded a similar welcome is probably explained by him not being a champion in 1908 – he was to win gold in Stockholm four years later and is commemorated today beside Hayes (and 1932 hurdles champion Bob Tisdall) in a triple statue near the town centre.

Political Divisions in Response to the Olympics
A quite divisive element after London arose with the staging of an international match at Ballsbridge, billed as 'Ireland v. America', making use of the fact that many of the American Olympic team were due to visit Ireland after the London Games. This was organised by the IAAA with, again, financial support from Richard 'Boss' Croker forthcoming to the tune of £25, in order to entertain the American visitors properly.[72] That the majority of the Irish-American athletes had no obvious difficulty with competing at an IAAA event was evidenced by the fact that there had been ongoing negotiations between the Irish American Athletic Club and the

Denis Horgan in competition outside of the London Olympics, wearing the entwined shamrocks logo of the IAAA on his vest. From Colm Murphy, *The Irish Whale*.

Irish body on the organisation of this event since before the Olympics themselves.[73] In the end, not only did champions like Flanagan, Matt McGrath and other Irish-Americans compete at Ballsbridge, so too did Ralph Rose, the athlete who had famously, or infamously depending on one's viewpoint, refused to dip the US flag to the king at the opening ceremony in London. As we will see in the next chapter, Rose had no Irish ancestry at all but was very good friends with the Irish weight-throwing members of the US team. The one leading Irish-American athlete who did not compete at Ballsbridge, and apparently for political reasons, was Martin Sheridan. Newspaper coverage of the Ballsbridge sports was more predictably in keeping with political viewpoints than was often the case. The *Freeman's Journal* was widely accused of having sold out to the Liberals against Sinn Féin in 1908, with many of its staff and contributors receiving government jobs.[74] Despite its normally paltry coverage of athletics, including the Olympics in London, the *Journal* was particularly supportive of the IAAA's initiative in organising the Ballsbridge contest.[75] By contrast, the reaction of extreme nationalism to the US athletes competing under IAAA rules came from a cynical *Sinn Féin*:

> We regret some of the Irish American athletes went to Ballsbridge under the auspices of a minor athletic body, but as the incident has served to make the premier position of the Gaelic Athletic Association clear it has not been without compensation.[76]

This event caused significant ripples in the political sphere as well, as will be seen shortly.

The 1908 Olympics were the first Games in which significant numbers of nationalist politicians showed an interest, some evidence of a growing realisation of the importance of sport in the public psyche. This was despite the fact that the first reaction of politicians to the Games seemed to be a negative one, as evidenced by the reaction at Westminster to Lord Desborough's appeal, through a telegram and reply form, to members for financial support for the Olympic Games:

> Many members, Irish and British, objected to this unusual way of asking for subscriptions, and a couple of members made no

The visit of John J. Hayes, winner of the marathon, to the House of Commons. Included are Michael J. Ryan, S. Duncan, Johnny Hayes, John Cullinan, William Joseph O'Malley and James Patrick (Jim) Sullivan. © National Portrait Gallery, London, NPG x131231.

secret of the fact that they would have subscribed but for the telegram, while others laughingly announced their intention of using the reply form for messages home to their families.[77]

Several Irish political figures responded to the victories in London. Significantly, however, in every single recorded case located to date this response was to an Irish-American victor, not an Irish-domiciled representative of Great Britain and Ireland. For example, marathon winner John Hayes and other American team members were taken on a tour of the House of Commons in the aftermath of the Games. While there, Hayes was introduced to the house by William O'Malley, MP for Connemara, and the athletes were hosted to tea by Joseph Devlin. Devlin, in turn, introduced Hayes to John Redmond. It would be excessive and wrong to see this event as a coup of some sort for a faction of the Irish Party. Devlin, for instance, was an Ancient Order of Hibernians and United Irish League leader, generally though not automatically deferential to Redmond.[78]

O'Malley had little in common with either, and had embarrassed the party by his involvement in a number of failed businesses.[79] The lack of some sort of nationalist aim to hosting the visit of the US team is perhaps best borne out by the fact that Hayes was welcomed by many non-Irish members as well:

> . . . members of both sides of the house coming over to meet him . . . Mr. O'Malley procured for Mr. Hayes the signatures of many prominent politicians in his autograph book, including those of Mr. Asquith, Mr. Birrell, Mr. Lloyd George, Sir Acland Hood, Dr Macnamara, Mr. Keir Hardie and several Irish members.[80]

John Hayes's trip to the regatta of the Lee Rowing Club in Cork proved most interesting from a political point of view. For one thing, politicians were again out to support the occasion, and gain exposure for themselves too. Augustine Roche, erstwhile nationalist MP for Cork, who also happened

Members of the Irish American Athletic Club visiting the Commons: Tom Morrissey, Louis Tewanima, Charles Hall, Ray Ewry, John J. Dolan, Jim Sullivan, John Baxter Taylor Jnr, A.P. Henry, Mel Sheppard, G. King, Robert Cloughen, Michael J. Ryan. The fact that none of the known staunch nationalists among the club, such as Sheridan and Flanagan, visited the Commons may, of course, have political overtones. © National Portrait Gallery, London, NPG x33501.

to be president of the club, was on hand to present Hayes with a gold medal. Roche presented the medal on behalf of the citizens of Cork, not the rowing club alone.[81] Also in attendance were several members of the town council and the chairman of Cork County Council. One town councillor, William Kinmonth, travelled to the USA a few weeks later to present a gold watch and an illuminated address to Hayes, suggesting that the club had had insufficient time to get one made before the athlete's Cork visit.[82]

The most controversial issue for Irish politicians was the aforementioned arrival of Irish-American athletes in Dublin for the Ballsbridge challenge on 1 August. A number of the capital's councillors became embroiled in the issue, with Alderman J.J. Davis suggesting that the city bands should meet the athletes at Westland Row station and also that the lord mayor 'should take action'.[83] In the same edition of the *Irish Independent,* a Mr M.J. Clarke declared:

> I cannot understand why no move has yet been made to give a public reception to the Irish winners at the stadium, who are to reach Dublin on Thursday night. They have certainly, and in a remarkable way, proved the physical superiority of the Irish race, and their prowess should not be ignored by their own countrymen on their landing on these shores.

Mr Clarke appeared to be including both the Irish-domiciled and Irish-American athletes in his plea for a reception. While the IAAA itself, aided by Richard Croker and other benefactors, did eventually put on a demonstration of welcome on 30 July, complete with marching bands and hospitality, the absence of Dublin's lord mayor from the occasion was severely criticised by the Mayo MP, Conor O'Kelly:

> Sir – What has become of Irish hospitality? Some of America's leading athletes are here just now and, as far as I know, nothing has been done to give them a thoroughly Irish welcome. May I ask is there such a person as Lord Mayor of Dublin?[84]

When the lord mayor replied to this query, it began to emerge that a certain degree of political point-scoring had been at the root of his absence, with his declaration:

He would have been at the reception for Mr. Hayes but that a member of the Council who had taken a prominent action in organising that welcome, had written to him not to go there. He [the Mayor] saw that gentleman had gone himself, which he thought was dishonourable.[85]

In covering the event, the New York-based *Irish World* recorded that the arriving Americans were greeted again by Joseph Devlin MP:

> Mr Devlin spoke on behalf of the militant Nationalists in Ireland. He knew the services that had been rendered to the Irish cause in the United States by these men who had fought and beaten the Saxon on his own ground at Shepherd's Bush in London.[86]

Although Irish-based newspapers were not as specific in relation to the party allegiances of attending politicians, the Home Rule-oriented *World* also recorded that:

> The so-called representatives of the defunct Sinn Féin movement were conspicuous by their absence in welcoming the representatives of the Irish American Athletic Club to Ireland's capital. Not a single one of them put in an appearance.

Among those who attended the reception was Alderman Maurice Davin, who actually presided at the reception. That this shows the degree of sporting ecumenism which we have already noted in relation to Davin is unquestionable. The dignitaries also included William Duffy MP and councillors from moderate Home Rule backgrounds, like J.M.C. Briscoe of Dublin and T.C.J. Wyse Power of Waterford, as well as several IAAA representatives.

The result of the controversy, from the political perspective, was that Dublin Corporation decided that it would not be found wanting when another possible celebration of Irish-American success came, as it did the following week when Martin Sheridan arrived in the capital, en route from his home in Mayo to Dungarvan, where he was to compete against Tom Kiely in a five-event weight contest at the Fraher Field. That event drew 10,000 spectators and saw Sheridan best in two events, Kiely winning two others and the referee, Frank Dineen, declaring all their throws in the fifth event to be fouls, thus ensuring an honourable draw between the two great champions. The difference with this reception, however, was that Sheridan was vehemently opposed to the IAAA and was an extreme nationalist, so, in deciding to honour the greatest of the Irish-American Olympians, the corporation also made a political statement of its own, albeit unwittingly or unwillingly in some parts. The motion to accept an invitation to the GAA-organised reception for Sheridan was carried at the corporation meeting but not without some dissent. Mr M. Doyle referred to the dangers of being selective in supporting such receptions, that 'there was a serious difference of opinion between two organisations in Dublin, and if they as a Corporation took sides in the matter it would be regarded as an affront to the American athletes'. Another councillor, Mr Quaid (a one-time Sinn Féin member), thought it would be lowering the character of the council to identify itself with sporting events. On this occasion, however, the lord mayor favoured attendance and the motion, proposed by Daniel McCarthy and seconded by Dr McWalter, was carried.[87]

Sheridan's Impact in Ireland
In deciding to be represented at the reception for Martin Sheridan, Dublin Corporation gave its blessing for the most striking blow for more extreme nationalism which the Olympic Games had yet presented within the island of Ireland. Sheridan, as the coming chapter will show, played a very significant part in fanning the flames of Anglo-American discord during the London Games, as well as becoming the most successful Irish-born athlete of all time at the London Games, his third and final Olympics. It was Sheridan who also initially challenged the notion of Irish athletes competing under Great Britain's colours:

> Ireland he considered is strong enough in athletics to demand national recognition in these sports, and he thought her representatives should insist upon it. Others of the team expressed similar views, and all appeared to be agreed that the Irish athletes who have signified their intention of competing should sport Irish colours.[88]

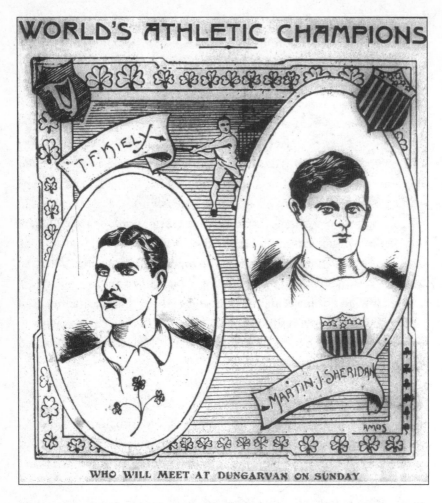

WHO WILL MEET AT DUNGARVAN ON SUNDAY

It was Sheridan, more than nationalist papers like *Sinn Féin* or the *Peasant*, who identified the Irish who competed under the Union Jack as some sort of athletic traitors:

> The only bitterness displayed by the boys of the Irish American Athletic Club is shown towards Leahy, of Dublin, who competed for the United Kingdom in the high jump, Horgan, of the New York Athletic Club, who also competed for the United Kingdom, Walsh of the Irish American Athletic Club, of New York, also in line for the United Kingdom, and Roche of the Gaelic A.A., whose score likewise goes to John Bull. All four of these men claim that they were scoring points for Ireland, but this

Two cartoons from the *Irish Weekly Freeman,* one from 25 July 1908 depicting the Irish-American Olympic champions and the other (opposite) from 15 August previewing the Kiely–Sheridan match at Dungarvan. Notice that Kiely has been drawn with the entwined shamrock emblem of the IAAA.

contention while patriotic is not practical because the very object they seek is defeated by themselves. The Irishmen want to beat England, and the only way they could do that would be to stay at home. The eight and one third points scored by those men were taken from the American team and recorded for England. No amount of patriotic argument can change that fact.[89]

There were factual inaccuracies here. There had, in fact, been two Leahys, neither from Dublin, competing in the high jump, while Walsh did not compete and James Patrick Roche of Ireland was knocked out in the two sprint events before his score could count at all.[90] The irony that one Irish-domiciled athlete who had scored most for the Great Britain and Ireland team, Tim Ahearne, was not cited by Sheridan at all even though he won a gold medal is explained by Sheridan's criticism being written while the Games were ongoing and three days before Ahearne's event took place on 25 July. Regardless, although Sheridan was writing for a US-based newspaper not widely circulated in Ireland, not even the extremities of *Sinn Féin* had resulted in the sort of naming and shaming of supposedly treacherous athletes as Sheridan indulged in here. Some of those being castigated by Sheridan were also long-standing clubmates in New York or acquaintances on the athletic field.

Sheridan in Dublin was a magnet for more extreme nationalists. The GAA immediately identified itself with him, even though almost all of Sheridan's athletic career and training had been with the GNYIAA in New York, after he had emigrated from County Mayo. J.J. Keane of the GAA Athletic Council presided over the preparations for the visit. Keane did not become president of the Athletic Council until the following year but may have been filling in for an unwell Frank Dineen. Having the tacit support of the lord mayor, who made his own carriage available to ferry Sheridan to the reception at the Gresham Hotel, was an added bonus. Sheridan, too, was very happy to identify himself with the GAA and to credit it with a major contribution to Irish athletic development. Sheridan even claimed that: 'He would be a cur and a dog if he did not adopt the principles of the Gaelic Association.'[91] In a subsequent interview, Sheridan elaborated:

> The Gaelic Athletic Association, he says, ought to control Irish athletics in a short time if they are alive to their opportunities, and to the necessity from a National point of view of their being on top. Every Irishman worthy of the name must come onto the Irish side of athletics.[92]

There was a clear sense of over-paraphrasing of Sheridan in some of the *Peasant*'s commentary, particularly where it had a chance to win GAA support from Griffith's rival nationalist publication. However, there was little doubt that these sentiments, if not necessarily all the words, were Sheridan's.

Along with the several addresses he was presented with in Dublin by the GAA, Sheridan also received one from Sinn Féin. He had become a member of Sinn Féin in New York and, given the paucity of the party's membership in 1908, it was keen to use him as a propaganda agent here. Nor did Sheridan disappoint, going further along the road of militant nationalism than even Sinn Féin might have felt comfortable with:

> He sees that new conditions have to be met in a new way and that Parliamentarianism as a force for achieving the independence of Ireland is useless . . . Sheridan knows well that only National Independence can put the Irish nation right, and he is one of those whose strength and sincerity are a national asset . . .[93]

A relatively new element which entered the national debate over Irish athletics was also found in the *Peasant*'s coverage of Sheridan's visit. There appeared the suggestion that the Irish language ought to be the language of athletic celebration. The degree to which this was the case in reality within the anglophone clubs of the GAA is uncertain; however, the newspaper expressed disquiet that the main language used on the occasion was English:

> It sounded rather curious to commend Irish games to the people and to do the greater part of the commendation in English. The revival of the games must go hand in hand with the revival of the language. We were glad to observe that unofficially the reception was much more Irish. Amongst the processionists as they marched through the city the Irish language was freely used. Some Irish choruses here and there, however, would be very welcome.[94]

In conclusion, the 1908 Olympics, from an internal Irish perspective, were seminal in the manner in which they saw considerable but largely unpublicised efforts by the IAAA, and to a lesser extent the GAA, to get

Another picture of the great Denis Horgan, again with the IAAA logo clearly visible on his vest. Courtesy of Colm Murphy.

representation for an Irish team, specifically an athletics team. These were also the Games which saw the largest Irish representation to date, and the largest Irish medal haul at thirty-three (eleven were in athletics), though those concerned were sometimes vilified for participating on the British and Irish team. The Games saw a major advance in terms of a bonding process between Irish and Irish-American athletes, though one which again caused considerable division in the context of both the Ballsbridge sports and various homecoming receptions. These were also the Games which, with varying degrees of impact, saw Irish political figures acknowledge for essentially the first time that Irish athletic achievement was something which could be harnessed for a political message. Yet, it was in the USA that the 1908 Olympic Games were to have the most profound impact on Irish social and political identity.

CHAPTER SEVEN

1908 AND THE TRIUMPH OF IRISH-AMERICA

Outside of the impact that Irish-American success at London had on Irish identity and nationalism in Ireland, the 1908 Games saw what can only be described as a huge dispute between America and Britain, and a very substantial impact on the position of Irish-Americans in the USA. The dispute manifested itself in sporting events but had origins and repercussions well beyond those events. One historian has suggested that the roots of the dispute lay in economic matters as much as anything else:

> By the beginning of the twentieth century . . . the stream of industrialisation was waning in Britain and the United States, with a seemingly endless supply of national resources, was beginning to rival and, indeed in some respects, surpass the economic achievements of England. Sport competition between the two rivals was viewed, at least by the newspapers, as a means of demonstrating the overall cultural superiority and promoting nationalism within both the United States and Great Britain.[1]

This chapter examines how the dispute involved the Irish element of American sport and, subsequently, how it affected Irish sporting, political and social status inside America.

Behind the Scenes
The rise of Irish-American sport and of the GNYIAA was already evident at the time of the 1904 Olympics. Between then and 1908, this powerful

sporting body changed its name to the Irish American Athletic Club (IAAC) and consolidated its position as the leading athletic club in the United States. One historian has identified sociological reasons for the Irish gravitation to such clubs:

> A high percentage of bachelors, delayed marriages, rigorous norms of premarital chastity, and traditions of segregation of the sexes made all-male groups far more important to the Irish Americans than to any other ethnic group. Whether married or unmarried, a male's status within the larger Irish community tended to rest on his membership and active participation in the bachelor subculture . . . The subculture furnished a refuge against loneliness, a substitute for the conjugal family, and served as an agency of social cohesion.[2]

Within Irish-American sport, 1908 was a year of some tension, though not tension which resulted in overt or divisive factions among Irish-Americans. In the latter decades of the nineteenth century, it was customary for the main sporting activities of Irish-America, including athletics, to be the preserve of independent Gaelic clubs and thereafter of the county associations in the main.[3] The arrival on the scene of the Greater New York Irish Athletic Association (later IAAC) had severely jolted the county associations by taking on board many of the new waves of Irish immigrants to New York via Ellis Island from the 1890s. The Celtic Park-based club favoured athletic pursuits clearly above the Gaelic games gaining ground in Ireland and increasingly the lifeblood of contests between county associations in the USA too. The effort by the county associations to remain independent of the IAAC and Celtic Park owners would see an attempted boycott by some of the counties of Celtic Park in 1909. In 1908, however, there was a very clear sense among the Irish, especially in New York, that:

> Sport was an important part of self-esteem for the Irish immigrant, and the US Olympic team received financial support from the county organisations in the era when the US team featured several well-known Irish-born athletes who often competed at Celtic Park.[4]

The realisation that success of Irish athletes for America in Olympic contests could assist the Irish in America was more of a unifying factor than rivalry between the counties and Celtic Park was a divisive one. Even as late as 1912, the *Irish American* reported:

> The Galway men feel that in aiding clean sport in this way [i.e. backing the Olympic team] they are promoting the interests of our race in this city and throughout the nation, it being a well known fact that America in large measure owes her devotion to track athletes to the Irish and Irish-American race within her borders. This is a matter for self-gratulation to every Irishman, who sees thus sustained all the claims of his race in manly sport, and thereby refuted many of the ignorant calumnies cast upon us by our enemies, who have tried to depict us as a debauched and inferior race.[5]

A form of watershed in Anglo-American relations was reached by 1908. Throughout the nineteenth century, Britain sought to maintain its rule of the waves, its status as the 'workshop of the world' and its Empire on which the sun never set. By 1908, all three of these 'givens' in modern British history had come under serious threat – the Germans had begun a great 'naval race' under Wilhelm II, parts of the Empire were beginning to hive off or seek greater freedom – not least Ireland – and Britain's industrial might was being threatened by Germany in Europe and, even more spectacularly, surpassed by the USA.

From its foundation, and despite its occasional pleas to the contrary, the British Olympic Association had a socio-political agenda as well as a merely sporting one. It is no accident that it was set up in a committee room of the House of Commons, that its first chairman was a Conservative MP, or that:

> ... from the beginning it was controlled by an elite of aristocratic and bourgeois sportsmen who often held positions of power in wider state structures, such as parliament, colonial administration, and the Church of England.[6]

Among the list of those invited to join the BOA's governing Council was Sir Edward Grey, the foreign secretary. Grey, although a Liberal, was the most influential figure in British diplomatic circles, especially in his determination that Britain's future lay in friendship with France and in fear of Germany.[7] Even though Grey played little subsequent part in the BOA, his invitation to join is strong evidence that the BOA saw its role as a diplomatic and not just a sporting one.

For the BOA, hosting the Olympic Games of 1908 was an opportunity to show what British organisational and sporting tradition was all about. The promotion of United Kingdom unity, traditionally British sports and colonial friendships were important aims. Hosting the Games was an opportunity to reinvigorate British sport, which was seen as the backbone of much of British success in world affairs. Wellington had suggested that Waterloo had been won on the playing fields of Eton; Theodore Cook and other members of the BOA were determined that this would continue and believed that: 'athletic traditions are in our blood, and athletic framework is constantly being bred into the best of our boys.'[8] With the Olympics under the umbrella of the great Franco-British Exhibition of 1908, the prospect of the Games helping to strengthen ties with relatively new-found allies was also an enticing one. Britain had formed its Entente Cordiale with France in 1904 and this had subsequently developed into the Triple Entente, including Russia, by 1907. Ample evidence has been unearthed to show that the British Foreign Office did quite a lot, considering the laissez-faire attitude generally to sport in government circles, to promote Anglo-French harmony through the London Games. The British organisers' reluctance to tolerate any demonstrations of Finnish separatism during the Games will, likewise, be seen as promoting new-found friendship with Russia, despite the irony of Britain also having a formal alliance with the Japanese, who had defeated Russia in a major war only three years earlier.[9]

The British Establishment and the Irish-American Challenge

In late 1907, the Amateur Athletic Union of the USA pledged its 'heartiest support' to the London Games and resolved:

> That James E. Sullivan, President of the Amateur Athletic Union be appointed to represent the Amateur Athletic Union as its Commissioner with full power at the Olympic Games in London.[10]

News of Sullivan's appointment to lead the US athletics team in London was not a surprise for the British Olympic Association. It was not, however, welcome news. Sullivan's brash and aggressive manner in Athens, his fervent 'Americanism', his obvious linkage with commercialism through the Spalding company and his antipathy towards aristocratic traditions made his appointment a cause of instant concern to the BOA. That Sullivan was to receive a special Olympic medal from Baron de Coubertin himself, chiefly for his work in organising the St Louis Games of 1904, while in London, did not help matters either. Curiously enough, Sullivan's involvement with the Spalding sports goods firm did not arouse much concern with Baron de Coubertin. In one letter to the baron, dated 29 April 1908, Sullivan converses on matters such as an outstanding bill which the company owed, presumably to the IOC, for 1907, and plans (encouraged by de Coubertin) for the establishment of a Spalding depot in Paris.[11]

James Sullivan made few if any overt statements on his own Irishness or on Anglo-Irish affairs. Yet, his background was very typical of early twentieth-century Irish-America. He was the son of a Kerry-born construction worker, left school at sixteen and became a self-made man, firstly through journalism and subsequently as president of the American Sports Publishing Company, a major subsidiary of Spalding.[12] Sullivan's Irishness was an additional reason for him being disliked by establishment figures, both in America and Britain. In commenting on his journalistic work for the *New York Morning Journal,* the *Spirit of the Times* declared: 'Mr. J.E. Sullivan degrades modern journalism. He is a renegade Irishman, the purveyor of shameful and malicious falsehoods.'[13] In a letter to de Coubertin, the BOA honorary secretary described Sullivan as 'un personage odieux, un intrigant de plus détestables', and felt clear amazement that the man was the official nominee of the president of the USA.[14] Most damning of all was the analysis of American IOC member William Sloane, who again latched on to Sullivan's working-class/Irish background: 'We all know Sullivan well, his great faults are those of his birth and breeding.'[15] Sloane, of old Anglo-American stock, was without doubt referring to Sullivan's Irish roots here, and his university professorship at Princeton and subsequently Columbia University would have made Sloane all the more likely to look down on Sullivan's class.

If Sullivan did not consistently emphasise his own Irishness, others did it for him. With both Sullivan and American team trainer Mike Murphy of Irish descent, it was automatic that their Irishness became mixed up with their positions as official envoys from the USA. Certainly, their statements and actions in London would reflect on America.[16] Mike Murphy, incidentally, the son of County Limerick parents, had achieved national fame at this point as a college athletics coach and later wrote one of the first published books on athletic conditioning, called *Athletics Training*, published in 1914. Sullivan emphasised a competitive, indeed combative spirit and a focus on track and field rather than other sports, both of which appealed greatly to Irish-American sports enthusiasts. He reported to de Coubertin prior to London:

> Great interest is being taken in them [the Olympic Games] in this country; I think we will have a very strong team. Of course you know what I mean by that, I mean track and field.[17]

For Americans generally, track and field was the be all and end all of the Olympics, whatever de Coubertin and others might wish. With the Irish American Athletic Club winning its third successive AAU club championship in 1908, and with some 30 per cent of the American athletes for London drawn from its members alone, Sullivan was quite intentionally setting the scene for confrontation between the old world and the new at London's Shepherd's Bush. With the Irish-Americans competing substantially in the track and field athletics events, combined with the US interest in athletics above all other elements of the Olympics, it was not surprising that the American team came to be considered as the 'Irish-American' team. Martin Sheridan, the Mayo-born discus champion and American captain, declared, somewhat exaggeratedly: 'Indeed if one were to go right through the team the difficulty would be to pick out those who haven't at least some strain of Irish blood in them.'[18] When Sullivan appealed to President Roosevelt for funds (which were declined) and for the president to become honorary president of the American team (which he accepted), he made it quite clear what was at stake: 'Please help us, Mr President. The sinews of athletic war, of national pride rather than individual honor, are at stake.'[19] The *New York Times* itself became both a barometer and instigator of American opinion on the London Games, with headlines like: 'Britishers

Fear Yankee Athletes' and 'We Will Knock the Spots Off the Britishers.' Historian S.W. Pope commented that: 'Such audacious declarations signalled what became a nationalistically charged showdown between the old industrial and imperial power of the world and the emergent one.'[20] Another historian of American Olympism has suggested that in 1908:

> The United States . . . perceived itself to be a young and growing power, rising in strength based on a new system of government. When American athletes fresh from the farms or factories defeated European aristocrats with nothing to do except organise their own leisure, the lesson learned was that the new world was rising at the expense of the old.[21]

The Irish in America certainly saw the London Games as a chance to do battle with and defeat Britain, simultaneously on behalf of the USA and of Ireland:

> Fit as so many Warriors, four score and three, bronze-faced, red-blooded soldiers of the track and field made up the list. They were prepared for battle but not with guns or cannon. Instead their implements of combat are speed, strength and a confidence that they will conquer the world in the London stadium.[22]

Even among old-stock Americans, the athletic ability of the Irish-American population was slowly helping to raise the status of Irish-America when contrasted with the perceived athletic – and, by definition, racial – weakness of the new immigrants from southern Europe. In a most influential article a year before the London Games, Charles Woodruff identified this very concern, specifically having examined the performances of athletes at the 1906 Athens Games:

> The stature and musculature of Europeans decrease from north to south, so that the south of Europe had exceedingly few winners in such events [jumping and throwing].[23]

Although Woodruff was reluctant to admit it directly and certainly preferred the idea of Germanic-Scandinavian immigration, for many of the old stock, the Irish, for all their perceived faults as immigrants, were now more acceptable as Americans, because:

. . . if America is to be at the front of civilisation with the other advanced nations, its blood must be constantly recruited from Northern Europe . . . Athletic decay is the first step in the process of physical decline, as in the case of the Homeric Greeks.

Controversy from the Outset

Much has been written about the events of the opening ceremony in London, specifically on how it damaged Anglo-American relations. Some of this has been exaggerated. The British organisers' failure to display the US flag at the opening ceremony caused outrage. The man responsible for the oversight, exhibition director general Imre Kiralfy, previously lived in America and had a son named Edgar who was on the American team in London, competing in the 100 metres. It is highly unlikely that the US flag was a deliberate omission on his part.[24] Yet, in the charged atmosphere of Anglo-American relations, this mattered little. Gustavus T. Kirby, a close ally of Sullivan's though with more obscure Irish connections, attacked the omission of an American flag in a celebrated pamphlet immediately after the Games.[25] Ironically, although the US flag was inadvertently omitted from the stadium display, part of the BOA Council's reply to the accusations referred to the fact that separate flags of Ireland and Scotland were displayed, but not of England itself.[26]

The second controversy of the opening ceremony has a stronger link to the Irish contingent. While all other teams dipped their national flags when saluting the personage of King Edward VII, the Americans did not. Some sources have suggested, incorrectly, that the American flag-bearer was Martin Sheridan.[27] However, most experts believe the flag-bearer was Ralph Rose, the giant shot putter. Sheridan, in fact, was subsequently quoted in the *Irish World:* 'Ah! When I saw the Stars and Stripes go marching by without going down, my heart took a great leap for joy.'[28] Rose was not an exiled and disgruntled Irishman; he was, however, heavily influenced by the Irish-American contingent. For one thing, Rose was a member of the Irish American Club. For another, he was clearly friendly with the 'Irish Whales' on the American team, as shown by his plan to accompany them to Ireland after the London Games and compete in Ballsbridge.[29] Martin Sheridan may not have been the US flag-carrier but

The front entrance to the Olympic Museum and Library, collectively known as the Olympic Studies Centre at Lausanne, Switzerland. Courtesy of the IOC Research and Reference Service, image number AABBH001.

This plaque from County Tipperary shows the degree to which parish pride in the local hurlers was developing in the 1890s. Ultimately, within a further decade, county hurling teams became truly countywide and contributed greatly to the growth of field games in the GAA and, arguably, to the decline of GAA interest in athletics.

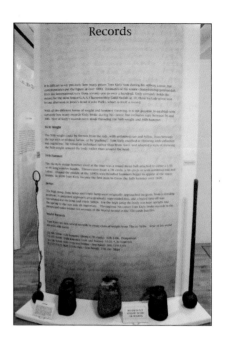

Top left: An image of the famous monument to John O'Grady on the Tipperary road out of Limerick. While focusing on the Irish involvement in the Olympic Games from 1896 to 1924, it should not be forgotten that before and during that period, the country produced a host of other great athletes who never made it to the Olympics.

Top right: The Irish weight-throwing tradition in particular was far ahead of most of the rest of the world as the Olympics dawned. Here is a collection of weights and hammers from South Tipperary County Museum in Clonmel.

Bottom left: The plaque at Lyre, County Cork commemorating Denis Horgan's achievements.

Bottom right: Tim Ahearne's gold medal from the 1908 Games.

The James B. Connolly statue in South Boston. Courtesy of Lily and Michael O'Donovan.

The certificate awarded to John Pius Boland for his victory in the tennis singles competition. Courtesy of Dr Cyril White.

Top left: The statue to John Flanagan which now stands outside his home parish church in County Limerick.

Top right: Matt McGrath's statue in front of the Courthouse at Nenagh.

Below: This is believed to be the Mannix Gate, jumped by teenager Con Leahy on his way from school.

This detail from the Kiely memorial at Ballyneale, County Tipperary shows a number of different events that the athlete competed in at St Louis.

Garda Sergeant Ned Tobin of Ballylooby, County Tipperary was another great athlete of the post-1924 era, commemorated in this massive memorial in his native village today.

The commemorative certificate presented to Michael Walker of Ireland upon his completion of the cycling race at the Stockholm Games. Courtesy of Michael Walker Jnr.

The Olympic Medal for the All Round Championship at St. Louis, 1904.

Due to an oversight, Tom Kiely's name was omitted from official Olympic records for many years. Following representations in the 1950's, by Dr. Ferene Mexo of Hungary and an examination of the medal itself, the record was finally corrected and his name reinstated as an Olympic All Round Champion of 1904.

The medal won at St Louis by Tom Kiely, with the bar inscription reading: '1904 Universal Exposition Olympic Games' and the medal itself inscribed with 'All Round Athletics Champion of the World' on one side and 'Amateur Athletic Union of the United States MDCCCLXXXVIII [1888]' on the other. The green ribbon is not the original but everything else is as it was in 1904. Courtesy of South Tipperary County Museum.

The Martin Sheridan memorial in his home village of Bohola, County Mayo.

The official certificate which Tim Ahearne received for his victory in the 1908 hop, step and jump. He is designated as a 'Member of the United Kingdom of Great Britain and Ireland team' and the certificate is signed by Lord Desborough, President of the British Olympic Council. Courtesy of Tim Quaid.

The winged Mercury memorial to Tim and Dan Ahearne at Athea, including author Tom Aherne on the left and long-standing athletics leader Ronnie Long on the right.

Top left: There were very few Irish women competitors at the Olympic Games prior to 1924. However, Sophie Peirce is commemorated in Newcastlewest as an aviator, in particular, but she also played a major role in the 1920s in furthering the involvement of women in the Olympic Games. Noel Henry's *From Sophie to Sonia* carries the full account of her remarkable Olympic involvement.

Left: The inscription on the statue to Dr Pat O'Callaghan of Derrygallon, near Banteer, who continued the great Irish hammer tradition by winning gold in 1928 and 1932.

Below left: A stylised American picture card depicting Marathon champion Johnny Hayes. Courtesy of South Tipperary County Museum.

Bottom: While the great Olympic days were over by the 1920s, several Irish athletes like Garda Seoirse Breathnach (George Walsh) of Castlemaine, County Kerry and later of Coachford, County Cork, enjoyed major success at AAA and other championships into the 1930s. Courtesy of Breathnach's Bar, Coachford.

A cartoon from the *Irish World*, 25 July 1908, depicting Ralph Rose's refusal to lower the US flag in 1908 as being akin to the American revolutionaries in 1776.

he was the acknowledged captain of the US team. Tradition has it that he was heard to declare: 'this flag dips for no earthly king' as the American team began its parade. Given what is known of Sheridan's political views, and his status among the American athletes, there must be considerable substance to this story. It became the basis of a tradition of US teams not lowering the Stars and Stripes at subsequent Olympic ceremonies.[30]

In the USA, the newspaper which most avidly dealt with this flag incident was the *Evening World*. This was also the newspaper which had contracted Martin Sheridan to send it regular reports from the Olympic Games and was to be the most vitriolic of the anti-British press in America. In covering the incident, the *Evening World* mocked the purported disdain of King Edward VII: 'My word, what an affront! Holding aloft the Stars and Stripes.'[31] The paper also mocked the supposed British amateur ethos in sport which had nonetheless seen many British companies receive royal patronage in the advertisement hoardings around the Shepherd's Bush arena:

> The King of England sat in his royal box yesterday morning, fat, happy and smiling . . . The King sat calmly, surrounded by his people, and set off in relief by a background of advertising signs . . . every sign announces 'purveyor to the King', which goes as a compliment and a guarantee. If people doubt the efficacy of a medicine they can look at the King and see how he stands it.

The *Irish World* carried coverage of the Anglo-American hostilities across its front page, with a magnificent cartoon of the flag incident showing Rose holding the flag aloft and the ghost of a patriot from 1776, possibly Washington, doing exactly the same thing beside him. The caption underneath read: 'Inspired by the Spirit of '76.'[32] The issue of whether or not the flag was lowered, whether or not Sheridan was involved, and so on, was only semi-relevant. What was central was that it typified both the tensions in Anglo-American relations of 1908 and the degree to which Irish anti-monarchical sentiments were indistinguishable from popular American ones at this time. The action of the flag-bearer, incidentally, horrified old-stock Americans, who saw Rose as representative of 'caddish, boorish manners . . . of which Americans should be heartily ashamed.'[33] Without being glib about it, these same manners were, it would seem from the earlier comments of people like William Sloane, also those of James Sullivan et al.

Problems in the Sporting Arena

In the sporting contests themselves, the initial argument between America and Britain came in the tug of war contest and the involvement of Irish-Americans in this controversy was central. Given the American focus on athletics, in some respects the concern they showed over a tug of war competition for which they were ill-prepared anyway was surprising. Tug of war, on the other hand, was a popular sport in Ireland. In addition, the Americans packed their team with leading athletes, particularly those of the heavier variety such as John Flanagan, Matt McGrath and Ralph Rose. Thus, the competition became a sort of early test of American athletics, by default. With a makeshift team, it was unsurprising that the USA was defeated very easily by an experienced Liverpool Police team. However, the Americans protested most vigorously over the footwear of the Liverpool outfit, turning the few seconds of competition into a virtual *casus belli*. Martin Sheridan did not compete in the tug of war although it is fascinating that a man (James Clarke) from Sheridan's tiny home village, Bohola, County Mayo, was on the opposition Liverpool Police team. Clarke's team eventually won the silver medals, beaten in the final by the City of London Police, who had Kerryman Edward Barrett in their ranks, as we saw in the previous chapter. Sheridan did witness and write about the USA–Liverpool incident in a celebrated article published in the *New York Evening World* during the Games:

> The American team was handed a real sour lemon here this afternoon when the tug-of-war event was announced. When our men went out into the stadium for the event they wore regulation shoes, without spikes or projecting nails or tips, as laid down in the rules for the contest. What was our surprise to find the English team wearing shoes as big as North River ferryboats, with steel topped heels and steel cleats in the front of the soles, while spikes an inch long stuck out of the soles. The Englishmen had to waddle out on the field like a lot of county Mayo ganders going down to the public pond for a swim. The shoes they wore were the biggest things over here and were clearly made for the purpose of getting away with the event by hook as well as by crook.[34]

The American reaction was excessive by all unbiased accounts of the day. The Liverpool team offered to re-pull the contest in bare feet if the Americans so wished, but all offers of rematches were spurned by the USA, with the main track and field athletic events by now under way. Yet, the stoking of the flames of discord by Sheridan was significant. They were

Two New York cartoons relating to the tug of war contest, the top one from the *Evening World* of 18 July 1908 and the other from the *Irish World* of 25 July.

fanned further by James Sullivan, though more on his return to the USA than while in London, when he wrote in the same breath of 'the prepared shoes worn by the Liverpool policemen in the tug-of-war, and the work that dishonest officials did in the committee rooms'.[35]

The tug of war issue did not even make the official list of US complaints compiled by Gustavus Kirby after the Games. In this report to the Inter-Collegiate Association of Amateur Athletes of America, dated 8 September 1908, Kirby cited thirteen reasons for American dissatisfaction with the London organisers.[36] Yet the tug of war was an incident which extremist Irish-America seized upon instantly through the *Gaelic American*, bonding with the US team in a swarm of mutual anglophobia:

> The explanation that the Liverpool policemen representing England in the tug-of-war wore only 'their usual boots' is a characteristic instance of English hypocrisy. Lord Desborough might just as well have said, 'Why, my dear sir, these are exactly the same boots that Lancashire men kick their wives with,' for all its relevancy to the charge of unfairness.[37]

The usually less extreme *Irish World* was just as vehement on the tug of war incident, again turning to its cartoonist, showing a British lion being pulled by an Uncle Sam character, the dates 1776 and 1812 tagged on to rope knots on the lion's tail and the caption 'Uncle Sam Can Win Without Spikes'.[38]

Here were some fine examples of how Irish-America empathised with the US Olympic experience and, when the opportunity arose, used the Games to highlight what its spokespeople had been telling America about Britain since the Irish began arriving in the USA. The incident was also the springboard for Irish-America to attack British injustice all over the Games, while they were still in progress. The highly influential Clan na Gael supporter and Irish-American advocate, Judge Daniel Cohalan, commented:

> Oh, no one who knows the English will be surprised at this little matter of favouritism in letting a team wear spiked shoes. It's quite typical of the English, who are always talking about fair play, that they don't know the meaning of the word, and would go far out of the way to keep from learning it . . .[39]

Another major cause of aggravation between the Americans and British arose over the disqualification of the American runner Carpenter for alleged lane infringements in the 400 metres. The British officials decided that the race ought to be re-run, the US team refused to participate, resulting in the strange sight of the British runner, Hallswelle, running the race on his own to claim the gold medal. Not one member of the Irish-American athletic fraternity was involved in this incident, yet again it was seized upon by the *Gaelic American* to promote American hostility towards the British:

> Hallswelle is a lieutenant in the British army and the British army broke the world record for running in the Boer War, as they also did in the matter of flags of truce; using white handkerchiefs, or any other old thing that was white, when regulation flags were not available . . . It was a case of appealing against the Devil with the court in hell and his Satanic majesty himself on the bench.[40]

Without doubt, the sporting event which contributed most to the American, including Irish-American, sense of antipathy towards the British was the marathon. The story of the diminutive Italian, Dorando Pietri, collapsing upon entering the Shepherd's Bush stadium, only to be assisted to the finish ahead of the American Johnny Hayes and then disqualified has been told and retold. Many Americans firmly believed that the British officials had deliberately tried to help Pietri not because of his suffering, or indeed his diminutive frame, but more simply because they wished to prevent an American from winning at all costs.[41] Ray Ewry, one of the American team members (though not of Irish background) declared on his return from London:

> I believe if those who had been following the runner around the course had seen that it was a runner from the United Kingdom who was in second place they would have been willing to hit Dorando over the head rather than have him cross the line. But it was an American who was in second place, so they wanted the Italian to win.[42]

Irish-America seized on Hayes's win not only as a vehicle for triumphalism against the supposed treachery of the old enemy but also for Irish assimilation into American national identity, perhaps inspired by the fact that Hayes, unlike Sheridan or Flanagan, was actually born in New York:

> From Windsor, the home of their kings,
> To London, he ran with the heart of the heroes
> Of Ireland, the legs and the fire of them.
> If America gave him a birthplace, he carried
> Her flag to the front, nor stumbled nor tarried
> A step on the way.
> For his fathers were sons of Tipp'rary . . .[43]

On a slightly different note, it has already been noted that the greatest hostility to those Irish athletes who were competing in London on the Great Britain and Ireland team came, at least in published form, from Irish-America through such as the writing of Martin Sheridan for the *Evening World*. Further evidence of this came from a meeting of New York Sinn Féin during the Games, where one of the resolutions was:

> That the action of those Irish athletes who competed contrary to the decision of the Gaelic Athletic Association, knowing in advance that their scores would be credited to England, deserves the severest condemnation of all Irish Americans who believe in Ireland's right to separate nationhood and in the principles of Sinn Féin.[44]

Johnny Hayes on his way to a controversial marathon victory in 1908 (© IOC Lausanne).

The more overt extremism of Irish nationalism in the USA is demonstrated by the fact that no such criticism has been found in Irish-based newspapers. Even the *Irish World* in New York, a Redmondite supporter in the main, carried negative coverage of the Irish thought to be competing for Britain:

> The Irishmen on our team and, in fact, all Irishmen are bitter against their countrymen who are competing under the colors of Great Britain and her colonies. The men are Cornelius Leahy, Thomas Kelly, Cornelius Walsh and Denis Horgan.[45]

The attack of P.J. Conway, the IAAC president, on the Irish athletes who competed for Britain gave an insight into the sense that those in Ireland who had competed for Britain had not just let Ireland down but had also hindered the triumph of America (and Irish-America) at the Games to an extent:

> Not only the Irish American Athletic Club, but the whole Irish race, have reason to be proud of the performance of the Irish-American athletes . . . if four or five Irishmen had not disgraced themselves by making points for England that no Englishman could have made, England's record would have been lowered by fully 20 points . . .[46]

Managing the News in New York

As American athletes achieved success after success in London, it brought tremendous joy to the Irish American Athletic Club in particular. Not only were its athletes beating Britain's, they were also surpassing those from other American clubs, particularly those of the New York Athletic Club (NYAC). While no special arrangements were reported from the NYAC for relaying the news of how its athletes were doing in London, the story was different at the Irish American Club following the triumphs of Sheppard and Flanagan:

> . . . the headquarters of the organisation, 163 East Sixtieth Street, presented a lively appearance last night, the clubhouse being filled and bulletins on the events eagerly sought . . . repeated cheers from the members greeted any mention of either athlete's name.[47]

> ## *Olympic Representatives*
> ### *Congratulate the I. A. A. C.*
> The following cablegram dated the Stadium, London, was received in this city to-day::
>
> P. J. Conway, President Irish-American Athletic Club, No. 163 East Sixtieth street, New York:
>
> We congratulate the Irish-American Athletic Club on the important part its athletes took in winning the track and field championship of the world. We are all proud of them.
>
> JAMES E. SULLIVAN,
American Commissioner to the Olympic Games.
GUSTAVUS KIRBY.
BARTOW S. WEEKS.
>
> The Irish-American club members scored 58½ points out of the total American score of 115 points.

The congratulatory message received by the IAAC in New York at the end of the 1908 Games. From the *Evening World*, 25 July.

While the *Evening World* counselled in one edition that not all of the Irish American Athletic Club athletes were of Irish descent, on the very same page the newspaper acknowledged the huge impact of the Irish at London through a cartoon. The illustration depicted Reggie Walker of South Africa, who had just won the 100 metres, denying the USA another victory. One spectator in the background is seen to comment: 'King Eddie was just tickled silly when Walker copped the 100 metres from America.' However, his interlocutor, who is a discus-carrying athlete (undoubtedly Sheridan) is seen to reply: 'Sure he's Irish. That's only a Philadelphia sunburn.'[48]

Irish-America used the London Games as a vehicle for Irish detestation of Britain to manifest itself. The *Gaelic American* could not hide its glee. Clan na Gael had not hitherto been particularly successful in marrying Irish and American nationalist causes; the common detestation of England at the time of the London Games was a perfect opportunity. Article upon article was written, often on events which had no Irish or Irish-American participants but always events which showed the purported British lack of fairness towards its enemies or rivals – the supposed unfairness of heat draws, the major controversy over the disqualification of the American sprinter Carpenter, constant disrespect for American symbols and representatives were highlighted by reports from Sullivan and others:

> They were friendly to every nation they could beat that was represented, and would raise their flags upon the smallest pretexts. When an American, however, finished, the raising of the Stars and Stripes, which was obligatory, was received in silence. Now, shouldn't everybody take their hats off to the American boys who went into the enemy's country and realized such glorious results?[49]

It was vital to remind Americans in general that in the forefront of the battle against this enemy at Shepherd's Bush was the Irish contingent. The victory of America was also a victory for Ireland, the Irish were the Americans, etc.:

> So let the Eagle scream, me boys, from 'Frisco to New York
> From Dublin town to Galway Bay, from Derry down to Cork.
> Hang out the starry banner and never take a dare,
> For they still raise brawny Yankees in Donegal and Clare.[50]

Once again, while more extreme Irish nationalists were to the fore in attacking the British on the Olympic front, it would be wrong to suggest that more moderate organs were lagging far behind either. Patrick Ford's *Irish World* devoted nearly as much space to the Games as the *Gaelic American* did, using headings like 'British "Fairness" in Olympic Games', 'England Gets Mollycoddle Title' and 'English Lies and Calumnies' while, under the heading 'John Bull Unmasks', was the editorial comment:

> The glaring unfairness of the English officials, whose decisions were final, has made the boast of 'English fair play' a matter of derision for the representatives of the nineteen non-English nations who took part in the London athletic contests . . . The Olympic Games have not alone demonstrated the superiority of American skill, brawn and muscle. They have done much more than that. They have stripped John Bull of the mask of friendship he assumed for his own self purpose and have shown him to be as thoroughly anti-American as he ever was in the past.[51]

Where Irish-American nationalists found it easier to attack the Irish-based athletes than the Irish press had done, the opposite was to be the case when a note of discord entered the Irish-American ranks themselves. As noted in the previous chapter, the IAAC had agreed to have some of its prominent athletes compete at the IAAA sports in Dublin before returning to the USA. Under significant pressure from the GAA and nationalist bodies, the IAAC then decided to tell its athletes to withdraw, literally as they were having breakfast on the morning of the Ballsbridge event:

> A cable despatch was received from Dublin Nationalists . . . ref to IAAA sports . . . President Conway promptly cabled his men and last Tuesday received a despatch assuring him that they would give the shoneen sports a wide berth.[52]

The American athletes did not give the IAAA event the wide berth that the IAAC and GAA had hoped for, the vast majority of them competing as an 'American' team, not as members of the Irish American Athletic Club. The *New York Sun* reported glowingly on the event itself:

> Not since the Carter–Conneff matches in 1887 has so much enthusiasm been roused by an athletic contest in Ireland as was seen today at Ball's Bridge [sic] in the games held under the auspices of the Irish Amateur Athletic Association.[53]

The article referred to the involvement of Mel Sheppard, Robert Cloughan, J.P. Sullivan, J.B. Taylor and G.V. Bonhag of the Irish American Athletic Club competing, while 'John J. Hayes, Irish American AC, who won the Marathon race at London, ran an exhibition mile in 5 minutes 40 seconds'. Yet in terms of the Irish-American press, neither the *Gaelic American* nor the *Irish American* made the slightest reference to the Americans competing at Ballsbridge despite instructions from their athletic masters not to, closing journalistic ranks when the nationalist politics of Irish-America might have been seen to offer a less-than-united front. The *Irish World* carried a lengthy account of the event but again with no reference to discord in Irish-American athletics.

The sheer impossibility of documenting every Olympic participant in 1908 who had Irish connections has been alluded to already. At least seventeen members of the IAAC took part in the London Games, with only six of these not recording a medal success of some sort. John Flanagan, as we saw, won his third hammer title and also, because of the timing of his event, became the first athlete to receive the new gold medal for victory. Martin Sheridan brought his overall total of Olympic placings to nine, with gold medals in the freestyle discus (his speciality) and the Greek-style discus, and a bronze medal in the standing long jump. Johnny Hayes, as we saw, won gold in the marathon, while Matt McGrath of Nenagh, who became a New York police inspector later in life, took silver in the hammer behind Flanagan. Cornelius (Con) Walsh, third in the hammer as we saw in the previous chapter, had been criticised by the *Irish World* as one of the Irish athletes competing under British colours, even though he had left Ireland, settled in Seattle and joined the Canadian team for London.

Things get more complex when we look at the other IAAC athletes. The club, as previously intimated, accommodated athletes who had no Irish backgrounds at all, including the great American Jew Myer Prinstein and the German-American Alvin Kraenzlein. It would continue to do so after 1908, with the mighty Finnish runner Hannes Kolehmainen winning

Martin Sheridan about to win his third Olympic freestyle discus championship, at Shepherd's Bush (© IOC Lausanne).

the senior metropolitan cross country championship in IAAC colours in 1914.[54] Perhaps the most significant non-Irish member of the IAAC in 1908 was John Baxter Taylor, who became the first African-American athlete to win a gold medal for the USA, as part of the 1,600 metres medley relay team. Taylor, sadly, died later in 1908 from typhoid fever.[55]

In terms of the Olympic triumphs of Irish-American athletes providing a highly significant boost to Irish identity in the USA, some of the other post-London developments were quite predictable. Celtic Park became, once again, a mecca for athletic contests, with the Olympic heroes as before headlining fundraising picnics and sports for Irish causes. The Ancient Order of Hibernians, for example, held a carnival there which the *New York Times* advertised with the heading: 'Members of Olympic Team will compete in AOH Games Sunday.'[56] Men like W.E. Robbins and Ralph Rose had no Irish backgrounds but their presence, along with the likes of Mel Sheppard of the IAAC, merely reflected the extent to which athletics meetings and the Irish in New York were by now synonymous.[57] Sheppard has been deliberately omitted from the listing of Irish athletes in the 1908 Games above. However, it is highly possible that he had some Irish connections, when one considers him coming from New Jersey, attempting to join the New York police force (and failing due to a weak heart) and joining the IAAC. If evidence does emerge that Sheppard was of Irish extraction, it will increase the 'Irish' Olympic medal haul substantially, given that he won three gold medals in London, in the 800 metres, 1,500 metres and 1,600 metres relay where he received the baton from Taylor on the last lap.

The use of Irish-American and other athletes' names was a deliberate attempt to attract crowds, not necessarily to put on athletic contests of the highest calibre. In the end, the AOH games attracted 15,000 spectators, but of the four Olympic athletes who did attend, two of them (John Hayes and Sheppard) did no more than exhibition jogs on the day.[58] The Clan na Gael of Connecticut advertised its field day for 29 August with the declaration that:

> Never again will there be such a chance to see those athletic celebrities compete, and the reason that we are now in a position to offer them to the public is the fact that we are getting them

Two pictures of Con Walsh, bronze medallist in the 1908 hammer. It is not clear if the action shot is from the 1908 Games, although the athlete in the background looks quite like John Flanagan. The image on the right definitely shows Walsh wearing the Seattle Police vest. Both pictures come courtesy of Con Walsh's nephew, Edward (Ned) Walsh of Carriganimmy.

just on their return to New York from the Olympic games in London.[59]

Similarly, the Irish American Athletic Club scheduled its own annual sports for Celtic Park just after this, with the promise (despite the great Martin Sheridan being still in Ireland) that:

> It is almost certain that at this meet many of the victorious athletes who fought shoulder to shoulder in the American Olympic team in London will find themselves in friendly rivalry.[60]

Irish-American assimilation was certainly given a huge boost by the Games. The *Irish World* enjoyed reminding all Americans of the debt owed to Irish athletes by producing, yet again, a telling cartoon showing Flanagan, Sheridan and McGrath with shamrocks on their vests, factually erroneous but emotively telling nonetheless. The same cartoon carried a poem poking fun at Britain and all other nations (with apologies to France) and later had 'England's New Anthem', employing the air of 'God Save the King' but now called 'God Save Our Boots', in reference to the tug of war.[61]

An intriguing episode in terms of the greening of America's Olympic success occurred at the Knickerbocker Theatre owned by George M. Cohan, where eighty-five of the US athletes were invited to a special performance. George Cohan was one of the USA's top entertainers at the time but, despite the name, was not Jewish but second-generation Irish, his name being an Americanisation of the common Galway surname, Coen.

During the second act of 'The Yankee Prince', an actor dressed as Uncle Sam came on stage and distributed Irish-American flags to the athletes in the boxes. The *New York Herald* recounted: 'The flag was formed by cutting off a section of Old Glory and adding the harp of Ireland. It was neatly printed on silk.'[62] As if the flag was not sufficient as a manifestation of America's acceptance of Ireland's contribution to its athletic glory, there followed an exchange between audience members which set the issue in even clearer relief:

> Before a dozen of the flags had been tossed into the boxes a young woman sprang from her seat and shrieked to Gregory [the actor] to stop. 'I am a daughter of the American Revolution,' she shouted in a clear, shrill voice, 'and I protest against this desecration of the American flag. I shall have you arrested. It is a shame and an outrage!' Far back in the audience a man jumped up and cried: 'I am an American soldier and I say it's all right. That flag doesn't mean anything but a compliment to the boys . . .'

According to the paper, the audience's response to the confrontation was so supportive of the soldier's defence of the flag that the young lady who had objected ran from the theatre. Cameo incident as this may have been, it was symbolic of the impact which the Irish-American Olympic successes

"FLANAGAN, — SHERIDAN, — McGRATH."

Flanagan, Sheridan, McGrath,
And "Kelly and Burke and Shea"—
Anglo-Saxons, Ha! ha! ha!
True Anglo-Saxons are we.

Great Hammer-Throwers are we,
Flanagan, Sheridan, McGrath;
We have just come over the sea
And hammered them all, tra la!

English and Scottish and Dutch,
Russians and French and Jews,
We ask their pardon as such,
And hope they will please excuse.

We're sorry they had no chance,
But hope that the times will mend—
We're sorry for old friend France—
This thing we did not intend.

Brave "Kelly and Burke and Shea,"
Flanagan, Sheridan, McGrath,
True Anglo-Saxons are we—
Ha, ha, ha, ha, HA, HA!

The *Irish World* (8 August 1908) gives Irish vests to the three Irish-born Olympic champions, who had all won gold for the USA.

had on the consciousness of New Yorkers, when a theatre, putting on a play celebrating old Yankee pride, becomes a scene of public endorsement of Irish-American assimilation, even accommodating some 'greening' of 'Old Glory' itself.

Going beyond Sport

Irish-American politicians were campaigning against American-British rapprochement for a number of years prior to 1908. The Ancient Order of Hibernians typified this, particularly in forging an alliance between the Irish and German communities in the USA. At an AOH national convention in Indianapolis, Timothy Hogan, candidate for attorney general of Ohio on the Democratic ticket, linked the AOH's anti-British philosophy directly to the reports of the Olympic Games being held in London. 'Why don't the Irish like the English?' he asked, answering himself thus: 'It's because of England's lack of the spirit of fair play, her lack of consideration for others.'[63]

Unsurprisingly, the mouthpiece of Clan na Gael was not slow in adding its voice to the Olympic-generated sense of hostility towards Britain. John Devoy declared the head of the American team to be a patriot who had helped to open American eyes to the folly of any purported closeness with Britain:

> James E. Sullivan . . . as an American citizen . . . should be one of the proudest men in the world. What learned editors, analytical academicians and Irish ex-patriates have failed to do by speech and other propaganda, he has accomplished, he and his fellows, automatically . . . The bubble of English friendship for America has been pricked in the most unexpected way. The Britons have shown their dislike for us by resorting to tricks that have made a comedy of that boasted though non-existent sentiment – known as British love of fair play.[64]

Devoy was masterly in his appeal to American history. He immediately linked the Olympic experience of America to warfare and, more pertinently, to an event which was designed almost automatically to raise the hackles of Yankee New Yorkers. The returning athletes were, in Devoy's eyes, as deserving of welcome as an American army returning in triumph from battlefield victory against the old foe:

> . . . if you are true Americans, go out and welcome home those gallant sons of America, whether of Irish extraction or no . . . for they ventured with the American flag in the lion's mouth, while it snarled and growled whenever by victory they glorified it. The English 'boos' and hisses which greeted every American victory were as strongly indicative of British love for the

A savage *Gaelic American* cartoon, from 17 October 1908, linking the British treatment of Ireland with its 1908 treatment of India.

American people as the British sovereigns which were abundantly subscribed in London in 1861 to break the back of the American Republic while it engaged in the life and death struggle of the Civil War.[65]

There is no doubt that the Olympics boosted the Clan na Gael campaign which sought to turn American policy against any potential US–British alliance. Later that year, Devoy was in a position to report on a great meeting of German-Irish societies in New York, including the AOH:

> Considering that English diplomacy to-day is mainly exerting itself in the Old World mainly to bring the United States into the anti-German combination, this German-Irish Alliance to checkmate England is of the first importance, especially as it has the active sympathy of large masses of native Americans and citizens of other races.[66]

The impact of such Irish- and/or German-American viewpoints within the USA prior to 1914 should not be underestimated. Any American leader who did not take cognisance of the views of his Irish and German electorate would not be destined for political longevity; it was that simple.[67]

In some British circles, too, the damage which the Olympic disputes had done to Anglo-American relations was very evident. When Thomas Rugby Burlford published his amazing attack against America, inspired by the Olympic controversies in 1908, he had no difficulty in linking the American behaviour with Irish anti-British sentiment. His pamphlet announced his intention to publish in the near future another entitled *Facts for American and Irish Liars,* and listed what he considered as provocative and biased headlines against Britain from American newspapers covering events in Ireland – 'Ireland plundered by the British', 'Irish Government is still a Tyrant's rule', 'Erin's last century of Gloom and Misery', etc.[68] Burlford was also at pains to point out the threat to Britain which came from the great melting pot of the USA:

> If we ignore the coloured population, the three great elements in the United States are: the native-born Americans, the Irish-Americans and the German-Americans. These three elements are not merely the most numerous and influential, they absolutely dominate the United States. They control both the wealth and the political power of the country. And these three elements are all anti-British. The native-born Americans and

And they call themselves Sportsmen.

American wins, Britons call it no race.

A British cartoon, from the pamphlet by Thomas Rugby Burlford, depicting how the Americans were felt to be constantly complaining at London.

the Irish are taught from infancy to hate the British, while the German-Americans, although they have long resented the claim that Americans are Anglo-Saxon, have developed their race prejudice into actual hatred in recent years . . .[69]

Returning Heroes

Given that a huge proportion of the American team had east coast bases, most of them in New York, the formal return home of the athletes saw the city *en fête*. The dominance of Irish-American political and judicial figures in the greatest of American cities also ensured that the return was used to endorse the contribution of Irishmen to the American triumph. Equally, the more anti-British elements of Irish-America used the occasion to turn the knife in any anglophilia it noted. The *Gaelic American* had, for four years prior to the Olympic Games of 1908, fought a campaign to keep the more militaristic and anti-British parts of the national anthem. When it spied the opportunity in August 1908, it returned to the same subject but this time with a more earnestly listening audience. Prior to the great parade of the victorious team, the paper noted with horror:

> The English National Anthem, 'God Save the King,' is to be sung under the thin disguise of 'America' by five hundred schoolchildren of Greater New York instead of the American National Anthem . . . If they will not withdraw this part of the performance then those present should drown the English National Anthem in a storm of hisses. That will administer a lesson to the Anglomaniacs that they will remember for some time to come.[70]

When the time came for the singing of American anthems at the victory celebration, 'The Star-Spangled Banner' in full and a de-anglicised version of 'America' were deployed. It is impossible to decipher what influence the likes of the *Gaelic American* had on this development but it is certainly one which showed how much American and Irish-American public opinion was in unison following the Olympics. Devoy subsequently reported:

> After the presentation of the medals, 1,200 children from the various schools, who were grouped in front of the viewing stand, sang the National Anthem, 'The Star Spangled Banner.' After the National Anthem they rendered 'America' to a new air composed by Professor Giacomo Quintano. This is significant of the new spirit, and it is the first time that this song has not been sung to the air of the English Royal Anthem, 'God Save the King.'[71]

If New York was going to celebrate America, it was going to celebrate Ireland too. Just as in the Knickerbocker Theatre, the notion of displaying

American emblems alongside Irish ones came very easily to New Yorkers, perhaps more easily than ever before and quite possibly more easily than it would ever be again. Devoy gloated at the amazing sights of Irish assimilation and acceptance along the Olympic parade route:

> Not since the reception to Admiral Dewey, after his return from the epoch-making victory of Manila Bay, has such a spectacle been witnessed in this city . . . The buildings along the route of the parade were decorated with American flags, and the American flags were carried by many of the paraders and spectators. The Irish flag was also in evidence, and the bands played 'The Star-Spangled Banner,' 'Hail, Columbia' and 'The Wearing of the Green' . . . All the regiments of the State National Guard and the Irish Volunteers were in line . . . a magnificent float . . . was decorated with American and Irish flags. In the centre the Marathon prize was displayed . . .[72]

Naturally enough, Irish-American leaders whipped up the old hatred, linking athletics with military prowess:

> That English King who, when he heard of the victorious charge of the Irish Brigade at Fontenoy, cried, 'Cursed be the laws which deprive me of such subjects,' might have a prototype today in some sprig of English royalty who, seeing the victories won for the United States by Irish-Americans, might well exclaim against the tyranny which drove those men or their ancestors from Ireland to seek asylum in this country.[73]

On the occasion referred to above, several weeks after the great New York parade, Martin Sheridan was in attendance, having returned from Ireland later than the others due to a family illness. In fact, this greatest of Irish Olympians would never see home again, being destined to die of pneumonia just ten years later. On the same occasion, James Sullivan found a most unique way of expressing Irish-American delight at the victory in London, bringing a lion cub on a chain to the reception, the lion symbolising British defeat, naturally. James Brendan Connolly had long seen the opportunity which athletic success offered to America as it sought to establish itself against the old world: 'For no country can find greater use for it than our own, which is standing now, awake and eager, where old Greece once slept – on the threshold of the world's leadership.'[74] Voicing the degree to which Irish athletes, and indeed athletes from other ethnic backgrounds, had copper-fastened their assimilation, Connolly reported on the Games of London and assured his readers that the American champions were 'typically American, of the Americans who are shaping the future rather than living in the past, and only America just now seems to be producing these remarkable athletes in any numbers'.[75]

Near-unanimous Approval

In all of the celebration of the American and Irish-American victories, one sour note was voiced in public. The left-wing newspaper, the *New York Evening Call,* had long been an opponent of the Tammany Hall (and Irish) control of New York politics, with all of the corruption and power-mongering that even many Irish-Americans had come to despise. When it was reported in the *New York Times* that $10,000 had been promised for the parade and banquet, the *Call* predicted that the public would be coerced into making 'voluntary' contributions. Tammany Hall's pressure on local employers, the *Call* maintained, would simply result in 'a sudden interest in the underpaid and hard-working employees denying their families the pleasure of a Sunday at the shore in order to give "voluntarily" the money necessary to entertain the Olympic athletes and their bourgeois patrons'. The *Call* condemned the effort as a ploy by 'a bunch of ward heelers, political grafters, and artistic plunderers' who aimed to 'steal the city's scant supply of real money to eat up and drink up in a political exploitation of a pseudo-reception to the Irish-American Olympic team'. In other words, as the *Call* explained, the 'spontaneous' enthusiasm for America's athletic exploits abroad was not equally visible to all social classes.[76]

There is no doubt that the *Call* had a point. Its voice remained an isolated one in the euphoria of late August 1908. The *Sun* had previously been quite ready to attack Irish-American politicians and mock barbarity on hurling and football fields. Now, however, it jumped to the defence of the athletic reception:

> If any sour and dyspeptic criticisms of to-day's parade and reception to the American athletes who took part in the

Olympic Games have been made they have been so faint as to escape general notice. The fact is that most of the people of New York are glad of the opportunity to see and to cheer the men who made such a notable record in the stadium in London ... Powerful men, skilled men, champions: New York will show them to-day how great the number of their admirers is, how powerful are their lungs and what a delighted populace thinks of the victorious Olympic team of 1908.[77]

The excellent research of John Schaeffer has shown that the entirety of the New York media, not just the Irish-American press, was besotted with the athletic victory in London.[78] Schaeffer has produced empirical evidence of how newspaper coverage saturated New York with the exploits of Irish-American victors and the despicable deeds of the English. 'Every New York newspaper carried daily accounts of the Games. The *Evening Post* had front-page coverage 80 per cent of the time. The *New York Times* had front-page coverage once. On two days, the *Herald* printed articles on its third page (the first two pages of the newspaper were advertisements). The *Sun* contained front page coverage three days.' The typical New Yorker was apprised of the happenings of the Games, and the Olympics were viewed with a lot more interest than a mere sports story. There was little difference between the coverage in the Irish-American weeklies and the established New York dailies. The central difference, as Schaeffer pointed out, was that the Irish papers continued the sentiment conveyed in the coverage to its logical end and called for a break in diplomatic relations with England.[79]

Political figures were, naturally, mindful of the kudos to be gained from association with the American victory, if not with the more vehement anglophilia of some quarters. Both candidates for presidency – W.H. Taft and W.J. Bryan – sent letters to the reception committee expressing their regret that they would be unable to attend the ceremonies. Outgoing President Roosevelt had long been an admirer of the Olympics. He found himself in a quandary in 1908 when the athletes returned. For the retiring president was, on the one hand, a founding member of the American Irish Historical Society and acutely aware of the need for Irish-American support in politics. On the other hand, he had also long pursued a course of anglophilia in his diplomacy and was certainly not going to be drawn too much into a war of words over the Games. Roosevelt received the returned athletes at Oyster Bay, his New York retreat, admonishing them to cease complaining of British unfairness. 'We don't need to talk,' the president gloated, 'we've won.'[80] Roosevelt continued:

> . . . the feat that this team has performed has never been duplicated in the history of athletics. I think it is the biggest feat that has ever been performed by any team of any nation, and I congratulate all of you.[81]

Some insight into the tightrope the president had to walk, however, is found when, after drinking the health of the athletes at Oyster Bay, Roosevelt seated himself near a window, James Sullivan on one side, John Hayes on the other, the rest standing around.

> Someone recalled the charges of fraud and foul raised by the British, and the President in reply made one or two strong remarks, but with the caution that he should not be quoted in the newspapers.[82]

Further indelible evidence of the degree to which the American triumphs in London had impacted on American high society is shown by the list of members of the financial committee appointed to raise funds for the celebration. They included many leading members of 'old-stock' New York society. Included were Samuel L. Bloomingdale (John Hayes's employer/sponsor), Stuyvesant Fish, William Randolph Hearst, Cornelius Vanderbilt, Oscar Hammerstein and George Gould, whose son Jay was one of the world's top tennis players of the time.[83]

> All doubt about the scarcity of money to defray the expenses of the celebration was dispelled yesterday by the receipt of a check for $2,500 from George W. Kessler who gave a big dinner in honor of the American athletes at Richmond on the Thames, near London, shortly after the Games. Sir Thomas Lipton's representative, Mr. Melville, turned over the £500 donated by the Irish baronet. The total amount subscribed up to last night

was $7,802, and it is expected that this will increase to $10,000 before the close of the celebration.[84]

In conclusion, the 1908 Games had brought Irish-America closer to sporting, social and political acceptance in the USA than ever before. The mutual hostility of both Irish-America and mainstream Americans to Britain, and the mutual exultation in what all perceived as a victory for the USA over the old-world power helped forge a bond within which Irish-American athletes and administrators achieved a degree of importance and acceptance which had not hitherto been evident. Some of this bonding was transitory – the euphoria of the moment would give way, some of the individuals most heavily involved in the promotion of Irish-America would not be active by the time of the next Games, the competitive edge generated by the Games being London-based would not be repeated. Yet, if we are to seek a high point for Olympian promotion of Irish identity within the USA, the summer of 1908 is that high point. It gave a simultaneous and huge boost to Irish pride, to American acceptance of the Irish as 'Americans' and, indeed, to the Irish embracing of their American identity.

CHAPTER EIGHT

THE 1912 OLYMPIC GAMES AT STOCKHOLM

T he 1908 Olympics at London marked a high point in Irish and Irish-American Olympism. Yet, in the years between 1908 and the next Olympics at Stockholm, it became evident that this high point was not going to be approached again. Nor would the overt displays of Irish nationalism which had characterised the 1904, 1906 and, in several ways, the 1908 Games ever be tolerated again. This would happen because of very thorough work mainly but not exclusively by British officialdom, because of internal disputes (again) in Ireland and because of a noticeable decline in some very important quarters of Irish and Irish-American athletics.

The British Olympic Association Tightens its Control
In the aftermath of London, the BOA moved to copper-fasten its regulations, ensuring that only acceptable sporting bodies could affiliate with it and thus compete under its umbrella at the Stockholm Olympics. In January 1909, the BOA agreed that among its defined objectives were:

> To secure that the views of the National Associations governing Sport in the United Kingdom shall have their due weight and influence in the organization of the Olympic movement . . .
>
> To promote the participation, both in Olympic Games and in such other International Games of similar character as may be approved, and also in International Athletic Congresses, of representatives properly accredited by the National Athletic and

Sporting Associations, and to facilitate the attendance of such
representatives . . .'[1]

The broadening of the BOA's remit beyond the mere entry of a team
for the Olympics was important. Here, it was also seeking to control other
international sporting competitions and gatherings. These same objectives
listed, among the governing bodies entitled to nominate representatives
to the governing body of the BOA, the Irish Amateur Athletic Association,
the Irish Cyclists Association and the Irish Amateur Swimming
Association. No Welsh organisations were included but both the Scottish
AAA and the Scottish Cyclists' Union were listed.

It was clear from the BOA's stated objectives that there would never
be a door open to an organisation like the GAA, should it decide to seek
links with the BOA. Seven months later, things were further clarified
when an alteration to Rule 3 saw the organisations who could have
members on the BOA restricted to the existing list of bodies and to
'representatives nominated by such other bodies as may be invited by
the council to nominate such representatives'.[2] Thus, British Olympism
became formally self-perpetuating and 'closed' to outside influence. De
Courcy Laffan explained subsequently to de Coubertin that this policy
of relying heavily on accredited associations was also an important
defence mechanism in the fight to maintain the 'amateur' ethos of the
Games.[3]

Further evidence from this same BOA meeting showed that any
possibility of admitting new Irish representation was very unlikely. The
attendance of the representatives of the three Irish organisations at BOA
council meetings became very infrequent from this time on, perhaps due
to the distance in time to the next Games in Stockholm and the difficulties
in travelling to London for meetings, which also tended to be held on week
nights. Examination of the attendances at BOA Council meetings shows
that, out of a total of twenty-three meetings, Irish representatives made
six, with Dr Bulger of the IAAA accounting for four of these, and Messrs
Metcalf of the ICA and Leighton of the IASA making just one meeting
each. It is worth noting that the Scots, with the issue of travelling to
London for meetings being almost as complex, fared little better. The
Scottish AAA, in fact, never saw its representative attend one meeting,

although J. Blair of the Scottish Cyclists' Union managed to attend on fifteen occasions (perhaps he was London-based).[4]

In seeking out possible barriers to Irish representation in 1912, we also find that the BOA's new legal adviser was G.S. Robertson, old adversary of Boland and Irish representation. The notion that Robertson would in any way fail to block attempts at separate representation for nations within the United Kingdom at future Olympic Games was barely imaginable. Nevertheless, a very important communication arrived at the BOA from the IAAA early in 1911, pleading the case for Irish representation on the IOC prior to Stockholm. Coinciding with the first appearance in some time of Dr Bulger at a Council meeting, the minutes of the BOA noted that a letter had been received from the IAAA suggesting:

> That the time has now come when the BOA as at present formed should be dissolved, and that the British representatives on the International Olympic Committee should endeavour to obtain separate representation for England, Scotland and Ireland on the Committee.[5]

This did not go as far as to request accreditation for a separate Irish team at the next Games but was clearly designed to be the initial step towards such an outcome. Given that Ireland did not meet the acceptable criteria for Stockholm participation on other grounds, the IAAA saw the route of having separate representation on the IOC as the most logical one to follow if Irish athletics were to have representatives on the track and field of Stockholm.[6] Following discussion, the BOA minutes shut the door very firmly on such an idea, with the committee recommending (and the word 'recommend' in bold type) that the secretary be instructed to reply:

> . . . that by the constitution of the International Olympic Committee the United Kingdom forms a single nation, in the same way as Germany or the United States of America form a single nation, and that it is not within the province of the Council of the BOA to propose alterations in the constitution . . .

BOA reluctance to consider separate Irish or Scottish representation on the IOC was completely at odds with its stance on other issues. It feared a growing clamour for the establishment of national organisations in athletics, which could easily threaten the hegemony of the AAA and other Olympic-affiliated bodies. De Courcy Laffan wrote to de Coubertin of his concerns on the very issue of the possible formation of an international athletics movement, and of individual national associations, stating:

> Personally I am not inclined to regard with satisfaction the formation of these international federations in various sports. We have had in this country more than one instance of how they tie the hands of national associations and hamper their actions.[7]

That it did, ultimately, accede to the push for separate Irish and Scottish cycling teams in Stockholm was mainly because there was no threatened breakaway group likely to enter a separate cycling team from these countries, as the BOA-affiliated cycling organisations could be trusted politically. More of the answer came from the difficulties the BOA saw in relation to the 1909 Swedish proposals to allow separate football teams from England, Scotland, Wales and Ireland in Stockholm. Although there appears to have been significant support for this proposal, notably from Mr Wall of the FA, the status quo in terms of keeping British Olympic representation homogeneous and under BOA control was maintained, with the input from the legal expert being central:

> Mr. Robertson pointed out that under this rule no British team could enter, inasmuch as there was no National Football Association for the whole of the United Kingdom, and on the other hand England, Scotland, Ireland and Wales are not recognised as separate nations by the IOC.[8]

The International Context of the BOA's Activities

Some broader issues, particularly political ones, were linked to continued BOA opposition to recognition of Ireland at the Stockholm Games. For one thing, considering the substantially Tory base of the BOA, the moves towards Irish Home Rule after 1910 were a matter of major concern to its leading members. A very significant communication from de Courcy Laffan to de Coubertin in late 1910, coinciding with the preliminaries of the Parliament Act, showed just how much the prospect of both Irish Home Rule, inextricable from advancing socio-liberalism and destruction of the Lords, frightened this bastion of the sporting establishment. The Parliament Act due in 1911, with the Liberals in power needing the support of the Irish to stay there, meant the possible end of the union and the beginning of change designed to distribute wealth more equitably through old age pensions and so on:

> Thank you for your wishes for this unhappy country. You already know the election results – the more things change, the more they stay the same. We are where we were and it seems all depends on the King. It is, I think, certain that Asquith will do everything he can to get from him the promise of creating enough peers to turn the House of Lords into a government satellite. Whether the King consents or not, we will very soon find an even more dangerous crisis on our hands.[9]

This letter was certainly a response to one of similar sympathies which de Coubertin had sent in the first place. Whatever sympathies a Frenchman might or might not have felt for Britain – and de Coubertin's were strongly positive ones – the matter of what was perceived as advancing social destruction was as much a cause of concern for the baron as it was for the BOA.

The BOA also sought to ensure that IOC representation for what it considered to be reliable members of the Empire would be secured, even if it was unwilling to pursue a similar course of action for the Irish or even more 'reliable' Scots or Welsh prior to 1912. It was just a few short years since the Devolution Crisis, where such consideration of autonomy for different areas of the United Kingdom had previously been discussed, much to the concern of the Tories in particular.

The closeness of the BOA to its predominantly anglophile Empire nations, such as Australia, New Zealand, South Africa and Canada, was evident from the very first Olympic Games. For a fleeting moment in the build-up to Stockholm, an opportunity arose which might have seen Britain unite in one team with its Empire:

> The Chairman . . . [referring to an IOC meeting in Budapest last May] reported a proposal by Mr R. Coombes of the AAU of Australasia that the representatives of the Empire should

compete not as several nations but as one 'Empire Team.' This proposal was felt to be very interesting and attractive but it was decided that it was too late to take steps to carry it out in the present Olympiad.[10]

The same closeness was evident, too, as the BOA made its final preparations for travelling to Stockholm:

> I think it is very likely that the Australian and New Zealand teams and also the Canadians will come over to England, and we shall all go to Stockholm together. The British Olympic Council will have somehow to make provision for sending out some 300, which will cost about £6,000 – as far as we have ascertained . . .[11]

It was on the issue of IOC representation that the BOA's stance was the clearest. De Courcy Laffan had no problem with Monaco having a team at the London Games, despite its very tenuous claims to nationhood under the IOC guidelines. Yet, this issue of representation on the IOC, so readily denied to Irish applications, was actively sought for 'reliable' empire members:

> Monaco certainly has the right to send a team or individual participants as long as they will be citizens of Monaco. We hope to have representation from Canada and South Africa . . .[12]

It was equally important that when an Empire nation obtained representation on the IOC, someone who was likely to be anglophile would be the chosen representative. In the case of Canada, the BOA actively proposed the appointment of the British army officer Sir John Hanbury-Williams as the Canadian representative, using his former position as president of the Olympic Committee of Canada as his link with the country and even citing the fact that he was, by 1911, domiciled in Britain as a distinct advantage to Canada:

> For Canada, I expect that we will certainly have a candidate to propose to you. We do not wish to represent the British Empire ourselves, the difficulty is to find a suitable candidate who may also be able to attend the sessions [of the IOC].[13]

In another communication, de Courcy Laffan explained the history of Canada's application for IOC membership, quoting from the original letter (dated 6 December 1910) of N.H. Crow, secretary of the Canadian Amateur Athletic Union:

> I am directed to write to you for information with regard to securing representation for Canada on the International Olympic Committee. We are not aware of the regulations of this committee and therefore do not know whether we are regarded as a colony with representation through the United Kingdom or whether we are eligible for representation and membership as a nation . . .[14]

Laffan had replied to Crow on 21 December, telling him that:

> Canada is for Olympic purposes a nation and as such is entitled to a representative on the International Olympic Committee. Members are elected to the International Olympic Committee by the International Olympic Committee and not by national bodies.

Laffan also recommended in the same letter that the Canadians contact the British IOC members with the name of their nominee and the British would then bring his name to the IOC. De Courcy Laffan was at pains to stress to de Coubertin that Hanbury-Williams was the Canadian nominee and that the BOA had nothing to do with it. However, he was also clearly very happy with the choice and pushed for his acceptance with de Coubertin:

> We would have found ourselves facing an enormous difficulty if we had to tell the Canadians that the IOC refused to accept the candidate which they wanted to nominate [Originally: *Nous nous trouverions vis à vis d'une difficulté énorme si nous avions à dire aux Canadiens que le CIO refusait d'accepter le candidat qu'ils désiraient vous nominer* . . .]

Hanbury-Williams was appointed as Canada's IOC representative in April 1911, although some Canadian Olympic historians remain quite dubious as to his credentials to truly represent the country at that time.[15]

The Decline of Irish-American Influence

With the BOA taking steps to ensure that Olympism remained a support to British and imperial unity, thereby acting as a barrier to possible Irish Olympic identity, some very significant moves were also afoot in the USA between the 1908 and 1912 Games. Some old-stock Americans were quite appalled at the events of London in 1908, both in terms of how the American team had apparently been treated but also by the behaviour of some of the American contingent. In the immediate aftermath of the 'Battle of Shepherd's Bush', William Sloane wrote to de Coubertin:

> It grieves me that the American athletes were subjected to such severe criticism, which worries me though I am sure it was in part, perhaps in great part, deserved. Considering the walk in life from which they come it is a matter of congratulations that things did not turn out worse . . . he [Sullivan] is unfortunately a representative man and holds the organised athletics of the clubs in the hollow of his hand . . . So as usual, dear Pierre, I come exactly to your way of thinking though I resent the pretended virtue of British sport. Its jealousy of the Irish, whether native-born or of Irish descent, is patent to all and natural, though not generous. They are, once and for all it must be admitted, foremost in certain lines and we have to make the best we can of their bitterness towards the English.[16]

Amid the backhanded compliments to the Irish in America and criticism of British sport, one issue shone through Sloane's analysis. The behaviour of Irish-led America in London was an embarrassment to 'respectable' America and steps would be taken to avoid any repetition in Stockholm. Sloane also suggested a solution. On the matter of a proposed international management committee for Stockholm, he identified a way forward for US Olympism without the same degree of input from Sullivan or Irish-America as had obtained in London: 'I feel that two intelligent active American members could hereafter mitigate if not abolish the evils that have been perpetrated in the American name.' In subsequent correspondence, Sloane acknowledged the wave of anglophobia which the London Games had unleashed, even appealing to de Coubertin's own national origin for understanding:

> Dispassionate friends are very few – with singular unanimity the Americans returning from London have spoken bitterly of the British management as both jealous and exasperating . . . I regret to say it but the same profound distrust the French people once felt for Albion is entertained in a high degree by the vast majority of my countrymen.[17]

Yet Sloane knew too that, when the dust settled and when Americans had gone back to their pre-existing 'understanding' with Britain, the issue was really one of quenching the Irish-American fire: 'Irish blood runs hot but it cools after a while.'[18] Sloane's own ancestry was Scottish Presbyterian. By early 1909, Sloane moved to consideration of how best to get more 'respectable' Americans into positions of power in the American Olympic movement and to weed out the combative and triumphalist approach with which Sullivan had led the AAU and, by relation, American Olympism:

> They [the British] have learned what it means for gentlemen to deal with self-seeking, semi-professional, self-styled 'amateurs' [i.e. Sullivan et al.] . . . As to America and American athletes we spend our lives in that as in many other directions bringing our adopted fellow-citizens to clearer and clearer comprehension of what their new allegiance means. We make very slow progress in eradicating ideas they have brought from their old homes: but we do make progress . . .[19]

By 1911, even with James Sullivan still at the helm of the AAU, the selection of an old-stock American as the US representative on the proposed Olympic management committee had Sloane gloating:

> Evert Jansen Rendell is of our best stock, English and Dutch. His family is very opulent, owning much land on this island. He has culture, refinement and delightful manners: a gentleman sportsman, our best known amateur actor, influential in all athletics, especially those of Harvard and Yale, persona gratissima in British athletic circles . . .[20]

Some historians have cast doubts on the degree to which Sullivan regarded himself as 'Irish'-American. To an extent, this is irrelevant, as it was the attitude of his adversaries to him, compounded by their attitude to the Irish generally, which is at issue here. It bears pointing out too that Sullivan did, in fact, take at least one opportunity to visit the land of his ancestors, on his way back from Stockholm in 1912. He is recorded as having visited the Davin home in south Tipperary, staying there for a few days. Of the visit, Sullivan later wrote:

> I never met a finer old man than Mr [Maurice] Davin. He had so much to tell me that I just sat there and listened with rapt attention. He was mighty interesting.[21]

We can only speculate that the near neighbour and relative of the Davins, Tom Kiely, made his way from his new home in Dungarvan to greet the man who had organised the St Louis Olympics. Among the group which visited Davin was Sullivan's cousin, Matt Halpin, who had judged at the infamous long jump competition between O'Connor and Prinstein in Athens 1906. Sullivan also visited his father's family home, in County Kerry, before returning to the USA and death in 1914, partly brought on by a car accident, at the young age of fifty-four.[22]

Although James Sullivan would control the AAU and remain the most influential administrator in the US Olympic movement until after 1912, the influence of Irish-America itself on the 1912 Games would pale by 1908 standards. That many of the great Irish-American athletes, such as Sheridan, Hayes and Flanagan, were past their best and not in Stockholm was a contributory factor in this. The Games being in neutral Sweden rather than in the cauldron of the White City, as well as the poor standard of the British opposition in Stockholm, meant that the same nationalistic edge, whether Irish-British or American-British, just was not to be found in 1912.

Another huge blow to Irish-American identity at the Stockholm Games came from the fact that athletics among the Irish in New York and elsewhere was in decline in terms of both popularity and quality. Great champions like Sheridan and Flanagan had not been replaced by other Irish-American athletes, even though the American team was at least as strong as it had been in 1908. In significant sporting respects, Irish-America had begun to go the way of Ireland, in that the team games of the GAA began to outpace athletic contests. In the *Gaelic American* in the period from June to August 1912, the adverts for the Claremen's and Mayomen's picnics featured headline hurling and/or football matches but neither mentioned athletic contests.[23] The same happened in the newspaper's 3 August edition which previewed the Irish Volunteers Games for 11 August. The Gaelic League Feis attracted 15,000 people to Celtic Park but featured no athletic contests.[24] When the Brooklyn Clan na Gael's carnival was previewed, the first and foremost sporting activity discussed was a football match. In fact, the only *Gaelic American* article or advert for an Irish-linked sports day over this three-month period which headlined athletic rather than GAA sports was after the Stockholm Games, when the Eccentric Firemen's advert announced as part of its promotion: 'World Champions will compete.'[25]

The *Gaelic American* certainly celebrated the US team's success in Stockholm, and gave an account of the victory parade. Yet, the Irish athletes in the American team were not celebrated, no gloating about victories for the old country or descriptions of green-flag-waving supporters during the victory parade appeared anywhere. This could be taken as evidence that even the *Gaelic American* had become assimilated as American by 1912 but this would not be correct. The newspaper's coverage of Irish political events like the Home Rule Bill was extensive, attacking Redmond's endorsement of Home Rule by declaring in Devoy's editorial:

> Irish citizens of the United States to obey orders from London, help secure unity of understanding and action with English-speaking Republic of America and be servant of England – Redmond accepts Home Rule Bill as final settlement, makes this promise and bids England go ahead with her foreign projects. His 'monumental gall' unparalleled in history – speaks for American Irish.[26]

Equally undiminished was its anglophobia, as shown in its continuing efforts to promote a Hiberno-German alliance in the USA.[27] But the great weapon that had been the Irish-American Olympic prowess was virtually consigned to history.

Disputes within Irish Athletics

If what was going on in London, Lausanne and New York between 1908 and 1912 was to have a detrimental effect on any possible effort to enter an Irish team in Stockholm, what occurred in Ireland during the same period made absolutely sure that this would be the case. Following a period of relative harmony between the GAA and IAAA/ICA, relations between the organisations plummeted in the period before 1912. At the core lay the issue of each organisation refusing to recognise or accommodate athletes from the other side at their own meetings. Thus, the GAA refused to allow athletes who had competed for the IAAA or at IAAA meetings (on the grounds that those meetings involved participation alongside RIC, DMP and army personnel). The IAAA, meanwhile, had as a resolution the right to suspend any of its athletes who competed at GAA meetings.

Because the IAAA had the only Irish athletic connection with the British Olympic Association, and because its activities by 1912 had dwindled to a very small number of meetings in Dublin and some surrounding counties, there were precious few Irish athletes of high quality in any position to achieve places on the next British and Irish team. The poor state of IAAA athletics was highlighted just prior to the Stockholm Games by a GAA writer. While his views might have been jaundiced, none of the substantial IAAA correspondence in subsequent editions denied that:

> Outside of their own official meetings in Dublin their other meetings are confined to the DMP, RIC, and the Tramway Sports, so that in Leinster, Munster and Connaught up to the present the IAAA and ICA have only five [meetings]. Three of these have been held and two are to be held. There may be another meeting under their rules somewhere, but so far I have not seen it announced . . . The IAAA and ICA have working agreements with English and Scottish Associations to keep Gaelic athletes and cyclists from competing in England or Scotland. That is the only asset they have left . . .[28]

The dispute between the GAA and IAAA as the Stockholm Games approached was, obviously, no help to Irish athletics. The matter was

J.J. Keane, himself a great GAA athlete, became president of the Athletic Council of the GAA in 1909. Courtesy of Larry Ryder, Dr Cyril White and J.J. Brophy, Ballinasloe.

essentially now one of control over athletic sports and less about political differences. Even in the midst of the 1912 press tirades, the GAA proponent acknowledged that the stumbling block of the GAA ban on police and army would be gone once Home Rule came:

> This dispute will settle itself. The moment that Bill [i.e. Home Rule] becomes an Act, the DMP will de facto be eligible to compete under GAA laws. The entente cordiale will do more than that, for when the RIC come under Home Government

they also will be eligible to compete under Gaelic laws. Only Mr Thomas Atkins [i.e. British soldiers] will be then left to the ICA and IAAA . . . I have written the above without consultation with any member of the Gaelic Athletic Association, but I know their views as well as any man. There can be no settlement at present . . . The Gaelic Association is bounding ahead, and to join with any other association would be to retard its progress and to nullify its distinguishing characteristics as a national association.[29]

The writer felt that most GAA opinion would accept both Home Rule and RIC membership once the time came, due to the seemingly imminent demise of the IAAA. Given that this sentiment was expressed in the middle of the 1912 Home Rule Bill debate, it suggests that there was quite a deal of moderate nationalist sentiment within the ranks of the GAA at this time.

The IAAA side was presented by several commentators, citing the GAA's ban and its lack of an international agenda as the two main obstacles to progress:

If an Irishman ambitions athletic fame and honour outside the geographical limits of his own country he must perforce detach himself from the GAA, assuming he belongs to it, and compete under the IAAA laws. Then, if he is up to the requisite standard of athletic ability, he will be chosen to represent his country against the pick of England or Scotland, or the world – as at Stockholm today in the Olympic Games. But while he continues to compete only under GAA laws no such opportunity will ever be given to him. From this it is clear to the meanest intelligence how unrepresentative must be every team chosen to represent Ireland in international athletic contests.[30]

There was a sense too that on the IAAA side, a realisation of the damage being done to Irish athletics was dawning, with the same commentator wistfully longing for a united Irish team:

Think what an athletic force this country could pit against all comers with a union between the GAA's best talent and such men as Kirwan, Newburn, O'Neill, Carroll, Barrett, Flanagan, Horgan, and the many cyclists and excellent sprinters lost to the country for lack of thorough local rivalry by being forced into camps of limited competition.

With the GAA confident that victory in the dispute would be its lot eventually, there was little likelihood of a solution to the athletic dispute coming from its ranks. One GAA writer even proposed that the association ought to move soon to take control of Irish rowing as well.[31] In terms of athletics, it remained for another IAAA proponent, T.W. Murphy, to bemoan the situation in 1912 by harking back to previous times of purported harmony:

> When both sides were working in harmony an athlete from Ireland could compete abroad in the English championships and at the Olympic Games without first having to make a choice as to which ruling body he would support at home. There have been numerous instances of men closely identified with the GAA competing in England and elsewhere, and it must always remain to the credit of the IAAA that when it selected a team to represent Ireland – not to represent itself – in an international contest, it never hesitated to ask the members of the GAA to come forward, if it happened that at the time the GAA had in its ranks better men than those in the ranks of the IAAA.[32]

None of the Irish-based athletes who had competed in the Olympic Games prior to this was exclusively a GAA athlete. Kiely, Holloway and Daly were substantially but not exclusively GAA athletes, with Daly's participation in 1906 quite possibly being under the AAA banner, as previously seen.[33] What Murphy stated here was, however, considerably more true of the annual match with Scotland, where GAA and IAAA athletes frequently lined out side by side.

Irish Cyclists at Stockholm

For reasons touched on earlier, a separate Irish cycling team for the Stockholm Games was allowed by the BOA and was supported financially too. At a meeting of the BOA in late 1911:

A photograph of five of the Irish cycling team on board the *Saga,* crossing the North Sea to Stockholm in 1912. Michael Walker, the top Irish finisher, is second from the left. Courtesy of Michael Walker Jnr.

. . . it had been intimated that the Irish Cyclists Association would probably desire to enter a team, and Mr. Blair explained that the regulations permitted the entry of teams from England,Scotland and Ireland.[34]

The six Irish cycling team members, decked out in ICA jerseys, taken after their return from Stockholm in 1912. Courtesy of Michael Walker Jnr.

The minutes recorded no stated dissension from this idea, not even from G.S. Robertson, who was in attendance, and despite the fact that the issue of separate representation in football remained a burning one for the committee at the very same meeting. Some months later, the committee had a further application before it from the Scottish Cyclists' Union, and

> . . . recommended that the BOA defray the expenses of four Scotch and four Irish competitors, leaving the Cycling Associations of these countries to provide for any further competitors that they wished to send.[35]

It is recorded that there were no Irish representatives present to plead the ICA case on this occasion, suggesting how positively disposed the BOA was to the ICA even without lobbying. It was also true that the council stood committed before any applications were received from Scotland or Ireland to defray the expenses of a team of eight from the National Cyclists' Union, possibly making it harder to say no to two other BOA-affiliated bodies, despite the additional expense it would incur. The minutes made it clear that the ICA had made an application for such support prior to this, even asking if the money would be conditional on the ICA finding additional funds to make up a full squad of six cyclists, i.e. funding two from their own resources:

> It was agreed that the grant should be unconditional, but that it should be suggested to the ICA that if at the eliminating trials the team were found to be not likely to do so well as the ICA had expected, it might be well to send only two or three competitors to take part in the individual competition.[36]

There was far from unanimous support within the ranks of the ICA for the sending of an additional pair of cyclists. The Dublin and Belfast centres of the Irish Road Club, for instance, passed a motion at their annual conference, asking that the ICA send six riders.[37] When the ICA's Records and Championships Committee met to organise the Olympic trial, the issue of sending two additional cyclists was discussed, as was the Road Club's support for it, yet the committee ultimately 'decided to take no action on the matter'.[38] This was hardly a resounding endorsement of the representation of Irish cycling at the Stockholm Olympics. In the end, six Irish cyclists did compete in Stockholm, with the BOA apparently absorbing some of the additional costs.[39] The highest-placed Irish cyclist was multiple national champion Michael Walker in sixty-seventh place, with the other five team members occupying places in the last twenty of a total of ninety-one finishers. This left Ireland with a team position, based on the first four riders home, of eleventh. It is also important to state that this was an endurance test beyond belief. The cyclists started individually at two-minute intervals, from 2 a.m. onwards, and the first Irish cyclist home took over twelve and a half hours to finish.[40]

There is no further explanation in the BOA minutes concerning the association's decision to support separate English, Irish and Scottish cycling teams for Stockholm. More remarkably, the Swedes were taken completely by surprise, it appears, by the arrival of three separate cycling teams when in every other event, as per the BOA's own regulations, 'Great Britain' had only one recognised team. On the day before the cycling road race, France lodged an objection to what it, and many other nations, regarded as a clear breach of the rules on national representation. The cycling committee noted that they

> ... regretted that this concession had been made, but declared at the same time that, as the teams from the countries in question had come to Sweden to take part in the event, the Swedish Cycling Committee did not wish to prevent them from doing so, and that the Swedish Cycling Association intended to take the responsibility for their so doing on its own shoulders, should any steps be taken in the matter by the Union Cycliste Internationale.[41]

The decline in the fortunes of Irish athletics, even in the four years since London, is mirrored in the decreased coverage of the Olympics by the Irish media. *Sinn Féin* was reduced to a few short paragraphs bemoaning the fact that Irishmen continued to be victorious but only as representatives of foreign states. In fact, the main focus of Griffith's attention on Stockholm was the opportunity to reinforce one of the Sinn Féin party's central tenets, its buy-Irish campaign, using the aforementioned cyclists:

> One remarkable record comes to Ireland. In the long distance (team) cycle race, the only team all of whose members finished was the Irish team. Two thirds of its members were mounted on Lucania bicycles – bicycles completely manufactured in Dublin. The riders of the Lucania raced on them for twelve hours in competition with the world ... In the case of every other team most of the riders had to change bicycles during the progress of the race. The Irish Lucania bicycle had thus made a world's record. And still in the city in which it is manufactured twenty foreign and inferior machines are purchased to every one of the Irish machines which beat the world at Stockholm. What slaves and what fools to our own interests we continue to be.[42]

Later, *Sinn Féin* quoted a letter from one of the Irish participants, detailing the very difficult conditions which the cyclists (and cycles) had dealt with and reinforcing the buy-Irish message quite forcefully. At no point did the issue of where the cyclists had placed in the race, or how

Michael Walker poses with what we may presume is a Lucania bicycle. Opposite a picture of the old Lucania works in South King Street. Both images courtesy of Michael Walker Jnr.

clearly their Irish identity had been displayed or recognised, come into the equation:

> None of us had the slightest trouble with our machines, although we had several bad falls, and I can tell you that numerous of our competitors' machines broke in two and forks, etc. gave way during the course of the race, and as we were the only team who had no spare machines, our machines had to bear very close scrutiny from the other competitors, both native and foreign who seemed surprised at the confidence we expressed in the ability of our machines to get through without any trouble. The result justified our confidence.[43]

How Ireland Saw the Games

Irish newspapers had little to celebrate about Stockholm. *Sport* carried a full list of results in the athletics contests, plus photographs of two DMP men who had taken part.[44] *Sinn Féin*, as previously intimated, had little athletic achievement to concern itself with, so it took a somewhat different tack. Firstly, it rebuked the non-representation of Ireland on the athletic track, presumably a jibe at the IAAA's acceptance of Irish athletes being part of the British team:

MATT McGRATH

"THE MAN who held the world's hammer-throwing record for twenty-four years, the great, kind giant who at fifty-one barely missed making the Olympic team as a weight thrower, is dead at sixty-four after two-score years on the New York police force. Hero of four Olympic games, one of the finest craftsmen in the none-too-finely taught science of throwing weights for distance, Matt dived into ice-cold rivers to rescue would-be suicides, subdued a gunman by heaving a dinnick at him, fought many a fight under what he called "the Marquis of Kilkenny" rules and in the sunset of his professional life as a cop rose to the high rank of inspector. He still held the world record for tossing the fifty-six pound weight (he threw one forty feet in 1911) and his hammer throw of almost 180 feet has been bettered fewer times than the fingers on one hand, unchallenged at all until 1936 at Berlin. An expert on how to untangle a fight crowd on Eighth Avenue, this 240-pound Tipperary cop will be missed by every sports writer who ever talked to him and by all of the police and news men who hang out for a living along Centre Market Place. As much for keeping alive the tradition of Irish strong men (it is said they were the basis for early fairy tales of prodigious English giants) as for being an honest and decent policeman for forty years, Matt McGrath slips away, leaving a trail of good will and friendly recollection seldom left by any man."

Matt McGrath went on to a long and distinguished career as a New York policeman before dying of pneumonia at the age of sixty-four. The police picture here accompanied the *New York Herald Tribune* obituary to him on 30 January 1941. The action shot (opposite) of McGrath comes from Colm Murphy, *The Irish Whale*.

Ireland was not officially represented at the Olympic games in Stockholm. Finland was. The Finns were denied the right to use a national flag, but they went there, marched in the parade without a flag, by that fact attracting even more attention and carried off many prizes.[45]

The paper further commented on the several Irishmen who had been successful under the flags of other nations, such as South Africa and the USA, with the lament that: 'As in the eighteenth century Irish valour was sold into the service of foreign countries, so now is Irish muscle.' The less extreme press harped on the same theme of Ireland's lost generations, delighting in the success of athletes like Matt McGrath from Nenagh (hammer), Pat McDonald the 6 foot 8 inch giant from Clare (shot) and Kennedy McArthur of Dervock, near Ballymoney in Antrim (marathon).

All three of these victors, the first two for the USA and the last for South Africa, were Irish emigrants representing their adopted countries. Matt McGrath had finished a close second to John Flanagan in the 1908 hammer but really came into his own in Stockholm. The shortest of his six throws in winning gold – 173 feet 4 inches – was almost fifteen feet longer than anyone else's throw and was over nine feet longer than Flanagan had thrown in 1908. The Olympic record set by McGrath in Stockholm lasted for twenty-four years.[46] McDonald, yet another New York policeman who had emigrated there from Ireland, caused a major shock by beating the giant Ralph Rose to win the shot with an Olympic record of 50 feet 4 inches. Nor was this a fluke victory, as McDonald, born McDonnell, had won the AAU title in the USA in 1911 and would do so again in 1912 and 1914. He won the Stockholm gold with his first throw. McDonald and Rose also played out an intense rivalry in the two-handed shot put event, where each participant took three puts with the right and left hand, the winner having the best aggregate distance. Rose beat McDonald with his last throw here, in an event which was never held before or since Stockholm.[47] When McGrath and McDonald visited their families in Ireland en route from Stockholm back to the USA, 'F.B.D.' of *Sport* met up with them and reported:

> McGrath told me that if all the Irishmen from all over the world combined and formed a team of their own they would at least

be second in the Olympic Games. He spoke enthusiastically of McArthur, of Co. Antrim, who won the Marathon race for South Africa, and of other Irishmen who were representing other countries.[48]

McArthur is actually still the tallest man ever to win an Olympic marathon title, at over 6 feet 1 inch. McArthur had lived in South Africa for nearly a decade by the time he competed in Stockholm, but had been little heard of even there. His greatest claim to fame in South African athletics was beating Charles Hefferon, the eventual silver medallist in London (1908), in the first marathon he ever ran, and winning five-mile and ten-mile South African championships. For winning in Stockholm, McArthur also won the challenge trophy which Johnny Hayes had received in London, a trophy presented by the king of Greece.[49] As a mildly nationalistic aside, *Sport* drew attention to the fact that the most celebrated and eventually most tragic victor in Stockholm, Jim Thorpe, had some Irish blood in his veins through a grandfather being an Ulster Scot:

> James Thorpe, who won the All-round Championship at the Olympic Games, and who a few weeks ago won the American All-Round Championship, in an interview stated that he was not a full-blooded Indian. His father was half Irish and half

Kennedy McArthur on his way to victory in the Stockholm marathon of 1912 (© IOC Lausanne).

Indian, and his mother was half French and half Indian. How is that when it is boiled down![50]

Although no Irish-based newspapers appeared to be surprised by the notion that John Flanagan was originally due to represent Britain in Stockholm, the athlete himself moved to dispel this illusion. Flanagan had been less extreme in his stance than Sheridan in 1908, happily competing in Ballsbridge at the controversial sports after the London Games. Yet, under no circumstances was he happy to accept even the rumour, unfounded as it was, that he was interested in representing Britain after his return to Ireland in 1910. Flanagan wrote to the *Gaelic American*:

> I saw where it was reported that I was to compete for England at the Olympic Games. NEVER! . . . If I were in form at the present time I would be only too glad to compete under the Starry Banner. Please give this all the circulation you possibly can as I want to refute statements in the press that I am competing for England.[51]

Perhaps it bears reiteration at this point that at least one member of Flanagan's maternal family, the Kincaids, had strong Fenian links in the USA and almost certainly knew John Devoy, as indeed John Flanagan himself did in the big village that was Irish New York. In fact, Devoy wrote to John Flanagan years later, declaring:

> It is one of my pleasant memories to stand in Celtic Park watching John's splendid figure whirl the hammer and send it flying into space. You have done more credit in the athletic field than any other Irishman, except perhaps Martin Sheridan, and I always held you as the fresh type of old Gallowglass, winning glory for Ireland . . . so long as Ireland produces John Flanagans there is hope for the future. You have no better well wisher in the world, than your old admirer, John Devoy.[52]

Falling Standards, Both in Britain and in Ireland

A particular fascination within much of the Irish reports of the Stockholm Olympics focused on the poor showing of British athletes. This came as little surprise to many athletic commentators, with Charles Otway of the *Sporting Life* declaring:

The latest news on the subject of the team does not tend to reassure those of whom are doubtful as to our prospects at Stockholm. The withdrawal of W.A. Stewart, F.G. Black and J.J. Flanagan from the list disposes of three who might be regarded as certain point-winners. P. Kirwan and T.J. Leahy do not appear in the jumping lists after all and they again would have been the probable scorers. . . . So it comes to this, in half of the events we have little if any chance, in the others we shall have to meet opposition of a far higher class than was arrayed against us in 1908 . . .[53]

The fact that three of the five likely point-scorers which Otway listed were really Irish was surely music to the ears of those critics of the Irish who had previously competed for Britain in 1908. Magnificent athletes as the likes of Percy Kirwan and T.J. Leahy were, it is unlikely that their best efforts would have been good enough to win Olympic medals in Stockholm. Even the regular columnist in *Sport* admitted as much:

England's chances of beating the world at Stockholm are not very rosy on the form displayed [i.e. at the AAA champion-ships]. The performances were well up to the average, perhaps a little above; but then that degree of excellence won't win the day in the great games . . . America will have it all her own way in that particular line.[54]

Sinn Féin was particularly gleeful afterwards at the failure of many of Britain's athletes to compete with any success, especially against the again-mighty Americans:

The strange state of mind into which the English have been thrown by their collapse at Stockholm is illustrated by the publication of a message from Prince Henry of Prussia. The Prince has telegraphed to the London 'Daily Mail' that England may console herself by looking back on her past record in athletics, for the realization that she is no longer equal to other nations. This epitaph made in Germany on England as an athletic nation has been accepted as a compliment by the British Press.[55]

What is considerably more surprising is that no commentator in the Irish press appears to have noticed that, for the first time since the inauguration of the modern Olympic Games, not one Irish-based sportsperson had come in the first three places in any event. The successes of Irish-born athletes for other countries were, of course, still highlighted, as we have seen. Many of the best of Ireland's athletes had retired by 1912 – Kiely, Horgan, O'Connor. Exceptions to this were the Ahearne brothers, Tim and Dan, from Athea, County Limerick. Tim won the hop, step and jump in 1908 and Dan was in 1912 the world record holder in the same event. Both, however, had emigrated to the USA by the time Stockholm came around. Dan won the AAU championships in 1910 and 1911 but neither of the brothers was on the US team for the Swedish capital. The attendance at Stockholm of Kirwan, Leahy and possibly some others might have made a difference to the outcome from an Irish perspective. Denis Carey of the DMP, from the same area of County Limerick as the great John Flanagan, competed in the hammer at Stockholm. He had actually thrown the hammer over 170 feet, on to the running track, at the AAA championships in June. He came a disappointing sixth in Stockholm, however, with some of the blame for his failure to win a medal being given to the use of an 'absurd guard board' at the front of the throwing circle.[56] However, it is very hard to argue with statistics when one looks for reasons for this Irish failure, whether as Irish or as British representatives. In the thirty-three years from the start of the AAA championships in 1880 up to 1912, Irish victories in traditionally strong Irish events numbered as follows: hammer – sixteen, shot – twenty-two, long jump – twenty-two and high jump – thirteen. By contrast, in the fifty-eight years of competitions after 1912, the Irish scores were: hammer – four, shot – three, long jump – zero and high jump – two.[57]

Perhaps the most clear-cut evidence that 1912, or perhaps more accurately 1908 before it, was a watershed in Irish athletics comes from the Olympics themselves. From 1912 to the present day, with the magnificent exception of Dr Pat O'Callaghan in 1928 and 1932, not one wholly Irish-trained athlete has won any Olympic title. Such statistical analysis, inevitably, has a benefit of hindsight which commentators of the day could not have. However, one contemporary journalist, F.B. (Frank) Dineen, did show an awareness that things were not as they had been, in attending the GAA annual championships at Fermoy, immediately after the Stockholm Olympics. This is all the more significant in that the highly respected Dineen was the original owner of the Jones's Road stadium and is still the only man to hold office as president and secretary general of the GAA at different times. Given that none of the Irish athletes who had gone to Stockholm was a GAA affiliate, it stood to reason that the standard on show would represent the best the GAA had to offer. Yet Dineen was moved to comment:

> It does not seem so long, yet it is four years, since the championships were held in Fermoy. Four years is not much in the life of an athlete, and yet, it would be maddening and saddening to go into detail of the ravages that four years have brought about.[58]

With no new talent emerging, Dineen felt as if he was watching the death throes of Irish athletics. Frank Dineen was a passionate advocate of athletics within the GAA, literally from its foundation. By 1912, he must have been terribly saddened by the striking irony that he had himself been an administrator over the organisation which probably bore most culpability for reneging on Ireland's athletic heritage:

> A friend of mine said they were a crowd of 'has beens.' I thought it cruel that men who were Erin's greatest glory on the athletic field should be so described, but such is fate, and such is the cynic.

The GAA's Athletic Awakening

There is considerable evidence from 1912 that many of those involved in Irish athletics had begun to realise that the demise of athletics, and cycling, had reached crisis point. That the decline in athletics was in direct contrast to the fortunes of hurling and football has been well documented. Over 18,000 watched the All Ireland football final of 1912, when the gate of £510 was the highest ever for a GAA match. Two weeks later, 20,000 paid a new record of £600 to see the hurling final. The 1910–12 period as a whole, when viewed in retrospect, was one of substantial overall progress in the spread of Gaelic games. Bigger crowds than ever attended the major fixtures, and they were entertained by standards of play that in both codes were higher than ever. Both football and hurling became permanently established on an inter-county basis, with the provincial and All Ireland championships being recognised as the principal annual competitions.[59] That their rise occurred at the expense of athletics, because of a deliberate GAA focus on developing team sports and seeing athletics as merely a weapon with which to beat the IAAA is in little doubt either. A motion, which was defeated, at the Belfast conference of the GAA in 1911 had sought the abolition of the Athletic Council because of its failure to promote athletics. The following year saw the formation of the Gaelic Athletes' and Cyclists' Union in Dublin in a breakaway effort to promote the relevant sports. This body also favoured co-operation with the ICA.

Athletic division within the GAA widened in March 1912, with the formation of the Munster Athletes' Protection Association (MAPA), due to dissatisfaction at the whole system of managing GAA athletics. J.J. Walsh was elected chairman of the MAPA and he declared:

> . . . that he was glad and proud that the athletes of Munster had a sufficiency of intellect and business ideas to combine for their own common welfare, and he considered that the time was opportune when a combination of this kind for the protection of cyclists and athletes should take place.[60]

Mr Thomas Leahy, presumably Thomas J. Leahy of the Charleville family, went a little further, clearly showing that athletes and cyclists were dissatisfied with the GAA's management of their sports and were now doing it for themselves:

> . . . the want of such an association was felt as far back as 1905. Cyclists and athletes were constantly grumbling that the Association was badly managed, and that they themselves were not properly represented on the governing body (hear, hear).

A motion from the Cork County Board on the agenda for the GAA annual convention, to be held on 7 April 1912, asked: 'That the Athletic Council be instructed by this Convention to open negotiations with all athletic governments outside Great Britain with a view to bringing about an international understanding.'[61] Nothing was to come of this motion; indeed, the fact that the IAAA and ICA controlled the international recognition of Irish athletes and cyclists would have been a stumbling block to any development anyway. With the Stockholm Olympics over and done with, and not one GAA-affiliated athlete participating, the clamour for change did not die down within GAA athletic circles. The Munster Athletes' Protection Association meeting in Dungarvan during October 1912 heard some harsh but forward-looking words from vice-president Beckett:

> The present Athletic Council was not representative of athletics. It was nominated by hurling and football men, and most of the Council didn't know how to lace a running shoe. They did not care a brass farthing about athletics.[62]

A significant development in athletics came about in the aftermath of the Stockholm Games. Basically, the mumblings about the need for a rapprochement, which began to emerge more and more from the athletes caught on both sides of the dispute, reached a volume that could not be ignored by even the most intransigent of foes. At the very same meeting where Beckett had criticised the GAA's running of athletics, he also pointed to the future:

> . . . they there present urged that at the proposed conference with the IAAA, a kindly mutual feeling should prevail, and the policy of 'open door' should be urged . . . No member of either ruling body, GAA or IAAA, had attended a meeting in the South for a number of years, and Irish athletic prestige had gone down. The object of the Protective Association was to raise the status and prestige of athletics in the South of Ireland, and to help towards the creation of an Irish national team for the next Olympic Games in Berlin.[63]

From August 1912, writers on both the IAAA and the GAA sides were arguing for a meeting to settle the dispute. T.W. Murphy, formerly of the GAA and ICA, discussed many of the issues of concern to the different parties on the pages of *Sport*, stressing that lack of international competition was the major deficit facing the GAA:

The knowledge that a request for an agreement might be refused has prevented the GAA asking for it in the past. But once it settles its differences with the IAAA it will be quite free to ask the AAA and the SAA for an agreement. I am sure the IAAA will not object. It may even support the application.[64]

Murphy ended with an impassioned plea for reconciliation:

Hang the details, let's settle the principles, and the details will take care of themselves. If three men, one from each association, got their legs under the Lord Mayor's mahogany at the Mansion House, surely a little matter like this could be settled in a few hours – I mean the principles of the matter.[65]

The dispute poisoned the holding of the Grocers' Sports in Dublin during July 1912, resulting in the Athletic Council of the GAA banning any of its athletes who had competed in the sports under IAAA auspices. That the council was finding itself increasingly out of touch with grassroots sentiment is shown by the emotional open letter from J.J. Holloway, relative of the Tipperary athlete who had competed alongside Tom Kiely at St Louis, who found himself one of the banned athletes:

By the decision of that body [Athletic Council] I am to be driven from the GAA for ever. To be accurate, I am suspended for three years, and at the expiration of that period, if I make application to the Athletic Council, I may be allowed back to the sphere of activity again, but as long as the constitution of that Council remains unaltered, so long shall I remain in my present state of retirement.[66]

For rank and file members of both ICA and GAA sides, a quick resolution to the dispute was the preferred option. *Sport* reported:

On Friday, Mr. Stephen Holland, who was one of the deputation to the committee of the night previous, had interviews with some of the cyclists, and then interviewed Mr J.J. Keane, with the result that a special meeting of the Committee was called for Friday night, for there was a desire on both sides that the trouble which had arisen at the Grocer's meeting should be tidied over, so as to allow the *Freeman* Staff meeting to run smoothly.

If anyone was, J.J. Keane was the central figure in the Athletic Council and, ultimately, would become the central figure in the future Irish Olympic Council, as well as becoming Ireland's first member of the International Olympic Committee.[67]

Another commentator, A.A. Moloney, wrote suggesting a round table conference, and the men who should represent the different organisations at the conference, men who:

> . . . represent the highest in the athletic and cycling life of the country – men of long experience whose judgment can be relied upon as were the Brehon judges of old . . . 'Sport for the whole and no exclusions' should be the motto of all bodies.[68]

Moloney certainly identified the main personalities on the different sides on his list of likely attendees – Keane, Crowe, Dineen, Murphy and others. Yet even he struggled with the mathematics of it all, failing to calculate how three GAA representatives could deal on equal terms with a total of six IAAA and ICA representatives. The suggestion of the services of the editor of *Sport* as chairman (with casting vote) would not necessarily have been appealing to the GAA either. In the end, it was the lord mayor of Dublin, Lorcan Sherlock, whose proposal and facilitation of a meeting between the heads of the different bodies was central to the move towards resolution of the athletics dispute. That Sherlock was seen by people on both sides in this dispute as an acceptable mediator is an important point. A Home Ruler, though one whom Redmond had passed over for a parliamentary nomination in 1910, Sherlock had by 1912 significantly aligned himself with a nationwide Catholic 'literature crusade'. Yet, no more than members of the GAA had a problem with Sherlock being a political moderate did the IAAA have an overt difficulty with the lord mayor's anti-Protestantism. The inference must be made that the GAA was not, in fact, as politically extreme in 1912 as it might subsequently have claimed, nor was the IAAA as unionist as its opponents asserted.[69]

By October, J.J. Keane received Central Council approval for the Athletic Council to represent the views of the entire GAA organisation.

This happened despite Keane being seen as a major contributor to the divisions within GAA athletics.[70] Yet, his role in the dealings with the IAAA and ICA was to be central. It was widely accepted that the GAA had emerged strongest from the dispute with the IAAA and ICA, but also that the GAA's ultimate goal had to be international recognition:

> The ICA and the IAAA have the power and influence to settle the dispute, for all minor questions are mere matters of detail, if the road is paved for direct recognition of the GAA by the English and Scottish authorities. That will be the price of peace by the GAA, and judging by Mr. T.W. Murphy's views, as expressed in *Sport,* there will not be much trouble with the home bodies in that respect.[71]

In anticipating a settlement, *Sport* also considered the way forward internationally, assuming the GAA ban on 'Tommy Atkins', if retained, did not prove a stumbling block with organisations like the AAA or the British Olympic Association:

> . . . they have won here in Ireland, as admitted all round . . . With the Gaelic Athletic Association having direct international recognition, smaller, but at the same time important points must be attended to . . .
>
> For international contests both Athletic Associations form an International Board; Cycling Internationals – Same . . . A joint body of the three Associations to gain for Ireland national representation at the Olympic Games. This body could also act in the organising of a team for the Olympic Games, bring off trial meetings, etc.[72]

It was clear that the various offshoots of disaffection within GAA athletic ranks could more easily be brought back into line by the prospect of international and Olympic competition being opened up to their members. At a meeting in Cork of the Munster Athletes' Protection Association, the following resolution was passed:

> Seeing that Messrs Keane and Crowe are to attend the conference with the representatives of the IAAA, presided over

by the Lord Mayor of Dublin, we call upon those gentlemen to
do all in their power, consistent with the dignity and principles
of the GAA, to bring about a settlement.[73]

As 1912 drew to a close, there was reason to expect that the
Stockholm Olympics could become the last ones not to have an
individual and all-embracing Irish team. The political signs were
particularly good. Even though the latter half of 1912 is seen historically
as the explosion of the 'Home Rule crisis', the evidence suggests that the
GAA, far from going in a more extreme direction, was moving more
towards a rapprochement with the IAAA and ICA. While moves towards
agreement with the IAAA would continue to meet with mixed responses,
one commentator summed up the role which the GAA might well play
before the next (1916) Olympics, citing the achievements of Finland in
using the Games to demonstrate its separation from Russia as the
example to follow:

> The dignified and patriotic stand of Finland has set a precedent
> which we in Ireland could follow with beneficial results. Four
> years of a progressive and an aggressive policy on the part of the
> GAA should enable Ireland to be creditably represented at Berlin
> in 1916. A series of championships, tournaments, with this
> object in view, would develop the material which we
> undoubtedly possess, and a claim put forward by the premier
> athletic organisation of Ireland, with the case of Finland as a
> precedent, would in all probability be upheld by the Olympic
> Committee, provided however that Ireland's claim be presented,
> not as a petition but as a national demand. In that event,
> England must either recognise our claim or appear in her true
> colours as a tyrant and a hypocrite.[74]

The sporting difficulties would not be as readily overcome – the decline
which was under way in Irish athletics would not be reversed as easily as
those seeking alignment between the disparate sporting bodies might have
hoped. The year 1916 itself, as a target date for a possible resurgence of
Irish Olympic performance and separate identity, would be fraught with
difficulty. Around the corner from the Stockholm disappointment lay

turmoil both in Ireland and in Europe which would destroy the prospects of staging the next Olympic Games at Berlin, and of bringing cohesion to Irish athletics.

CHAPTER NINE

THE ANTWERP GAMES OF 1920

The Olympic Games emerged from the depths of the Great War determined to carry on, with Antwerp being selected as host city. The Games were austere, to say the least, with accommodation and services quite spartan in the environs of war-ravaged Belgium. Nevertheless, twenty-nine countries sent representatives and over 2,500 competitors made it to Antwerp.[1] These Games, from an Irish perspective, would be more important for what happened around them rather than at them, perhaps, although there were a number of notable performances by Irish and Irish-American athletes to applaud too.

Although there had definitely been moves around the time of the Stockholm Games to generate athletic unity in Ireland, both within the GAA and between it and the IAAA, this was to become something of a false dawn as early as 1913. Within the GAA, its official historian has laid much of the blame for the festering fragmentation prior to Stockholm at the feet of J.J. Keane, president of the Athletic Council of the association. Ironically, Keane would go on to be the central figure in Irish athletics after independence, the man behind the setting up of the Irish Olympic Council and as member for Ireland on the International Olympic Committee for over two decades afterwards.[2] However, Keane

> ... had been permitted by the association to run athletics almost single-handed, justifying the demands for a more democratic system of management. Whatever justification he had in

refusing to treat with the GACU [Gaelic Athletes' and Cyclists' Union], a disgruntled group without clear aims, Keane's domineering and obstinate attitude to the MAPA [Munster Athletes' Protection Association], consisting largely of old associates in the GAA, only served to put off the day when the GAA found itself forced to concede the claims of the Munster athletes to a bigger voice in their own affairs . . .[3]

Statistical evidence also suggests that whatever moves had begun in 1912 to place athletics, and by correlation Irish Olympism, on a firmer footing were going to fail. It has already been seen that IAAA meetings had been plummeting in popularity, number and in the general quality of performance. GAA athletics was stronger, certainly, but in decline as well, with the number of GAA athletic meetings falling to 154 in 1913 and to 131 in 1914. The outbreak of the Great War could only have had minimal effect on this latter figure, with most GAA meetings traditionally being well over by the time serious hostilities involving Irish participants had begun in 1914. The 1914 figure was similar to what had been customary prior to 1905, before the rift with the IAAA developed but at that time the quality of performances at both GAA and IAAA meetings had been world class, to use a modern phrase.[4]

One of the positive outcomes of the GAA's struggle with the Munster Athletes' Protection Association was the push it gave to the idea of Olympic participation.[5] It has been suggested that the Athletic Council of the GAA agreed to support participation at the Berlin Olympics in 1916 and that Keane hoped to make an announcement on the matter of unification of Irish athletic bodies.[6] News of the proposed unification reached the British Olympic Association in May 1913 when

> Mr Fisher [secretary of the AAA and the AAA representative on the BOA] reported that the two great athletic organisations in Ireland had come to a mutual agreement. The Committee expressed a strong wish that these two bodies should co-operate in carrying out the Scheme [for preparing athletes] and that members of both Associations should have equal facilities.[7]

A week later, the BOA's enthusiasm for Irish athletic unification appeared to have intensified:

> Arising out of the minutes Mr Fisher stated that no official confirmation had reached him of the agreement arrived at between the two Irish Athletic Associations. At the Committee's request he promised to make official enquiries and to report the result.[8]

The common perception has been that the outbreak of the Great War ended both the ideas of Irish athletics unification and of separate Irish participation in the next Olympic celebration. The war did, quite obviously, prevent the Irish or any other national entity from competing at the next scheduled Olympiad. However, a closer examination of the proceedings of the British Olympic Association suggests that this anticipated new dawn for Irish Olympism would have foundered on the rocks of recognition for Ireland as a separate entry anyway.

The BOA and Irish Preparation Schemes for Berlin, 1916
The meeting at which the British Olympic Association was first informed of a possible liaison between the Irish athletic bodies was also one at which the different sporting bodies affiliated to the BOA presented their individual schemes for preparing athletes, cyclists, swimmers, etc. for the 1916 Berlin Games:

> Dr. Bulger presented the scheme submitted by the Irish Amateur Athletic Association, and after careful consideration a general approval was given . . . The estimated cost of the scheme was £900 with an initial payment of £30 for cost of apparatus.[9]

This IAAA scheme was particularly thorough, referring to plans for setting up an Irish schools' championship, encouraging the holding of provincial Olympic championships, the establishment of a training headquarters and the appointment of trainers, and the creation of a register of approved athletes who were to receive special training and advice. This scheme had nowhere within its aim the development of a separate Irish team for Berlin. The BOA decided, in the aftermath of the debacle of Stockholm, to encourage the different regional and national bodies within its remit to develop localised training schemes which the BOA would then part fund. The thoroughness of the IAAA's proposals is reflected by it being over three and a half times as costly as the scheme proposed by the Scottish AAA. It is, however, very clear that the BOA had no intention of going beyond the granting of this element of autonomy to Ireland, Scotland or anywhere else. There would be one, and only one British team at the next Olympic Games. The BOA's Special Committee for the Berlin Games, furthermore, also called on the Irish Amateur Swimming Association and its Welsh and Scottish counterparts to submit separate training schemes. It accepted plans for co-operation between the Irish Cyclists Association, the Scottish Cyclists' Union and the National Cyclists' Union towards trials for a British team in Berlin.[10] No separate Irish cycling team would compete again under BOA auspices, unlike what had happened at Stockholm in 1912. Interestingly, as a counterpoint, photographic evidence of the Great Britain and Ireland aquatic representatives at the 1920 Olympics, held in the Olympic Museum, Lausanne, shows that the representatives of England, Ireland and (apparently) of a club wore swimming costumes emblazoned with the logos of their countries, not of Great Britain overall.[11]

The BOA's efforts to ensure a better performance at the 1916 Games could only have been enhanced had the cream of Ireland's GAA athletes as well as IAAA representatives been available for selection. This explains the committee's enthusiasm for the news of possible hatchet-burying in Ireland. However, there was no evidence of a chink appearing in the BOA's armour in relation to accepting a separate Irish team. The Berlin preparatory committee proceeded with its regionalised structure, affording Ireland every support it could but most certainly in the context of helping it prepare athletes to compete on behalf of one Great Britain and Ireland team. Early in 1914, a sum of £3,000 had been proposed as payment for trainers:

> Mr W.R. Knox as Chief Trainer at £400 per annum and £150 per annum travelling expenses, and nine supplementary trainers for two years (26 weeks in the year) at about £3 each per week. These supplementary trainers will be located, two for Scotland,

two for Ireland, two for the North of England, one for the Midlands, and two for the South and South East of England.[12]

Even this was better from the Irish perspective than it might have been, given that one BOA representative had previously proposed that the job of training a Great Britain team for Berlin should be handed over to the army, navy and Board of Education, abandoning any reliance on governing associations at all.[13] With the proposed rapprochement between the GAA and IAAA not coming to fruition in 1913–14, the commitment of the BOA to regional preparation but for one Great Britain team for Berlin contributed, unsurprisingly, to a parallel decision that came in 1914. With the formation of the International Amateur Athletic Federation (IAAF) immediately after the Stockholm Olympics, the definition of a nation for the purposes of Olympic competition was reinforced by the new organisation, blocking any possibility of Irish recognition within the IAAF either, should it be pressed, and the IAAA 'agreed, with some reluctance, to the formation of the International Federation and the inclusion therein of the United Kingdom of Great Britain and Ireland as one nation'. Further evidence of the co-operative regional approach which suited the BOA too is provided by the fact that the Ireland–Scotland match planned for 11 July that year was now to be a triangular one including England. The possibilities of this match becoming a form of Olympic trial for Berlin by 1916 must have been high, had the Great War not intervened.[14]

As in 1912, murmurings to the BOA about entering one British Empire Olympic team surfaced in 1913.[15] The response of the BOA to the idea was quite lukewarm. It is unclear from the minutes whether the proposal sought to include Great Britain and Ireland within such an Empire team. If so, it would certainly have been one capable of taking on the Americans and all other comers at Berlin. However, it is highly unlikely that the BOA would ever have agreed essentially to diminish its own importance or the identity of Britain at the Olympic Games. It found suitably reasonable reasons to decline progressing the notion any further:

> With reference to forming an 'Empire Team' it was decided that a reply should be sent to Mr. Hugh D. McIntosh to the effect that the British Olympic Council were approached by the Oversea

[*sic*] Dominions requesting that they be kept entirely separate; also to point out that Australia has been represented on the International Olympic Committee longer than any other of the Colonies, and that the question should have been raised then. Nevertheless, the Committee wished to express their desire to offer every facility for training to the Colonies previous to the Olympic Games.[16]

An important reason behind the BOA's defence of independent representation for nations like Australia and, as seen previously, Canada and South Africa came from later minutes. At the IOC conference held at the Sorbonne in Paris in 1914, there were no non-English delegates among the ten BOA representatives. In addition:

> The Canadian Olympic Committee were not able to send the full number of representatives which they were entitled, and Mr C.J. West and Capt. F.W. Jones were allowed to attend the Congress as Canadian delegates. Capt. F.W. Jones acted as Secretary to all the Delegates from the British Empire, for whose use a room at the Hotel Regina was set apart.[17]

Having in its own right ten English delegates at the Sorbonne conference already gave the BOA significant influence. Being able to add more English (or at least 'reliable') delegates in place of absentee Empire ones further strengthened that influence. With the BOA providing secretarial support and organising accommodation for the Empire delegates, further circumstantial evidence of its influence, or at least potential influence, over more Sorbonne delegates is provided. Behind the scenes too, a push was maintained to ensure representation for Empire-based British states on the International Olympic Committee itself. A personal plea to de Coubertin was made by the BOA secretary on behalf of the South Africans:

> The S. African Cee [*sic*] is very desirous of being represented at the Congress of Paris but in the absence of a representative of S. Africa on the IOC they are, I suppose, not yet a National Olympic Cee according to the definition in ?? [illegible] of the regulations of the Congress.

> I am therefore writing to ask if I may (as representing meanwhile Great Britain and such of her colonies as have not yet a representative on the IOC) put in *pro forma* a notice that the South African Olympic Cee [*sic*] will desire to be represented at the Congress of Paris by its representative on the IOC and five delegates.[18]

That such a proposal was designed as much to ensure the 'right' sort of representative as it was to ensure South African representation in itself is clear from Laffan's résumé within this letter of the likely representative's background:

> Matters have gone so far that the S. African Cee [*sic*] has expressed a wish to be represented by Mr Sidney H. Farrar, of the London Wall Buildings Company, a member of a prominent firm of S. African financiers, and brother of Sir George Farrar, who has been for many years one of the leading men in Johannesburg . . .

The BOA managed to ensure that a significant proportion of delegates at the Olympic Congress and on the IOC were committed to the status quo in terms of Olympic philosophy and national recognition. Little wonder, then, that the BOA's own proposals of January 1914 in relation to defining a nation or nationality were subsequently adopted virtually word for word at the Sorbonne.[19] Ireland would remain part of the 'United Kingdom of Great Britain' for the foreseeable future, regardless of growing moves towards political self determination.

After the Great War

The outbreak of the Great War finished all planning for the 1916 Berlin Games.[20] From the perspective of Britain and Ireland, the aftermath of the 1916 Rising then changed the political and indeed sporting landscape completely. The IAAA, ICA and other sporting bodies were still in existence but were, in many respects, in their own death throes. After 1916, however, the IAAA's overall affiliation to British sporting bodies meant that it became much more an object of odium among nationalists. Correspondingly, whatever leanings the GAA demonstrated before 1916 towards conciliation with moderate nationalist and unionist opinion were now dissipated. The political landscape placed the sporting emphasis among nationalists very firmly on the GAA, witnessed by the presence of Sinn Féin leaders like Griffith, Collins and even rugby man Éamon de Valera at countless GAA matches from 1917 onwards. By this time, the GAA became even more focused on its team games ethos and whatever moves it was to make towards leading an Olympic entry or athletics revival would be limited to the efforts of a small group of officials. Indeed, the drive to form an Irish Olympic Council and have it recognised in Lausanne was essentially the work of just one such administrator, the aforementioned J.J. Keane.[21] One connection between Sinn Féin and the Olympic proponents deserves mention at this stage. Apart from Michael Collins's relationship by marriage to the great Martin Sheridan, he had also been a member of the Geraldines GAA club in London, a sister club of the Geraldines club of Dublin. J.J. Keane was a founding member of the Dublin club, increasing the likelihood that the two men at least knew each other prior to the War of Independence.[22]

After the Great War, with a major Irish independence struggle commencing in early 1919 and a more global sense of imperial decline beginning to hit the British establishment's consciousness, the BOA's attitude towards anything at the Olympic Games which might smack of decline or fragmentation was a highly cautious one. For example, when the old issue of the different football associations within the United Kingdom having separate teams at the hastily convened Antwerp Games of 1920 came up, the BOA expressed its concerns, not least that this could create a precedent in other sports, presumably including the blue riband athletics contests:

> The Hon. Gen. Secretary reported that the Football Association asked that the definition of a 'country' be that of the International Football Federation. The Hon. Gen. Secretary explained that this would mean that England, Ireland, Scotland and Wales could each enter a separate team. It was felt that this would probably cause considerable difficulty in other sports, and it was unanimously decided to delete all reference to Association Football in the letter.[23]

As in 1912, the notion that four possible teams could be entered from the United Kingdom in some team sports was also something which troubled other Olympic associations, meaning that, in the end, the Antwerp Games saw no sports at all having separate English, Scottish or, of course, Irish teams entered. A French Olympic committee report on Antwerp subsequently argued that:

> . . . in team (or crew) sports ['sports par équipes'] our friends across the Channel should only be represented by a single team or crew for Great Britain . . . The Union has perhaps desired the innovation that in a tournament, say of Rugby Football, Great Britain should not be entitled to a team each for Scotland, Ireland, Wales and England.[24]

The association football situation had become considerably more complicated when, in early 1919, the football associations of England, Ireland, Scotland and Wales withdrew from the Federation of International Football Associations (FIFA) and formed their own 'Federation of National Football Associations'. Eventually, and despite opposition from the USA and France among others, a Great Britain football team, unaffiliated to FIFA, was allowed to compete at Antwerp. The Great Britain team contained no Irish members as far as can be ascertained and was knocked out in the opening round of the competition by Norway on a 3–1 scoreline.[25]

British officialdom was not ready to yield to any suggestion that a separate Irish entry be tolerated at Antwerp. Although never mentioned, even incidentally, in BOA minutes, the Sinn Féin election victory of November 1918 and the subsequent independence struggle from 1919 to 1921 must have fuelled the more establishment-oriented BOA members in this resolve. The decline in the IAAA is also evident in its lack of involvement in the BOA immediately after the war. For example, as training and selection programmes for Antwerp were being sanctioned in London, the BOA developed a list of organisations supporting, not supporting or not yet responded to its invitation to get involved in the Antwerp Games. The Scottish AAA was supporting involvement but there was no indication either that an invite had been sent to or an acknowledgement received from the IAAA, or any other affiliated body.[26]

The minutes of the BOA's meetings also record no Irish attendee in the period from early 1919 to the Antwerp Games.

Irish-American Decline in the USA

While Irish-America was central to much of the sporting and political involvement of Irishmen in the Olympic Games prior to the Great War, the decline of Irish influence in athletic and Olympic circles in the USA was, if anything, more pronounced than the apparent decline of the IAAA. Some of the great antagonists of British Olympism, like James Sullivan and Martin Sheridan, were dead by the time the preparations for Antwerp began.[27] The predominance of both the Irish in American athletics and of athletics among the sporting Irish themselves continued to decline after Stockholm. Yet, the exploits of Paddy Ryan, Matt McGrath, Pat McDonald and Pat Flynn maintained an Irish presence on the US athletics squad for Antwerp. McGrath was desperately unfortunate in Antwerp, injuring his knee in the second round of the hammer and having to withdraw from both that event and the 56-pound throwing event. In the hammer, McGrath and Paddy Ryan dominated the American AAU championships, with Ryan winning eight titles and McGrath seven between 1908 and 1926. At Antwerp, with McGrath out, Ryan won easily with a distance well short of either his own world record, set in 1913, or McGrath's Olympic record from 1912.[28] Ryan's world record, at 189 feet 6 inches, was to last for twenty-five years and was not beaten as an American record for half a century.[29]

We saw Pat McDonald winning the shot put in Stockholm. He only managed to finish fourth in the event in Antwerp, where his Stockholm mark would easily have won gold again had it been repeated. In the 56-pound weight throw, however, McDonald came into his own and, with a winning throw of 36 feet 11.5 inches he set two records which still stand. The first was the 56-pound record and, given that this was to be the last Games in which the event was held, the Olympic record McDonald broke on 21 August 1920 technically still stands. Furthermore, at forty-two years and twenty-six days old, he also became the oldest Olympic track and field gold medallist in history, a record he still holds.[30] It has been mentioned previously that McDonald was born 'McDonnell'. The name change has generally been explained by the fact

An action shot here of Paddy Ryan from Colm Murphy, *The Irish Whale*. There is a statue of Paddy Ryan beside the main road through Pallasgreen, with, beside it, a plaque carrying the words he spoke before his winning throw in Antwerp.

that his sister had emigrated to New York before him and the immigration clerk at Ellis Island wrote her name down incorrectly. Fearing deportation, allegedly, Ms McDonald said nothing and her other family members who landed subsequently, including Pat, kept the same

A rather grainy image of Pat McDonald in action, courtesy of Larry Ryder. McDonald eventually rose to the rank of precinct captain in the New York police force, dying in 1954 at the age of seventy-five, forty years after his last visit home. The action shot is from Colm Murphy's *The Irish Whale*.

spelling. Paddy Ryan finished second to McDonald in the 56-pound event in Antwerp, with a possible Irish clean sweep again being denied by Matt McGrath's injury. McGrath held seven AAU 56-pound titles, one fewer than McDonald.[31]

Pat Flynn hailed from Bandon, County Cork, and emigrated to the USA after the Great War. He was American AAU champion in the steeplechase in 1920, an event which by this time had settled at a 3,000 metres distance. In Antwerp, Flynn finished second to Percy Hodge of Britain, with an Italian named Ambrosini in third place. No times were recorded but it was estimated that Hodge won by close to 100 metres, with Flynn about forty metres ahead of the third-placed athlete.[32]

In rowing, John (Jack) Kelly of Philadelphia, and of Mayo stock originally, won the single sculls and double sculls with his cousin, Paul Costello. This gave Kelly some compensation for his not being allowed to compete at the Diamond Sculls at Henley. Kelly and Costello would win in the double sculls again in Paris at the 1924 Games, while Costello would win a third such title with a new partner in 1928. Tradition has it that Kelly had been refused the right to compete at Henley because he was a

Jack Kelly of the USA defeating Jack Beresford of Britain in the Antwerp single sculls final (© IOC Lausanne).

bricklayer. In fact, his Vesper Boat Club of Philadelphia was not granted an entry at Henley because of an infringement of the amateur rules when the club had previously competed there, back in 1905. Kelly, of course, was the father of Grace Kelly, the actress and later princess of Monaco, while his bricklaying work eventually made him a millionaire contractor and company executive in Philadelphia.[33]

Coverage of the Antwerp Games in the *Gaelic American* was virtually non-existent. Even with Sinn Féin president de Valera touring the USA on a fundraising drive in 1919–20, there are no accounts of the famous athletic picnics of old being used to help in any fundraising. Before the infamous split between de Valera and leading Irish-Americans like John Devoy and Daniel Cohalan, articles in Devoy's newspaper detailed the fundraising campaign. Several nationalist clubs are mentioned in the organisation of fundraising events. However, no reference at all has been found to a sporting body being involved at any such function nor to the use of a sporting event to raise funds.

The career of James Brendan Connolly after 1896 has been alluded to earlier. At this point, his journalism provides one further point of interest in 1920 which he, as well as the *Gaelic American* more generally, identified. In a massive article for the *Gaelic American* in January, he attacked the anti-Irish Admiral Sims, an American naval officer.[34] Connolly refers to Sims repeating 'atrocious lies about the treatment of American sailors in Cork and Queenstown . . . part of the British propaganda against Ireland . . .' According to the newspaper, 'Mr. Connolly's citation of the number of marriages between American sailors and Irish girls shows the utter absurdity of the Admiral's falsehoods . . .' Connolly also referred to Sims promoting Winston Churchill, telling a dinner in London:

> Let me assure you gentlemen here tonight that there is not one American citizen but who stands ready to shed the last drop of his blood before he will see the British Empire go down.[35]

The restoration of old-stock Americans to the leadership of the US Olympic Committee provided one further challenge to the position of Irish-America at the Antwerp Games. The first intimation of a problem came from an Irish-based newspaper:

... a little incident in Antwerp with regard to Irish-American competitors was quite in keeping with the general attitude of the American authorities towards those who contribute so largely to the renown of American Athletics.[36]

The issue here appears to have been some harsh treatment of an Irish athlete in American ranks, concerning the brother of the 1908 hop, step and jump gold medallist:

Daniel Ahearn [*sic*] was lucky to be able to compete at all in the event. The American team was less than pleased with their

Dan Ahearn of Athea, world hop, step and jump record holder at the time of the Antwerp Olympics. Courtesy of Tim Quaid.

accommodations in Antwerp, which were in an old school building. The team members protested to their officials, to no avail. The athletes had a 10 p.m. curfew, but one night, Ahearn [*sic*] did not return at all, having rented a room for himself in a tavern, in protest against his sleeping quarters. For this he was removed from the Olympic team. In response, the 200 members of the US Olympic team signed a petition demanding better accommodations and that Ahearn [*sic*] be reinstated, threatening to withdraw en masse if their demands were not met. Eventually Ahearn [*sic*] was returned to the Olympic team and was thus able to compete.[37]

This dispute may have arisen partly because some Irish-American competitors, described by the *New York Times* as 'the big weightmen' were being treated better than others. Yet the vehemence of the athletes' support of Ahearn(e) was such that:

A certain few of the athletes have informed the American Olympic Committee that they will not compete in the stadium events unless Ahearn is reinstated. 'Go ahead, we will get a better committee,' and other similar comments were shouted at judge Weeks. The outburst of the athletes seemingly left the committee stunned.[38]

The anger of the American team members was exacerbated by the fact that their accommodation in the main was on board a ship which had been used for carrying laden coffins during the Great War. One way or another, the incident shows a different relationship between Irish-American athletes and US officialdom than ever obtained in the halcyon days of Sheridan–Sullivan dominance. Before we leave the Ahearn(e) story, it is worth noting that both brothers had emigrated to the USA and had become prominent in athletics there. Timothy, the 1908 hop, step and jump winner, did not compete at Antwerp and Dan, who dropped the 'e' at the end of his surname, eventually finished sixth in the hop, step and jump. Dan actually held the world record in that event from 1909 until 1924, when it was broken by a quarter of an inch by an Australian athlete, Nick Winter, at the Paris Olympics. Dan Ahearn may well be the greatest

Irish athlete of the twentieth century not to win even a medal at the Olympics. He broke the world record in the hop, step and jump in 1909, 1911 and 1915, and also in the variation event, two hops and a jump (1910), which is no longer held, so technically he remains the record holder in that event. He won eight AAU hop, step and jump titles in all, and two Canadian championships. By 1920, although again American champion, he was simply a little past his best and finished a foot and a half behind the winner.[39]

Olympic Coverage in Ireland
In neither national nor local press has a single article of significance, either previewing or reviewing Irish sporting performances in Antwerp, been found. The *Cork Examiner* was fairly typical, relying on generic Reuters reports with no Irish-specific references at all. *Sport* expressed concerns about the non-inclusion of Ireland's Tim Crowe on the British athletics team and referred to the number of Irish names among the published US team.[40] During the Games, *Sport* had more lengthy coverage of Antwerp results than the *Examiner* but the Irish material it covered was nil, beyond one reference to the existence of Irish-American competitors in weight-throwing events. Not one of the national newspapers examined has shown a recognition of Anton (Francis) Hegarty from County Derry, who finished in the top five in the cross country race won by the great Finn Paavo Nurmi and collected a silver medal as part of the British team.[41] The paucity of the material *Sport* worked with during the Antwerp Games is further reflected by its reliance on one reflective article dealing with Kennedy McArthur's marathon victory in 1912, with the comment that 'the Irishman's greater strength and stamina prevailed', and a very lengthy article on the achievements of Tom Kiely nearly two decades previously. This article was repeated in full just seven weeks later.[42] The *Nationalist*, voice of Clonmel and south Tipperary, carried no coverage at all of the Olympic Games between July and October 1920. The *Irish Independent* was perhaps the newspaper which gave the Games most coverage in terms of detailing the events themselves, but making no reference to the Irishness of any weight-throwing medallists and ignoring or not realising the Irish connections with Jack Kelly in the single sculls and of Kelly and his cousin Paul Costello in the double sculls.[43] Yet, the same newspaper carried very

This picture has been previously captioned as 'swimmers'. However, the number of swimmers here, seven, plus the facts that there is clearly an Irishman among them and all wear similar bathing hats except for the probable goalkeeper, suggest that this is actually the water polo team and the Irishman here must be Noel Purcell. There was no Irish representative on the swimming squad (© IOC Lausanne).

significant coverage of the Gaelic League's Oireachtas in mid-1920, including the athletic events under its auspices between July and August 1920. The implication from all this must be that interest in athletics had declined but was not extinct, while the Olympic Games from the viewpoint of Irish successes or even participation in competition was reduced to a peripheral existence in the Irish sporting psyche, more or less as it had been back in 1896.

What changed very significantly in Ireland was the attitude among nationalists to the Games as a political vehicle. Few nationalists in the separatist tradition had realised the potential for national identity which the Olympics could offer. It was now too late to let the quality of Irish athletic performances create this identity in the optimum fashion, by winning for Ireland. However, with the War of Independence increasing in momentum in mid-1920, the time was certainly ripe for using the Olympics to establish Irish identity abroad.[44] *Sport* noted with some satisfaction that the traditionally unionist Irish Swimming Association was now more troubled than previously by not having separate Olympic representation, although its misgivings came to nothing concrete in the end:

> We were glad to see the question of Ireland's international status
> in relation to the Olympic Games raised at the meeting of the
> Irish Swimming Association; and are satisfied with the decision
> come to, though it looks like shelving. Surely, Irish athletes of
> all kinds should be tired of seeking the world arena through the
> back door of England? Hope of an athletic revival while we lack
> the incentive and thrill of international rivalry is futile and, all
> ideas of racial self-respect apart, this is a vital issue for us.[45]

The *Irish Independent* subsequently confirmed that the Swimming
Association's AGM had indeed considered the matter of separate
representation but that it was deferred. The newspaper's sporting editor
also sneered (4 August) at the non-nationalist credentials of 'our single
representative in the water polo'; interestingly, the representative in
question, who was Noel Mary Purcell, went on to become the only person
from the 1920 Games to represent Ireland when it made its Olympic debut
as a nation at Paris in 1924.[46] More of a flutter was created in Irish athletic
and journalistic circles when news came, via Chicago for some reason,
that Irish athletes due to compete in Antwerp were threatening a boycott
in search of separate representation:

> A telegram from Brussels to the *Chicago Tribune* says that Irish
> athletes have refused to compete at the Olympic Games under
> the British flag. They wrote the executive to the effect that they
> were willing to enter the series of events only if allowed to do so
> as members of an independent nation. The committee
> corresponded with the British committee and decided that the
> Irish could not be admitted on the footing demanded.[47]

The more polarised nationalism of 1920 Ireland is typified by the scant
regard the *Irish Independent* showed for this protest, given that: 'The Irish
athletes concerned are not named and those selected by Great Britain are
IAAA men, and therefore not likely to take up such an attitude as reported.'
The newspaper's sports editor here was clearly forgetting that the majority
of Irish athletes to attend any previous Olympic Games and demand
separate Irish recognition could all have been termed 'IAAA men' in the
past. Other newspapers gave similar reports of this Irish protest at

Antwerp, in considerably more detail than they dealt with any of the athletics events themselves. The rejection of the protest was laid squarely at the door of the BOA:

> A telegram from Brussels to the *Chicago Tribune* says: 'The Irish athletes have refused to compete at the Olympic Games under the British flag. They wrote to the Executive Committee to the effect that they were willing to enter the series of events only, if allowed to do so, as members of an independent nation. The Committee, in face of this delicate situation, corresponded with the British Committee and then, after duly considering the matter, decided that the Irish could not be admitted on the footing demanded.'[48]

Apart from the *Irish Independent,* the effort by the Irish athletes appears to have inspired a positive response from most nationalist organs. The day after it first reported the incident, the *Freeman's Journal* waxed lyrically about the glory days of Irish athletics, the Tailteann Games and the desire for international recognition via the Olympics:

> This year our native contests precede the Olympic events, and being still denied the right of self-respecting participation, we must turn our attention to the home championships, which are the survival of athletic contests of renown far ante-dating even the historic Isthmian games of which the modern Olympiads purport to be a revival . . . if we fall short of the brilliancy of achievement that distinguished the years around 1904, there is the material and impulse still amongst us that have made the name of Gaelic athletes world known . . .[49]

Sport chipped in with some derogatory analysis of the poor prospects of British athletes for Antwerp and bemoaned that the English AA (i.e. the AAA) permitted just three Irish athletes to compete at Antwerp while 'the mass of Irish athletes . . . are denied recognition except at the price of their national self-respect'.[50] The more republican *Tipperary Star* joked that Britain herself ought to be barred from Antwerp:

> It is of interest that at a moment when one of the former members of the Comité International Olympique is suggesting

the withdrawal of British teams from the Olympic games on the ground, amongst others, that as Germany is not admitted the Olympiad can hardly be called international.[51]

The *Limerick Leader* had been surprisingly quiet on athletics over the previous decades, despite the fact that County Limerick had produced more Olympic champions and medallists than any other county. Yet now, it too was aroused by the issue of Irish participation, its editor using an allusion to Lord Byron's *The Isles of Greece* to make his somewhat romanticised point:

> Poor Byron! How he would revolt at the new order of things . . . out of the four and a quarter millions of the grandchildren of Desla, who in the fourth mythic cycle of Ireland's invasions led his Greek clansmen into the Emerald Isle to sling the shot and hurl the stone discus, only four athletes could be found fit to wear the shamrock for the Faenna in the foreign and far away field of Flanders! . . . Could we but weep o'er days more blest, when Jim Mitchell and Jack Flanagan were preparing to invade America . . .[52]

An aside in the same *Limerick Leader* editorial comes with the comment: 'It is a melancholy reflection that Irish athletes must go to America to be finished in the modus operandi essential to a professional athlete.' The *Leader* laid some of the blame for athletic decline firmly on the GAA:

> The Gaelic Athletic Association has done well in the hurling and football arenas, and, let it be written to its credit, has fostered a beautiful spirit in the sons of Ireland, and kept alive the best traditions of its forebears. But the members of this august body – good men and true men – should know that for the general development of the Gael the two national pastimes do not necessarily meet with the requirements of the international athlete . . . if the association took a keener and a more lively interest in the field sports the young men of this city and, indeed, for that matter the provincial Gaels, would be of a better calibre than they are today.

In the USA, John Devoy's *Gaelic American* made no more efforts to mock the purported nationalism of the few IAAA athletes at Antwerp. This may be an early sign of Devoy's moderation as a nationalist in his final years, which may well have been partly in reaction to de Valera, with whom he and Judge Cohalan had significant differences of opinion in the latter half of de Valera's tour of the USA. As previously mentioned, when John Devoy made his first, and last, return to Ireland in the twentieth century, it was to attend the Tailteann Games of 1924 in Dublin, under the auspices of the Cumann na nGaedheal government. Thus, his lack of ridicule of the IAAA athletes here may now be more understandable than his sporting extremism during earlier Olympic celebrations would have suggested. The *Gaelic American* saw the throwing out of the Irish athletes' protest in 1920 as merely further evidence of what it considered to be Britain exercising influence over smaller nations for its own purposes:

> That official Belgium is still dominated by England is proved by the following dispatch from Brussels, dated July 21: 'after an exchange of correspondence with the British Olympic committee, the Executive Committee of the Olympic Games has refused Ireland permission to participate in the seventh Olympic as a separate nation.'[53]

The Irish Olympic Council

A short time before the Antwerp Olympics, J.J. Keane of the GAA spearheaded the move to establish an Irish Olympic Council, achieve membership of the International Olympic Committee and enter an Irish team at the Olympic Games.

At least one prominent Olympic historian has suggested that General Eoin O'Duffy was centrally involved in the push to form the Irish Olympic Council (IOC) but no documentary or newspaper evidence of this has been found in the course of research for this publication. The same source also suggests that:

> The exact date of the foundation of the Irish Olympic Council – the Olympic Council of Ireland as it is known today – cannot be traced due to the absence of minutes for its early years but the likelihood is that it came into existence in the summer of 1923.[54]

While it is reasonable to state that it was 1923 before the OCI was fully accepted internationally, there is no doubt from cross-referenced and contemporary newspaper evidence that it was founded, and by J.J. Keane, in 1920. Keane was in fact summoned to a meeting with Michael Collins and Arthur Griffith during 1920 at Vaughan's Hotel in Dublin, at which he was encouraged in his efforts to get IOC recognition for Ireland at Antwerp.[55] O'Duffy's first known entry into the Keane inner circle did not come about until he replaced Andrew Harty as president of the Handball Association in 1926.[56] Circular letters signed by Keane to prospective members of the Irish Olympic Council referred to the 'anomalous and unworthy position' which Ireland found itself in as a nation due to its non-recognition by the International Olympic Commitee. Keane was, however, also mindful that Olympic involvement was vital for the future of Irish athletics in purely sporting terms, referring to how 'the more immediate and practical benefit would be a quickening of Irish athletic activities – now restricted and corrupted by the incubus of continued singularity'. In essence, the potential members of the Irish Olympic Council were told:

> We shall deem it a great favour for your permission to add your name to the Committee about to be formed: (1) to seek formal recognition of Irish civilian amateur competitors under the Regulations of the International Committee of the Olympic Games and (2) to take such steps as will secure the proper presentation and consideration of this claim.[57]

According to the *Limerick Leader,* the aim of the new Council was simple:

> The formation of an Irish Olympic Council that is completely and influentially representative of the Irish nation . . . At the first meeting of the newly formed Council the movement was discussed in all its aspects and, while the difficulties were fully acknowledged, it was unanimously agreed that the time was opportune and the necessity urgent for formulating Ireland's right to participate as a distinct national entity in such world competitions as the Olympic Games . . .[58]

Another edition of the newspaper recalled of Limerick that: 'It was once the foremost city in Ireland for the developing of champions, and from

the evergreen field of the Markets the finest and best of men sported silk
for the fame and fortune of the Maiden city . . .'[59]

In noting that the *Limerick Leader* had taken a keen interest in the
fledgling Irish Olympic Council, we may note that the county of Limerick
was not just a centre of athletic excellence but also of coaching and
administration. Both Tom Flanagan and Mike Murphy, leading US
coaches in 1908, were Limerickmen, as indeed were Frank Dineen, the
only man to hold office as president and secretary general of the GAA,
and J.J. Keane himself.

An insight into the origins of the Olympic Council is given by the
headed notepaper adopted by the Council after its formation. It lists the
mayors or lords mayor, as applicable, of eleven Irish conurbations in all,
including 'Terence McSweeney' [*sic*], the presidents of UCD and UCC,
the president and secretary of the GAA and the president and secretary
of the Leinster Council of the GAA. Douglas Hyde, Oliver St John Gogarty,
Arthur Griffith TD and J.J. Walsh TD were also members.[60] Although the
letter here dates from some two years after the formation of the Council,
it still contained the names of the original members, even though those
who had been in mayoral positions in early 1920 could not possibly have
retained office in 1922. Terence McSwiney, of course, died later in 1920
while the other holders of mayoral office relinquished their positions in
mid-1920, as per tradition. Searches through the files of the corporations
of Clonmel and Waterford, whose mayors were listed, and documentary
collections of Douglas Hyde and Oliver St John Gogarty have failed to
locate any letter of response, or indeed a copy of the initial invitation from
Keane prior to April 1920.[61]

A number of points can be made about the initial composition of the
Council. Firstly, not one mayor, lord mayor or university president from
a unionist background is listed. Queen's University, Trinity College, Belfast
Corporation and so on had no representative. While no evidence of an
official response from any mayor or corporation has been found, all of
those mayors listed must have given their consent to being included on
the Olympic Council. A trawl through the minutes of Clonmel
Corporation during this period, for example, shows the members, and
mayor, embroiled in nationalistic issues and likely to be very receptive to
any invitation to participate in yet another declaration of independence,

this time in sporting terms. The corporation also displayed an awareness of the importance of spreading the message of Irish identity to a more global audience.[62]

That there was no obvious IAAA or ICA representative also suggests that the Irish Olympic Council was to be representative of the separatist tradition only. The involvement of the presidents of Irish universities is symptomatic of the hope, expressed previously in IAAA circles even more forcefully, that the universities would take a lead in the development of Irish athletics.[63] The GAA personnel on the Council are somewhat more puzzling. Clearly, Keane's own GAA contacts were in Leinster mainly. The difficulty in the representation on the 1920 incarnation of the Olympic Council was that it had been eminently clear throughout the history of GAA athletics and Irish Olympic athletics that the hotbed of athletic excellence in Ireland was central Munster; yet for some reason no Munster GAA representative was to be found on the OCI.

The Council's personnel, apart from mayoral, GAA and university representatives, is not terribly surprising. Arthur Griffith had long championed the cause of an Irish Olympic identity, apart from being a leading member of Dáil Éireann.[64] J.J. Walsh was another TD with a pedigree on athletic involvement and would, in 1924, be the government minister given responsibility for overseeing the revival of the Tailteann Games. Douglas Hyde's papers in the National Library of Ireland contain no direct reference to an interest in athletics or Olympism but it is worth recalling that Hyde was one of the individuals identified by Roger Casement back in 1907 as a suitable member of such a council.[65] Gogarty's papers, likewise in the National Library, do not refer to a sporting interest in this area but he was to play a central role in the organisation of the Tailteann Games in Dublin in 1924.[66] That neither of these was merely a token member is also refuted by the fact that both literary figures are recorded as having attended the inaugural meeting they were invited to.[67]

Winning the Battle for Recognition?
The formation of the Irish Olympic Council was one significant step towards recognition of Irish Olympic integrity, even though somewhat flawed by being wholly nationalist in its composition. There was considerable expectation in 1920 that the achievement of that same

recognition was also imminent, with some quarters anticipating that an Irish team of some description might well make it to Antwerp for the August Games. Keane sent a communication to de Coubertin, outlining details of the formation of the Irish Olympic Council and of Ireland's desire to enter an Olympic team:

> The Baron acknowledged receipt of this communication in sympathetic terms and advised that the Belgian committee should be informed of Ireland's desire to participate, and intimating that the matter would come before the International Committee in general meeting which would be held in Antwerp during the progress of the Games.[68]

No copy of this letter has been found in either the Keane or de Coubertin files at Lausanne. However, it is very likely that the letters passed in May 1920. The baron's sympathetic ear led him to refer the matter of Ireland's possible Antwerp entry to the Belgian committee which, in turn, replied that the acceptance of entries from new states was outside their jurisdiction and referred the Irish body to the English [*sic*] Olympic Committee in London. The Irish Council wrote back to the Belgians pointing out the inappropriateness of this course of action. Certainly, no receipt of any such request has been recorded in the BOA minutes from this time, nor indeed has any evidence been found of the BOA discussing the Irish issue at all in its deliberations.[69] It is symptomatic of the likely response which would have emanated from the BOA, and probably of the desire to demonstrate independence of action from the British association, that the Irish decided to write back to the Belgians rather than to London. Time appears to have slipped by, with the prospects of getting an Irish team to Antwerp slipping too. It was August – too late for athletes to be organised – before the next step was possible:

> Mr J.J. Keane, President of the Athletic Council, was sent to Antwerp on the 10th inst, to forward Ireland's claim before the Olympic Executive in Belgium. 'He is already assured', a report regarding the matter says, 'of valuable support and assistance from representative American and European friends, so that, at last, the Olympic council will have an adequate conception

of Ireland's Athletic renown and status and be enabled to adjudicate thereon with all the facts and circumstances before them.' Mr Keane has returned from Antwerp, and we are glad to see that his mission, as far as can be judged up to the present, has been a gratifying success.[70]

Elsewhere, too, the mood was very optimistic, with the *Tipperary Star* assuring its readers that while 'formal recognition has yet to come', its own information was 'to the effect that the official recognition is to come at once'.[71] The *Star* also felt confident that access to the Olympics would have a far-reaching effect on athletics, with the encouragement of the nation to 'put forth her best effort and to send teams to compete in future Olympiads which will be worthy of the dignity of the nation'. The *Freeman's Journal* was even more certain that the longed-for moment was at hand: 'Pending an official announcement, it can be said that Ireland's right to distinct representation has been recognised, and all the conditions attaching to this recognition will be known within a few days . . .'[72] Later in the same interview, Keane referred to 'the altered attitude of the Olympic delegates in respect of Ireland's claim for international recognition' and in particular to 'the friendly interest of the Olympic President, Count de Coubertin, whose appreciation of Ireland's position was in keeping with his recognition of our athletic prestige'.

Closer scrutiny of the documentary evidence from the Olympic movement itself shows that the political battle for Olympic recognition was not, in fact, over. Even the ebullient *Freeman* admitted that the anticipated support from the United States had not materialised:

> While paying tribute to the considerate and indeed sympathetic attention given by the Olympic delegates as a whole to Ireland's case, it is regrettable to have to except the American representatives from this acknowledgement. For reasons best known to themselves, the US delegates adopted an attitude of indifference, if not of antagonism . . .[73]

In post-war Europe, the International Olympic Committee was never going to be to the fore in accepting or encouraging the new international order of things. While being happy to bar the defeated nations of the Great

War from Antwerp, it was very wary of opening the floodgates of national recognition too widely. One resolution declared:

> Every Olympic Committee which is constituted by the IOC or its members from that country, by mutual agreement, is considered an Olympic Committee. The recognition lasts as long as their agreement lasts. If the International Committee notes that this accord no longer exists, the recognition also ceases.[74]

Any nations which were not already part of the Olympic family were not easily going to be adopted by it now. A hint of this conservative stance is seen in the response to a Hungarian application for IOC membership in August 1920, basically that no change to the IOC status quo could be considered.[75] That Ireland was in the midst of a political and military struggle against Britain would do nothing to make it seem more acceptable to the IOC than the Hungarians were at this point. Yet the double standards which have been evident in IOC dealings with national identities were very evident elsewhere in the same document. Because Russia had overthrown its czar, defected from the Allied cause in the Great War and established a communist state, it could hardly have been more odious to the IOC. When then an application for IOC membership from Armenia came to the Antwerp meeting, it was deemed acceptable, presumably because it suited the IOC's political viewpoint:

> Armenian athletes desire to take part in the Olympic Games 'as Armenians.' After a discussion on the matter (in which Baron de Lavelaye, Prof. Sloane, Rev. de Courcy Laffan and the Compte Clary took part) the proposition of Baron de Coubertin was accepted to admit the Armenians to the Olympic Games as soon as the Armenian Athletes Union is established and the state finds itself properly organised.[76]

A case for representation for non-belligerent Iceland was also made, this time by one of the more vocal British delegates, even though the head of state of Denmark was still the Icelandic head of state as well: '*M le Col. Hansen feut remarquer que l'Islande, devenu un pays indépendent et n'ayant rien de commun avec Danemark que le Roi, a le droit d'être représenté au*

CIO. In other words, Iceland was fully eligible for admission. Yet, when the matter of Ireland's appeal, even for recognition as a separate group while still under the British flag, was made, the response was in the negative, with the British and conservative American delegate leading the opposition:

> The demand of Ireland to participate at the Olympic Games under the British flag but as a distinct Irish group raised some objections from Messrs de Courcy Laffan and Sloane. While there was a certain analogy here with the issue of the Czechs and the old Austrian Empire in Stockholm (Messrs General Balck, Dr Guth-Sarkovsky), it was decided on the proposition of Mr de Courcy Laffan to suspend all decision until the moment when the Irish question would be solved politically.[77]

The more one reads the IOC minutes and correspondence from this period, the more obvious it becomes that the same five or six delegates tended to dominate all significant proceedings and decision-making in Lausanne. By the time of this eighteenth IOC session, of course, the Antwerp Olympic Games were over. The best that Ireland's new Olympic Council could hope for was to achieve IOC membership and recognition as soon as possible, with a view to participating as a nation at the 1924 Paris Games. There would, even then, be a number of obstacles to overcome before this would be achieved.

CHAPTER TEN

FROM ANTWERP TO PARIS, 1920–24

Well after the stalling of Irish efforts at Olympic entry in 1920, the powers that were in the British Olympic Association still maintained significant influence in the Olympic movement generally. Their success was mixed, however. De Coubertin, for example, was struck by the fact that Britain had, in 1921, apparently failed to find even one representative to attend an IOC meeting, despite the previous IOC meeting in Paris, 'where the English participated forcefully and with great enthusiasm'.[1] At that same Paris meeting, the British delegates had, as previously, sought to ensure that the British political viewpoint also became the Olympic viewpoint, as with the IOC's decision to bar Germany from future Games.[2] British influence behind the scenes at the IOC may also have turned towards the Irish question again. This would, at least, help to explain why de Coubertin gave a list of people he was proposing for IOC membership but which contained no reference at all to J.J. Keane, despite all of the latter's efforts to get Irish recognition at the IOC and Antwerp just nine months previously.[3] It could also have been the case that the fledgling Irish Olympic Council had not functioned beyond the months around the push for admission at Antwerp, although it is unlikely that Keane personally had relented in his efforts.

Following the ratification of the Anglo-Irish Treaty and subsequent withdrawal of Crown forces, J.J. Keane wasted little time in writing to de Coubertin, advising him that Ireland was now an independent nation and was intent on pursuing its application for recognition from the Olympic movement:

Cumann na ꝺCleaꞃ lút nꝼaeꝺealaċ

Irish Olympic Council.

COUNCIL:

J. J. Keane,
President, Athletic Co., G.A.A., Chairman
Most Rev. Dr. Harty, D.D.,
Archbishop of Cashel
L. O'Neill,
Lord Mayor of Dublin
T. McSweeney,
Lord Mayor of Cork
Ml. O'Callaghan,
Mayor of Limerick
Dr. V. White,
Mayor of Waterford
R. Corish,
Mayor of Wexford
D. F. O'Meara,
Mayor of Clonmel
H. C. O'Doherty,
Mayor of Derry
P. De Loughrey,
Mayor of Kilkenny
P. Monaghan,
Mayor of Drogheda
T. Fitzpatrick,
Mayor of Sligo
T. Walsh, M.D., B.Sc.
Mayor of Galway
Sir T. Myles, C.B., M.B., F.R.C.S.I.
Douglas Hyde, LL.D., D.Litt.
Dr. D. J. Coffey, M.A., M.B., LL.D.
President, University College, Dublin
J. Creed Meredith, M.A., K.C.
Dr. O. St. J. Gogarty, M.D., F.R.C.S.I.
P. J. Merriman, M.A.
President, University College, Cork
Arthur E. Clery, LL.D.
H. Hughes, B.L.
Ald. A. Byrne
A. Griffith, T.D.
J. J. Walsh, T.D.
P. J. Devlin
Ald. J. Nowlan
President, G.A.A.
D. MacCarthy
President, L. Council, G.A.A.
L. J. O'Toole
Secretary, G.A.A.
J. F. Shouldice
Secretary, L. Council, G.A.A.
W. Hely

A. C. HARTY,
Secretary

68 Upper O'Connell Street,

Dublin, ... 10th April ...... 192 2.

Baron Pierre de Coubertin,
President,
Comité International Olympique,
Lausanne, Switzerland.

Monsieur,

J'ai l'honneur de vous demander encore de la part de l'Irlande d'être reconnue dans les jeux Olympiques prochains, comme concurrente à titre indépendant. Après nous être rencontrés a Anvers, vous nous avez informés que la demande de l'Irlande serait reconnue aussitot que l'autonomie politique lui serait accordée.

J'ai grand plaisir à vous annoncer formellement que mon pays est maintenant un "Etat Libre", et qu'il jouit, sur un pied commun, des memes droits comme état autonome dans l'empire brittanique, que le Canada, l'Australie, l'Afrique du sud etc. La condition posée par vôtre Comité comme essentielle a l'admission de la demande de l'Irlande se trouve donc remplie.

De ce que mes compatriots ont prévu la possibilité de notre admission, il est déjà résulté un développement considérable d'activités athlètiques en Irlande. Des clubs se forment partout. Pendant 1 mois d'août prochain, des jeux olympiques pour la rac

I have the honour of asking you again on behalf of Ireland, to be recognised in the coming Olympic Games, as an independent nation. After our meeting in Antwerp, you told us that the Irish demand would be recognised as soon as political autonomy had been granted. I have great pleasure in telling you that my country is now a 'Free State', and that it holds, on a common footing, the same rights as an autonomous state in the British Empire as Canada, Australia, South Africa etc. The condition

Cumann na zcleat lút nzaedealac

Irish Olympic Council.

COUNCIL :

J. J. Keane,
President, Athletic Co., G.A.A., Chairman
Most Rev. Dr. Harty, D.D.,
Archbishop of Cashel
L. O'Neill,
Lord Mayor of Dublin
T. McSweeney,
Lord Mayor of Cork
Ml. O'Callaghan,
Mayor of Limerick
Dr. V. White,
Mayor of Waterford
R. Corish,
Mayor of Wexford
D. F. O'Meara,
Mayor of Clonmel
H. C. O'Doherty,
Mayor of Derry
P. De Loughrey,
Mayor of Kilkenny
P. Monaghan,
Mayor of Drogheda
T. Fitzpatrick,
Mayor of Sligo
T. Walsh, M.D., B.Sc.
Mayor of Galway
Sir T. Myles, C.B., M.B., F.R.C.S.I.
Douglas Hyde, LL.D., D.Litt.
Dr. D. J. Coffey, M.A., M.B., LL.D.
President, University College, Dublin
J. Creed Meredith, M.A., K.C.
Dr. O. St. J. Gogarty, M.D., F.R.C.S.I.
P. J. Merriman, M.A.
President, University College, Cork
Arthur E. Clery, LL.D.
H. Hughes, B.L.
Ald. A. Byrne
A. Griffith, T.D.
J. J. Walsh, T.D.
P. J. Devlin
Ald. J. Nowlan
President, G.A.A.
D. MacCarthy
President, L. Council, G.A.A.
L. J. O'Toole
Secretary, G.A.A.
J. F. Shouldice
Secretary, L. Council, G.A.A.
W. Hely

A. C. HARTY,
Secretary

68 Upper O'Connell Street,

Dublin, ... 192

(2)

irlandaise seront tenus à Dublin et le programme
olympique sera suivi au complet. Des irlandais de
tous les pays du monde ont déjà exprimé l'intention
de prendre part aux concours d'équipe et d'individus.
Le nouveau gouvernement a voté 20,000 livres vers
les frais.

Il n'y a guère besoin de dire que l'admission
de l'Irlande serait pour nos activites athlétiques
un encouragement des plus vifs. Je serai donc très
reconaissant de recevoir votre réponse au plus tôt.

J'ai l'honneur de vous présenter mes
salutations cordiales et respectueuses.

J.J. Keane.

Président, Gaa

Starting on the page opposite and continuing above is the two-page letter which J.J. Keane sent to Baron de Coubertin in April 1922, pressing for Irish Olympic admission and outlining plans to hold the Tailteann Games. Courtesy of OSC, Lausanne.

laid down by your committee as essential for acceptance of Ireland's application is thus complied with.[4]

It is notable that Keane used the IOC's own previous acceptance of British dominions as independent nations to press the Irish case here. Keane, as we saw in the previous chapter, had an unrecorded meeting with both Arthur Griffith and Michael Collins in 1920, with the leaders of the Provisional Government pressing the cause of Irish recognition further.[5] This made sense on a number of levels. Obviously, Olympic recognition would solidify the international perception of Ireland as an independent state. We should also remember that Griffith had been a long-time proponent of Irish Olympic involvement, while Collins was, as we saw, a member of the sister club of J.J. Keane's, Dublin Geraldines. Elsewhere in the Keane letter to de Coubertin quoted above, he referred to great interest in Ireland in new clubs being formed and that plans for '*des jeux olympiques pour la race irlandaise seront tenus à Dublin et le programme olympique sera suivi au complet . . .*' ('The Irish Race Olympics [i.e. Tailteann Games] will be held in Dublin and the full Olympic programme of events will be followed'). That the Irish Olympic Council was very

This picture of J.J. Keane dates from around the time of the founding of the Irish Olympic Council. Courtesy of Ryder, White and Brophy.

definitely nationalist and separatist in its sentiments was reinforced by Keane signing as 'President, GAA'.

The baron's response to Keane has not been preserved in known records but it certainly seems to have accepted the case for Irish entry in future Olympics, from the reply of Keane to it: *Je suis prié de vous remercier de la part de mon Conseil de ce que l'Irlande a reçu le droit de prendre part aux jeux olympiques à son proper titre.*[6] Dr Cyril White has also pointed out that Keane was known by this stage to have struck up a strong friendship with J. Sigfrid Edström of Sweden, a powerful supporter to have at the IOC. Keane also informed the baron that he had been selected by the Irish Olympic Council as its nominee to the IOC at Easter, at which time the Council also recorded Irish appreciation of the baron's *'intérêt bienveillant'* in Ireland's search for Olympic recognition. This may show a little naivety on Keane's part, because as we saw it was custom and practice for the IOC to appoint its own 'members' and then appoint them as members for countries, making the members effectively the ambassadors of the IOC to the countries concerned, not the other way around.[7] Debatable as de Coubertin's support for Ireland might have been, what Keane did not expect, however, was the negative reaction of de Coubertin to the idea of Olympic Games for the Irish race (Tailteann Games) to which Keane had referred, fearing they might be in some sort of competition with the actual Olympics. The baron's concerns moved Keane to respond very quickly with assurances that the Tailteann Games were in no way intended as a challenge or alternative to the Olympic Games:

> . . . there is no intention on our part to create a rival Olympic organisation or to act in a fashion contrary to the interests of the international Olympic movement. We have already remarked to you about the disarray caused to our teams and athletic organisations by the political events of recent years. It is in order to remedy this situation and to reinvigorate the enthusiasm of the young people of our race, spread across the world, that we have prepared, in advance of Paris [i.e. the Olympics of 1924], this project for the athletes of the Irish race.[8]

The following month, prior to departing for the IOC congress in Paris and in the midst of forwarding two other names for possible IOC

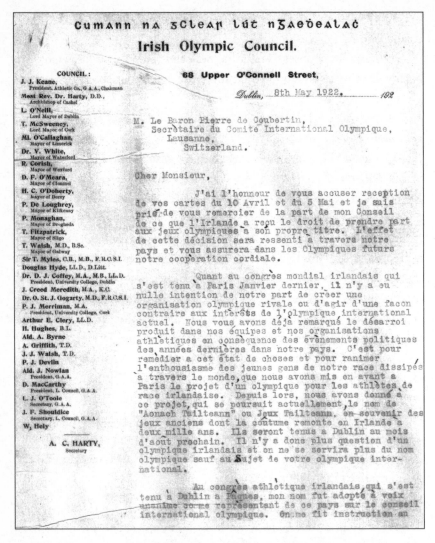

Cumann na ₃Cleaɼ Lúṫ nₔaeᵭealaċ

Irish Olympic Council.

COUNCIL:

J. J. Keane,
President, Athletic Co., G.A.A., Chairman
Most Rev. Dr. Harty, D.D.,
Archbishop of Cashel
L. O'Neill,
Lord Mayor of Dublin
T. McSweeney,
Lord Mayor of Cork
Ml. O'Callaghan,
Mayor of Limerick
Dr. V. White,
Mayor of Waterford
R. Corish,
Mayor of Wexford
D. F. O'Meara,
Mayor of Clonmel
H. C. O'Doherty,
Mayor of Derry
P. De Loughrey,
Mayor of Kilkenny
P. Monaghan,
Mayor of Drogheda
T. Fitzpatrick,
Mayor of Sligo
T. Walsh, M.D., B.Sc.
Mayor of Galway
Sir T. Myles, C.B., M.B., F.R.C.S.I.
Douglas Hyde, LL.D., D.Litt.
Dr. D. J. Coffey, M.A., M.B., LL.D.
President, University College, Dublin
J. Creed Meredith, M.A., K.C.
Dr. O. St. J. Gogarty, M.D., F.R.C.S.I.
P. J. Merriman, M.A.
President, University College, Cork
Arthur E. Clery, LL.D.
H. Hughes, B.L.
Ald. A. Byrne
A. Griffith, T.D.
J. J. Walsh, T.D.
P. J. Devlin
Ald. J. Nowlan
President, G.A.A.
D. MacCarthy
President, L. Council, G.A.A.
L. J. O'Toole
Secretary, G.A.A.
J. F. Shouldice
Secretary, L. Council, G.A.A.
W. Hely

A. C. HARTY,
Secretary

68 Upper O'Connell Street,

Dublin, 8th May 1922. 192

M. Le Baron Pierre de Coubertin,
Secrètaire du Comite International Olympique,
Lausanne,
Switzerland.

Cher Monsieur,

J'ai l'honneur de vous accuser reception de vos cartes du 10 Avril et du 5 Mai et je suis prié de vous remercier de la part de mon Conseil de ce que l'Irlande a reçu le droit de prendre part aux jeux olympiques à son propre titre. L'effet de cette décision sera ressenti a travers notre pays et vous assurera dans les Olympiques futurs notre cooperation cordiale.

Quant au congrès mondial irlandais qui s'est tenu à Paris Janvier dernier, il n'y a eu nulle intention de notre part de créer une organisation olympique rivale ou d'agir d'une facon contraire aux interêts de l'olympique international actuel. Nous vous avons déjà remarqué le désarroi produit dans nos équipes et nos organisations athlétiques en consèquence des évènements politiques des années dernières dans notre pays. C'est pour remédier a cet état de choses et pour ranimer l'enthousiasme des jeunes gens de notre race dissipés a travers le monde, que nous avons mis en avant a Paris le projet d'un olympique pour les athlètes de race irlandaise. Depuis lors, nous avons donné a ce projet, qui se poursuit actuellement, le nom de "Aonach Tailteann" ou Jeux Tailteann, en souvenir des jeux anciens dont la coutume remonte en Irlande à deux mille ans. Ils seront tenus à Dublin au mois d'aout prochain. Il n'y a donc plus question d'un olympique irlandais et on ne se servira plus du nom olympique sauf au Sujet de votre olympique international.

Au congrès athlétique irlandais qui s'est tenu à Dublin à Pâques, mon nom fut adopté à voix unanime comme représentant de ce pays sur le conseil international olympique. On me fit instruction a

membership, Keane still found it necessary to placate the baron further about the intention behind the Tailteann Games:

> We would be very upset if we have given you the impression that we were acting against the rules of the IOC, which we fully respect. It is a misunderstanding on the part of our Council, in suggesting a representative for your committee. Please consider this as merely a symptom of our enthusiasm than any desire on our parts to pre-empt the decision of your committee.[9]

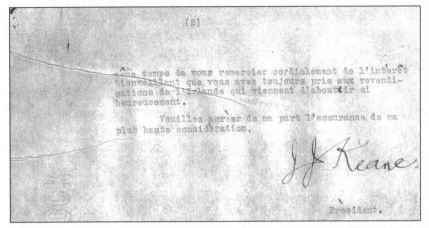

J.J. Keane's letter to Baron de Coubertin in May 1922, explaining that the planned Tailteann Games were no threat to the Olympic movement and that he, Keane, had been chosen by the Irish Olympic Council (later Olympic Council of Ireland) as its representative, should the International Olympic Committee accept the Irish case. Courtesy of OSC, Lausanne.

At the IOC session in Paris, even with the baron's concerns about the Tailteann Games now resolved, once more the stumbling block of a British Olympic representative was encountered. De Coubertin, probably prompted by Edstrom, reminded the session that they had agreed to re-examine the Irish campaign for representation at this meeting, even proposing '*la candidature de m. J.J. Keane, president du Comité Olympique Irlandais*'.[10] The executive committee agreed but then heard the concerns of the British delegate:

> Colonel Kentish thinks that the Irish situation is still too uncertain for it to be possible to proceed with the election proposed. A decision was required on the subject. In the end, Colonel Kentish suggested that, while accepting the principle of appointing an Irish member, this decision should be referred to a later meeting. It was thus decided.[11]

The following day, Keane requested the committee to hear his and Ireland's case again. Keane outlined all of the progress that he and the Irish Olympic Council had made, including the unification of the different athletic bodies and reorganisation of Irish sporting federations to the point that there were now at least 365 athletic clubs in Ireland. He verified for de Coubertin that the Irish Council was 'ouvert à tous sans distinction religieuse ou ethnique'.[12] Unsurprisingly, given Keane's strong GAA background, the questioning which his adversary of the previous day engaged in related to the national agenda and relations with Ulster. Replying here to Kentish's concerns as to what would happen should relations break down between the Free State and Ulster, Keane responded that he did not concern himself with politics.[13]

Keane at this point was thanked by de Coubertin and then retired. We may never know the details of what happened later that evening, beyond the certainty that Keane and Kentish met to discuss the issue of Irish representation on the IOC and, naturally, of Irish admission to the Olympic fold. Whatever unfolded, it was enough to satisfy Kentish by the following session:

> Colonel Kentish announces that the question of Ireland had been discussed again, he was revising his opinions of the previous evening following a conversation with Mr Keane. He thinks that it is now acceptable and had merely made his previous declaration in the interests of peace as well as sport.[14]

Given the nature of the IOC president, there is every likelihood that de Coubertin was involved in some of the behind-the-scenes discussions between Kentish and Keane too, and influenced the British representative to back down. Thus, finally, Keane and Ireland were welcomed with open arms. The irony of the welcome deserves to be noted. After ignoring the campaigns for Irish recognition on its own sporting merits, which went back at least to Peter O'Connor in 1906, the Olympic Committee now reminded itself of the *valeur olympique* of Ireland.[15] Here – though not used by de Coubertin himself – was finally an official reference to the Irish athletic tradition, at a time when it was at possibly its lowest ebb in twenty years. When Irish athletes had been supreme in at least eight Olympic events, the country's case for recognition had never resulted in acknowledgement by the IOC of this same tradition. De Coubertin compounded the irony by reminding the 1922 congress of how this so-called *valeur olympique* was a central reason why other non-independent states had been accorded IOC recognition in the past:

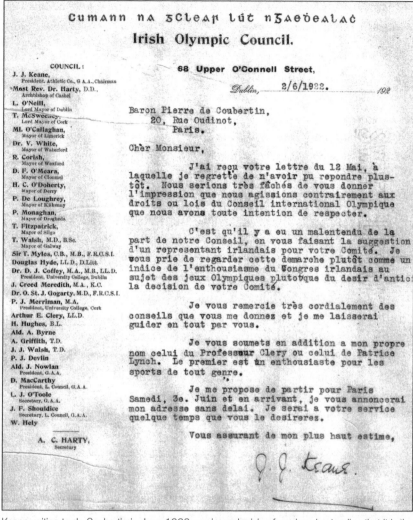

Cumann na ȝCleap Lúᴄ nȝaeòeaLaᴄ

Irish Olympic Council.

COUNCIL:

J. J. Keane,
President, Athletic Co., G.A.A., Chairman

Most Rev. Dr. Harty, D.D.,
Archbishop of Cashel

L. O'Neill,
Lord Mayor of Dublin

T. McSweeney,
Lord Mayor of Cork

Ml. O'Callaghan,
Mayor of Limerick

Dr. V. White,
Mayor of Waterford

R. Corish,
Mayor of Wexford

D. F. O'Meara,
Mayor of Clonmel

H. C. O'Doherty,
Mayor of Derry

P. De Loughrey,
Mayor of Kilkenny

P. Monaghan,
Mayor of Drogheda

T. Fitzpatrick,
Mayor of Sligo

T. Walsh, M.D., B.Sc.
Mayor of Galway

Sir T. Myles, C.B., M.B., F.R.C.S.I.

Douglas Hyde, LL.D., D.Litt.

Dr. D. J. Coffey, M.A., M.B., LL.D.
President, University College, Dublin

J. Creed Meredith, M.A., K.C.

Dr. O. St. J. Gogarty, M.D., F.R.C.S.I.

P. J. Merriman, M.A.
President, University College, Cork

Arthur E. Clery, LL.D.

H. Hughes, B.L.

Ald. A. Byrne

A. Griffith, T.D.

J. J. Walsh, T.D.

P. J. Devlin

Ald. J. Nowlan
President, G.A.A.

D. MacCarthy
President, L. Council, G.A.A.

L. J. O'Toole
Secretary, G.A.A.

J. F. Shouldice
Secretary, L. Council, G.A.A.

W. Hely

A. C. HARTY,
Secretary

68 Upper O'Connell Street,

Dublin, 2/6/1922. 192

Baron Pierre de Coubertin,
20, Rue Oudinot,
Paris.

Chèr Monsieur,

J'ai reçu votre lettre du 12 Mai, à laquelle je regrette de n'avoir pu repondre plus-tôt. Nous serions très fâchés de vous donner l'impression que nous agissions contrairement aux droits ou lois du Conseil international Olympique que nous avons toute intention de respecter.

C'est qu'il y a eu un malentendu de la part de notre Conseil, en vous faisant la suggestion d'un representant irlandais pour votre Comité. Je vous prie de regarder cette demarche plutôt comme un indice de l'enthousiasme du Congres irlandais au sujet des jeux Olympiques plutôque du desir d'antici la decision de votre Comité.

Je vous remercie très cordialement des conseils que vous me donnez et je me laisserai guider en tout par vous.

Je vous soumets en addition a mon propre nom celui du Professeur Clery ou celui de Patrice Lynch. Le premier est un enthousiaste pour les sports de tout genre.

Je me propose de partir pour Paris Samedi, 3e. Juin et en arrivant, je vous annoncerai mon adresse sans delai. Je serai a votre service quelque temps que vous le desirerez.

Vous assurant de mon plus haut estime,

J. J. Keane.

Keane writing to de Coubertin in June 1922, again apologising for misunderstanding that it is the IOC who chooses its members from different countries, and not for a country like Ireland to nominate its member first. Courtesy of OSC, Lausanne.

The President replied that it had always been thus and that this was the reason why Bohemia from the outset and then Finland had been among the list of IOC members, which has not always been easy for Austria or Russia to accept. [*Le président répond qu'il a toujours été ainsi et que c'est la raison pour laquelle la Bohème dès l'origine et par suite la Finlande ont figuré sur la liste du CIO privilège qui n'a pas été toujours aisé à faire accepter en Autriche ou en Russie.*][16]

Keane was, nevertheless, proposed for election by the baron himself and thus it was that Ireland was effectively admitted to the Olympic family, over twenty-eight years after that same family had first been formed.

The Aftermath of Olympic Admission

In looking at events in Ireland through 1922–3, there were some grounds for optimism in relation to the future Olympic prospects of an Irish team. Moves were afoot which would bring about an unprecedented unification in Irish athletics. For one thing, the Great War dealt a hammer blow to an already struggling IAAA. It held no track and field championships between 1914 and 1919 and other activities were very much reduced during the same period. These championships did recommence in 1919, as did an international match with Scotland, with a cross country championship beginning again in 1920. These events masked, however, what were significant numerical weaknesses and differences of opinion within the IAAA, between the southern and northern branches and relating to visions for the future of athletics on the island.[16]

Under de Valera, Dáil Éireann had expressed interest in reviving the Tailteann Games and this interest was maintained by the Griffith-led Free State. This is unsurprising, given that Griffith was one of the few nationalist political figures before 1916 who had seen the value of pushing for Irish representation in the Olympic arena. The government's organising committee for the Tailteann Games, headed by J.J. Walsh, had some funding available and also managed to broaden the issue beyond the usual GAA–IAAA conflict by getting the backing of the Irish universities. Traditionally, university athletic clubs had been quite strongly IAAA in their leanings, despite the naming of several university presidents on the first Irish Olympic Council. The involvement of the universities may well have helped to ease fears that many IAAA members had of rapprochement:

> The decision taken by the IAAA was 'the AGM of the IAAA, having considered the invitation from the Inter University Athletics Association to discuss with that Body and the Gaelic

Athletics Association how athletics could be benefited in Ireland, expresses its willingness to enter into such a conference, and is of the opinion that there should be no insuperable obstacle to coming to a working agreement between the two Associations'.[17]

The initial response of the GAA to the universities' proposal of unity was more lukewarm than the IAAA's response. The GAA anticipated complete victory over the IAAA very soon anyway. However, it has already been noted how important the portrayal of a united front of Irish athletics was for Keane at Paris in June 1922. That the new body would retain a clear nationalist ethos was also not in doubt, with the southern branch of the IAAA accepting an exclusion rule, banning British military and members of the RIC from membership.[18] Keane was at Paris in early June as both president of the Irish Olympic Council and as 'President GAA'. Although Keane was only the president of the Athletic Council of the GAA, there is no doubting that de Coubertin's aristocratic sentiments were impressed by such titles. Yet Keane was also well aware that the IAAA was substantially rowing in behind the unification, having heard a GAA appeal 'not to wreck the agreement for the sake of a few Ulster Specials'.[19] From the GAA's own perspective, Keane worked hard in the early months of 1922 to persuade the GAA itself to abandon the old Athletic Council which had had such a chequered history with its own athletes:

> ... within weeks of the ratification of the Treaty he had moved into action. Overcoming the understandable opposition of some members to the prospect of releasing control of athletics to any other body, Keane got authority to draw up a detailed scheme, to be submitted for its approval to the GAA congress at Easter, for a new Irish athletics body independent of the GAA.[20]

The success of Keane in persuading the GAA of the merits of unification can be seen in the fact that forty-nine of the fifty delegates to a special Athletic Council meeting agreed that the Council would cede control of GAA athletes to a new body, set up in the early summer of 1922 as the National Athletic and Cycling Association of Ireland (NACAI). It was to this same body that the IAAA would eventually affiliate in July.

That northern athletics would secede from the rest of Irish athletics was made more likely by the coming into being of Northern Ireland in 1920 and then the Free State in early 1922. That this was not inevitable is shown by the fact that the Irish Rugby Football Union remained intact, as did other sporting bodies. In athletics, however, the significantly nationalist presence of the GAA in the new athletics proposals might have become tolerable to southern IAAA members but not to northerners in the main. When the Northern Branch of the IAAA met on 14 June 1922, days after Keane's triumph in Paris, it announced:

> That the Northern IAAA, while of the opinion that the proposed NACA would be of benefit to athletics generally, regret that the proposed Constitution debars soldiers, sailors and police on active service in Ireland from competing at meetings of the new Body. Unless this clause is withdrawn the Northern Branch cannot see their way to advise delegates to support the IAAA who recommends the clubs to join the new Association.[21]

The IAAA proceeded with the process of dissolution, and on 18 July 1922 it ceased to exist as a corporate body. On 28 July the Northern Branch of the IAAA renamed itself the AAA(I), open to all Ireland and willing to join the NACAI if the exclusion rule was changed. On the IAAA's dissolution and merging with the GAA in the NACAI, the *Irish Independent* commented:

> To all genuinely interested in the furtherance of Irish athletics, the above news will make pleasant reading and it is to be hoped that the fusion of forces will be welded into a joint [body] that will endure for long.[22]

The year 1922 saw the removal, or at least diminution within the twenty-six counties, of the political and organisational obstacles which had dogged Irish athletics generally and Olympism specifically since the mid-1890s. The immovable force that was the British Olympic movement, the IOC's own reservations about calls for Irish representation and the internecine feud within Irish athletics were officially ended within a few short weeks in the early summer of that year. Even the old GAA indifference to athletics seemed no longer to matter with the establishment of the new National Athletic and Cycling Association, dedicated to restoring Irish athletic and cycling prowess, at home and internationally. The early signs were very promising, beginning with a successful application for Ireland to join the IAAF in early 1923.[23] There was also a very successful if delayed inaugural Tailteann Games in 1924, and the first involvement of a recognised Irish team at the Paris Olympic Games the same year.[24]

The Paris Olympics of 1924

Subsequent sporting history shows that there was no sudden reversal of fortunes for Irish Olympism following on the nonetheless momentous developments of 1922. Ireland did compete in Paris, and as 'Ireland' rather than the 'Irish Free State'. The use of the term 'Ireland' rather than the 'Irish Free State' left all sorts of doors open for all-Ireland co-operation in Olympic sports. When the rules were changed in the early 1930s, requiring Olympic representation to be directly aligned with nation-state boundaries, it would spark a major crisis in the Irish Olympic movement and lead to our non-participation at the Berlin Games of 1936, among other difficulties which are not our direct concern here.

Ireland came away from Paris with no athletic or other sporting medal successes at all. The official report on the Paris Games suggests that although there was a definite Irish team, as many Irish entrants failed to take their places as did so, while the absence of a team photograph from the opening ceremony also suggests that this great opportunity for national identity may well have been diminished.[25] The official report does not acknowledge the participation of an Irish team in the opening ceremony at Paris, with no actual listing of teams which participated but pictures of thirty-nine of the countries participating being included in the report, mostly in alphabetical order. One page includes Greece, Haiti, Holland, Hungary, India and Italy but no reference to Ireland or pictures of an Irish team have been found. However, other evidence has been offered to show that Ireland marched in twenty-fifth position among the forty-five nations present, led by high-jumper Larry Stanley, who also won two All Ireland football medals with Kildare in his day.[26] It is difficult to believe that gaps in Irish representation can be explained by mere budgetary constraints. The annual general meeting of the NACAI in May

This parade scene from the 1928 Tailteann Games at Croke Park shows Pat O'Callaghan directly behind the flag-bearer, Tom Kiely, with a hat-wearing Peter O'Connor further to the right at the rear and John Flanagan with J.J. Keane on the further right, both in hats, flanking an unidentified visiting US athlete. The young man at the front right with the wolfhound is Mitchel Cogley. Courtesy Dr Cyril White.

1925 reported that the net loss incurred in sending athletes to Paris had been just over £10 in all.[27]

The Irish boxing squad consisted of eight members, essentially one boxer entered at each of the weights available, again not evidence of financial issues curtailing entries where competitors of standing were available. One Irish boxer, Paddy Dwyer, was beaten in the welterweight semi-final at Paris but was not awarded a bronze medal as this tradition of awarding losing semi-finalists a bronze was not established in Olympic boxing until much later.[28]

The only Irish representatives to win medals in the 1924 Paris Games were in the cultural events, with Jack B. Yeats earning the distinction of becoming the first official Irish Free State medallist by winning a silver medal in art for his painting, generally now called *The Liffey Swim* but referred to simply as *Swimming* in the official report. Oliver St John Gogarty became the only member of the inaugural Olympic Council of

Ireland to compete for Ireland at the Olympic Games, his poetry entry for 1924 being awarded joint third place.[29] Irish-America had something of a last hurrah at Paris, with Matt McGrath winning a fantastic second place in the hammer, to add to his previous gold and silver from the pre-war days. Jack Kelly and Paul Costello won another gold medal for the USA in the double sculls, making Kelly the first oarsman to win three Olympic titles. An interesting Irish success was recorded in association football, where the first-ever Irish team victory post-independence was recorded as the Irish beat Bulgaria 1–0, losing 2–1 in the quarter-final afterwards to the Dutch, after extra time.[30] It is ironic that Ireland's first team victory at an Olympic celebration came in a sport which had been anathema to the GAA before and after for so long.

Many of the old differences between the GAA and the IAAA continued after unification. With the tightening of Olympic regulations on the definition of 'Ireland', the level of division in the Irish Olympic movement showed itself to be so significant that the General O'Duffy-led Council failed to enter a team at all for the 1936 Games in Berlin.

Amazing as it may seem, the only time that Ireland has applied to host the Olympic Games themselves came within a decade of 1924. At the Los Angeles meeting of the IOC during the 1932 Games, on 29 July, it was recorded that nine cities in all had formally applied to host the summer Games of 1940. In black and white, the official report of the organising committee which eventually had the task of hosting those Games records that Tokyo won the Games from the challenge of five European cities, two South American cities, one North American and one African city. The five European cities are listed as Rome, Barcelona, Helsingfors (Helsinki), Budapest and Dublin.[31] Japan eventually lost the Games due to the outbreak of the Second World War, but this fascinating report still survives, perhaps testament to the ambitions of the new de Valera and Fianna Fáil government, with O'Duffy still its Garda chief, to show Ireland's independence and assist in Treaty-dismantling indirectly by hosting the Olympics. Had it succeeded, hosting the Games would have been the most dramatic opportunity yet to establish an Irish identity beyond doubt at the Olympics. The opportunity could, of course, also have bankrupted the country in the process!

CONCLUSION

G iven that the core sporting events around which Irish Olympic involvement revolved were athletic ones, it is important to take stock of how Ireland's athletic identity was affected by the Games and, indeed, how the Olympics impacted upon different versions of Irish identity in athletics.

Firstly, it is noteworthy that the most dramatic efforts at the Olympic Games to establish an Irish identity came from outside the control of either of the two main athletic bodies in Ireland. John Boland's post-Athens battle with G.S. Robertson over his Irishness had no connection with any Irish sporting association. Tom Kiely in 1904 went to St Louis as an individual and had connections with both athletic organisations in Ireland, as did Peter O'Connor in 1906, although O'Connor did carry Irish regalia at the instigation of the IAAA and Kiely was largely associated with the GAA in Ireland, even more so after St Louis.

From the organisational point of view, the IAAA was more consistent and persistent in its efforts to foster Irish involvement and identity at the Olympics than the GAA was. That this was achieved sporadically and not to the satisfaction of those who sought a more independent recognition of Ireland at the Games is also undeniable. Yet, in the period prior to the intensification and popularisation of separatist sentiment, i.e. before 1916, the IAAA's efforts were not out of sync with popular political sentiment in the main. Bear in mind, for instance, that the Irish Party won seventy-nine seats in the general elections of 1910, while Sinn Féin won none. The IAAA's choice of national symbols in fact reflected unionist, separatist and cultural perspectives, as has been witnessed with O'Connor in 1906. The first time that the Irish press which has been researched recorded any significant dissatisfaction with Irish athletes competing on a Great Britain and Ireland team was in 1908, and even then the dissatisfaction was more strongly expressed in Irish-American sources than within Ireland itself.

From the more nationalist perspective, the GAA had more or less abandoned its interest in athletics as the Olympic Games began to take hold. A former secretary general of the association, writing in modern times, summed this up:

> Athletics were almost completely neglected by the GAA and the field was left open to the IAAA. The situation had deteriorated to such a degree by 1900 that the national athletics championships were abandoned and even the recently revived all-round championship was allowed to lapse. It is true that it was proposed to inaugurate inter-county athletic contests, but the initiative was passed on to a few enthusiasts to put into practice.[1]

It has been clear that the GAA was not particularly interested in using the Olympic Games to establish an Irish separatist identity. Indeed, the evidence shows that, despite its IRB links, such a separatist identity was not always as strong within the ranks of the GAA as has been ascribed to it on the basis of its post-1916 positions. While the reasons for the failure to play hurling in Paris during the 1900 Games have not been verifiable, that the GAA had little international vision has been self-evident, at least prior to 1912. It has been even more evident that the GAA's interest in athletic sports was in itself very dubious. In many respects, it was the passion of Frank Dineen which kept GAA athletics alive at all. That it was largely the GAA which ultimately led the moves to found the Olympic Council of Ireland was a somewhat ironic turn of events, therefore, and may be testament to the forcefulness of J.J. Keane as an individual as much as to any change of view by the GAA more broadly. The association began to appreciate the need to foster an athletic and Olympic ambition from at least 1912, in part because of the pressures from within, from groups like MAPA and the Gaelic Cyclists. The IAAA was by then in a greatly weakened position because of the years of inactivity due to the Great War and the massive political shift which occurred after 1916. In many respects, its demise, and that of the ICA, in the early 1920s was inevitable.

That the Olympic Council of Ireland emerged as a mainly GAA inspiration, clearly linked to separatist politics, and that the new NACAI could not retain the support of northern athletics meant that the future of Olympic involvement from 1922 onwards would continue to reflect the political divisions which affected much of the period from 1896 to 1920. Neither Irish athletics nor the Irish Olympic movement would manage to bridge the divide created by the foundation of Northern Ireland and the Irish Free State in 1920–2. The political division of the island was not the cause of this sporting division. The Irish Rugby Football Union, for example, survived as a single body through all the political turmoil, partly because its members had sufficient socio-political common interests. The political divisions which permeated the Olympic story itself from the 1890s were simply too profound. It proved impossible to bridge the divide when the concept of Ireland as a single 'nation' was still there in theory at least. After 1920, the political division of the island merely reinforced a division which had been present and proved an insurmountable barrier to Irish athletic and Olympic unity from the very first Games. Within the twenty-six counties, and athletics therein, the old GAA–IAAA rancour was to take decades to die down, very much to the detriment of hopes to restore an athletic tradition which was shown to be in serious decline since at least 1908.[2]

The Broader Political Messages

Irish involvement with the Olympic Games sheds considerable light on several broader political issues. Firstly, the degree to which there were multiple interpretations of what Irish nationality meant in the 1890s and 1900s is very evident in the Olympic experience. John Boland's comfort in accepting his 'British' identity in 1896, until goaded into demonstrating his Irishness, is an interesting example. At a time of low ebb for the Home Rule cause, years of Tory rule and fluctuating efforts to generate a cultural revival, Boland's nationalism was effectively a latent one, submerged until it was challenged as being 'British'.

On the other hand, at least within Ireland at that time, the story of Tom Kiely had no challenge to his assertion of being Irish. More intriguing, however, was the degree to which Kiely achieved universal acclaim in Ireland, from both athletic associations and people of vastly different shades of political opinion. That this was essentially a personal endorsement for Kiely is undeniable. However, his popularity also shows the degree to which pride in Irish achievement was capable of unifying people of different political persuasions, thus suggesting that a greater effort to establish an international identity via the Olympics from the outset might have affected not only Ireland's standing internationally but also helped to generate a greater sense of cohesion in the national vision at a time when Ireland still had sufficient athletic might to make a real impact at the Olympic Games.

Kiely's impact within Tipperary, and to some extent that of James Brendan Connolly on South Boston, reinforces another aspect of Irish identity, in the sense that it inevitably had a strong local angle. This applied where the athlete was well known or where his sporting success was in a popular sport. By contrast, the achievements of John Boland or Harold Mahony were virtually ignored in their own localities, because the athletes were unknown, or represented the gentry to some extent, but certainly because their sporting success came in a non-popular event.[3]

The impact of Peter O'Connor's protests in 1906 highlighted the fact that Irish athletes might have been forced to compete as part of a British and Irish team but resented it and sought to establish a separate identity for themselves. Similar protests took place in 1908, and it is no exaggeration to suggest either that such demonstrations of independent aspirations also reflected the political aspirations for Home Rule, which had been somewhat reinvigorated in Ireland since the fall of the Conservatives in late 1905. Because the Irish representation at most of the early Olympics was small, sometimes individual and never a cohesive 'team', the concept of Irish identity never reached the level that the Finns achieved in their efforts to be seen as distinct from Russia. Nevertheless, they remained important. In fact, when the Finnish athlete Hannes Kolehmainen stood for his own victory celebration in 1912, forced to see a Russian flag raised in his honour rather than a Finnish one, he echoed very clearly the sentiments of Peter O'Connor six years previously when he commented to a friend: 'I would almost rather not have won, than to see that flag up there.'[4]

It is no coincidence that the immediate aftermath of O'Connor's Olympic achievements saw a number of important political figures beginning to realise the potential vehicle for political messages which the Olympics had to offer. Roger Casement realised the import of establishing such an identity internationally. So did Arthur Griffith, although in his case the message was more focused on wanting to prevent Irish successes being hailed as British ones and also, even in the midst of failure, on portraying the merits of the Sinn Féin 'buy-Irish' campaign. In 1908, in addition to some degree of awakening by national political figures to Irish-American Olympic achievements in particular, the scramble by local politicians to associate themselves with either the IAAA or GAA-led homecoming celebrations again showed the importance which the Olympics had now attained, particularly where such successes had been achieved against British opposition.

Finally, within Ireland, the moves by J.J. Keane and the GAA to set up an Irish Olympic Council in the early 1920s succeeded in galvanising much of the separatist political support among both the Dáil and local corporations. It was nationalist and separatist in its orientation, apart from the more moderate angle which some of the university representatives stood for. This development reflected the changed political environment in Ireland itself, as much as it stemmed from the demise of the IAAA, but the two developments combined ensured that the directions taken by Irish athletics and Olympism after 1920 reflected the division of the island into two political entities.

While the degree to which Irish identity and nationalism were furthered by Olympism was mixed, the impact of the Olympic Games on the identity of Irish-America was more clear-cut and profound. For one thing, there is little doubt that the involvement of first- and second-generation Irish athletes on US Olympic teams had a significant role in helping the Irish to assimilate with the broader US population and gain greater acceptance than had been the case heretofore. This happened particularly in 1908 but was evident from as early as the first American Olympic triumph, that of James Brendan Connolly. That Irish involvement and influence waned in later US teams is undeniable, but the evidence is there to suggest that Olympism did much for Irish identity in the USA, both in achieving a degree of acceptability as Americans and also in furthering pride in their Irish ancestry among the major Irish communities of cities like New York and Boston.[5]

The rise of Irish-American athletics and Olympic involvement coincided with the reinvigoration of militant Irish nationalism in the USA and has been shown to be of considerable importance. The Ancient Order of Hibernians, but more so Clan na Gael and John Devoy, made significant use of the successes of Irish-American sportsmen to promote the political philosophy of Irish republicanism. The evidence also suggests that Clan na Gael, and some other nationalist movements, used the Irish Olympians as a significant part of their efforts to raise funds and US-based recruits for the cause of Irish revolution. While the Clan certainly attracted financial support from a number of quarters, there is no doubt that the amount of money raised on the backs of Irish-American Olympians' attendance, sometimes purported attendance, at its picnics equated to a multiple of the funds it sent to assist the 1916 Rising. While substantial numbers of Irish-Americans never made it to Ireland to help in the independence struggle, these same picnics were certainly aimed at the recruitment of large numbers of men to assist in the cause of Irish nationalism. Important evidence of the influence of Irish-American militancy, using the springboard of Olympic successes, on the promotion of Hiberno-German friendship and anglophobia in some major American political circles has also been presented.

The International Impact of Irish Olympism

From an international perspective, it is clear that Irish identity failed to establish itself politically among the ranks of the International Olympic Committee for over two and a half decades after the IOC was founded. The nature of the IOC itself was partly to blame for this. From its first congress at the Sorbonne in 1894, the IOC became a very tightly knit group, dominated by Baron de Coubertin and, in many instances, people who were hand-picked by him. Although two IAAA representatives were in attendance at the Sorbonne, and we know that an invitation was sent to at least one of the Irish athletic associations, possibly both, for 1896, there is very little evidence of IOC interest in Irish representation after that. No evidence has been found to suggest that the IOC had any involvement in the decision to offer to stage a demonstration hurling game in Paris, or Irish sports in St Louis. Similarly, the IOC had no part in the acceptance of the Irish entries of Kiely and others in St Louis.

A picture of John Flanagan surrounded by family members in later life. Courtesy of the Flanagan Memorial Committee.

Overtly, at least, it was the local organising committee and Prince George of Greece who blocked the Irish demands for separate recognition in 1906, and certainly from 1908 to 1920 inclusive the main obstacles to Irish recognition came from the British Olympic Association.

All this said, the IOC cannot be completely absolved from the matter of preventing demands for Irish recognition at the Olympics from reaching fruition. For one thing, its 'ignorance' of Irish claims was suspect. Ireland's athletes held several world records during the period 1896 to 1920 and there was a tradition of Ireland having its own international team in athletics which pre-dated the 1894 Sorbonne congress. Accordingly, to suggest that Ireland should automatically be included with Britain, while at the same time de Coubertin was happy to accord separate recognition from 1896 to semi-independent Hungary and completely non-independent Bohemia, both under Habsberg rule until the end of the Great War, betrays either ignorance of the political situation or IOC bias in relation to it. De Coubertin's subsequent correspondence with members of the British Olympic movement and the American equivalent also suggest that he, the IOC and establishment figures within these movements were more than concerned about the danger of affording recognition to Ireland. Any moves which might contribute to a decline of establishment values or the old international order of things, or smack of tolerating the aggressive quasi-professionalism of Irish-America were anathema to most IOC leaders. The IOC's policy on nationality and national recognition was always uncertain and fraught with inconsistencies. That Irish efforts to achieve recognition failed should not be a surprise in this context. That they failed for so long, even though de Coubertin himself was ultimately to recognise the athletic tradition in Ireland in 1922, was due to the conservative values of the IOC in no small part, particularly in the manner in which it allowed itself to be heavily influenced by the British Olympic Association. 'Ultimately, participation in the Games became a public affirmation of international recognition.'[6] For over a quarter of a century, the IOC tacitly ignored what was, admittedly, a somewhat sporadically expressed Irish case for such recognition.

In turning to the British Olympic Association, it is clear that this body's role was central in the prevention of Irish efforts to establish a separate identity at the Olympic Games, particularly from 1906. While the BOA only came into existence after the St Louis Games, from 1896 individuals like Robertson and de Courcy Laffan were influential in either denying Irish identity or in seeking to ensure that the only Irish bodies who might achieve Olympic recognition of any sort would be ones considered reliable from the British perspective. Similarly, and again before the formalisation of the British Olympic Association, British correspondence with de Coubertin focused the baron's mind on the unacceptability of the Irish-American influence of James Sullivan and others in St Louis.

The Intercalated Games of 1906 were the first in which the BOA had a formal role, and these Games displayed very significant influence coming from the association against the efforts of Irish athletes to achieve independent recognition. The same happened in 1908 and 1912, both at the meetings of the BOA and of the IOC, and ultimately at the Olympic venues themselves. Neither the efforts of the Irish within the meetings of the BOA nor the actions of the athletes in the stadia caused the BOA to waver one bit from its position on Irish representation. Indeed, the only times when the BOA supported separate Irish identity at the Olympics were when it suited its own needs, as in the different and mostly British sports which needed team entries at the London Games, or the easiest way of keeping the different and trustworthy cycling bodies happy at the Stockholm Games. That the BOA's stance was based on British interests rather than Irish is quite understandable.[7] That it was a broadly imperialist agenda is also undeniable, as evidenced by its strong support for Olympic and IOC membership for appropriately chosen representatives of some of the Empire's more anglicised components, particularly Canada. That the most important stumbling block in the way of albeit disjointed Irish efforts to enter an Irish team, or achieve recognition on the IOC, remained the BOA until well after the formation of the Olympic Council of Ireland and the setting up of the Irish Free State remains certain.

A closing anecdote may help to sum up the position in relation to Irish identity and the BOA. In the 1990s, the BOA made an assertion that Britain was one of a small group of countries which had been represented at every summer Olympic Games since 1896.[8] In relation to the St Louis Olympics, for example, the BOA asserted:

> There is little doubt that as the two countries known as Britain and Ireland were combined at that time (1904) and that Irish athletes competed under the umbrella of Great Britain, the British Olympic Association can continue to claim to be one of three national Olympic committees to have attended all Olympic Games.[9]

This assertion was immediately challenged, not by the Olympic Council of Ireland but by the Australian Olympic Committee. Apart altogether from the fact that the BOA had not even been founded in 1904, the Australians' argument, at the time in defence of some quiz questions that had been generated in advance of the 2000 Sydney Games, was forceful:

> It is a little hard to take seriously the notion of athletes of Britain and Ireland combining at those Games under one banner. The evidence in fact is that people like Kiely strenuously resisted the offer of the umbrella. In simple terms, we believe it would be quite wrong to claim that such a man was a member of a United Kingdom or Great Britain team when he chose not to accept an

invitation to become one, even to the point of refusing to accept travel expenses . . . We cannot see the fact that Great Britain governed Ireland at the time as justification. In 1896 Australia was still a collection of colonies governed by Britain; that does not affect the status of Edwin Flack as an Australian competitor at the Athens Games . . .[10]

Perhaps the most remarkable thing about this latter correspondence is the date: February 2000. That Tom Kiely's national identity in the twenty-first century remains a source of some controversy is surprising and certainly makes it more difficult to demonstrate that others, whether they represented 'Great Britain', 'Great Britain and Ireland' or the 'United States of America', were, in fact, very important representatives of an Irish sporting tradition which battled to assert itself through whatever media it could between 1896 and 1920, restricted both by internal division and international obstacles. That they did so, in all of these guises, and still managed to leave a major imprint on the history of the early Olympic Games, winning the equivalent of nearly sixty medals in all up to 1920, has been one of the most remarkable feats of Irish sporting history. The Irish Olympic story up to the early 1920s is very deserving of commemoration in its own right and regardless of the political and diplomatic divisions which permeated the efforts of these great proponents of different forms of Irish identity. The *dénouement* arrived at in 1922, added to the failure of different sporting bodies to arrest athletic decline in the intervening years, meant that these glory days of Irish Olympism would not be restored, particularly in an increasingly competitive sporting world. Nor does this take from the marvellous individual achievements of those who came afterwards. Irish athletes, from O'Callaghan to Delany, Treacy, O'Sullivan and others have done remarkably well in international competition, considering the size of the country and pre-eminence of so many other sports. However, the combined efforts of the Irish and Irish-American Olympians contributed to a general growth in awareness of and pride in Irish identity, both at home and internationally. As Arthur Griffith himself pointed out, revolutions are slow and often barely perceptible things, and the gradual, and sporadic, raising of awareness of Ireland's identity which was achieved by Irish Olympians was a very important contribution to the cultural and indeed political revolution which was under way in Ireland up to 1922.[11]

A NOTE ON SOURCES

R esearch to date into sport and national identity in pre-independence Ireland has focused chiefly on the Gaelic Athletic Association and to a lesser degree on sports like association football, rugby and athletics. The role of the GAA particularly as a vehicle for promoting national identity has been well documented by historians like Pádraig Purséal and Marcus de Búrca. Within the work of these writers, the political focus has been almost entirely on the role of the GAA as an anti-British, Irish nationalist organisation, whose main impact has been within Ireland itself. Furthermore, the GAA's own sporting interests came to concentrate increasingly on the team sports of hurling and football, moving away from athletic and potentially international sports from as early as the first decade after its foundation. This has tended to influence the research of GAA writers also, who sometimes ignore the fact that the founding fathers of the GAA, like Davin and Cusack, were much more steeped in athletics than in the team sports of hurling and football, which later came to dominate the organisation's activities. On the other hand, the international team sports which have had some Irish-oriented research done on them have tended to be seen as anglicised sports, not fully reflective of either national identity or nationalism in late nineteenth- and early twentieth-century Ireland. The work of Mike Cronin and Edmund van Esbeck in association football and rugby respectively has gone some way towards identifying the particular political and national issues which permeated non-native sport. However, much remains to be done on the role of international sport in the evolution of an Irish national identity, and on the evolution of Irish nationalism itself.

With the exception of the early parts of a fine work in Irish by Séamus Ware, *Laochra na hÉireann agus na Cluichí Olimpeacha* (published by the author, 1996), the role played by the Olympic Games in the evolution of an Irish identity and nationalism prior to independence has been virtually ignored by Irish historians. Most Olympic histories which deal with Irish involvement have dealt chiefly with the post-independence period and, within that, with the achievements of the competitors rather than on matters of national identity. Excellent works by Johnny Watterson and Lindie Naughton include *Irish Olympians* (Dublin: Blackwater Press, 1992) and an updated and expanded version by the same authors called *Faster, Higher, Stronger* (Dublin: Ashfield Press, 2008); they are well worth the read. There are also several by famous Irish Olympic expert David Guiney that fall into this category, including *Gold, Silver, Bronze* (Dublin: Sportsworld, 1991) and *Olympic Facts and Figures* (Olympic Council of Ireland, 1992). Taking a refreshing perspective also is *From Sophie to Sonia* by Noel Henry (Noel Henry, 1998), on the emergence of women in Irish and Olympic athletics, again after independence. Tony O'Donoghue's *Irish Championship Athletics 1873–1914* (published by the author in Dublin in 2005) is an absolute must for anyone studying the athletics of this period in Ireland.

The research for this current book has encompassed a number of areas which have not been tapped into previously. It is important to bear in mind that many of the most relevant primary records relating to Irish Olympic involvement up to 1920 are held abroad. Over a series of visits to the Olympic Studies Centre in Lausanne, Switzerland, access has been gained to the considerable resources stored there. These include official International Olympic Committee (IOC) documentation and correspondence between the IOC head, Baron de Coubertin, and many British and American officials who had an influence on Irish Olympic involvement. Lausanne has also yielded up the then unpublished diary of Ireland's first Olympian, John Boland, the IOC's massive photographic archive and a vast array of books and articles which have never been used in published works on Irish Olympic involvement. Some of my most interesting research has been in the quiet corners of Ireland where our Olympic greats mostly came from. Whether in Mayo, west Limerick, north Cork or south Tipperary, I was privileged to meet some marvellous people who have done huge amounts of work on their local heroes, often including magnificent locally funded memorials and publications.

I have been a rather taciturn member of the International Society of Olympic Historians for the duration of this work and appreciate greatly the support mechanism which this society has put in place to further Olympic research in general. The research that people like Bill Mallon, David Wallechinsky, Ian Buchanan, Karl Lennartz and dozens of others have undertaken has been hugely valuable to me in my work, and it would be a signal honour to think that this humble offering of mine might one day sit on the same shelf as works by such giants of sports history as these. There is no doubt that the commitment to serious sports history by Olympic historians and by historians in a number of individual countries would put us in Ireland to shame. We have too long underestimated the importance of sport as a window on history, something which places like Australia, Germany and the USA have long accepted as 'legitimate' historical study. We are fortunate indeed that Ireland does have a small but hugely committed band of athletics historians, most of them members of the Hibernian Athletics Historical Society, who have kept the flame alive through writing articles, collecting huge amounts of archival material, organising talks on athletics history and other activities. Knowing these self-styled 'HAHAs' has been hugely valuable to my work.

The very important records of the British Olympic Association (BOA) were made freely available to me at the association's base in Wandsworth, south London, as indeed were the GAA's archives in Croke Park. On a visit to New York, the relevant resources of the American Irish Historical Society, New York University and the New York Public Library were sought out. The American Irish Historical Society has not only an impressive library of books and documents but also holds several of the trophies won by the Greater New York Irish Athletic Association in its heyday. The library of Trinity College Dublin and the manuscripts archive of the National Library of Ireland have also been scoured, though with more limited results, while the Olympic Council of Ireland was unable to provide any archival materials, given that its foundation essentially post-dated the period of my research. A near-complete history of the Olympic Council of Ireland from its foundation in 1920, written by the late David Guiney, has as yet not been published. I have been privileged to gain access to a number of individual collections, including the Tom Kiely collection at South Tipperary Museum in Clonmel, the Martin Sheridan collection in the Cheshire Home in Bohola, County Mayo, and material from relatives and local experts on athletes like the Ahearnes, John Flanagan and others.

Over the many evenings when my job has taken me away from home, the National Library of Ireland at Kildare Street, Dublin, and local library services in places like Cork, Tralee, Thurles, Waterford and Galway have been searched for newspapers and other material relevant to the Olympic Games. The newspaper archives of both the New York Public Library and the British Library (Colindale) have also been visited for several days each, chiefly to access Irish-American and some British sources. While national newspapers have indeed been a rich source of evidence, the focus has been at least as much on local or sectoral newspapers in compiling this work. It has been suggested, though admittedly with more modern media in mind, that 'the nationalistic symbolism of sport is needed . . . by the media so that they can construct a national battle that can be sold'.[1] The Irish Olympic experience from 1896 to 1920 has been frequently at odds with this generalisation. For one thing, the Irish newspaper industry between 1896 and 1920, in sporting terms, was hugely focused on its pet sports, none more so than horse racing. At times, the degree of bias for some sports over others in the Irish national press had a political basis. Some national newspapers never covered sports which did not have an anglicised element to them. Outside of these, the story differed not significantly. The *Freeman's Journal*, for instance, was a relatively moderate nationalist newspaper, sharing the views of many GAA members in the 1880s and 1890s but having major differences and clashes with leading GAA personalities like Michael Cusack, and therefore rarely did the newspaper cover GAA events. At other times, extreme press views, such as those of *Sinn Féin* or the *Peasant*, might well comment on sporting and indeed Olympic matters but in a very jaundiced fashion, being particularly anxious to criticise any Irish athletes who competed on 'Great Britain and Ireland' teams. It must also be factored into the equation that news of Olympic competitions was not as readily available as it would be in modern times and, perhaps even more significantly, that Irish national newspapers depended almost exclusively on international or British news sources for their Olympic material.

Given these circumstances, it took some time for the Irish press to alert itself to the Olympics, let alone use them 'to construct a national battle that can be sold'. Coverage of Olympic issues was largely confined to the months prior to and weeks after specific Games, at least until 1908. Ultimately, it was the Irish local press, and to another extent the Irish-American press, which provided much of the evidence of a growing sense of Irish identity as the Olympic movement impacted the nation's sporting consciousness. Local newspapers, for instance, often had more available column space, more time to explore stories (given their weekly rather than daily deadlines), more detailed insights into feats of athletes from their own areas and, in the case of western and southern papers particularly, more inclination towards some national drum-beating when the opportunity arose. The research of Marie-Louise Legg has shown too that readership of local newspapers increased quite significantly around the turn of the nineteenth century, commenting that 'the habit of reading a newspaper was entering its golden age'.[2] Legg also notes that many local papers took on an increasingly nationalist tone in terms of the events they covered:

> The Irish provincial press should not . . . be considered as subsidiary or inferior to the national press. It performed an essential role in the development of the idea of the nation and in understanding its parts and varieties.

It will be seen that this eventually became the case in Olympic coverage as well, perhaps even more clearly than in national newspapers from the same period. It was also the local press which provided the truest reflection of people's sentiments. The local press reflected the views of its readership; if not, these small newspapers would not have survived. Hence, in an examination of the emerging sense of Irish identity through the Olympic movement, the local press can be, and has indeed been, a veritable goldmine.

Clearly, the involvement of the Irish in the early Olympic Games has not been accorded the historiographical attention of other Irish sporting activities of the time. Yet, early Irish Olympism has a store of potential research avenues, from local sources to international ones, which surpass what is available in almost any other facet of Irish sports history, including the records of the GAA itself. It is these sources which have been the platform of the research undertaken for this work over the past years and which, hopefully, provide a new insight into the Irish involvement in the Olympics prior to independence and the impact of that involvement on Irish identity and nationalism.

APPENDIX

IRISH AND IRISH-LINKED OLYMPIC MEDALLISTS BY COMPETITION, 1896–1920

I rish athletes who competed before the foundation of the British Olympic Association in 1905 are listed here by their county of origin or residence. Thus, from 1906 onwards, they are listed both by county and with whatever national team they were officially recorded on. This is invariably either as Great Britain (GBR), Great Britain and Ireland (GBR–Irl) or as Ireland (Irl), depending on the circumstances as explained in the body of the book.

For the Irish representing the USA, etc., the coding may appear somewhat more complex. If an athlete was Irish born and on the USA team, for example, you will see the county of origin followed by the national team represented. If the athlete was second-generation Irish, and thereby not born in an Irish county, then the number 2 (for second generation) is inserted before the nationality, as in 2Canada, 2USA, etc.

The sheer number of Irish-associated medal winners in London has led me to develop two lists for the 1908 Games, one for athletes representing Ireland or Great Britain and Ireland, and another for those representing the USA or Canada. It is also practically impossible to be sure that all athletes of Irish origin or descent are included in a table like this, so the apologies of the author are freely offered if any omissions have occurred.

1896 ATHENS

Singles Tennis
1. **John Boland** (Dublin) beat
2. Demis Kasdaglis (Greece) 7–5, 6–4, 6–1

Doubles Tennis
1. **John Boland** (Dublin) and Fritz Traun (Germany) beat
2. Demis Kasdaglis and Demetrios Petrokkinos 6–2, 6–2

Hop, Step and Jump
1. **James Connolly** (2USA): 13.71 M
2. Alexandre Tuffere (France): 12.70 M
3. Ioannis Persakis (Greece): 12.52 M

Long Jump
1. Ellery Clark (USA): 6.35 M
2. Robert Garrett (USA): 6.18 M
3. **James Connolly** (2USA): 6.11 M

100 Metres
1. **Thomas Burke** (2USA): 12.0 seconds
2. Fritz Hofmann (Germany): 12.2 seconds (estimated)
3. Alajos Szokolyi (Hungary): 12.6 seconds

400 Metres
1. **Thomas Burke** (2USA): 54.2 seconds
2. Herbert Jamison (USA): 55.2 seconds
3. Charles Gmelin (GBR): 55.6 seconds

Hammer
1. **John Flanagan** (Limerick/USA): 49.73 M
2. Thomas Truxton Hare (USA): 49.13 M
3. Josiah McCracken (USA): 42.46 M

Shot Put
1. **Richard Sheldon** (2USA): 14.10 M
2. Josiah McCracken (USA): 12.85 M
3. Robert Garrett (USA) 12.37 M

Discus
1. Rudolf Bauer (Hungary): 36.04 M
2. Frantisek Janda-Suk (Bohemia): 35.14 M
3. **Richard Sheldon** (2USA): 34.60 M

High Jump
1. Irving Baxter (USA): 1.90 M
2. **Pat Leahy** (Limerick): 1.78 M
3. Lajos Gönczy (Hungary): 1.75 M

Long Jump
1. Alvin Kraenzlein (USA): 7.18 M
2. Meyer Prinstein (USA): 7.17 M
3. **Pat Leahy** (Limerick): 6.95 M

Hop, Step and Jump
1. Meyer Prinstein (USA): 14.47 M
2. **James Connolly** (2USA): 13.97 M
3. Lewis Sheldon (USA): 13.64 M

Men's Singles Tennis
1. Hugh Doherty (GBR) beat
2. **Harold Mahony** (Kerry) 6–4, 6–2, 6–3
3. Reginald Doherty (GBR)
3. A.B.J. Norris (GBR)

Men's Doubles Tennis
1. Reginald Doherty (GBR) and Hugh Doherty (GBR) beat
2. B. Spalding de Garmendia (USA) and Max Decugin (France) 6–1, 6–1, 6–0
3. **Harold Mahony** (Kerry) and A.B.J. Norris (GBR)
3. A. Prévost (France) and G. de la Chappelle (France)

Mixed Doubles Tennis
1. Charlotte Cooper (GBR) and Reginald Doherty (GBR) beat
2. Hélène Prévost (France) and **Harold Mahony** (Kerry) 6–2, 6–4
3. Hedwig Rosenbaum (Bohemia) and Archibald Walden (GBR)
3. Marion Jones (USA) and Hugh Doherty (GBR)

Polo
1. Foxhunters, Hurlingham (GBR): Alfred Rawlinson, Frank Mackey, Foxhall Keene, **Dennis St George Daly** (Galway), **John George Beresford** (Waterford)
2. Club Rugby (GBR/USA)
3. Bagatelle Paris (France/GBR)

Discus
1. **Martin Sheridan** (Mayo/USA): 39.28 M
2. Ralph Rose (USA): 39.28 M
3. Nicolaos Georgantas (Greece): 37.68 M
   (Sheridan won on a throw-off after he and Rose tied)

Hammer
1. **John Flanagan** (Limerick/USA): 51.23 M
2. John de Witt (USA): 50.26 M
3. Ralph Rose (USA): 45.73 M

56-pound Weight
1. Etienne Desmarteau (Canada): 10.46 M
2. **John Flanagan** (Limerick/USA): 10.16 M
3. **James Mitchell** (Tipperary/USA): 10.13 M

All-Round Championship (Decathlon)
1. **Tom Kiely** (Tipperary): 6,036 points
2. Adam Gunn (USA): 5,907 points
3. Thomas Truxton Hare (USA): 5,813 points

Steeplechase (2,590 M)
1. James Lightbody (USA): 7 minutes 39.6 seconds
2. **John J. Daly** (Galway): 7 minutes 40.6 seconds
3. Arthur Newton (USA): time not recorded

Association Football
1. Canada (Galt Football Club)
2. USA (Christian Brothers College), including **Joseph Lydon** (Mayo)
3. USA (St Rose School)

Boxing (Welterweight)
1. Albert Young (USA) beat
2. Harry Spanger (USA)
3. Jack Eagan (USA)
3. **Joseph Lydon** (Mayo/USA)

Tug of War
1. USA (Milwaukee Athletic Club), including **Pat Flanagan** (county uncertain)
2. USA (St Louis Southwest Turnverein #1)
3. USA (St Louis Southwest Turnverein #2)

1906 ATHENS

Triple Jump
1. **Peter O'Connor** (Waterford/GBR–Irl): 14.075 M
2. **Con Leahy** (Limerick/GBR–Irl): 13.98 M
3. Thomas Cronan (USA): 13.70 M

Long Jump
1. Meyer Prinstein (USA): 7.20 M
2. **Peter O'Connor** (Waterford/GBR–Irl): 7.02 M
3. Hugo Friend (USA): 6.96 M

High Jump
1. **Con Leahy** (Limerick/GBR–Irl): 1.775 M
2. Lajos Gönczy (Hungary): 1.75 M
3. Themistoklis Diakidis (Greece): 1.725 M
3. Herbert Kerrigan (USA): 1.725 M

Discus
1. **Martin Sheridan** (Mayo/USA): 41.46 M
2. Nicolaos Georgantas (Greece): 38.06 M
3. Werner Järvinen (Finland): 36.82 M

Shot Put
1. **Martin Sheridan** (Mayo/USA): 12.325 M
2. Mihály Dávid (Hungary): 11.83 M
3. Eric Lemming (Sweden): 11.26 M

Standing High Jump
1. Raymond Ewry (USA): 1.60 M
2. **Martin Sheridan** (Mayo/USA), Léon Dupont (Belgium)
   and Lawson Robertson (USA): all at 1.40 M in a three-way tie

Standing Long Jump
1. Raymond Ewry (USA): 3.30 M
2. **Martin Sheridan** (Mayo/USA): 3.095 M
3. Lawson Robertson (USA): 3.05 M

Stone Throwing
1. Nicolaos Georgantas (Greece): 19.925 M
2. **Martin Sheridan** (Mayo/USA): 19.035 M
3. Michel Dorizas (Greece): 18.585 M

1,500 Metres
1. James Lightbody (USA): 4:12
2. **John McGough** (Monaghan/GBR–Irl): 4:12.6
3. Kristian Hellstrom (Sweden): 4:13.4

Marathon
1. **William Sherring** (2Canada): 2 hours, 51 minutes, 23.6 seconds
2. John Svanberg (Sweden): 2 hours, 58 minutes, 20.8 seconds
3. William Frank (USA): 3 hours, 46.8 seconds

1908 LONDON

(Representing GBR–Ireland or Ireland)

Triple Jump
1. **Timothy Ahearne** (Limerick/GBR–Irl): 14.92 M
2. J. Garfield McDonald (Canada): 14.76 M
3. Edvard Larsen (Norway): 14.39 M

High Jump
1. Harry Porter (USA): 1.905 M
2. George André (France), **Con Leahy** (Limerick/GBR–Irl), István Somodi (Hungary), tied at 1.88 M

Shot Put
1. Ralph Rose (USA): 14.21 M
2. **Denis Horgan** (Cork/GBR–Irl): 13.62 M
3. John Garreis (USA): 13.18 M

3-mile Team Race
1. GBR (including **Joseph Deakin** (Dublin/Wicklow), placed first in 14 minutes, 39.6 seconds)
2. United States
3. France

Tug of War
1. GBR (City Police), including **Edward Barrett** (Kerry)
2. GBR (Liverpool Police), including **James Clark** (Mayo)
3. GBR (K Division Metropolitan Police)

Freestyle Wrestling (Super Heavyweight)
1. **George Con O'Kelly** (Cork/GBR–Irl))
2. Jacob Gundersen (Norway)
3. **Edward Barrett** (Kerry/GBR–Irl)

Men's Doubles Tennis
1. George Hillyard (GBR) and Reginald Doherty (GBR) beat
2. **James Parke** (Dublin/GBR–Irl) and Josiah Richie (GBR) 9–7, 7–5, 9–7
3. Charles Cazalet (GBR) and Charles Dixon (GBR)

Free Rifle Shooting
1. **Joshua Milner** (Ulster/GBR–Irl): 98 points
2. Kellogg Kennon Casey (USA): 93 points
3. Maurice Blood (GBR): 92 points

Archery (Ladies Double National Round)
1. Sybil Newall (GBR): 688 points
2. Charlotte Dod (GBR): 642 points
3. **Beatrice Hill-Lowe** (GBR/Irl): 618 points

Men's Hockey
1. England beat
2. **Ireland** 8–1. Irish team: **E.P.C. Holmes** (Antrim); **Henry Brown** (Dublin); **Walter Pearson** (Dublin); **William Graham** (Dublin); **Walter Campbell** (Dublin); **Henry Murphy** (Dublin); **C.F. Power** (Dublin); **G.S. Gregg** (Dublin); **Eric Allman-Smith** (Dublin); **Robert Kennedy** (Down); **W.G. McCormick** (Dublin)
3. Scotland

Polo
1. GBR (Roehampton)
2. GBR (Hurlingham)
3. **Ireland** – **H. Lloyd** (Kildare); **J. McCann** (Dublin); **P. O'Reilly** (Westmeath); **A. Rotherham** (Dublin)

(Representing USA or Canada)

Discus
1. **Martin Sheridan** (Mayo/USA): 40.89 M
2. Merritt Giffin (USA): 40.70 M
3. Marquis Horr (USA): 39.44 M

Hammer
1. **John Flanagan** (Limerick/USA): 51.92 M
2. **Matthew McGrath** (Tipperary/USA): 51.18 M
3. **Cornelius Walsh** (Cork/Canada): 48.52 M

Greek-style Discus
1. **Martin Sheridan** (Mayo/USA): 38.00 M
2. Marquin Horr (USA): 37.33 M
3. Werner Järvinen (Finland): 36.48 M

Standing Long Jump
1. Raymond Ewry (USA): 3.335 M
2. Constantin Tsiklitrias (Greece): 3.235 M
3. **Martin Sheridan** (Mayo/USA): 3.23 M

Marathon
1. **John Hayes** (2USA): 2 hours, 55 minutes, 18.4 seconds
2. Charles Hefferon (South Africa): 2 hours, 56 minutes, 6 seconds
3. Joseph Forshaw (USA): 2 hours, 57 minutes, 10.4 seconds

100 Metres
1. Reginald Walker (South Africa): 10.8 seconds
2. James Rector (USA): 10.9 seconds
3. **Robert Kerr** (Fermanagh/Canada): 11.0 seconds

200 Metres
1. **Robert Kerr** (Fermanagh/Canada): 22.6 seconds
2. Robert Cloughen (USA): 22.6 seconds
3. Nathaniel Cartmell (USA): 22.7 seconds

1912 STOCKHOLM

Hammer
1. **Matthew McGrath** (Tipperary/USA): 54.74 M
2. Duncan Gillis (Canada): 48.39 M
3. Clarence Childs (USA): 48.17 M

Shot Put
1. **Pat McDonald** (Clare/USA): 15.34 M
2. Ralph Rose (USA): 15.25 M
3. Lawrence Whitney (USA): 13.93 M

Two-Handed Shot Put
1. Ralph Rose (USA): 27.70 M
2. **Pat McDonald** (Clare/USA): 27.53 M
3. Elmer Niklander (Finland): 27.14 M

Marathon
1. **Kennedy McArthur** (Antrim/South Africa): 2 hours, 36 minutes, 54.8 seconds
2. Christopher Gitsham (South Africa): 2 hours, 37 minutes, 52 seconds
3. Gaston Strobino (USA): 2 hours, 38 minutes, 42.4 seconds

Tug of War
1. Sweden
2. GBR (including **Mathias Hynes**, Ireland)
   No third place awarded

1920 ANTWERP

Hammer
1. **Paddy Ryan** (Limerick/USA): 52.875 M
2. Carl Lind (Sweden): 48.43 M
3. Basil Bennet (USA): 48.25 M

56-pound Weight
1. **Pat McDonald** (Clare/USA): 11.265 M
2. **Paddy Ryan** (Limerick/USA): 10.925 M
3. Carl Lind (Sweden): 10.255 M

3,000 Metres Steeplechase
1. Percy Hodge (GBR): 10:00.4
2. **Pat Flynn** (Cork/USA): @100 M
3. Ernesto Ambrosini (Italy): @50 M further

Cross Country Team Event
1. Finland: 10 points
2. GBR, including **Anton Francis Hegarty** (Derry): 21 points
3. Sweden: 23 points

Polo
1. GBR, including **F.W. Barrett** (Cork)
2. Spain
3. USA

Water Polo
1. GBR, including **Noel Purcell** (Dublin)
2. Belgium
3. Sweden

Rowing – Single Sculls
1. **Jack Kelly** (2USA): 7:35.0
2. Jack Beresford (GBR): 7:36.0

Rowing – Double Sculls
1. **Jack Kelly** and **Paul Costello** (2USA): 7:09.0
2. Erminio Dones and Pietro Annoni (Italy): 7:19.0
3. Alfred Plé and Gaston Giran (France): 7:21.090

NOTES

Notes to Introduction

1. Peter Lovesey, *The Official Centenary History of the Amateur Athletic Association* (Guinness Superlatives, 1979), Preface.
2. *Chronicle of the Olympics 1896–1996* (Dorling Kindersley, 1999), p. 9.
3. Alfred Senn, *Power, Politics and the Olympic Games* (Human Kinetics, 1999), p. 22.
4. Mike Cronin, *Sport and Nationalism in Ireland* (Four Courts Press, 1999), p. 63. This matter is discussed in an international context in J. Hargreaves, 'Olympism and Nationalism: Some Preliminary Considerations', *International Review for the Sociology of Sport*, vol. 1, no. 27, 1992, pp. 119–35.
5. Allen Guttmann, *The Olympics* (University of Illinois Press, 2002), p. 2.
6. Guttmann, op. cit., p. 12. It is worth noting that the maintenance of amateurism as an Olympic principle owed more to the IOC generally than it did to ancient Olympic traditions or indeed to de Coubertin's personal viewpoints, which were quite indifferent to the matter at times.
7. Although of less concern here, it should be pointed out that a cogent argument has also been made about the use of sport by the Irish, among other immigrant groups, as a ladder for socio-economic advancement. See Ralph Wilcox, 'Irish Americans in Sport: The Nineteenth Century', in J.J. Lee and Marion R. Casey (eds.), *Making the Irish American* (New York University Press, 2006), pp. 443–56.
8. *Gaelic American,* 9 July 1904.
9. Cronin, op. cit., p. 30.
10. Ironically, the New York Athletic Club was not at all the main haven for Irish-American athletes in the metropolis. The club had quite an austere and non-immigrant ethos and, by the end of the decade, most of the prominent Irish athletes in New York had become members of the Greater New York Irish Athletic Association (GNYIAA), which later became the Irish American Athletic Club (IAAC).

11. *Sport,* 10 August 1895.
12. ibid., 25 September 1895.
13. ibid.
14. ibid., p. 9.
15. Lovesey, op. cit., pp. 185–8.
16. J.J. Lee, *The Modernisation of Irish Society 1848–1918* (Gill and Macmillan, 1973), pp. 138–40. Lee referred specifically to Douglas Hyde in this instance but it is a point which holds true of the GAA in the 1890s as well, to a considerable extent.
17. *Freeman's Journal,* 20 February 1899.
18. *Sport,* see 25 May and 20 July 1895, for respective examples. It should be pointed out at this early juncture that *Sport* was a by-product of the *Freeman's Journal.* As such, it might be expected to present a more extreme viewpoint in nationalistic terms than other nationally published papers. This said, the *Journal* itself was grappling with its own political demons in the early years of the 1890s, caught up in the internal wranglings of the Irish Party, changing its allegiance from Parnellism. As such, the viewpoints from either the *Journal* or *Sport* in this period tend to be neither consistent nor necessarily clear. The best account found of the confusion within the *Freeman's Journal* at this time lies in F.S.L. Lyons, *The Irish Parliamentary Party, 1890–1910* (Faber and Faber, 1950), pp. 38–44. It should also be kept in mind that relations between the *Journal* (and by corollary *Sport*) and the GAA had not been very warm either since Cusack's day. See Marcus de Búrca, *The GAA: A History* (Gill and Macmillan, 1999 edn), pp. 27–8.
19. Colm Murphy, *The Irish Championships – The 1873–1884 ICAC and DAC Championships* (privately published and undated), p. 1 of Introduction.
20. Cronin, op. cit., pp. 84–5.
21. *Sport,* 20 July 1895.
22. ibid.

Notes to Chapter One

1. Bill Mallon and Ture Widlund, *The 1896 Olympic Games* (McFarland, 1998), p. 1.
2. F.S.L. Lyons, *The Irish Parliamentary Party, 1890–1910* (Faber and Faber, 1950), p. 62.
3. Quoted in a lecture by Dr Cyril White, 'The Irish–French Sporting Connection', delivered at the 'Ireland and France: Heroism in Sport' conference at Trinity College Dublin, 9 July 1998.

4. ibid.

5. Interview with Dr Cyril White and Larry Ryder of the Hibernian Athletic Historical Association, at the Avoca Café, Kilmacanogue, on 10 November 2008. Hereafter referred to as White–Ryder Interview.

6. Séamus Ware, *Laochra na hÉireann agus Cluichí Olimpeacha 1896–1996* (author-published, 1996), p. 19. Ware suggests that the late Olympian and Olympic historian, Dave Guiney, believed that the GAA was invited to the Sorbonne in 1894 but the documentary evidence for this is not thought to be extant. Magee was, in fact, the brother of Louis Magee, captain of the rugby team which won the Triple Crown in 1899, referred to in the previous chapter.

7. Details of Walsh's, Bulger's and Magee's sporting careers all come from an unpublished article by Dr Cyril White, entitled 'Edward J. Walsh: One of Ireland's Outstanding Sportsmen and Sports Administrators'. Walsh and Bulger also played together on the first Lansdowne RFC team to win the Leinster Senior Cup in 1891.

8. Marcus de Búrca, *The GAA: A History* (Gill and Macmillan, 1999 edn), p. 54.

9. *Sport*, 12 January 1895.

10. Mike Cronin, *Sport and Nationalism in Ireland* (Four Courts Press, 1999), p. 79.

11. Alvin Jackson, *Home Rule: An Irish History, 1800–2000* (Phoenix: 2003), p. 117.

12. T.P. Curtis, 'High Hurdles and White Gloves', *The Sportsman*, vol. 12, no. 1, July 1932, p. 60.

13. *Sport*, 12 October 1895.

14. Lindie Naughton and Johnny Watterson, *Faster, Higher, Stronger: A History of Ireland's Olympians* (Ashfield Press, 2008), p. 14. The term 'record' is used by the authors, and by this author generally too, although it would be the second decade of the twentieth century before official International Amateur Athletic Federation (IAAF) records were to be formalised.

15. *The Guardian*, 7 April 1896.

16. De Búrca, op. cit., p. 54.

17. Séamus Ware, *Laochra na hÉireann agus Cluichí Olimpeacha 1896–1996* (author-published, 1996), p. 22.

18. *Sport,* 14 December 1895.

19. These figures come from a number of newspaper accounts of the convention. It is also worth noting that the receipts were significantly down on what had been recorded in earlier years (de Búrca, op. cit., p.

35), adding to the sense that the GAA was in a serious period of financial contraction at the time of the Athens Olympics.

20. *Irish Independent*, 4 April 1896.

21. ibid., 7 April 1896.

22. Bob Withers, *Tom Kiely: For Tipperary and Ireland* (South Tipperary County Museum, 1997), p. 15. The author also makes the interesting point that this was the first interprovincial hurling match since 1786. Perhaps this again proves the rather peripheral nature of hurling and football in the early GAA, as this was fully twelve years after the organisation was founded.

23. For the accompanying statistics I am indebted to Tony O'Donoghue, *Irish Championship Athletics 1873–1914* (author-published, 2005), pp. 85–90. David Wallechinsky, *The Complete Book of the Olympics* (Penguin Books, 1984 edn) is the source of the comparative Olympic records but these are available in many publications and in the official report.

24. Investigations with Boston University have failed to establish the Irish roots of Burke, but his name itself makes his ancestry a certainty.

25. *Irish Independent*, 7 April 1896.

26. ibid., 10 April 1896.

27. Bridget Boland, *At My Mother's Knee* (Bodley Head, 1978), pp. 29–30.

28. Patrick Maume, *The Long Gestation* (Gill and Macmillan, 1999), p. 18.

29. ibid.

30. Dr Cyril White offers a lot of fascinating biographical detail about Boland in 'John Pius Boland: Ireland's First Olympic Champion', *Tennis Ireland*, August–September 1998, pp. 8–9.

31. See, for example, Mallon and Widlund, *1896*, p. 108.

32. Boland, op. cit., p. 31.

33. Mallon and Widlund, *1896*, pp. 73 and 108–9.

34. Naughton and Watterson, op. cit., p. 227.

35. John Boland's diary (unpublished and untitled), held at the Olympic Studies Centre, Lausanne. This entry relates to Friday, 10 April 1906 and is found between pages 102 and 103 of the manuscript. The existence of this same diary was quite unknown until the latter years of the twentieth century. Authenticated by Dr Cyril White of the HAHA, this will hereafter be referred to as Boland's Diary.

36. Heiner Gillmeister, *Tennis: A Cultural History* (Leicester University Press (translated), 1997), pp. 230–1.

37. *Official Report on the Olympic Games* (1896), vol. 2, p. 99.

38. ibid., p. 115.

39. Mallon and Widlund, *1896*, pp. 126 and 129.
40. Boland's Diary, pp. 108–9, referring to 10 April.
41. See Gillmeister, op. cit., p. 227 and notes on p. 367 for discussion on this point.
42. ibid., p. 230, quoting from Boland's Diary, pp. 122–4. It may be of interest to note that the *Official Report* carries a photograph of the victors on the last day, carrying the large diplomas and other items which Boland mentions here. See *Official Report* (1896), vol. 2, p. 104.
43. Boland's Diary, p. 31.
44. Subsequent to my research being completed, Dr Heiner Gillmeister's excellent edition of Boland's Diary appeared, entitled *From Bonn to Athens, Single and Return* (Academia Verlag, 2008). While Gillmeister, whom it has also been my pleasure to meet in person, clearly explains the Irishness of this purchase, he also shows the absence of such a sash in the remaining photographic evidence, pp. 150 and 269–7 on.
45. Boland's Diary, pp. 104–5, referring to 10 April.
46. ibid., p. 116, referring to Monday, 13 April.
47. ibid., p. 120, referring to Wednesday, 15 April. The host on this occasion was none other than the famed archaeologist of Troy, Heinrich Schliemann, who had settled in Athens some years previously.
48. Jackson, op. cit., p. 121. Jackson discusses the great range of contradictions and accommodations evident in Irish nationalism in considerable depth here.
49. ibid., p. 97.
50. *Irish Independent*, 10 April 1896.
51. ibid., 13 April 1896.
52. *The Guardian*, 9 and 13 April respectively.
53. Charles Little and Richard Cashman, 'Ambiguous and Overlapping Identities', in Richard Cashman, John O'Hara and Andrew Honey (eds.), *Sport, Federation, Nation* (Walla Walla Press, 2001), pp. 81–2.
54. *Oxford Magazine*, 13 May 1896. Boland completed the latter pages of his diary with a sort of scrapbook, containing cuttings relating to his letters with Robertson. For the sake of record, these cuttings will also be given page references in Boland's Diary. This particular one is on p. 169.
55. *Oxford Magazine*, 20 May 1896 and Boland's Diary, p. 173.
56. *Oxford Magazine*, 20 May 1896 and Boland's Diary, p. 175.
57. White–Ryder Interview.
58. *Oxford Magazine*, 20 May 1896 and Boland's Diary, p. 175.
59. *Oxford Magazine*, 27 May 1896 and Boland's Diary, p. 177.

60. See Cronin, op. cit., p. 79 *et seq.*

61. *Irish Independent*, 25 April 1906.

62. Ware, op. cit., pp. 28 and 31.

63. Wallechinsky, op. cit., pp. 3 and 17.

64. *Irish Independent*, 11 April 1896.

65. See the *Pilot* on 15 and 17 February 1896 and 22 April 1896, for example.

66. ibid., 22 February 1896.

67. ibid., 15 February 1896.

68. ibid., 28 March 1896.

69. ibid., 23 May 1896.

70. Letter from T.E. Burke to Dean Edmund H. Bennet, undated, the extract graciously supplied by Boston University Archives.

71. James B. Connolly, *The First Olympic Champion* (1924), p. 79.

72. Kevin Kenny, *The American Irish: A History* (Pearson Education, 2000), p. 148. Kenny is here identifying a long-standing tenet, propounded according to him in Kerby A. Miller, *Emigrants and Exiles* (Oxford University Press, 1985), p. 533 and Arnold Schrier, *Ireland and the American Migration, 1850–1900* (University of Minneapolis Press, 1958), pp. 105–7.

73. *Boston Herald*, 8 April 1896.

74. Letter to James A. Healy from Annapolis, Maryland, dated 7 March 1959. Found in the James A. Healy Papers, National Library of Ireland, MS 21,246.

75. James Brendan Connolly Papers, Colby College collection, code n.d. (f), p. 4.

76. *New York Times*, 7 April 1896.

77. *Boston Post*, 7 April 1896.

78. TG4 is to be commended for an excellent programme on Connolly and his background, transmitted a few times in recent years as part of its *Laochra Gael* series.

79. White–Ryder Interview.

80. Connolly Papers, code n.d.(a), pp. 1–4.

81. Healy Papers, MS 18,423 (undated).

82. Unpublished Connolly manuscript entitled 'The English as Poor Losers' (1908).

83. The *Evening Herald* did in fact do a feature on Boland when he returned but a copy has not been located during the course of this research.

84. Connolly, 'The English as Poor Losers'.

Notes to Chapter Two

1. Bill Mallon, *The 1900 Olympic Games* (McFarland, 1998), p. 1.
2. ibid., p. 6.
3. *Cork Examiner*, 16 July 1900 (denoted as being via 'Special Cable').
4. It is not at all unreasonable, given the degree of correspondence which passed between Herbert and de Coubertin up to the former's incapacitation through illness, to describe Herbert as de Coubertin's right-hand man when it came to British Olympic involvement.
5. Letter from Charles Herbert to de Coubertin (undated), in Correspondance Charles Herbert 1894–1906 held at the Olympic Studies Centre, Lausanne. Hereafter known as Correspondance Herbert.
6. For instance, see the *Kerry Sentinel*, 11 July 1900; *The Irish Times*, 16 July 1900.
7. Mallon, *1900*, p. 28.
8. See the file CIO Paris 1900.
9. *Waterford News*, 8 June 1900.
10. ibid., 15 June 1900.
11. *Belfast Newsletter*, 2 July 1900.
12. ibid.
13. *United Irishman*, 2 June 1900.
14. ibid., 30 June 1900.
15. *Pilot*, 14 July 1900.
16. For those interested, there is a marvellous film of both Peter O'Connor and Tom Kiely competing at the 1901 AAA championships in Huddersfield. It is part of the Mitchel and Kenyon series of BBC DVDs, entitled 'Edwardian Sport'. Kiely's hammer-throwing style in particular is more than favourably compared with the styles of his adversaries in the film.
17. My very sincere thanks to Michael McGrath and Mary Burke for their assistance with this story in Charleville, and to Michael for the guided tour of the Mannix gate and Leahy homestead around Cregane.
18. *Pilot*, 14 July 1900.
19. Attributed to the *Referee*, quoted in Mallon, *1900*, p. 7.
20. Letter from Charles Herbert to de Coubertin (undated), Correspondance Herbert.
21. *Sport*, 14 July 1900.
22. *Limerick Leader*, 30 July 1900.
23. *Cork Examiner*, 10 July 1900.
24. *Waterford News*, 27 July 1900.

25. *Kerry Sentinel*, 18 July 1900.
26. *United Irishman*, 14 July 1900.
27. ibid.
28. ibid.
29. Kraenzlein (variant spelling, sometimes Kraelinzlein) won the 60 metres, 110 metres high hurdles, 200 metres low hurdles and long jump.
30. *Sport*, 23 June 1900.
31. ibid., 21 July 1900.
32. *Waterford News*, 3 August 1900.
33. *Sport*, 28 July 1900.
34. ibid.
35. ibid., 18 August 1900.
36. Mallon, *1900*, p. 51.
37. My sincere thanks, again, to Dr Cyril White of HAHA for his insights and information here. White–Ryder Interview.
38. Séamus Ware, *Laochra na hÉireann agus Cluichí Olimpeacha 1896–1996* (author-published, 1996), p. 38.
39. ibid., p. 39.
40. Ted O'Riordan, 'The Unsurpassable Leahys of Charleville', *Charleville and District Historical Journal*, vol. 3, 1988, p. 8.
41. See, for example, the *Journal of Olympic History*, Special Edition December 2008, compiled by Karl Lennartz, Tony Bijkerk and Volker Kluge, pp. 38–9.
42. ibid.
43. See Mallon, *1900*, pp. 52 and 68n.
44. *Sport*, 21 July 1900.
45. Mark Quinn, *The King of Spring* (Liffey Press, 2004), pp. 76–9.
46. Kilfinane (Coshlea) Historical Society, *John Flanagan: His Life and Times* (2001), p. 29.
47. *Sport*, 21 July 1900.
48. ibid., 28 July 1900.
49. My thanks to local Flanagan expert Patsy McGrath for his assistance with this and more background information, and congratulations to the local committee on a truly wonderful memorial.
50. Mallon, *1900*, p. 38.
51. ibid., pp. 53–4.
52. ibid., p. 54 and 69n.
53. Ware, op. cit., p. 37. See also David Wallechinsky, *The Complete Book of the Olympics* (Penguin Books, 1984 edn), p. 72.
54. Mallon, *1900*, p. 57.

55. Lennartz, Bijkerk and Kluge, op. cit., p. 42.

56. Reuters report in *Cork Examiner*, 9 July 1900.

57. Mallon, *1900*, p. 207. Mahony would, undoubtedly, have been a significantly more successful international tennis player were it not for the dominance of the Doherty brothers of Britain in both singles and doubles events around this time.

58. *The Irish Times*, 9 July 1900.

59. I am indebted to Bansha's Olympic historian Michael O'Dwyer for this information on Mahony.

60. Lennartz, Bijkerk and Kluge, op. cit., pp. 86–7.

61. Mallon, *1900*, pp. 143–4.

62. Mallon, *1900*, argues that the event should be considered official whereas the work of Lennartz, Bijkerk and Kluge, op. cit., suggests by complete omission that polo was not a recognisable Olympic sport in 1900.

63. Whether or not Dillon-Cavanagh finished sixth or seventh remains unclear from official reports. See Mallon, *1900*, p. 124. Most sources, however, have him as seventh.

64. Lennartz, Bijkerk and Kluge, op. cit., p. 28.

65. Tony O'Donoghue, *Irish Championship Athletics 1873–1914* (author-published, 2005), p. 110. The author also cites a poor August harvest as a mitigating factor.

66. White–Ryder Interview.

67. See O'Donoghue, op. cit., p. 109, and *Chronicle of the Olympics 1896–1996*, published by Dorling Kindersley (1996), p. 214, for respective tables.

68. There is a discrepancy between the Paris hammer distance reported in *Chronicle of the Olympics*, p. 214 (49.73 m) and in Mallon, *1900*, p. 55, where it is given as 51.01 m, but the basic point made here is not affected by it.

69. Mallon, *1900*, p. 140.

70. *Kerry Sentinel*, 23 June 1900.

71. *United Irishman*, 16 June 1900.

72. No record of any description relating to the supposed invitation sent to the Cork County Board has been found, despite the considerable efforts of some Corkonians on this matter, which are nonetheless greatly appreciated.

73. *United Irishman*, 21 July 1900.

74. *Kerry Sentinel*, 12 September 1900.

75. ibid., 29 September 1900.

76. ibid.
77. Arnd Kruger, 'The Origins of Pierre de Coubertin's Religio Athletiae', *Olympika*, vol. 2, 1993, claims that Lynch was first elected in a by-election in 1899. Patrick Maume offers much fascinating detail about Lynch, a real political maverick, but implies that his election to parliament took place later, in either 1900 or 1901. See Patrick Maume, *The Long Gestation* (Gill and Macmillan, 1999), pp. 233–4 particularly.
78. Kruger, op. cit., pp. 94–8.
79. John P. Boland, *Some Memories* (Cahill and Co., 1928), p. 21. As if to reinforce my point above, there is not a single reference in this small book to the author's own Olympic exploits, even though it is essentially a personal memoir produced for the benefit of family and friends.
80. Arthur Lynch to William O'Brien, 11 February 1924, quoted in Maume, op. cit., p. 218, letter originally sourced in the Library of University College Cork, Code AT205.

Notes to Chapter Three

1. Bill Mallon, *The 1904 Olympic Games* (McFarland, 1999), p. 1.
2. Letter from de Coubertin to the *New York Sun*, published 13 January 1901.
3. Letter from de Courcy Laffan to de Coubertin, 10 June 1904. Correspondance Rev. Robert de Courcy Laffan at Olympic Studies Centre, Lausanne. Henceforth called Correspondance de Courcy Laffan.
4. Letter from de Courcy Laffan to de Coubertin, 28 December 1902. Correspondance de Courcy Laffan. The original French version of this comment read: 'Cette décision me paraît des plus regrettables . . . Aujourd'hui l'impression que fera le Comité de Chicago – je ne dis pas sur nos collègues mais sur l'opinion publique en général – sera celle de vouloir se débarrasser d'une charge désagreable . . . la conjonction des Jeux Olympiques avec une Exposition Universelle n'est pas faite pour rehausser la dignité de ceux-ci. La célébration des Jeux Olympiques doit être, selon mon avis, indépendente de toute autre réunion . . .'
5. Charles P. Lucas, *The Olympic Games 1904* (Woodward and Tiernan, 1905), p. 15.
6. *Chicago Tribune* – undated but must be 1901 – *File CIO JO 1904S* at OSC Lausanne.
7. See Mallon, *1904*, p. 166.
8. *Brooklyn Eagle*, New York, 21 July 1903, Coupures de presse des Jeux Olympiques de Saint Louis 1904–1900–1903, File CIO JO 1904S at OSC Lausanne.

9. *St Louis Republic,* 12 August 1903, *File CIO JO 1904S* at OSC Lausanne.
10. Kevin Kenny, *The American Irish: A History* (Pearson Education, 2000), pp. 105 and 145.
11. ibid., p. 179.
12. *Irish American,* 21 February 1903.
13. *Devoy's Post Bag,* ed. William O'Brien and Desmond Ryan (C.J. Fallon, 1953), vol. 2, Editorial comment, p. 330.
14. See the *Irish American,* 20 April 1903. *The Playboy of the Western World* was actually dragged through the courts for similar reasons by disgruntled Irish-Americans in Philadelphia, when the Abbey Theatre toured there in 1911, according to Dennis Clarke, *The Irish in Philadelphia* (Temple University Press, 1973), p. 148. Incidentally, John Devoy was to take opposition to *The Playboy* to an almost personal level, calling its 1911 US debut a 'vile libel on Irish womanhood and a gross misrepresentation of their religious feelings' and denounced Synge as 'foul, gross and vulgar,' *Gaelic American,* 14 September 1911, quoted in Terry Golway, *Irish Rebel* (St Martin's Press, 1998), pp. 185–6.
15. Clarke, op. cit., p. 144.
16. Mallon, *1904,* p. 166.
17. Séamus Ware, *Laochra na hÉireann agus Cluichí Olimpeacha 1896–1996* (author-published, 1996), p. 49. The author suggests that Lydon may well be the only Olympian to have won medals in both association football and boxing, certainly at the same Games.
18. Mallon, *1904,* pp. 62–3.
19. Ware, op. cit., p. 86.
20. Sheridan Memorial Committee, *The Martin Sheridan Story* (n.d.), p. 20.
21. ibid., p. 22.
22. Ralph C. Wilcox, 'The Shamrock and the Eagle', in George Eisen and David K. Wiggins (eds.), *Ethnicity and Sport in North American History and Culture,* no. 40, 1994, pp. 57–8, is particularly good on the Irish-American prize-fighting tradition.
23. *Spalding's Official Athletic Almanac* (American Sports Publishing Co., 1905), p. 209.
24. Mallon, *1904,* pp. 96–7.
25. ibid., p. 166.
26. ibid., p. 209.
27. *Gaelic American,* 6 August 1904.
28. ibid.
29. ibid. This is also based on the evidence of John J. Murphy of the Connecticut AOH.

30. ibid., 9 July 1904.

31. ibid., 16 July 1904.

32. Terence Dooley, *The Greatest of the Fenians* (Wolfhound Press, 2003), p. 124.

33. *Devoy's Post Bag.* There are many examples of Devoy's scrupulousness over Clan na Gael accounting in this collection, including a letter from Tom Clarke to Devoy, referring to Clarke's fears that money sent to the IRB by Clan na Gael over the previous two years had not reached its intended destination (dated 25 May 1909, p. 382) and a letter from Clarke about money he owed to the *Gaelic American*. He had paid off $100 and promised the remainder as soon as possible (10 February 1910, p. 395).

34. Dooley, op. cit., pp. 131 and 139.

35. *Gaelic American*, 24 September 1904.

36. ibid., 27 April 1907, quoted in Golway, op. cit., p. 183.

37. Dooley, op. cit., p. 126.

38. *Devoy's Post Bag.* See Devoy's speech in Boston, 8 March 1921, vol. 2, pp. 489 and 495.

39. Kenny, op. cit., p. 142 (my estimate is based on Kenny's figure for 1890 of 110,935 Irish living in Philadelphia).

40. *Gaelic American*, 9 July 1904. It was on the basis of such long-term aspirations that Luke Dillon, the old dynamiter jailed in Canada for many years, announced immediately after the 1916 Rising – and before any executions had taken place – that there were 100,000 Irishmen in the United States who would fight to avenge the men of 1916. See Clarke, op. cit., p. 151.

41. *Gaelic American*, 2 July 1904.

42. ibid., 24 September 1904.

43. Interview with Patsy McGrath, Flanagan historian, on 6 November 2008.

44. Sheridan Memorial Committee, *The Martin Sheridan Story*, p. 10.

45. *Gaelic American*, 16 July 1904. Lonergan spoke at the outing and games of De Soto Council, Knights of Columbus, at College Point, Long Island.

46. ibid., 3 September 1904.

47. ibid., 10 September 1904.

48. Dooley, op. cit., p. 133. Devoy's association with these games, in 1924, has sometimes been portrayed as a propaganda coup by the Cosgrave government. It undoubtedly was, but it was also a letter from Devoy's niece, suggesting that he come for the Tailteann festival, which actually prompted Devoy, then aged eighty-two, to make the journey. Devoy

actually wrote that 'As my visit is entirely personal and for the Aonach Tailteann, I wish to avoid public demonstration.'

49. *Gaelic American*, 23 July 1904.
50. *Sport*, 27 August 1904.
51. *St Louis Star*, 24 July 1904.
52. *Gaelic American*, 9 July 1904.
53. *Sport*, 20 August 1904.
54. *Gaelic American*, 1 October 1904.
55. *New York Daily News*, 22 October 1904. With Kiely on his journey to the ship was William Prendergast of Clonmel and latterly of the Oak Street police station, a central figure in the founding of Celtic Park.

Notes to Chapter Four
1. *United Irishman*, 10 September 1904.
2. GAA Central Council Minutes, 3 July 1904, show a typical anti-unionist decision: 'The action of the southern branch of the Irish Cyclists Association in still refusing to grant Mr Bourke his licence was under consideration and the Council decided not to have any further meetings with either body – the ICA or IAAA – in reference to proposed conference until Mr Bourke was granted his licence.'
3. *United Irishman*, 30 July 1904.
4. Marcus de Búrca, *The GAA: A History* (Gill and Macmillan, 1999 edn), p. 69.
5. *Waterford News*, 12 July 1901.
6. The best account of this row is in Mark Quinn, *The King of Spring* (Liffey Press, 2004), pp. 134–41.
7. *Waterford News*, 15 July 1904.
8. ibid., 29 July 1904.
9. *Gaelic American*, 27 August 1904. Obviously, for 'Hogan' here we should read 'Horgan', while the 'Leary' brothers must be interpreted as the 'Leahy' brothers from Charleville.
10. *Kerry Sentinel*, 20 July 1904.
11. See Quinn, op. cit., pp. 100 and 152.
12. One account from 1893 had even reported: 'It is also said that Jim's excursion [refers to Manhattan athletics promoter Jim Robinson] will include Carrick on Suir, Ireland, where he hopes to annex T.F. Kiely, considered by many to be the greatest all-round athlete in the world . . . I do not exactly know that Kiely will go to America with the Manhattan manager for the odds are greatly against him at present, and though I should be delighted to see the Gaelic Athletic Association represented

at the World's Fair Sports, I cannot keep from my mind the terrible injury the departure of Kiely would be to athletics in this country'. From the *Daily Herald* in the Tom Kiely scrapbook (Clonmel Museum archives), p. 11, dated just '1893'.

13. Quinn, op. cit., pp. 106–7.
14. ibid., pp. 146–7. (Mark Quinn is, in fact, a grandson of Peter O'Connor.)
15. *The Irish Times,* 8 July 1904. The term 'World's champion' was probably referring to Horgan's holding of the world record at that time.
16. Bill Mallon and Ian Buchanan, *The 1908 Olympic Games* (McFarland, 2000), p. 90.
17. Bob Withers, *Tom Kiely: For Tipperary and Ireland* (South Tipperary County Museum, 1997), p. 19.
18. ibid.
19. *Cork Examiner,* 6 July 1904.
20. On top of his athletic exploits, Kiely had even played, as did John Flanagan the hammer thrower, in the first GAA-organised Munster–Leinster hurling match, at Stamford Bridge in 1896. Withers, op. cit., p. 15.
21. Unattributed article from late 1890s – Kiely scrapbook (Clonmel Museum archives), p. 41.
22. Seán O'Donnell, *Clonmel 1840–1900: Anatomy of an Irish Town* (Geography Publications, 1998), p. 285.
23. Canon P. Fogarty, *Tipperary's GAA Story* (Thurles, 1960), p. 27.
24. Mallon, *1904,* pp. 63–6. Mallon also insists on including Kiely's event in the main Olympic athletics events, not with the non-Olympic events in different sections of a magnificent reference work.
25. See Karl Lennartz, *Die Olympischen Spiele 1904 in St Louis* (Kassel, 2004), p. 182.
26. *Chronicle of the Olympics,* p. 25. The picture is in the possession of the Karl Diem Institute for Olympic Studies, Cologne. Nor is it possible that the photograph in question was taken during the Irish sports rather than the all-round championship. Kiely, in fact, had his gear stolen at the time of the Irish sports and shared the same outfit with Holloway for the duration, neither one appearing in competition simultaneously as a result. See Withers, op. cit., p. 19.
27. *Spalding's Official Athletic Almanac* (1904) (Spalding and Co., 1904), p. 163.
28. *Sport,* 27 August 1904.
29. ibid., 3 September 1904.
30. Mallon, *1904,* p. 56.
31. The picture mentioned lies in the *1904 Spalding Athletic Review* while

the assertion that Daly wore green is made in Ware, op. cit., p. 54.

32. Minutes of a special meeting of the Athletics Committee, 17 July 1904, found within the GAA Central Council Minutes.

33. *St Louis Star*, 1 September 1904.

34. *Gaelic American*, 5 November 1904.

35. *Sport*, 17 September 1904.

36. *Clonmel Chronicle*, 13 July 1904.

37. ibid., 27 August 1904.

38. *Nationalist*, 6 July 1904.

39. ibid., 16 July 1904.

40. ibid., 30 July 1904.

41. ibid., 6 August 1904.

42. Letter from James Hahesy of Boston, published in the *Nationalist*, 1 October 1904.

43. ibid., 20 August 1904.

44. Headed 'An appreciation by P.R. Cleary, Tipperary', ibid., 23 July 1904.

45. De Búrca, op. cit., p. 65.

46. *Nationalist*, 27 July 1904.

47. ibid.

48. ibid., 8 October 1904.

49. *The Irish Times*, 6 July 1904. Admittedly, the coverage was sandwiched in between a lengthy article on the Waterford Bicycle Club's sports and one on the South of Ireland Imperial Yeomanry Sports.

50. Supplement to the *Waterford News*, 8 July 1904.

51. Letter to the *Nationalist*, 23 July 1904.

52. ibid., 10 August 1904.

53. ibid., 13 August 1904.

54. O'Donnell, op. cit., p. 238. See also *St Mary's Hurling Club, Clonmel* (Clonmel, 1989), pp. 10–13, by the same author.

55. *Waterford Star*, 29 July 1893, found in Tom Kiely scrapbook.

56. *Waterford Star*, probably 12 August 1893.

57. *Nationalist*, 8 October 1904.

58. ibid., 13 August 1904.

59. Dan Fraher both contributed to and helped organise a County Waterford fundraising drive for the *Nationalist*'s testimonial fund.

60. *Gaelic American*, 6 August 1904.

61. *Cork Examiner*, 12 July 1904.

62. Central Council Minutes, 17 July 1904. It deserves reiterating that this is the only reference to Kiely or the Olympic Games found in Central Council minutes between 1896 and 1908.

63. Illuminated address presented by the GAA to Tom Kiely. This now hangs in the excellent South Tipperary County Museum in Clonmel.

Notes to Chapter Five

1. *Journal of Olympic History*, Special Edition December 2008, compiled by Karl Lennartz, Tony Bijkerk and Volker Kluge, p. 2.
2. *United Irishman*, 11 April 1903.
3. ibid.
4. *Wicklow People*, 17 March 1906.
5. *Waterford News*, 4 May 1906.
6. Mark Quinn, *The King of Spring* (Liffey Press, 2004), p. 161.
7. For the speculation referred to, see Séamus Ware, *Laochra na hÉireann agus Cluichí Olimpeacha 1896–1996* (author-published, 1996), p. 61. The speculation refers to the Athletic Council being led by J.J. Keane but Keane did not succeed Frank Dineen at the Athletic Council until 1909.
8. Letter from O'Connor to Séamus Ó Ceallaigh, kindly supplied by the GAA museum, Croke Park.
9. *Wicklow People*, 10 March 1906.
10. *Galway Express*, 7 April 1906.
11. Letter to the paper from L. O'Neill, president of the ICA. *Waterford News*, 30 March 1906.
12. Quoted in Quinn, op. cit. There is some excellent photographic evidence in the book's inserts of this 'uniform' and of the six-foot by four-foot flags, emblazoned with 'Erin Go Brágh', a harp and sprig of shamrock which the IAAA equipped both Leahy and O'Connor with for the trip. O'Connor also had the patriotic foresight to get formal photographs taken of himself (wearing his blazer) and his wife in Athens, with the 'Erin Go Brágh' flag as a backdrop.
13. Michael Kenny, *The 1798 Rebellion* (Country House, 1996), p. 23.
14. ibid., p. 31.
15. *Wicklow People*, 24 February 1906.
16. Quinn, op. cit., p. 166.
17. ibid. Footnoted to 'a story told by Con Power, who heard it from Maurice Leahy, Con Leahy's brother'.
18. Colm Murphy, *The Irish Champoinships – The 1873–1874 ICAC and DAC Championships* (privately published and undated). See entry on unnumbered page under Robert 'Bob' Coll towards the end of the book.
19. Quinn, op. cit., p. 166.

20. *Irish Field*, 24 February 1906.

21. ibid., 3 March 1906.

22. ibid., 10 March. Proof of the newspaper's lack of genuine interest in the Games is shown by the solitary reference in its columns to them over the next two months, a brief article on 19 May on how Greeks living in Turkey had been victimised by having their Greek-language newspapers confiscated, denying them news of the Athens events.

23. Quinn, op. cit., p. 168.

24. Theodore A. Cook, *The Cruise of the Branwen* (published privately, 1908). A poem printed within this book as 'The Song of the Branwen' also suggests that Lord Desborough, who competed in the fencing at Athens, did so with the Grenfell family crest on his chest (Stanza VII). The poem is reprinted in Bill Mallon, *The 1906 Olympic Games* (McFarland, 1999), pp. 171–4.

25. *Waterford News*, 6 April 1906.

26. ibid., 13 April 1906.

27. Quinn, op. cit., p. 168 – not footnoted to any particular newspaper.

28. *Waterford Chronicle*, 18 April 1906.

29. *Wicklow People*, 28 April 1906.

30. The *Freeman's Journal*, by contrast, had just two short Reuters-derived reports on the entire Games, missing the actions and achievements of O'Connor completely.

31. *Irish Independent*, 25 April 1906.

32. Letter from Rev. de Courcy Laffan to de Coubertin, 6 February 1906, found in Correspondance Pierre de Coubertin – Robert de Courcy Laffan 1902–20, pp. 18–19, at OSC Library, Lausanne.

33. Minuted note dated 24 May 1905, in the file denoted Correspondance British Olympic Association, 1892–1923, Olympic Studies Centre, Lausanne.

34. Jiří Kössl, 'Origin and Development of the Czechoslovak Olympic Committee', *Citius, Altius, Fortius*, vol. 2, no. 3, Autumn 1994, p. 12.

35. De Coubertin to the editor of *Allgemeine Sportzeitung*, Vienna, in *Revue Olympique*, April 1911, p. 51–2.

36. Mallon, *1906*, introductory pages xi–xiv.

37. *Sinn Féin*, 5 May 1906.

38. Exhaustive searches at IOC headquarters have failed to locate a copy of the original entry lists, or indeed of O'Connor's subsequent appeal for Irish representation.

39. Quinn, op. cit., p. 176.

40. See, for example, Ted O'Riordan, 'The Unsurpassable Leahys of Charleville', *Charleville and District Historical Journal*, vol. 3, 1988, p. 13.
41. Quinn, op. cit., p. 173.
42. *Waterford News*, 4 May 1906.
43. ibid., 11 May 1906.
44. *Gaelic American*, 19 May 1906.
45. *Irish World*, 5 May 1906. Patrick Ford's newspaper's full title was *The Irish World and American Industrial Liberator* but it will be hereafter known simply as *Irish World*.
46. Mallon, *1906*, pp. 49–50.
47. ibid., p. 53.
48. White–Ryder Interview.
49. Quinn, op. cit., p. 181.
50. Quinn offers us the example of the commentary of John A. Buttery, writing from Athens for the *Glasgow Daily Record*: 'Thus the curious spectacle was afforded of Mr Halpin the American athletic manager judging and measuring the long jump and deciding between his own man Prinstein and O'Connor the Irishman as to what was a foul and what was a fair jump. I do not say that O'Connor ought to have won as he avers, but to say the least it was scarcely the correct thing that the judge should be an acknowledged partisan. Meanwhile the eyes of the English judges were glued to a horizontal bar at the other end of the arena.' (Not footnoted). Op. cit., p. 196.
51. O'Connor interview in *Limerick Leader*, 25 August 1956.
52. Quinn, op. cit., p. 181.
53. ibid., 28 April and 1 May 1906, respectively.
54. Letter from O'Connor to Séamus Ó Ceallaigh, GAA Museum, Croke Park, dated 1951.
55. Quinn, op. cit., p. 199.
56. *Wicklow People*, 12 May 1906.
57. *Sinn Féin*, 12 May 1906.
58. ibid.
59. *Gaelic American*, 5 May 1906. Two separate articles in this edition cover the flag incident.
60. *New York Sun*, 3 May 1906. The notion that O'Connor actually demonstrated twice makes total sense, although the flagpole climbing was the more dramatic event, naturally. Victory in the hop, step and jump, with no further events he could be barred from or suffer the alleged wrath of officialdom, would be a more obvious platform for a

demonstration than after the long jump, where he could have been accused of not accepting his beating by Prinstein. Bill Mallon has assumed that an ageing O'Connor simply mixed up the events when recounting his story to the *Limerick Leader* in April 1956 but O'Connor remained very sharp to the day he died and was not likely to have made such a mistake. There may well have been two flag protests, one more dramatic than the other, but I remain to be corrected on this proposition. See Mallon, *1906*, pp. 52–3. David Wallechinsky, *The Complete Book of the Olympics* (Penguin Books, 1984 edn), p. 88, has argued that the flagpole climbing occurred after the hop, step and jump.

61. *Irish World*, 5 May 1906.

62. Leahy and O'Connor are pictured in the photograph section between pages 148 and 149 of Quinn, op. cit. Sherring of Canada is there too, complete with shamrock on his vest.

63. *Waterford Chronicle*, 25 April 1906.

64. *Waterford News*, 2 May 1906.

65. *Wicklow People*, 5 May 1906.

66. *Cork Examiner*, 1 and 2 May 1906.

67. *Cork Constitution*, 18 April 1906.

68. *Freeman's Journal*, 21 April 1906.

69. *Sinn Féin*, 5 May 1906.

70. *Waterford News*, 18 May 1906.

71. Quoted in Mallon, *1906*, p. 14.

72. ibid., pp. 55–6.

73. ibid., pp. 53–4, 56–7.

74. *Gaelic American*, 2 June 1906. Naturally, the writer excluded any British points won by Irish, Canadian or Australian athletes in this calculation.

75. Joseph I.C. Clarke, 'When Sheridan Hurled the Discus', *Gaelic American*, 9 June 1906. There are sixty or so lines in this poem.

76. *Irish World*, 12 May 1906.

77. See, for instance, Kenny, op. cit., p. 148.

78. *Gaelic American*, 11 August 1906.

79. For a time in the summer of 1906, such advertising of picnics received another boost with the arrival of Tom Kiely from Ireland. Kiely had definitely been scaling down his athletic activity but went back to the USA in 1906 to compete in, and win, another AAU all-round championship, after which he was persuaded to attend some athletic picnics.

80. *Gaelic American*, 7 July 1906.

81. ibid., 14 July 1906.

82. ibid., 14 April 1906.
83. Terry Golway, *Irish Rebel* (St Martin's Press, 1998), p. 183.
84. *Gaelic American*, 2 June 1906. See *Irish World*, 12 May 1906.
85. *Gaelic American*, 2 June 1906. One small but interesting example of a degree of culinary assimilation at least is found in the newspaper's 11 August edition, where we find the Owen Roe Club running its picnic at Celtic Park, with the athletics being followed by a very American clambake!

Notes to Chapter Six

1. Bill Mallon and Ian Buchanan, *The 1908 Olympic Games* (McFarland, 2000), pp. 2–3, suggest that there were also financial considerations involved in the decision to abandon Rome, with the Italian government being reluctant to underwrite the cost of the Games.
2. Letter from Robert de Courcy Laffan to Baron de Coubertin, 1 November 1906. Correspondance British Olympic Association, Olympic Studies Centre, Lausanne.
3. Minutes of the British Olympic Association (henceforth MBOA), 20 December 1906.
4. In rural clubs, it was not uncommon to find members of the local gentry and business community rowing side by side with local fishermen. The club in the writer's home town of Cappoquin at this time had a crew of national renown which was comprised of a factory worker, a baker, a postman, a landlord and, as cox, a dry goods merchant. The first three were definitely nationalists, the latter two unionists.
5. MBOA, 20 December 1906.
6. Peter Lovesey, *The Official Centenary History of the Amateur Athletic Association* (Guinness Superlatives, 1979), p. 47.
7. MBOA, 4 February 1907.
8. See letter from Lord Desborough (chairman of BOA) to Baron Godefroy de Blonay, 22 January 1907. Correspondance British Olympic Association, Olympic Studies Centre, Lausanne.
9. ibid.
10. MBOA, 18 February 1907.
11. ibid., 11 March 1907.
12. ibid., 24 April 1907.
13. ibid., 8 May 1907.
14. ibid., 17 February 1908.
15. *Official Report on the 1908 London Olympic Games* (International Olympic Committee, 1908), p. 29, although the definition is available

in the minutes of the Hague meeting (25 May 1907) and in other sources at Lausanne. Although Regulations 19 and 20 of the Hague conference appeared to offer the possibility of a form of dual Olympic citizenship, these were governed by Regulation 6 in any event, so made little difference in the cases of Ireland or Scotland. See page 31 of the official report for these.

16. MBOA, 7 June 1907, containing a report submitted by the hon. secretary on the Hague conference. It is also clear from the minutes of the 24 April meeting that there had been communication between the BOA and H.L. James, premier of Cape Colony, in advance of the Hague decision.

17. Robert Barney, Malcolm Scott and Rachel Moore, 'Old Boys at Work and Play', *Olympika*, vol. 3, 1999, p. 82.

18. MBOA, 27 March 1907.

19. Electronic versions of these pictures are held at the Olympic Studies Centre in Lausanne. The two most interesting pictures of the Irish village are coded 1908 – nos. 0035557 and 0035562.

20. See the correspondence in *Cork Sportsman* between 22 August and 29 September 1908.

21. *Irish Independent*, 12 June 1908.

22. For details on the political ethos of the *Irish Independent* at this time, Frank Callinan, *T.M. Healy* (Cork University Press, 1996), pp. 438–9 has some interesting insights.

23. The peripherality of the *Freeman's Journal*'s Olympic interest is perhaps also indicated by its solitary identification of Irish competitors in London, namely the bicycle polo team! (14 July 1908).

24. Séamus Ware, *Laochra na hÉireann agus Cluichí Olimpeacha 1896–1996* (author-published, 1996), p. 44.

25. Mallon and Buchanan, *1908*, pp. 319–22. The authors give comprehensive coverage here of an ironic controversy in which the Americans protested that Longboat was a professional, while the British accepted the Canadian Olympic Association's plea that he was not. Hanbury-Williams's influence in the affair was central. It is also worth noting that Longboat had significant backing, both in terms of finances and moral support, from the Canadian parliament (*Cork Examiner*, 17 July 1908).

26. Alvin Jackson, *Home Rule: An Irish History 1800–2000* (Phoenix, 2003), p. 116. A unity campaign by the *Irish People*, seeking to bridge the gap between Irish Party nationalists like William O'Brien and Sinn Féin, generated little more sense of direction beyond some lively rallies

around Munster. See Patrick Maume, *The Long Gestation* (Gill and Macmillan, 1999), , p. 95.

27. *Irish Independent*, 14 July 1908. That there was a protest is supported by Mallon and Buchanan, *1908*, op. cit., p. 314, quoting David Wallechinsky's BOA cuttings file, though ascribing no other date or source details. 'The Irish athletes have expressed dissatisfaction because the Olympic Committee has refused to permit them to enter a separate team on the ground that Ireland is not a nation, thereby compelling them to compete as part of the British team.'

28. MBOA, 24 October 1907 and 3 February 1908 respectively. Interestingly, Leighton was one of those who later opposed the admission of a representative of the Welsh swimming body to the Programme Committee, although the wording of the resolution suggests that this was largely due to the difficulties of accommodating more committee members at too late a stage of preparation. See MBOA, 31 March 1908.

29. *Irish Independent*, 16 July 1908.

30. Per Jorgensen, 'From Balck to Nurmi: The Olympic Movement and the Nordic Nations', *International Journal of the History of Sport (IJHS)*, vol. 14, December 1997, no. 3, pp. 87–8.

31. MBOA, 2 December 1907.

32. Marcus de Búrca, *The GAA: A History* (Gill and Macmillan, 1999 edn), readily accepts that the GAA by then 'actively initiated no competitions whatever' and describes the 'almost total neglect of athletics by the Association', see pp. 80–1.

33. In the *Peasant*, 27 June 1908, for example, the paper voices its concerns that tug of war contests were happening in Dublin without the competitors being GAA affiliates, while completely ignoring the fact that the Olympic Games were due to start in London with no GAA presence.

34. *Sinn Féin*, 7 March 1908. An even more scathing attack on the athletic failure of the GAA was launched on 4 July.

35. Open letter to F.B. Dineen, dated 26 April 1907 – W.G. Fallon Papers, containing draft letters on various topics, National Library of Ireland, MS 22,577.

36. Bulmer Hobson Papers, dated 1908 and in National Library of Ireland, MS 13,159. It was written in August 1907, according to an annotation from Hobson. The article is very heavily edited, suggesting it was in preparation for publication.

37. *Sinn Féin*, 6 June 1908.

38. *Irish World*, 11 July 1908.

39. Mallon and Buchanan, *1908*, p. 75. The team win is denoted as GBR, not GBR–IRL, as Deakin was domiciled in Britain. He had also been born there, in Stoke-on-Trent.

40. See Lindie Naughton and Johnny Watterson, *Faster, Higher, Stronger: A History of Ireland's Olympians* (Ashfield Press, 2008), p. 225.

41. Tom Aherne, *Ahearne Brothers Athea: Olympic and World Champions* (2008), pp. 42–3.

42. Mallon and Buchanan, *1908*, p. 86.

43. ibid., p. 90. I am hugely indebted to Con Tarrant of Banteer for his background information on Horgan, given in personal discussions with me and also in his article 'Denis Horgan: Shot Putter Supreme' in *Seanchas Duthalla 1986* (Duhallow Historical Society, 1986), pp. 81–2. Con suggests, based on local evidence, that the actual birthdate of Horgan lay in 1869, not the 1871 given by Mallon and Buchanan. This means that he may well have been in his fortieth year when winning silver in London.

44. De Búrca, op. cit., p. 81.

45. See David Wallechinsky, *The Complete Book of the Olympics* (Penguin Books, 1984 edn), p. 12, for the athletic details on Kerr, and Ware, op. cit., p. 81, for the reference to his representing Ireland in 1909. Tony O'Donoghue, *Irish Championship Athletics 1873–1914* (author-published, 2005) has the fullest details on all of these international contests.

46. Mallon and Buchanan, *1908*, p. 189.

47. ibid., p. 219.

48. Naughton and Watterson, op. cit., p. 230.

49. ibid., p. 224.

50. *Irish Independent*, 9 July 1908.

51. Mallon and Buchanan, *1908*, pp. 42–3.

52. Naughton and Watterson, op. cit., p. 224.

53. *Evening World* (New York), 14 July 1908.

54. *Cork Examiner*, 27 July 1908.

55. *Cork Sportsman*, 25 July 1908.

56. ibid., 1 August 1908.

57. ibid.

58. *Sinn Féin*, 8 August 1908.

59. Mark Quinn, *The King of Spring* (Liffey Press, 2004), pp. 202–10.

60. *Cork Sportsman* 29 August 1908.

61. See *Freeman's Journal* editions of 21 and 24 July. The *Irish Independent* of 21 July had a like tone.

62. *Irish Independent*, 15 July 1908.
63. David Guiney, *Gold, Silver, Bronze* (Sportsworld, 1991), p. 9.
64. Dr Cyril White in an interview dated 23 November 2008.
65. *Cork Examiner*, 16 July 1908.
66. Ware, op. cit., p. 76.
67. I am hugely indebted to Edward (Ned) Walsh, nephew of Con Walsh, for his hospitality and helpfulness when I called to Carriganimmy. Ned told me that Con Walsh's medal for the Gaelic football long kick, for a distance of 84 yards, came to light by accident only a few years ago. A lovely plaque also now stands at the front of the Walsh home, commemorating Con's Olympic success, although his bronze medal is thought to be with family members in Seattle.
68. See Ware, op. cit., p. 75, and also Peter Lovesey, 'Conan Doyle and the Olympics,' *Journal of Olympic History (JOH)*, vol. 10, December 2001–January 2002, p. 6.
69. *Cork Sportsman*, 1 August 1908. The *Evening Telegraph*'s commentary was reproduced in the *Cork Examiner* of 27 July 1908.
70. *Irish Independent*, 27 July 1908.
71. *Irish World*, 15 August 1908.
72. *Irish Independent*, 20 July 1908. Croker's political sentiments were essentially moderate nationalist, probably closest to those of Redmond, whom he stood beside at the inauguration of the Parnell memorial in Dublin in 1911.
73. ibid., 10 July 1908. John Flanagan had, in point of fact, even contemplated representing the IAAA's Ireland team against Scotland in a pre-Olympic international match but was forced to withdraw by the American management to avoid risk of injury or over-exertion.
74. Maume, op. cit., p. 92.
75. *Freeman's Journal*, 18 and 25 July 1908.
76. *Sinn Féin*, 8 August 1908.
77. *Connaught Telegraph*, 11 July 1908.
78. Maume, op. cit., p. 225. A small point of note here is that the No. 11 division of the New York County AOH, in a submission to join with the Irish AOH around this time, declared: 'We recognize in Hon. John E. Redmond and Hon. Joseph Devlin, the recognized leaders of the Irish people . . .' *Irish World*, 15 August 1908.
79. Maume, op. cit., p. 239.
80. *Irish Independent*, 27 July 1908.
81. *Cork Sportsman*, 15 August 1908.
82. ibid., 29 August 1908.

83. *Irish Independent*, 29 July 1908.
84. *Connaught Telegraph*, 8 August 1908.
85. ibid., 15 August 1908. The reception was held for more than Mr Hayes on the night, but it remains unverified as to whether the IAAA's own athletes who had returned from London were invited or there.
86. *Irish World*, 15 August 1908.
87. ibid.
88. ibid., 11 July 1908.
89. Sheridan, writing for the *New York Evening World*, 22 July 1908.
90. Mallon and Buchanan, *1908*, pp. 442–3.
91. As reported in the *Connaught Telegraph*, 22 August 1908.
92. *Peasant*, 22 August 1908. Although echoing similar extreme sentiments to *Sinn Féin*, the *Peasant* was, by this time, quite a competitor of Griffith's publication in terms of seeking to capture and direct the opinions of the nationalist readership. See Maume, op. cit., pp. 84–7.
93. ibid.
94. ibid.

Notes to Chapter Seven

1. George R. Matthews sums this up in 'The Controversial Olympic Games of 1908', *Journal of Sports History (JSH)*, vol. 2, no. 2, Summer 1980, p. 40.
2. Steven A. Reiss, *City Games: The Evolution of American Urban Society and the Rise of Sports* (University of Illinois Press, 1989), p. 17.
3. John T. Ridge, 'Irish County Societies in New York 1880–1914', in Ronald Bayor and Timothy J. Meagher (eds.), *The New York Irish* (Johns Hopkins University Press, 1996), pp. 287–92, carries a fine summary of the rivalry between the county associations and the IAAC/Celtic Park proponents, which reached its height between 1907 and 1909.
4. ibid., p. 290.
5. *Irish American*, 18 May 1912.
6. Martin Polley, 'No Business of Ours? The Foreign Office and the Olympic Games, 1896–1914', *IJHS*, vol. 13, no. 2, August 1996, p. 98.
7. Grey's name appears in the minutes of the inaugural BOA meeting, held in Committee Room 12 on 25 May 1905. This list cites Grey as one of those who, although not present, was asked to form the council of the BOA. It is filed under Correspondance British Olympic Association 1892–1923 at the Olympic Studies Centre, Lausanne.
8. Theodore A. Cook, *The Cruise of the Branwen* (published privately, 1908), p. 91.
9. Polley, op. cit., pp. 102–3.

10. Noted as received in correspondence by the British Olympic Association, date unrecorded but logically it must have been shortly after 18 November 1908. Correspondance British Olympic Association at the Olympic Studies Centre, Lausanne.

11. Correspondance James E. Sullivan, Olympic Studies Centre, Lausanne.

12. While no biography of Sullivan exists, a most interesting portrait of him is found in John Lucas, 'The Hegemonic Rule of the American Amateur Athletic Union 1888–1914: James Edward Sullivan as Prime Mover', *IJHS* (Frank Cass Ltd), vol. 11, no. 3, December 1994, pp. 355–71.

13. Quoted in Bill Mallon and Ian Buchanan, *The 1908 Olympic Games* (McFarland, 2000), p. 10, but not footnoted otherwise.

14. De Courcy Laffan to de Coubertin, 1 October 1908, Correspondance de Courcy Laffan.

15. Letter from Sloane to de Coubertin, 16 August 1908, in Correspondance Pierre de Coubertin – William Sloane, 1897–1924, Olympic Studies Centre, Lausanne. Hereafter Correspondance Coubertin–Sloane.

16. John Schaeffer, 'The Irish American Athletic Club: Redefining Americanism at the 1908 Olympic Games', Archives of Irish America (electronic), NYU, p. 5.

17. Sullivan to de Coubertin, 29 April 1908, in Correspondance James E. Sullivan, OSC Lausanne.

18. Quoted in Schaeffer, op. cit., p. 4 and taken originally from 'Irishmen at Olympic Games', *Irish-American Advocate*, 18 July 1908, p. 4.

19. Sullivan's appeal to Theodore Roosevelt was published in the *New York Times*, 20 February 1907, and probably in several other publications as well.

20. S.W. Pope, *Patriotic Games: Sporting Traditions in the American Imagination 1876–1929* (Oxford University Press, 1997), p. 46.

21. David B. Kanin, *A Political History of the Olympic Games* (Westview Press, 1981), p. 34.

22. *Gaelic American*, 4 July 1908.

23. Charles E. Woodruff, 'The Failure of Americans as Athletes', *North American Review*, no. 186 (October 1907), pp. 200–4.

24. Mallon and Buchanan, *1908*, p. 9. The authors also point out that the Swedish flag was similarly omitted and led to a protest and partial Swedish withdrawal from the Games.

25. Gustavus T. Kirby, *To the Inter-Collegiate Association of Amateur Athletes of America*. While there is apparently no extant copy of this pamphlet, based on a speech given by Kirby on 8 September 1908, it is essentially reproduced in Mallon and Buchanan, *1908*, pp. 328–31.

26. Theodore A. Cook published a very lengthy *Reply to Certain Charges Made by Some of the American Officials* (1908), which is published in full in Mallon and Buchanan, *1908*. The flag incident is discussed on p. 381.

27. The most recent of these sources is Associated Press and Grolier, *Pursuit of Excellence: The Olympic Story* (Franklin Watts, 1979), p. 60.

28. *Irish World*, 1 August 1908.

29. *Irish Independent*, 20 July 1908, as noted in the previous chapter.

30. Bill Mallon and Ian Buchanan, 'To No Earthly King', *JOH*, vol. 7, no. 3, September 1999, pp. 21–8 is hard to beat.

31. *New York Evening World*, 14 July 1908.

32. *Irish World*, 25 July 1908.

33. Anonymous commentator, 'Chronicle and Comment: The Olympic Muddle', *The Bookman*, no. 28, October 1908, pp. 104–5. This is quoted in Mallon and Buchanan, 'To No Earthly King', p. 24.

34. *New York Evening World*, 18 July 1908.

35. *New York Herald*, 9 August 1908.

36. The list is reprinted in Mallon and Buchanan, *1908*, p. 329.

37. *Gaelic American*, 25 July 1908.

38. *Irish World*, 25 July 1908.

39. Cohalan is quoted in the *Gaelic American*, 25 July 1908, but the original interview with him was taken from an edition of the *Evening Post* 'a few days' earlier. Many commentators see Cohalan as a driving force of Irish-American assimilation.

40. John Devoy's editorial in the *Gaelic American*, 1 August 1908.

41. An irony in some of the American protests against the actions of the officials here was that one of the most criticised was Irishman Dr M.J. Bulger, the IAAA's representative on the British Olympic Council and senior medical officer for the 1908 marathon.

42. *New York Times*, 7 August 1908.

43. *Gaelic American*, 3 October 1908 poem by Joseph I.C. Clarke and read at the Waldorf Astoria dinner on 21 September.

44. *Gaelic American*, 1 August 1908.

45. *Irish World*, 1 August 1908.

46. *Gaelic American*, 1 August 1908.

47. *New York Times*, 15 July 1908.

48. *Evening World*, 23 July 1908.

49. James E. Sullivan, quoted in *Gaelic American*, 15 August 1908.

50. E.P. McKenna's poem, 'How the Yankees beat the World', appeared in the *Gaelic American*, 25 July 1908.

51. *Irish World*, 1 August 1908.

52. *Gaelic American*, 1 August 1908.

53. *New York Sun*, 2 August 1908.

54. *New York Times*, 22 November 1914.

55. Mallon and Buchanan, *1908*, p. 74.

56. *New York Times*, 28 August 1908.

57. It may well be taken as part of the athletic assimilation of the Irish that the early head coach at the GNYIAA was in fact a Swede, Ernie Hjertberg, who was personally responsible for recruiting many non-Irish, including Jews, into the Celtic Park fold. After Hjertberg, the Scot Lawson Robertson took over as head coach and maintained the tradition of accommodating Irish and non-Irish athletes at the IAAC.

58. *New York Sun*, 31 August 1908.

59. *Gaelic American*, 8 August 1908. In this instance, the scheduled date for the meeting was 29 August, which clashed with the great reception afforded the returning athletes in New York itself.

60. *New York Evening World*, 18 August 1908.

61. *Irish World*, 8 August 1908 and, for the new anthem, see 22 August 1908.

62. *New York Herald*, 29 August 1908.

63. *Gaelic American*, 8 August 1908.

64. ibid., 15 August 1908 (quoting from the *Morning Telegraph*, New York).

65. *Gaelic American*, 29 August 1908.

66. ibid., 10 October 1908.

67. It may be speculative to suggest that political awareness of the Irish and German influence was a factor in American reluctance to enter the Great War on Britain's side. However, even when President Wilson brought the USA into that war on 2 April 1917, he went to great pains to explain that the action was a declaration of war against the German government, not against the German people.

68. Thomas Rugby Burlford, *American Hatred and British Folly* (author-published pamphlet, 1908), p. 47. While it would be unreasonable to see Burlford's views as representative of the majority viewpoint in Britain, Burlford's pamphlet was most definitely inspired by the Olympic disputes. In fact, the copy of this pamphlet, with a very limited print run, which was obtained during the course of this research was found in the Olympic Studies Centre at Lausanne, having been presented to the library by the British Olympic Association.

69. ibid., p. 70.

70. *Gaelic American*, 22 August 1908.

71. ibid., 5 September 1908.

72. ibid.

73. ibid., 26 September 1908. Judge Victor Dowling was speaking on this occasion at a Waldorf Astoria banquet in honour of the athletes.

74. Mark Dyreson, 'America's Athletic Missionaries', *Olympika*, vol. 1, 1992, p. 82, quoting from Connolly, 'The Spirit of the Olympian Games', *Outing*, no. 48, April 1906, p. 104.

75. Dyreson, op. cit. This quotation from Connolly comes from 'The Shepherd's Bush Greeks', *Collier's*, no. 41, 5 September 1908.

76. *New York Evening Call*, 8 August 1908.

77. *New York Sun*, 29 August 1908.

78. Schaefer, op. cit., p. 3. It has also been shown that the difference between the coverage of the issues by *The* (London) *Times* and the *New York Times* was quite stark, with even these most 'respectable' of broadsheets getting embroiled in the taking of sides, without an Irish angle in sight. See Matthews, op. cit., pp. 40–53.

79. Schaeffer, op. cit., p. 6.

80. Dyreson, op. cit., quoting from the *New York Times*, 2 September 1908.

81. *New York Evening World*, 31 August 1908.

82. *New York Herald*, 1 September 1908.

83. *New York Times*, 7 August 1908.

84. ibid., 29 August 1908. According to the *Evening World* of 28 August, Kessler was at the time a guest of Richard Croker in Ireland and had sent a blank cheque for the committee to fill in as it deemed fit. Ronnie Long of Limerick has also traced Croker as being an officer in a Limerick athletic club not long after his arrival from the USA, suggesting that Croker had some genuine interest in athletics rather than a mere self-promoting one.

Notes to Chapter Eight

1. MBOA, Draft of Amended Rules suggested for the British Olympic Association as drawn up by the committee appointed for that purpose, January 1909.

2. MBOA, 16 July 1909.

3. In a letter to de Coubertin, dated 31 December 1909, Reverend de Courcy Laffan declared: 'Pour moi c'est aussi la question de l'amateurisme. Si les Olympiades étaient ouvertes à tous venant nous n'aurions pas à nous occuper des féderations. Mais dis que nous n'y voulons que des amateurs, comment pouvions nous constater la qualité d'amateur d'un concurrent quelconque si non en acceptant la décision de la féderation dont il fait part . . . L'abolition de l'autorité des

féderations serait la porte ouverte à tout faux amateur . . .'
Correspondance de Courcy Laffan.

4. Figures are based on MBOA from 25 February 1909 to 4 February 1913.

5. ibid., 25 April 1911.

6. *Sport* gave a very clear guide to how the Olympic movement defined a 'nation': 'A "nation" in the Olympic sense is any country having separate representation on the International Olympic committee, or, where no such representation exists, any country recognised as a "nation" at the last Olympic Games; and, further, any sovereign state not forming part of a states-union, as well as any states-union under one and the same sovereign jurisdiction.' See *Sport*, 6 April 1912.

7. See letter dated 14 to 18 December 1911, Correspondance de Courcy Laffan.

8. MBOA, 19 May 1909. None of the three Irish representatives was in attendance at this meeting. It is also worth recalling that none of the national football associations, being promoters of professional sport to differing degrees, had any representatives on the BOA anyway.

9. Letter from de Courcy Laffan to de Coubertin, 15 December 1910, in Correspondance de Courcy Laffan. This letter was originally in French: 'Merci de vos voeux pour ce malheureux pays. Vous avez déjà pris connaissance du résultat des élections – plus ça change plus c'est la même chose. Nous en sommes ou nous étions et il me semble que tout va dépendre du Roi. Il est, je suppose, certain qu'Asquith fera son possible pour obtenir de lui la promesse de créer un nombre de pairs capable de transformer la chambre des Lords en satellite du Gouvernemente. Que le Roi consente ou qu'il ne consente pas nous trouverons très prochainement une crise de plus dangereuse.'

10. MBOA, 18 July 1911.

11. Letter from Lord Desborough of Taplow to de Coubertin, 23 July 1911. Hereafter Correspondance Desborough. In French, it read as: 'Le Monaco a certainement droit à nous envoyer soit une équipe soit des concurrents individuels pouront qu'ils soient citoyens de Monaco. Nous lâcherons d'avoir un représentant du Canada et de l'Afrique du Sud.'

12. Letter from de Courcy Laffan to de Coubertin, 9 March 1908 in Correspondance de Courcy Laffan.

13. Letter from de Courcy Laffan to de Coubertin, 7 March 1911. The original French read: 'J'espère pour le Canada que nous avons sans peur un candidat à vous proposer. Ce n'est pas nous qui tenons à représenter l'Empire Brittanique, c'est la difficulté de trouver un candidat convenable qui soit à meme d'assister aux séances des CIO.' In a

subsequent letter, the same author referred to HanburyWilliams's Edinburgh base: 'et sera par cela plus apté à pouvoir assister aux séances du CIO que s'il avait domicile au Canada – c'est un soldat du premier rang et je crois que vous serez heureux de le voir proposer ... [. . . and will therefore be more able to attend IOC sessions than if he had been living in Canada – he is a soldier of the highest class and I think you will be happy to see him proposed], de Courcy Laffan to de Coubertin, 15 April 1911. Both Correspondance de Courcy Laffan.

14. Letter from de Courcy Laffan to de Coubertin, 18 April 1911. In Correspondance de Courcy Laffan.

15. See, for example, Robert Barney, Malcolm Scott and Rachel Moore, 'Old Boys' at Work and Play', *Olympika*, vol. 3, 1999.

16. William Sloane to de Coubertin, 16 August 1908, in Correspondance Coubertin–Sloane.

17. Sloane to de Coubertin, 16 October 1908, Correspondance Coubertin–Sloane.

18. Sloane to de Coubertin, 16 November 1908, Correspondance Coubertin–Sloane.

19. Sloane to de Coubertin, 26 January 1909, Correspondance Coubertin–Sloane.

20. Sloane to de Coubertin, 22 January 1911, Correspondance Coubertin–Sloane.

21. Quoted from an unidentified newspaper interview in Séamus Ó Riain, *Maurice Davin, First President of the GAA* (Geography Publications, 1994), p. 213.

22. White–Ryder Interview.

23. *Gaelic American*, 8 June 1912. There were athletic contests at the Claremen's picnic at least, because the *Gaelic American* carried a later small article on how Martin Sheridan came out of retirement to throw the discus during the event (29 June 1912).

24. ibid., 25 May 1912.

25. ibid., 17 August 1912. A follow-up article refers to Matt McGrath's and Pat McDonald's record throws not standing as the tape measure was too short.

26. ibid., 18 May 1912.

27. Take, for example, the coverage of the visit of the German fleet to New York, and the extensive coverage of the resolution: 'That we, the United Irish American Society of New York heartily welcome the officers and men of the German fleet to this, the commercial metropolis of the United States, of whose citizenship men of German and Irish blood

form a most important part, and we place on record our hearty good wishes for the success of the German Empire, its people and its ruler' (*Gaelic American*, 15 June 1912).

28. *Sport*, article by 'XP', 6 July 1912.
29. ibid.
30. *Sport*, article by 'Nomad'.
31. *Gaelic Athlete*, 29 June 1912. The point was initiated in response to the IARU using British-made trophies.
32. *Sport*, article by T.W. Murphy, 13 July 1912.
33. This bears in mind the fact that the only Olympic involvement of Kiely and Holloway had been as independent representatives in St Louis (1904) of 'Tipperary and Ireland', not of the GAA or IAAA.
34. MBOA, 28 November 1911.
35. ibid., 12 March 1912.
36. ibid., 16 April 1912.
37. *Sport*, 4 May 1912.
38. ibid., 25 May 1912.
39. BOA minutes, 14 May 1912, record that sending competitors was becoming a bit more costly than expected, adding that: 'In some cases the increase has been unavoidable, e.g. in the case of the Irish Cyclists Association . . .'
40. *Sport*, 20 July 1912, reported that Francis Guy was the first Irish cyclist home, in seventy-first place, but most official records have Walker four places ahead of this. See Bill Mallon and Ture Widlund, *The 1912 Olympic Games* (McFarland, 2002), pp. 139–52 for very detailed coverage of the cycling race.
41. *Official Report on the 1912 Olympic Games* (International Olympic Committee, 1920), p. 437. See also Mallon and Widlund, *1912*, pp. 139–40. No comments from either de Coubertin or the IOC have been located.
42. *Sinn Féin*, 20 July 1912. Lucania bicycles were then made by John O'Neill at the Lucania Works in South King Street, Dublin. An advertisement for the Lucania in a 1911 edition of *Sinn Féin* carried the information also that the company had won a contract to supply the post office with four hundred delivery bicycles.
43. ibid., 27 July 1912.
44. *Sport*, 20 July 1912.
45. *Sinn Féin*, 20 July 1912.
46. Wallechinsky, *The Complete Book of the Olympics* (Penguin Books, 1984 edn), p. 99.
47. Mallon and Widlund, *1912*, pp. 106–9.

48. *Sport*, 27 July 1912. In the case of Jim Thorpe, he was to lose his decathlon gold medal soon afterwards, being found to have accepted payment for playing minor league baseball some years before. He was only reinstated as champion after his death.

49. Mallon and Widlund, *1912*, p. 84.

50. *Sport*, 5 October 1912.

51. *Gaelic American*, 20 July 1912. This was published as it appeared in a letter to journalist Robert Edgren in New York.

52. Quoted in Kilfinane (Coshlea) Historical Society, *John Flanagan: His Life and Times* (2001), p. 31. The date of the letter is not given here but it is from sometime after 1924.

53. Quoted in *Sport*, 15 June 1912. Original date of publication in *Sporting Life* unknown.

54. *Sport*, 29 June 1912.

55. *Sinn Féin*, 20 July 1912.

56. See *Sport*, 29 June 1912 and 19 October 1912.

57. My calculations here are based on an analysis of the AAA's results given in Peter Lovesey, *The Official Centenary History of the Amateur Athletic Association* (Guinness Superlatives, 1979), pp. 185–8.

58. *Sport*, 20 July 1912.

59. Marcus de Búrca, *The GAA: A History* (Gill and Macmillan, 1999 edn), pp. 83–4.

60. *Sport*, 23 March 1912.

61. ibid., 30 March 1912.

62. ibid., 2 November 1912.

63. ibid.

64. T.W. Murphy, writing on 'The Athletic Dispute,' with the sub-heading of 'A Possible Basis for Settlement,' *Sport*, 3 August 1912. From the wider text of the article, it is clear that Murphy's reference to the GAA anticipating a refusal of recognition in Britain previously relates here to its ban on police and soldiers being a reason why the AAA or Scottish AAA might not deal with the GAA even if the IAAA and ICA did.

65. It should be pointed out here that the initial reaction of the GAA Athletic Council to letters proposing a settlement, from both Murphy and the lord mayor of Dublin, were received very coldly indeed and marked simply as 'read' by the executive. See *Gaelic Athlete*, 6 July 1912.

66. Letter to the editor, *Gaelic Athlete*, 24 August 1912. My thanks again to Bansha expert Michael O'Dwyer for his clarification that the Holloway

in question here is a close relative of the J.J. Holloway who competed with Tom Kiely in St Louis but that they are not one and the same man. The 1904 athlete, according to Michael's research, remained on in the USA after St Louis. Although unrelated in terms of cause, the Athletic Council's lack of sympathy for Ireland's former Olympians is also shown by its suspension of the great Tom Kiely from handicapping around this time. See also *Gaelic Athlete*, 6 July 1912.

67.   *Sport*, 3 August 1912.
68.   ibid., 10 August 1912.
69.   Patrick Maume, *The Long Gestation* (Gill and Macmillan, 1999), pp. 130–1. Maume also points out that Sherlock's right-wing Catholicism was subsequently tarnished when it transpired that he was secretly part-owner of a music hall, the very sort of establishment which the crusade had sought to condemn.
70.   Keane had arrived in Dublin from County Limerick to work as a junior clerk in the company of Christopher Dodd and Sons, grain merchants, of Smithfield. He eventually bought out the entire business.
71.   *Sport*, 5 October 1912.
72.   ibid.
73.   ibid., 19 October 1912.
74.   'The GAA and the Olympic Games' by 'Cluain Tarbh', New York, August 1912, quoted in the *Gaelic Athlete*, 7 September 1912.

Notes to Chapter Nine

1.   Bill Mallon and Anthony Th. Bijkerk, *The 1920 Olympic Games* (McFarland, 2003), p. 15.
2.   The Irish Olympic Council was not known as the 'Olympic Council of Ireland' until 1956, when the original title was changed, apparently due to the clash of the acronym form of the organisation's name with the acronym for the International Olympic Committee.
3.   Marcus de Búrca, *The GAA: A History* (Gill and Macmillan, 1999 edn), p. 86.
4.   ibid.
5.   Olympic entry in 1916 has already been noted among the stated aims of MAPA in the previous chapter and its importance is reinforced in Séamus Ware, *Laochra na hÉireann agus Cluichí Olimpeacha 1896–1996* (author-published, 1996), p. 115.
6.   Ware, op. cit., p. 117.
7.   MBOA, 21 May 1913 (Meeting of the Special Committee for the Olympic Games of Berlin, 1916).

8. MBOA, 27 May 1913 (Special Committee for the Olympic Games of Berlin, 1916).

9. MBOA, 21 May 1913.

10. MBOA, 27 May 1913. The ICA's scheme was subsequently recorded as having been received in the BOA Minutes of 27 June 1913.

11. OSC Lausanne archive: photograph file number XAAI0033.

12. MBOA, 15 January 1914. Some interpretation of this minute is needed but it seems clear that the money was to be administered by the Amateur Athletic Association as the umbrella body, further evidence of the denial of Irish autonomy even in the area of financial administration. See MBOA, 27 June 1913.

13. MBOA, 27 June 1913. The proponent here was a Captain W. Wright.

14. Pádraig Griffin, *The Politics of Irish Athletics 1850–1990* (Marathon Publications, 1990), p. 55. Griffin here is quoting from the IAAA annual general meeting, held on 28 March 1914.

15. MBOA, 2 April 1913. This suggestion came from a Mr Bosanquet not otherwise identified in the minutes although most likely to be the same man who was on the BOA finance committee in 1913 and also the man who, as a cricketer, was credited with inventing the 'googly'. See Peter Lovesey, 'Conan Doyle and the Olympics', *JOH*, vol. 10, December 2001–January 2002, p. 8.

16. MBOA, 16 October 1913.

17. ibid., 22 January 1914.

18. De Courcy Laffan to de Coubertin, 28 April 1914. Correspondance de Courcy Laffan.

19. MBOA, 22 January 1914. Australasia, Canada and South Africa were all considered 'nations' in this resolution.

20. While the Great War disrupted the holding of the Olympics until 1920 and of the AAA championships in Britain until 1919, and saw the deaths of many prominent athletes as well, the impetus it gave to physical training allied to the introduction of physical training in the British national school system gave a considerable boost to athletic activity. New athletic clubs affiliated to the AAA at the rate of 100 a year in the immediate post-war period. See Lovesey, 'Conan Doyle', pp. 65–6.

21. See Ware, op. cit., pp. 114–21, and de Búrca, op. cit., pp. 124–5.

22. White–Ryder Interview.

23. MBOA, 20 November 1919. This would mean that the suggested four teams from each country, put forward by the Belgian Olympic committee, would stand, which would no doubt meet the views of the

football association (re a letter about to be sent by the BOA to the Belgian organisers of the Antwerp Games).

24. *The Report of the Secretary General of the French Olympic Committee on the Olympiad of Antwerp* (OSC Lausanne, 1920).

25. Mallon and Bijkerk, op. cit., p. 187.

26. MBOA, 23 September 1919.

27. Sullivan died after Stockholm, in 1914, failing to recover from a serious accident, while Sheridan retired from athletics but died at the young age of thirty-seven in 1918, having contracted pneumonia. Ralph Rose, non-Irish but the celebrated flag-bearer at London, was also dead by 1920.

28. Mallon and Bijkerk, op. cit., p. 81.

29. David Wallechinsky, *The Complete Book of the Olympics* (Penguin Books, 1984 edn), p. 99.

30. ibid., p. 123.

31. Mallon and Bijkerk, op. cit., p. 82.

32. Ware, op. cit., p. 110.

33. ibid., pp. 224–6.

34. *Gaelic American*, 31 January 1920.

35. Churchill was 'one of our best-selling little novelists', according to Connolly in the same work.

36. *Freeman's Journal*, 23 August 1920.

37. Mallon and Bijkerk, op. cit., p. 78. Originally footnoted to Sandor Barcs, *The Modern Olympic Story* (Corvina Press, 1964), pp. 72–3.

38. *New York Times*, 14 August 1920.

39. Tom Aherne, *Ahearne Brothers Athea: Olympic and World Champions* (no publisher, 2008), pp. 51–3.

40. *Sport*, 17 July 1920.

41. My thanks to Michael O'Dwyer's scholarship again for spotting Hegarty's Irish birth, and for the sad detail also that the Derryman died later in a fall from a bicycle, just as the 1900 tennis player Harold Mahony had done.

42. *Sport*, 21 August 1920. See the editions of 8 May, 15 May and 3 July respectively.

43. *Irish Independent*, 20 August and 30 August 1920 respectively.

44. Following the murder of Thomas McCurtain, the next lord mayor of Cork, Terence McSwiney, was arrested and went on hunger strike. Newspaper reports in Ireland throughout the period of the Antwerp Olympics reported on the declining health of McSwiney, predicting his imminent death for a number of weeks before he eventually died.

45. *Sport*, 29 May 1920.
46. *Irish Independent*, 24 May 1920.
47. ibid., 4 August 1920.
48. *Freeman's Journal*, 4 August 1920.
49. ibid., 5 August 1920.
50. *Sport*, 14 August 1920.
51. *Tipperary Star*, 28 August 1920. The weekly editions of this newspaper around this period also carry very interesting accounts which show how the GAA was under threat from martial law in Tipperary, as elsewhere, with the banning of matches and crowd assembly by the authorities.
52. *Limerick Leader*, 18 August 1920.
53. *Gaelic American*, 31 July 1920. It may also be worth remembering that Devoy supported acceptance of the Anglo-Irish Treaty in late 1921.
54. David Guiney, *Olympic Facts and Figures* (Olympic Council of Ireland, 1992), p. 37.
55. Undated interview with Keane, from the *Irish Independent*, 1952.
56. White–Ryder Interview.
57. *Freeman's Journal*, 19 August 1920. The journal quotes from the letter at great length but it has not been possible to trace a copy of the original letter, sent in April 1920.
58. *Limerick Leader*, 23 August 1920.
59. ibid., 18 August 1920. Another edition of the newspaper, on 30 August, gives us the detail that the first meeting of the new Olympic Council of Ireland took place at the Gresham Hotel on 27 April.
60. Letter from J.J. Keane to Baron de Coubertin, 10 April 1922, Correspondance J.J. Keane (OSC Lausanne).
61. Details from the *Limerick Leader*, 30 August 1920, suggest that the decision to invite representatives of the various corporations was taken at a second meeting of the Irish Olympic Council on 3 May.
62. The corporation's resolution of support for Dáil Éireann on 7 April 1920, for example, carried with it the decision: 'That copies of this resolution be forwarded to the Irish Republican Minister for Foreign Affairs for transmission to the Governments of Europe and the President and Chairman of the Senate and House of Representatives of the United States [*sic*] America.'
63. Pat O'Callaghan of UCC was the first and so far only graduate of an Irish university to win an Olympic athletics medal after graduating.
64. Griffith was, of course, destined to die before seeing the first Irish team compete at Paris in 1924.
65. We note again Casement's unpublished 1907 article on Ireland and the

Olympic Games – contained in the Bulmer Hobson Papers (National Library of Ireland, MS 13,159).

66. See Ulick O'Connor, *Oliver St John Gogarty: A Poet and his Times* (Jonathan Cape, 1964), pp. 210–14. O'Connor also points out that Gogarty had taken up archery prior to the 1924 Tailteann Games and finished third in the competition.

67. *Limerick Leader*, 30 August 1920, listing the men who attended the Gresham Hotel meeting on 27 April.

68. *Limerick Leader*, 30 August 1920.

69. The BOA's minutes around the time of the Antwerp Games are dominated by the mundane matters of finding transport and suitable accommodation for athletes in war-torn Belgium.

70. *Limerick Leader*, 23 August 1920.

71. *Tipperary Star*, 28 August 1920.

72. *Freeman's Journal*, 23 August 1920.

73. ibid.

74. *Comité International Olympique 1920–21. Règlements et Protocole de la célébration des Olympiades Modernes et des Jeux Olympiques Quadriennaux. Adresses des Membres,* at OSC Lausanne. [This translates roughly from the original: Est considerée comme Comité national reconnu, tout Comité olympique qui est constitué par le ou [Comité] les membres du Comité International pour le pays en question ou d'accord avec eux. La reconnaissance dure autant que l'accord entre eux. S'ils font part au Comité International que l'accord n'existe plus, la reconnaissance cesse *ipso facto.*]

75. *Procès-verbal de la 18ème Session du Comité International Olympique– Anvers 17 au 30 Août 1920.* Olympic Studies Centre, Lausanne. I found this document stamped with 'CIO' (i.e. the IOC logo in French, signifying Comité Internationale Olympique) although the minute is actually recorded on the headed notepaper of the Czechoslovakian Olympic Committee, author unknown.

76. *Procès-verbal de la 18ème Session du Comite International Olympique– Anvers 17 au 30 Août 1920.* [Translated from the original, which was: 'La communication que les athlètes armeniens désirent prendre part aux Jeux Olympiques "comme Armeniens". Après une discussion relative à ce sujet (dont prennent part: le Bar. de Lavelaye, Prof Sloane, le Bar. de Coubertin, rev. deCourcy Laffan, le Cte Clary) on accepte la proposition du Bar deCoubertin d'admettre les Armeniens aux Jeux Olympiques aussitôt que le siège de l'Union des Athlètes armeniens soit en Armenie, et l'état se retrouvera regulièrement organisé.']

77. In French, the message here was: 'La demande de l'Irlande qui voudrait participer aux jeux Ol. sous le drapeau britannique, mais dans une groupe irlandaise, séparée, soulève quelques objections de la part de MM deCourcy Laffan et Sloane. Quoiqu'il y avait une certaine analogie avec la question des Tcheques de l'ancienne Autriche à Stockholm (MM le Gen. Balck, Dr Guth-Sarkovsky) on décide sur la proposition de M de Courcy Laffan de suspender toute la décision jusqu'au moment où la question irlandaise sera politiquement solutionnée . . .'

Notes to Chapter Ten

1.   Letter from de Coubertin to Godefroy de Blonay, received 20 March 1921. In French, the phrase read 'où les Anglais participeront forcement en grand nombre et avec enthousiasme', Correspondance de Coubertin.

2.   Letter from de Coubertin to unknown, 30 March 1921. The baron was amazed at the vehemence of the British position and wrote: 'Les Anglais ont été follement anti-germains', Correspondance de Coubertin.

3.   ibid.

4.   Letter from J.J. Keane on behalf of the Irish Olympic Council to de Coubertin, 10 April 1922, Correspondance J.J. Keane. [This translates from the original: 'J'ai l'honneur de vous demander encore de la part de l'Irlande d'être reconnue dans les jeux Olympiques prochains, comme concurrente à titre independent. Après nous être rencontrés à Anvers, vous nous avez informés que la demande de l'Irlande serait reconnue aussitôt que l'autonomie politique lui serait accordée. J'ai grand plaisir à vous annoncer formellement que mon pays est maintenant un "Etat Libre" et qu'il jouit, sur un pied commun, des mêmes droits comme état autonome dans l'empire brittanique, que le Canada, l'Australie, l'Afrique du sud etc. La condition posée par votre Comité comme essentielle à l'admission de la demande de l'Irlande se trouve donc remplie.']

5.   White–Ryder Interview.

6.   Letter from J.J. Keane to de Coubertin, 8 May 1922. File Correspondance J.J. Keane.

7.   My thanks to Dr Cyril White for this clarification. White–Ryder Interview.

8.   Letter from J.J. Keane to de Coubertin, 8 May 1922. File Correspondance J.J. Keane. [Translates from: '. . . il n'y a eu nulle intention de notre part de créer une organisation olympique rivale ou d'agir d'une façon contraire aux intérêts de l'olympique international actuel. Nous vous avons déjà remarqué le désarroi produit dans nos équipes et nos organisations athlétiques in consequence des évènements

politiques des années dernières dans notre pays. C'est pour remédier à cet état de choses et pour ranimer l'enthousiasme des jeunes gens de notre race dissipés à travers le monde, que nous avons mis en avant à Paris le projet d'un olympique pour les athlètes de race irlandaise . . .']

9.   Letter from J.J. Keane to de Coubertin 2 June 1922, File Correspondance J.J. Keane. This reads in the original French as: 'Nous serions très fâchés de vous donner l'impression que nous agissions contrairement aux droits ou lois du Conseil international Olympique que nous avons toute intention de respecter. C'est qu'il y a eu un malentendu de la part de notre Conseil, en vous faisant la suggestion d'un représentant irlandais pour votre Comité. Je vous prie de regarder cette démarche plutôt comme un indice de l'enthousiasme du Congrès irlandais au sujet des jeux Olympiques plutôt que du désir d'anticiper la décision de votre Comité . . .'

10. *Session of the IOC at Paris, 7 to 10 June 1922. Official Report* at OSC Lausanne, 7 June, p. 4.

11. ibid. This reads in French: 'Le colonel Kentish pense que la situation de l'Irlande est encore trop incertaine pour qu'il puisse être procedé à l'élection proposé. Une decision s'engage à ce sujet. Finalement le colonel Kentish suggère que, tout en admettent le principe de la désignation d'un membre irlandais, cette désignation soit reportée à une séance ultérieure. Il en est ainsi decidé.'

12. *Session of the IOC at Paris, 7 to 10 June 1922. Official Report*, 8 June, p. 14.

13. *Session of the IOC at Paris, 7 to 10 June 1922. Official Report*, 8 June, p. 14 In French: 'Le colonel Kentish demande à M. Keane quelle serait la situation si l'entente ne se scellait pas entre l'Etat Libre et l'Ulster. M. Keane répond qu'il ne s'occupe pas de politique.'

14. *Session of the IOC at Paris, 7 to 10 June 1922. Official Report*, 9 June, p. 18. Kentish's acceptance translates from: 'Le colonel Kentish annonce que la question irlandaise devant de nouveau être discutée, il revient sur les opinions exprimées l'avant veille à la suite d'une convérsation priveé qu'il a eue avec M. Keane. Il pense qu'il sera juste de l'élire et fait cette déclaration dans l'intérêt de la paix comme du sport.'

15. ibid. This phrase was employed by the Russian prince Ouroussof.

16. Pádraig Griffin, *The Politics of Irish Athletics 1850–1990* (Marathon Publications, 1990), pp. 55–6.

17. 'The IAAA General Meeting of March 25 had before it a letter from the Universities Athletics Association inviting them to discuss with that Body and the GAA "how athletics could be benefited in Ireland".' ibid., p. 57.

18. ibid., Griffin makes the argument here that the southern branch members were of the opinion that the ban would not last long; that the success of the new body would result in the exclusion being dropped very quickly. It was, of course, to last for almost half a century.

19. ibid., The original document from which this quotation comes has not been located.

20. Marcus de Búrca, *The GAA: A History* (Gill and Macmillan, 1999 edn), pp. 124–5.

21. Griffin, op. cit., pp. 58–9. One leading northern club, Ulsterville Harriers, declared its approval of the NACAI provided the exclusion clause was withdrawn.

22. Quoted but not date-specified in Griffin, op. cit., p. 65.

23. See Séamus Ware, *Laochra na hÉireann agus Cluichí Olimpeacha 1896– 1996* (author-published, 1996), p. 118. Ware also makes the interesting observation that a group of GAA representatives but which included J.J. Keane, tried unsuccessfully in early 1923 to bring an end to the Irish Civil War, presumably by offering to act as intermediaries of some description. See page 117.

24. In examining the *Programme of Events and Regulations for the 1924 Tailteann Games*, found in Correspondance J.J. Keane, it is interesting to note that while athletics and cycling were governed by 'GAA Rules' (more correctly this should have read 'under NACAI rules'), the Irish Amateur Swimming Association was recognised as the body of arbitration in swimming.

25. *Official Report on the Paris Olympic Games* (International Olympic Committee, 1920), pp. 83–90. While all official reports for Olympic Games that exist can be accessed in the original languages at the Olympic Studies Centre in Lausanne, they are also available on the website of the Amateur Athletic Federation of Los Angeles at www.aafla.com.

26. Ware, op. cit., p. 128.

27. According to Griffin, op. cit., p. 77, 'The Treasurer reported that athletes had been sent to the 1924 Olympic Games in Paris and that the income had been £1,134–07 while the expenditure was £1,144–08–0.'

28. Ware, op. cit., p. 129.

29. There is confusion about Gogarty's result in 1924. Writers have sometimes attributed fourth place in the poetry competition to his *Ode pour les Jeux de Tailteann* but the *Official Report on the Paris Olympic Games*, p. 607, notes the conferral upon him of a bronze medal, there being two silver medal winners.

30. Ware, op. cit., p. 127.
31. *Report of the Organising Committee on Its Work for the XIIth Olympic Games of 1940 in Tokyo Until the Relinquishment*, pp. 2 and 4. This, like all other Olympic reports, as previously mentioned, can be accessed at www.aafla.com.

Notes to Conclusion

1. Séamus Ó Riain, *Maurice Davin, First President of the GAA* (Geography Publications, 1994), p. 209. Ó Riain was here using some evidence drawn from page 143 of a 1916 publication by T.F. O'Sullivan, entitled *The Story of the GAA*.

2. A great athlete from my own locality in west Waterford, Danny McGrath, has told of being invited to compete in a sports day to be attended by the then-president, Seán T. Ó Ceallaigh, in the late 1940s in Cappoquin. While he and other athletes who had had general associations with the IAAA side were competing, GAA supporters apparently stole their clothing and burned it. This was over a quarter of a century after the so-called unification of Irish athletics.

3. The best argument for how local insights can illuminate the national and global in history has been made by Joseph Amato in *Rethinking Home: A Case for Writing Local History* (University of California Press, 2002), p. 245. In this, he has invented and propounded the maxim that 'All history is local.'

4. Quoted in Alfred E. Senn, *Power, Politics, and the Olympic Games* (Human Kinetics, 1999), p. 29. Kolehmainen's own subsequent commitment to running for the Irish American Athletic Club in New York during 1914 may well have been inspired by the sense that the Irish had a kindred, independent spirit to his own Finland.

5. According to Larry McCarthy, 'Irish Americans in Sports' in J.J. Lee and Marion R. Casey (eds.), *Making the Irish American* (New York University Press, 2006), p. 468, 'The Irish were the first American ethnic group whose sports heroes were used to endorse products.' Unsurprisingly, the Spalding company was to the fore in using the athletes, particularly Martin Sheridan, to help sell its produce. This is further evidence of the importance which the American population generally gave to the Olympics, and of the respectability which had been achieved by Sheridan and others via their 1908 achievements in particular.

6. Senn, op. cit., p. 2.

7. It is important not to confuse the BOA's support of British imperialist and conservative values during the period of this study with a lack of political independence of British governments if it felt such independence was warranted. Perhaps the most clear-cut example of this BOA independence came in modern times when, although Margaret Thatcher's Conservative government favoured British abstention from the Moscow Olympic Games of 1980, the BOA voted by eighteen votes to five in favour of participating, thus defying the government directly. See Allen Guttmann, *The Olympics* (University of Illinois Press, 2002), p. 152.

8. The IOC Congress, held in Cairo between 10 and 18 March 1938, *Bulletin No. 2*, identified the countries as USA, Britain, Greece and Australia. Naturally, the abstention of the USA from the 1980 Games in Moscow reduced this purported number, then, to three.

9. Quoted in a letter by John D. Coates of the Australian Olympic Committee to Jean-François Pahud of the Olympic Museum in Lausanne, 23 February 2000.

10. Letter by John D. Coates of the Australian Olympic Committee to Jean-François Pahud of the Olympic Museum in Lausanne, 23 February 2000. Coates here was partly reiterating what he had said in 1993 and, latterly, adding new views on Flack as a point of comparison.

11. Griffith wrote in 1903: 'The taking of the Bastille was an upheaval. A revolution is not an upheaval. A revolution is the silent, impalpable working of forces for the most part undiscerned in their action.' Quoted in Owen McGee, *The IRB* (Four Courts Press, 2005), p. 300, taken originally from *United Irishman*, 27 June 1903.

Notes to 'Note on Sources'

1. Mike Cronin, *Sport and Nationalism in Ireland* (Four Courts Press, 1999), p. 62.

2. Marie-Louise Legg, *Newspapers and Nationalism: The Irish Provincial Press 1850–1892* (Four Courts Press, 1999), pp. 174–5.

BIBLIOGRAPHY

NEWSPAPERS

Belfast Newsletter, 1894–1900
Boston Globe, 1896
Boston Herald, 1896
Boston Journal, 1896
Boston Post, 1896
Brooklyn Eagle, 1908
Chicago Tribune, 1900–4
Clonmel Chronicle, 1904
Connaught Telegraph, 1904–8
Cork Constitution, 1894–6
Cork Examiner, 1894–1920
Cork Sportsman, 1908
Daily Herald, 1908
Freeman's Journal, 1894–1920
Gaelic American, 1896–1912
Gaelic Athlete – 1912
Galway Express, 1906
The Guardian, 1908
Irish American, 1900–12
Irish Field, 1906
Irish Independent, 1894–1922
The Irish Times, 1894–1904
Irish World, 1908
Kerry Sentinel, 1900
Limerick Chronicle, 1900
Limerick Leader, 1900–20

Nationalist (Clonmel), 1900–8

New York Daily News, 1904 and 1908

New York Evening Call, 1908

New York Evening World, 1908

New York Herald, 1908

New York Sun, 1908

New York Times, 1904–12

Peasant, 1900–8

Pilot (Boston), 1896–1900

St Louis Republic, 1903–4

St Louis Star, 1904

Sinn Féin, 1908–12

Sport, 1894–1920

The Times, 1908

Tipperary Star, 1920

United Irishman, 1900–6

Waterford News, 1900–6

Waterford Star, 1896–1906

Wicklow People, 1900–6

DOCUMENT COLLECTIONS

Boland (John) Diary (OSC Lausanne)

British Olympic Association cuttings compiled by David Wallechinsky (OSC Lausanne)

British Olympic Association (Minutes of) (British Olympic Association, London) (MBOA)

Burke, T.E. to Dean Edmund H. Bennet, undated letter (Boston University Archives)

Connolly (James Brendan) Papers (Colby College, Maine, USA)

Connolly (James Brendan) unpublished manuscript 1908: 'The English as Poor Losers'

Correspondance British Olympic Association, 1892–1923 (OSC Lausanne)

Correspondance Charles Herbert 1894–1906 (OSC Lausanne)

Correspondance James E. Sullivan (OSC Lausanne)

Correspondance J.J. Keane (OSC Lausanne)

Correspondance Lord Desborough (OSC Lausanne)

Correspondance Pierre de Coubertin – Robert de Courcy Laffan 1902–20 (OSC Lausanne)

Correspondance Pierre de Coubertin – William Sloane, 1897–1924 (OSC Lausanne)

Correspondance Rev. Robert de Courcy Laffan (OSC Lausanne)

Coupures de presse des Jeux Olympiques de Saint Louis 1904 (OSC Lausanne)

Devoy's Post Bag, ed. by William O'Brien and Desmond Ryan (C.J. Fallon, 1953)

Fallon (W.G.) Papers (National Library of Ireland)

GAA Central Council Minutes (Croke Park)

Healy (James A.) Papers (National Library of Ireland)

Hobson (Bulmer) Papers (National Library of Ireland)

Kiely (Tom) scrapbook (Clonmel Museum archives)

Official Report on the 1906 Olympic Games (International Olympic Committee, 1906)

Official Report on the 1908 London Olympic Games (International Olympic Committee, 1908)

Official Report on the 1912 Olympic Games (International Olympic Committee, 1912)

Official Report on the Paris Olympic Games (International Olympic Committee, 1920)

Procès-verbal de la 18ème Session du Comité International Olympique – Anvers 17 au 30 Août 1920 (OSC Lausanne)

Programme of Events and Regulations for the 1924 Tailteann Games (OSC Lausanne)

Réglements et Protocole de la célebration des Olympiades Modernes et des Jeux Olympiques Quadriennaux. Adresses des Membres, Comité International Olympique 1920–21 (OSC Lausanne)

Report of the Organising Committee on Its Work for the XIIth Olympic Games of 1940 in Tokyo Until the Relinquishment (1940)

Report of the Secretary General of the French Olympic Committee on the Olympiad of Antwerp (OSC Lausanne, 1920)

Session of the IOC at Paris, 7 to 10 June 1922. Official Report (OSC Lausanne)

JOURNALS

Charleville and District Historical Journal

Citius, Altius, Fortius

History Today

International Journal of the History of Sport (IJHS)

International Review for the Sociology of Sport

Irish-American Advocate

Journal of Olympic History (JOH)

Journal of Sports History

North American Review

Olympika

Oxford Magazine

Revue Olympique

Seanchas Duthalla

The Sportsman

ARTICLES, LECTURES AND PAMPHLETS

Barney, Robert, Scott, Malcolm and Moore, Rachel, 'Old Boys at Work and Play', *Olympika*, vol. 3, 1999

Burlford, Thomas Rugby, *American Hatred and British Folly* (author-published pamphlet, 1908)

Connolly, James B., 'The Capitalisation of Amateur Athletics', *San Diego Sun*, 1910

Connolly, James B., 'The Shepherd's Bush Greeks', *Collier's*, no. 41, 5 September 1908

Cook, Theodore A., *Reply to Certain Charges Made by Some of the American Officials* (pamphlet, 1908)

Curtis, T.P., 'High Hurdles and White Gloves', *The Sportsman*, vol. 12, no. 1, July 1932

De Coubertin, Pierre, 'To the editor of *Allgemeine Sportzeitung*, Vienna', *Revue Olympique*, April 1911

Dyreson, Mark, 'America's Athletic Missionaries', *Olympika*, vol. 1, 1992

Finn, Mike, 'The Realities of War', *History Today*, vol. 52, no. 8, August 2002

Frost, Warwick, 'Heritage, Nationalism, Identity: The 1861–2 England Cricket Tour of Australia', *International Journal of the History of Sport (IJHS)*, vol. 19, December 2002

Hargreaves, J., 'Olympism and Nationalism: Some Preliminary Considerations', *International Review for the Sociology of Sport*, vol. 1, no. 27, 1992

Jorgensen, Per, 'From Balck to Nurmi: The Olympic Movement and the Nordic Nations', *IJHS*, vol. 14, December 1997

Kilfinane (Coshlea) Historical Society, *John Flanagan: His Life and Times* (2001)

Kirby, Gustavus T. 'To the Inter-Collegiate Association of Amateur Athletes of America' (Speech, 1908)

Kössl, Jiří, 'Origin and Development of the Czechoslovak Olympic Committee', *Citius, Altius, Fortius*, vol. 2, no. 3, Autumn 1994

Kruger, Arnd, 'The Origins of Pierre de Coubertin's Religio Athletae', *Olympika*, vol. 2, 1993

Little, Charles and Cashman, Richard, 'Ambiguous and Overlapping Identities', in Richard Cashman, John O'Hara and Andrew Honey (eds.), *Sport, Federation, Nation* (Walla Walla Press, 2001)

Lovesey, Peter, 'Conan Doyle and the Olympics', *JOH*, vol. 10, December 2001–January 2002

Lucas, John, 'The Hegemonic Rule of the American Amateur Athletic Union 1888–1914: James Edward Sullivan as Prime Mover', *IJHS*, vol. 11, no. 3, December 1994

McCarthy, Larry, 'Irish Americans in Sports', in J.J. Lee and Marion R. Casey (eds.), *Making the Irish American* (New York University Press, 2006)

Mallon, Bill and Buchanan, Ian, 'To No Earthly King', *Journal of Olympic History*, vol. 7, no. 3, September 1999

Matthews, George R., 'The controversial Olympic Games of 1908', *JSH*, vol. 2, no. 2, Summer 1980

O'Riordan, Ted, 'The Unsurpassable Leahys of Charleville', *Charleville and District Historical Journal*, vol. 3, 1988

Polley, Martin, 'No Business of Ours? The Foreign Office and the Olympic Games, 1896–1914', *IJHS*, vol. 13, no. 2, August 1996

Ridge, John T., 'Irish County Societies in New York 1880–1914', in Ronald Bayor and Timothy J. Meagher (eds.), *The New York Irish* (Johns Hopkins University Press, 1996)

Schaeffer, John, 'The Irish American Athletic Club: Redefining Americanism at the 1908 Olympic Games', Archives of Irish America (electronic), NYU

Tarrant, Con, 'Denis Horgan: Shot Putter Supreme', *Seanchas Duthalla 1986*, Duhallow Historical Society, 1986

White, Dr Cyril, 'Edward J. Walsh: One of Ireland's Outstanding Sportsmen and Sports Administrators' (unpublished article)

White, Dr Cyril, 'The Irish–French Sporting Connection', delivered at the 'Ireland and France: Heroism in Sport' conference at Trinity College Dublin, 9 July 1998

White, Dr Cyril, 'John Pius Boland: Ireland's First Olympic Champion', *Tennis Ireland*, August–September 1998

Wilcox, Ralph C., 'Irish Americans in Sport: The Nineteenth Century', in J.J. Lee and Marion R. Casey (eds.), *Making the Irish American* (New York University Press, 2006)

Wilcox, Ralph C., 'The Shamrock and the Eagle', in George Eisen and David K. Wiggins (eds.), *Ethnicity and Sport in North American History and Culture*, no. 40, 1994

Woodruff, Charles E. 'The Failure of Americans as Athletes', *North American Review*, no. 186, October 1907

Sports Books

Aherne, Tom, *Ahearne Brothers Athea: Olympic and World Champions* (privately published, 2008)

Associated Press and Grolier, *Pursuit of Excellence: The Olympic Story* (Franklin Watts, 1979)

Barcs, Sandor, *The Modern Olympic Story* (Corvina Press, 1964)

Chronicle of the Olympics 1896–1996 (Dorling Kindersley, 1996)

Connolly, James B., *The First Olympic Champion* (1924)

Cook, Theodore A., *The Cruise of the Branwen* (published privately, 1908)

Cronin, Mike, *Sport and Nationalism in Ireland* (Four Courts Press, 1999)

De Búrca, Marcus, *The GAA: A History* (Gill and Macmillan, 1999 edn)

Fogarty, Canon P., *Tipperary's GAA Story* (Thurles, 1960)

Gillmeister, Heiner, *Tennis: A Cultural History* (Leicester University Press (translated), 1997)

(Since I completed my research, Dr Gillmeister has produced a wonderful edition of Boland's Diary. It is entitled *From Bonn to Athens, Single and Return* (Academia Verlag, 2008))

Griffin, Pádraig, *The Politics of Irish Athletics 1850–1990* (Marathon Publications, 1990)

Guiney, David, *The Dunlop Book of the Olympic Games* (Eastland Press, 1972)

Guiney, David, *Gold, Silver, Bronze* (Sportsworld, 1991)

Guiney, David, *Olympic Facts and Figures* (Olympic Council of Ireland, 1992)

Guttmann, Allen, *The Olympics* (University of Illinois Press, 2002)

Henry, Noel, *From Sophie to Sonia* (privately published, 1988)

Kanin, David B., *A Political History of the Olympic Games* (Westview Press, 1981)

Kemper, Erich and Mallon, Bill, *The Golden Book of the Olympic Games* (Vallardi & Associati, 1992)

Lennartz, Karl, *Die Spiele der III. Olympiade 1904 in St Louis* (Agon Sportverlag, 2004)

Llewellyn Smith, Michael, *Olympics in Athens 1896* (Profile Books, 2004)

Lovesey, Peter, *The Official Centenary History of the Amateur Athletic Association* (Guinness Superlatives, 1979)

Lucas, Charles P., *The Olympic Games 1904* (Woodward and Tiernan, 1905)

Mallon, Bill and Widlund, Ture, *The 1896 Olympic Games* (McFarland, 1998)

Mallon, Bill, *The 1900 Olympic Games* (McFarland, 1998)

Mallon, Bill, *The 1904 Olympic Games* (McFarland, 1999)

Mallon, Bill, *The 1906 Olympic Games* (McFarland, 1999)

Mallon, Bill and Buchanan, Ian, *The 1908 Olympic Games* (McFarland, 2000)

Mallon, Bill and Widlund, Ture, *The 1912 Olympic Games* (McFarland, 2002)

Mallon, Bill and Bijkerk, Anthony Th., *The 1920 Olympic Games* (McFarland, 2003)

Murphy, Colm, *The Irish Championships – The 1873–1884 ICAC and DAC Championships* (privately published and undated)

Murphy, Colm, *The Irish Whale* (privately published and undated)

Naughton, Lindie and Watterson, Johnny, *Faster, Higher, Stronger: A History of Ireland's Olympians* (Ashfield Press, 2008)

O'Donnell, Seán: *St Mary's Hurling Club, Clonmel* (Clonmel, 1989)

O'Donoghue, Tony, *Irish Championship Athletics 1873–1914* (author-published, 2005)

Ó Riain, Séamus, *Maurice Davin, First President of the GAA* (Geography Publications, 1994)

Osler, Tom and Dodd, Ed, *Ultra-marathoning – The Next Challenge* (World Publications, 1979)

Pope, S.W., *Patriotic Games: Sporting Traditions in the American Imagination 1876–1926* (Oxford University Press, 1997)

Puirséal, Pádraig, *The GAA in its Time* (Ward River, 1984)

Quinn, Mark, *The King of Spring* (Liffey Press, 2004)

Reiss, Steven A., *City Games: The Evolution of American Urban Society and the Rise of Sports* (University of Illinois Press, 1989)

Senn, Alfred, *Power, Politics and the Olympic Games* (Human Kinetics, 1999)

Sheridan Memorial Committee, *The Martin Sheridan Story* (n.d.)

Spalding's Official Athletic Almanac (Spalding and Co., 1904)

Spalding's Official Athletic Almanac (American Sports Publishing Co., 1905)

van Esbeck, Edmund, *One Hundred Years of Irish Rugby* (Gill and Macmillan, 1974)

Wallechinsky, David, *The Complete Book of the Olympics* (Penguin Books, 1984 edn)

Ware, Séamus, *Laochra na hÉireann agus na Cluichí Olimpeacha 1896–1996* (author-published, 1996)

Withers, Bob, *Tom Kiely: For Tipperary and Ireland* (South Tipperary County Museum, 1997)

GENERAL BOOKS

Bayor, Ronald and Meagher, Timothy J. (eds.), *The New York Irish* (Johns Hopkins University Press, 1996)

Bew, Paul, *John Redmond* (Dundalk, 1996)

Boland, Bridget, *At My Mother's Knee* (Bodley Head, 1978)

Boland, John P., *Some Memories* (Cahill and Co., 1928)

Callinan, Frank, *T.M. Healy* (Cork University Press, 1996)

Clarke, Dennis, *The Irish in Philadelphia* (Temple University Press, 1973)

Davis, Richard, *Arthur Griffith and Non-Violent Sinn Féin* (Dublin, 1974)

Devoy, John, *Recollections of an Irish Rebel* (New York, 1929)

Dooley, Terence, *The Greatest of the Fenians* (Wolfhound Press, 2003)

Farrell, Brian, *The Irish Parliamentary Tradition* (Dublin, 1973)

Golway, Terry, *Irish Rebel* (St Martin's Press, 1998)

Healy, T.M. *Letters and Leaders of My Day* (London, 1928)

Hobson, Bulmer, *Ireland Yesterday and Tomorrow* (Tralee, 1968)

Jackson, Alvin, *Home Rule: An Irish History 1800–2000* (Phoenix, 2003)

Kenny, Kevin, *The American Irish: A History* (Pearson Education, 2000)

Kenny, Michael, *The 1798 Rebellion* (Dublin, Country House, 1996)

Keogh, Dermot, *Twentieth Century Ireland: Nation and State* (Gill and Macmillan, 1994)

Ledbetter, Gordon T., *The Great Irish Tenor: John McCormack* (Town House, 2003)

Lee, Joseph J. *The Modernisation of Irish Society 1848–1918* (Gill and Macmillan, 1973)

Legg, Marie-Louise, *Newspapers and Nationalism: The Irish Provincial Press 1850–1892* (Four Courts Press, 1999)

Lynch, Arthur, *My Life Story* (London, 1924)

Lyons, F.S.L., *The Irish Parliamentary Party, 1890–1910* (Faber and Faber, 1950)

McGee, Owen, *The IRB* (Four Courts Press, 2005)

Mandle, W.F., *The Gaelic Athletic Association and Irish Nationalist Politics 1884–1924* (Gill and Macmillan, 1987)

Maume, Patrick, *The Long Gestation* (Gill and Macmillan, 1999)

Maye, Brian, *Arthur Griffith* (Griffith College Publications, 1997)

Miller, Kerby A., *Emigrants and Exiles* (Oxford University Press, 1985)

Moran, D.P., *The Philosophy of Irish Ireland* (Dublin, 1905)

O'Brien, William, *The Downfall of Parliamentarianism* (Dublin, 1918)

O'Connor, T.P., *Memories of an Old Parliamentarian* (London, 1929)

O'Connor, Ulick, *Oliver St John Gogarty: A Poet and his Times* (Jonathan Cape, 1964)

O'Day, Alan, *Irish Home Rule 1867–1921* (Manchester University Press, 2003)

O'Donnell, Seán, *Clonmel 1840–1900: Anatomy of an Irish Town* (Geography Publications, 1998)

O'Grady, J.P., *Irish-American and Anglo-American Relations, 1880–88* (Arno Press, 1976)

Schrier, Arnold, *Ireland and the American Migration, 1850–1900* (University of Minneapolis Press, 1958)

INDEX

Names of publications are in *italics*. Page numbers in *italics* refer to pages with photographs.